The Gothic
of Peter Straub

The Gothic Worlds of Peter Straub

JOHN C. TIBBETTS

Foreword by Gary K. Wolfe

McFarland & Company, Inc., Publishers
Jefferson, North Carolina

All drawings and paintings throughout the book
are by John C. Tibbetts.

ISBN (print) 978-1-4766-6492-7
ISBN (ebook) 978-1-4766-2733-5

LIBRARY OF CONGRESS CATALOGUING DATA ARE AVAILABLE

BRITISH LIBRARY CATALOGUING DATA ARE AVAILABLE

Front cover: (inset) Peter Straub illustration by John C. Tibbets;
background image by The Power of Forever Photography

Printed in the United States of America

McFarland & Company, Inc., Publishers
Box 611, Jefferson, North Carolina 28640
www.mcfarlandpub.com

To the writers, readers and publishers
of Arkham House, past and present

What do you feel? What do you see? Wonderful things, right? Extraordinary shows? Isn't this very beautiful? And terrible? And very dangerous?

—Charles Baudelaire, *Théâtre de Séraphim* (1860)

Table of Contents

Acknowledgments

My thanks, above all, to Peter Straub. Peter, I wish all readers of your works could know firsthand your kindness and sometimes antic humor. Your patience, moreover, with my many pesky questions in person, by letter, and on the phone has made this experience a particular pleasure. Your inspiration has also gotten me to revisit the works of Nathaniel Hawthorne and Henry James. And to Stephen King, your patience with my persistent requests for an interview is greatly appreciated. Your respect and affection for Peter and his work is something very special indeed! And to William Sheehan—Bill, this book would not have been possible without your generous support and assistance every step of the way. Your *At the Foot of the Story Tree: An Inquiry into the Fiction of Peter Straub* (2000) is an important, groundbreaking study that ably combines biographical detail with insightful commentaries on the novels and stories. Undeservedly out of print, it ranks among the best serious studies of writers and writing and belongs on the shelf of every Gothic enthusiast. My thanks to that redoubtable historian of all things weird and uncanny, S. T. Joshi, who first suggested this project. To Emily King and Rachel Greer, with the Fales Archive at New York University (fales.library@nyu.ed), where Peter Straub's papers are stored, goes my gratitude for your help in accessing for me the many boxes of files and photographs during my research trip to New York. I highly recommend this valuable resource, which is open to the serious scholar. Thanks to Ron Harris and his wife, Lila, who put me up during that trip. And to members of the Straub family—Susan Straub, thanks for an inspiring conversation about your wonderful "Read to Me" program; Benjamin Straub, I am grateful for your correspondence and we all hope that your efforts to bring Peter's work to film and television will continue. To Emma, I hope that we may meet soon; meantime, you have a new baby to bring up! Thanks go to Francis Nevins for reading the manuscript and to Stephen King's agent Chuck Verrill for facilitating the interview with King. Others who have taken their time to read and comment on the progress of this book include Peter's good friends and colleagues Thomas Tessier, Ramsey

Campbell, Jack Ketchum, William F. Nolan, and Gary K. Wolfe. Among other correspondents and readers, Michael Dirda, T.E.D. Klein, Jon Eller, Cynthia J. Miller, Bev Vincent, Brian Faucette, Barbara Goebel, Jason and Sunni Brock, Frank Thompson, and Josh and Stephi Wille have been very helpful. To Paula Courtney, Pam LeRow, and Elizabeth Stevens of the University of Kansas, I am grateful for your assistance in transcribing and formatting this manuscript. And my thanks go to my supportive colleagues in the Department of Film and Media Studies, University of Kansas, including Michael Baskett, department chair, Karla Conrad, executive secretary, Tamara Falicov, Madison Davis Lacey, Catherine Preston, Kevin Willmott, Germaine Halegoua, Robert Hurst, and Cathy Joritz. Finally, as always, my heartfelt appreciations to my partner, Mary Lou Pagano: You have patiently endured the stresses and strains of my writing this book. Thank you, my "LuLu." Where would this book be without your love and wise counsel?

Foreword:
Locating Peter Straub
by Gary K. Wolfe

It has been said, at various times and in various ways, that writers create their own antecedents. This is a somewhat more complex idea than Harold Bloom's much-discussed "anxiety of influence" and it is of particular relevance to writers who are associated with genre literature. Horror, fantasy, and science fiction writers have habitually sought to recommission earlier traditions in the service of lending historical *gravitas* to genres which are seen as having unfairly fallen off the radar of literary respectability; fantasy advocates want to reach back before Tolkien to find noble ancestors in medieval romances, or indeed in the entire scope of world mythology. Science fiction readers like to cite the speculative aspects of utopian or dystopian fiction from Plato to Aldous Huxley, along with fanciful speculations of space voyages from Lucian of Samosata to Jules Verne. Horror finds its forbears in folktales and legends as well as in Gothic romances and even *fin de siècle* decadence. But despite such genealogical ambitions, a more modest consensus history seems to persist among readers: modern science fiction begins with Verne and Wells, modern fantasy with Tolkien, modern horror with Poe and Lovecraft.

Such consensus histories can be useful in cementing a sense of continuity and community, but they can also promote a kind of tunnel vision in terms of a genre's history and of its possibilities. None of the major genres of fantastic literature are lacking in authors who are cheerfully content to work within those historical parameters, to color within the lines. For such writers, some of them excellent, fiction can become largely a matter of performance and repertoire rather than of testing boundaries or pursuing a unique artistic vision, and thanks to them, the core traditions of horror, fantasy, or science fiction—and, for that matter, of mysteries or romances—can remain vital from generation to generation, satisfying readers who know exactly what they want with, well, exactly what they want.

And then there are writers like Peter Straub, who does not hesitate to challenge his substantial base of loyal readers, expanding not only the available literary materials of his chosen mode, but also its future possibilities. I sometimes think of writers like Straub as fulcrums, key points on which an entire genre may pivot, leading to unexpected results and to unexpected negotiations with literary tradition. There are perhaps one or two such writers in a generation in a given genre. In 1960s science fiction, for example, writers like John Brunner and J.G. Ballard showed how the modernist or postmodernist techniques of John Dos Passos and William Burroughs could inform a new kind of science fiction, and the later impact of "New Wave" science fiction extended well beyond what had previously been viewed as the borders of the genre. Still earlier, writers like Dashiell Hammett, Raymond Chandler, and Ross Macdonald had redefined the mystery genre in a manner that incorporated elements of classic American realism, and what followed became an entire mode of narrative, sometimes conveniently labeled *noir*, that remains a vital form even today. Straub demonstrated, first through his fiction and later through edited anthologies and a few essays, that what is commonly labeled horror fiction could be enlarged and enriched by a broad understanding of writers as diverse as Chandler and Henry James and even poets such as William Carlos Williams and John Ashbery. Perhaps more than any author of his generation—Stephen King included—Straub extended the literary possibilities of horror fiction, and among the younger writers who have said that Straub, in one way or another, helped open up their own territory include figures as diverse as Kelly Link, Caitlin R. Kiernan, Brian Evenson, and Laird Barron, though the list is undoubtedly much longer than that, and would include the majority of contemporary writers of more traditional horror.

For a writer who serves as such a fulcrum between literary traditions, context is crucially important, and one of the many benefits of John Tibbetts's insightful study—apart from his clearly organized and thoroughly researched examinations of Straub's own works—is the manner in which he positions Straub in a grand tradition of fantastic literature that includes such figures as E.T.A. Hoffmann, Charles Brockden Brown, Nathaniel Hawthorne, Herman Melville, Charles Dickens, Edgar Allan Poe, and G.K. Chesterton, as well as Chandler, James, Lovecraft, and others I've mentioned. Tibbetts doesn't always claim such writers as direct literary influences on Straub's fiction, but he uses them to weave a kind of literary tapestry which reveals Straub's prominence in American literature in a way that a purely genre-oriented study cannot. With his multiple awards—including World Fantasy,

World Horror, Bram Stoker, and International Horror Guild lifetime achievement awards—Straub occupies a central position in the arena of modern literary horror that is indisputable. But his broader legacy is still being formed, while his own fiction continues to evolve and grow yet more adventurous, as the stories in his recent retrospective collection, *Interior Darkness*, attest. Supporting his arguments with research drawn not only from the full range of Straub's work, but also from his working papers, correspondence, and interviews, Tibbetts provides an invaluable roadmap to the complex, multileveled novels and stories that will eventually come to define Straub's legacy, and that already define the literary possibilities of the genre which, before Straub came along, was simply labeled horror.

Gary K. Wolfe is a professor of humanities in Roosevelt University's Evelyn T. Stone College of Professional Studies. He is the author of *Evaporating Genres: Essays on Fantastic Literature* (Wesleyan University Press, 2011).

Introduction:
"The Juniper Tree"

"You may be before a dwindling fire with your head full of pictures…."
— The Brothers Grimm

"I was looking at the pictures in the fire."
— Steerforth, *David Copperfield*

He knew that the street with its rising lawns and tall elms was only a picture over the face of a terrible fire.
— Peter Straub, "In the Realm of Dreams"

Alone at his desk, a man bends to a manuscript. "I live underground in a hidden room," he writes. "Before me, half unseen, hangs a large and appallingly complicated vision I must explore and memorize, witness again and again in order to locate its hidden corner." He looks around and takes inventory: "Everything is in its proper place. My typewriter sits on the study table. Beside the typewriter a cigarette smolders, raising a gray stream of smoke. A record revolves on the turntable, and my small apartment is dense with music…. Beyond my walls and windows is a world toward which I reach with outstretched arms and an ambitious and divided heart…." He pauses a moment. "[I listen to] the voices of sentences to be written this afternoon, tomorrow, or next month [which] stir and whisper, beginning to speak, and I lean over the typewriter toward them, getting as close as I can." A curious story unfolds that "boils" with "things that cannot be true, that must be inventions and fables," of "talking cats and silver boots filled with blood," and of "dismembered children buried beneath juniper trees" who rise and speak, "made whole once again."[1]

These passages from a short story by Peter Straub, "The Juniper Tree," describe the trauma of family dysfunction and childhood sexual abuse. The nameless writer is haunted by the memory, torn apart by the pain: "I dreamed that I was buried beneath a juniper tree, and the cut-off pieces of my body called out to each other and wept because they were separate."[2]

Imagine Straub himself, now, at the writing desk of his own "hidden room," his study. He's not tapping the keys of a typewriter but a word processor; not listening to a turntable but a compact disc player; not gazing out the window but closing the shutters ("I never look out the window unless I have to; I want artificial light here, not sunlight"). Cigarette smoke, jazz riffs, and operatic arias fill the room. The manuscript pages of "The Juniper Tree" lie scattered before him.

The story is Straub's own testament and confession. The metaphor of the Juniper Tree assumes a central place in all his work, appearing and reappearing in a variety of guises and contexts. "No story exists without its past," he says. "Things that are crucial and important in our childhood may be buried and repressed. But one day they come up, they speak again. Most of the central figures in my stories have denied or forgotten some crucial and determining event that still boils and smokes inside them."[3] Thus, like the scattered body parts of its namesake, the Grimm fairy tale, Straub's novels and stories recall, reawaken

Peter Straub (courtesy Jenny Calivas).

and reassemble the pieces of both public and private trauma, such as the violence of childhood sexual and emotional abuse, incest, serial killings, and the atrocities of war.[4] They are the bones that can but hint at a totality of meaning that will forever elude us. "Human beings need stories to make sense of their accident-ridden lives," says a ghostly character in Straub's *Mr. X.* "They're always telling one small fragment of the same huge story, and they'll never get it right."[5]

Throughout his long career, Peter Straub has been getting it right: "I would like to look at the emotional conditions that prevail in horror, which are striking and eccentric. Horror is very internal. It works with naked subconscious material.... I want to look into that."[6]

Unusual for a writer in the field of weird fiction, Peter Straub has garnered success and critical acceptance in both the popular and literary communities. In the opinion of historian Douglas E. Winter, "[He is] the premier stylist of the modern supernatural novel, a writer of rare wit and intelligence in a field beset with cynical potboilers."[7] He began his literary career with a BA at the University of Wisconsin and an MA at Columbia University. From 1966 to 1968 he taught English at a boys' school in Milwaukee. ("It was my only real job," he says.) During subsequent travels in Dublin and London, he wrote two volumes of poetry, *Open Air* (1973) and *Leeson Park and Belsize Square* (1983), and his first novels, *Marriages* (1973), *Under Venus* (not published until 1985), *Julia* (1975), and *If You Could See Me Now* (1977). In his "breakthrough" novel, *Ghost Story* (1979), which was adapted into a film in 1981, he took the elements of fantasy and horror that had been marginally present in his earlier work and developed them into the full-throated Gothic expression with literary pretensions that has marked all of his subsequent writing. "I wanted to bring whatever literary acumen and intelligence I could muster," he says, "to a very attractive and quirky form."[8] His subsequent works include five short-story collections and the novels *Shadowland* (1980), *Floating Dragon* (1983), two collaborations with Stephen King—*The Talisman* (1984) and *Black House* (2001)—*Koko* (1988), *Mystery* (1989), *The Throat* (1993), *The Hellfire Club* (1996), *Mr. X* (1999), *lost boy lost girl* (2003), *In the Night Room* (2004), *A Dark Matter* (2010), "*A Special Place* (2010)," and a forthcoming novel, tentatively titled *Hello Jack.* Straub has edited the Library of America volume of H.P. Lovecraft (2005) and several volumes of short weird fiction, and he has won the British Fantasy Award, the August Derleth Award, the World Fantasy Award, and numerous Bram Stoker Awards.

Transformative Gothic

For Straub the Gothic mode is no longer something that is *found* but something that is *created* and *recreated* in an ever-changing world. Genre structures are mere pivots for endless gestures of variation and invention. Straub's own literary "Juniper Tree," as it were, is a highly personalized meta-textual fiction whose self-conscious allusiveness, Gothic tropes, and baffling ambiguities deny the closure of the standard horror dynamic. Heir to Faustian pacts, buried secrets, damaged children, haunted places, dark magicians, ghosts, vampires, succubi, *Doppelgänger*, and embedded narratives, he commingles them into strange new shapes and effects. His strategy and method is perfectly conveyed in an episode in his novel *Shadowland*, itself derived from the Brothers Grimm: A boy finds a box and a key. After a struggle, he opens the box:

> Every story in the world, every story ever told, blew up out of the box. Princes and princesses, wizards, foxes and trolls and witches and wolves and woodsmen and kings and elves and dwarves and a beautiful girl in a red cape…. Then the wind caught them and sent them blowing away, some this way and some that…. But I wonder if some of those stories might not have blown into other stories. Maybe the wind tumbled those stories all together, and switched the trolls with the kings and put foxes's heads on the princes and mixed up the witch with the beautiful girl in the red cape.[9]

A windy mixture, indeed. Worlds made and unmade, captured in a vivid, *glowing* synaesthetic prose that teases the eye, ear, and nose. Supernatural horrors rush toward us headlong, and reluctantly retreat into the realms of the explicable, the rationally explained, and the psychologically grounded. Houses are haunted by *both* ghosts and people in *Julia*, *Ghost Story*, and *lost boy lost girl*. The living and the dead search for identity in "Hunger, an Introduction" and *In the Night Room*. The *Doppelgänger* frequenting *Mr. X* flow *into* and *out of* each other. The magicians in *Shadowland*, *A Dark Matter*, and *Floating Dragon* startle with magic and deceive with hoaxes. Writers like Tim Underhill, the fictional stand-in for Straub himself, Don Wanderley in *Ghost Story* and William Graham in *Floating Dragon* either *live* in their stories at the same time that they *write* them; or vanish altogether into their narratives, like Katherine Mannheim and Isobel Standish in *The Hellfire Club* and "Mrs. God," respectively. In the two collaborations with Stephen King, parallel worlds intertwine, their very existence hanging in the balance.

Straub's stories are like ambigrams, *Gothic* ambigrams, if you will. They can be understood, as Nathaniel Hawthorne once defined the effect, as dualities of images and ideas that can be "read" in multiple, even contradictory ways, but which ultimately suspend us in the space *in between*.[10] In Straub's novel *In the Night Room*, the character of Tim Underhill privileges this essential ambivalence: "I like the space between. The space between dreaming and wakefulness. Between imagination and reality. Between no and yes. Between is and is not. That's where the interesting stuff is. That's where you are. You are completely the product of the space between…. Where they both hold true, where they become one thing."[11] Straub has admitted in an interview that metatexts like this and many of his other stories "allow for inconclusiveness, ambiguity, and a general, accommodating recognition that in this particular universe no valid position can be final."[12]

Nor should it be. Like the poet Orpheus—the favored standard bearer for artists of the imagination—suspended on the threshold between life and death, we endure (perhaps enjoy) the ambiguity. "It was one of the essential features of the Orphic myth," writes historian John Fetzer, "in that one yearns for some higher realm but, at the same time, is caught in the reality of everyday, practical living." Perhaps, Fetzer continues, none of the Romantics—perhaps Straub himself?—really *wants* to achieve closure: "I personally don't think that the Romanticist ever attains—or even deep down wants to attain—that higher realm that he's yearning for. Or, maybe he does want to, but knows it's impossible. And that's often seen as the roots of what we call 'Romantic Irony' or 'Romantic Agony.' We can only stand there at the crossroads and find a way of life and understanding that adjusts to this basically tragic situation we're in."[13]

The Wound and the Bow

Straub's Juniper Tree has roots that burrow deep into a postmodernist, self-ironizing preoccupation with the transgression of the body. This has been dubbed "Affect Horror," i.e., the experience wholly given over to visceral affect, to "the atrocity of the thing itself."[14] Deviant behavior, even torture and sadism, transform the visceral responses of *grand guignol* into hitherto undreamt of extremes of affect. The *enjoyment* of the wicked Eva Galli regarding the tortures she inflicts upon her victims in *Ghost Story* comes to mind, of course, as well as the depictions of tortures in other stories to be presently examined in this book, notably *Koko*, "A Special Place," "The Blue Rose," and "Mr. Clubb and Mr. Cuff."

Straub's exuberant indulgence in this sort of thing—which he shares with many of his contemporaries, including Jack Ketchum (*The Girl Next Door*), Thomas Tessier (*Finishing Touches*), and Clive Barker (*Books of Blood*), etc.—is regarded in some quarters as controversial. "Peter Straub's personal voice," writes critic Roz Kaveney in a review of *Magic Terror*, "shows a compassion for the victimized that sometimes sits uneasily alongside his fascinated taxonomizing of the processes of victimization."[15] Yet, it belongs to a tradition harkening back to the bloody savagery of the archetypal serial killer "Bluebeard" in Perrault's fairy tale, the hideous descriptions by the Puritan Jonathan Edwards of the tortures that await the unregenerate in Hell, the Jacobean tragedy of John Webster's *The Duchess of Malfi*, and more latterly in the final scenes of Alban Berg's *Lulu*, Artaud's Theater of Cruelty, the raw and visceral screams of Francis Bacon's paintings, and the tangled shrieks of the music of the Beatles's *Revolution 9*.[16] Even in the works of those elegant Gothic stylists to whom Straub owes so much, including Nathaniel Hawthorne's dark allegories of satanic temptation and unpardonable sin and Henry James's ghost stories (recall the outcry "Oh, how delicious!" when one of the ladies in the prologue of *The Turn of the Screw* is warned that the tale to be told possesses sheer "ugliness and horror and pain")— the disturbing *frisson* of blood and pain prevails.

What seems most graphically relevant, however, are works by the brilliant Italian Baroque sculptor Gianlorenzo Bernini, whose "The Martyrdom of San Lorenzo" (1613) and "The Ecstasy of St. Theresa" (1644–1647) are studies in the evocation of simultaneous pain and pleasure, physical torture and spiritual transcendence. "It's this precise moment of transformation," writes art historian Simon Schama of the "Martyrdom"—"at once spiritual and carnal—Lawrence's body arched in a mysterious union of pan and pleasure—that Bernini tries to seize...."[17]

This is not to confuse this tendency in Straub with the recent filmic genre of "torture porn," a term coined by David Edelstein in 2006 describing a spate of post–Abu Ghraib atrocities in films such as the *Saw* and *Hostel* series. Their depictions of torture are unusual due to their pandering to the viewer's perverse *enjoyment* of torture.[18] To the contrary, contends Gary K. Wolfe, we find in Straub's characters "the seed of exaltation in extremity, of ... transcendence."[19] Damaging experiences, says Wolfe, "can help one accept and transcend those experiences." It is the notion, Wolfe adds, "that at the heart of horror is some kind of emotional truth ... the disturbing emotion that arises from glimpsing a reality that neither the characters (nor the reader) are fully prepared to deal with."[20] Straub has talked candidly about this in a recent interview:

> Nobody gets anywhere at all without some bit of *woundedness* about them. This idea is not original to me. There's a great book by Edmund Wilson called *The Wound and the Bow*.[21] It looks back to Greek myth ... and the idea that writers accrete fiction pearl-like around the places they've been hurt. I think there's a great deal of truth in that. I think the woundedness amounts to a separation, an awakening of the mind where you realize you and the world are very different.... Every single person on earth has experienced pain, grief, loss, and these things deepen them. There's a genuine humanity in the recognition that other people bear their own agonies and miseries and bandaged places through the world.[22]

He repeatedly describes this as an epiphany, a kind of *clarity*—a perception wherein, as he writes in "The Buffalo Hunter," "everything glows ... everything is organized to take you somewhere.... There's some force pushing away at all the details, making them bulge, making them sing" (177).

Who else but Straub could find in that most disturbing and baffling of his short stories, "The Ballad of Ballard and Sandrine," a *love story* arising from the mutilations the two titular characters inflict upon each other? "I liked the idea of these people doing this essentially barbaric, painful, terrible, mutilating thing to one another out of love and mutual respect and out of actual knowledge of where it was going and what was going to happen to them."[23]

Straub rarely loses sight of what is ultimately the most baffling, even horrific of monsters—the human animal. Nothing is more monstrous and inexplicable than a mind divided against itself. "'Unlike you and me,'" says serial killer Till Hayward to his protégé, Keith, in Straub's "A Special Place"— "'most people hide their real motives from themselves. They have no idea why they do the things they do. Oh, they talk all day long about what made them do this and that, but what they tell you isn't even close to the truth. Because they don't *know* the truth. And why is that? They can't let themselves know it. The truth is unacceptable. Every human being on earth tells millions of lies in the course of his life, but most of those lies are to himself about himself.'"[24] Hence his crowded gallery of wartime atrocities and the depredations of serial killers and child molesters in the so-called "Blue Rose" trilogy of novels, *Mystery*, *Koko*, and *The Throat*; the stories "The Juniper Tree," "Bunny Is Good Bread," "Blue Rose," "A Special Place"; and the current novel-in-progress, *Hello, Jack*. More than one reader has flinched at Straub's gruesomely detailed accounts of these visceral horrors. Yet Straub insists his preoccupation with the serial killer, in particular, provides opportunities to measure the stark confrontation of life and death, to relish "the passage into death [which] is an immense transition from the temporal into the eternal. I think there's a tremendous focused power involved in that particular moment."[25]

Serial killers conduct their lives as a Great Secret, of daylight anonymity and nocturnal evil: "If you run your life that way," says Straub, "the most important part of your life must be secret; everything else is a sort of code." A key to that code may be, as in Straub's aforementioned stories, "Bunny Is Good Bread" and "The Juniper Tree," the formative influences on serial killers of childhood trauma and abuse: "I always went back to that same conception that some people are made out of other people who have a great potential for good that was by cruelty and ignorance pounded out of them, so their lives turn into retribution. Unfortunately, the retribution is wreaked upon the innocent."

Further, "[their] whole childhoods are composed of such cruelties I feel empathy for them. What I feel for the man who grew up from that child—I feel a kind of extremity of pity. I think, 'You shouldn't be that way. Somebody made you that way.... For much of my work, when I look at the serial killer, in a way he's the most beloved character in the book. This surely must give my work an odd taste, but it's worth thinking about."[26]

Straub has revealed that the trauma of a debilitating accident suffered in childhood has profoundly impacted his own professional and private adult life. With the aid of a therapist, after many years, he recovered a forgotten near-death experience. "I opened and explored, often shaken and weeping, an internal seam of misery, sorrow, rage, and endless injury," he says. In a phrase that will be repeated several times throughout this book—indeed, it could be his testament—he confronted and embraced these horrors in his life and work: "*I wanted to wear my own blood.* I wanted to walk around in the costume of my worst, most decisive, most mysterious and appalling moment.... I wanted to plug myself back into the fearful story to recover what had been lost. The wish to dress myself in that ruined clothing, it strikes me now, represented a childish, cartoonlike attempt at self-analysis" (my italics).[27]

Hovering uncertainly between life and death, between substance and shadow, between the visible and the invisible, Straub eventually recovered not only the pain, the imminence of death, but also a kind of transcendence, or ecstasy, "which flooded into me and was instantly beyond my capacity for coping with it, even to contain it...."[28] Descriptions like this, couched in a language that "glows," is typical of Straub's distinctive tone and style. It is a synaesthetic prose style that "paints" like an artist, "sings" like a musician, and "dreams" like a poet.

"To think there really is no meaning in life is to live in an empty, dead world," Straub says. "Is the everyday a kind of blank, or does it reveal a transfiguration? Is there a hidden radiance or a hidden nothing?" Straub answers his own questions:

> There's no question which side of the duality I have chosen as the truth. I like the drawing by Chris Van Allsburg in his book, *The Mysteries of Harris Burdick* [1984]. It could have been from *The Talisman*. It shows some children pedaling a machine through a desert; and there before them is a huge palace. The caption says: "If it was anywhere, it was there." Although I don't really think there is a theological or supernatural motif that breathes through the world, what I really believe is that the world is its own meaning. If it's just dead matter, then we're left in a sort of pointless hell, it seems to me.[29]

A deeply felt grace and humane compassion illuminates the work of Peter Straub. An Emersonian to the core, Straub transcends the human without forsaking humanism.[30]

The Weird

This not to say that Straub doesn't occasionally indulge himself in the essentially *non-human* horrors of what writer China Miéville has dubbed "The Weird," which involves the dread of outer, unknown forces, of monstrous creatures.[31] Straub displays a certain prankishness, even an antic humor, here. What seems at first to be an "anti–Gothic" sensibility actually bears a passing affinity to the *Sagen* tradition of the European fairy tale (see the "Shadowplay" chapter), which revels in the horror of the physical universe, of the sorts of oozing, tentacled things that began to appear early in the last century in the horror stories of William Hope Hodgson (*Boats of the "Glen Carrig"*), M.R. James ("Count Magnus"), and H.P. Lovecraft ("The Call of Cthulhu" and "The Dunwich Horror"). Lacking "moral" and "instructional" agendas, these entities are not evil, but "predatory and cosmically amoral." Indeed, if they serve any morally heuristic purpose at all, Miéville adds, "it is precisely to undermine any religiose good/evil binary."[32] Thus, Straub serves up monstrous assaults on the village of Milburn in *Ghost Story*; Hampstead, Connecticut, in *Floating Dragon;* Edgerton, Illinois, in the Lovecraftian pastiche, *Mr. X.* A veritable apotheosis of the Affect transpires in the closing chapters of *Black House.* These are fun-house horrors, "savage sideshows" (the phrase is Rimbaud's).[33] The grotesque is laced with a mad, sardonic humor. "[This] excessive intensity," observes critic Terry Eagleton, is "in the manner of an obscene joke [which] allows us to indulge our repressed fantasies so unashamedly that we laugh at its very bare-facedness, quite independently of its content."[34] Straub has admitted as much in a 1985 interview, that *excess* was the whole point in *Floating Dragon*: "I sort of deliberately let out all the stops and made things as graphic, visceral, and physical as I could possibly do, because the point of the book was its demonstration of the effect of excess."[35] Thus, side by side with a more traditional brand of ghosting, Straub effects an "under-one-roof *co-existence* of the two"—a union Miéville wittily calls a kind of tag-team in which "*Hauntology deploys Weird as its sidekick.*"[36]

However Straub's Gothic may be classified—as Weird, Transgressive, Affect, Post-modernist Irony, or Transcendent—what has been wrought, admits a bemused Straub, is "barely classifiable at all—except as literature."[37] Historian Douglas Winter agrees. However we define it, he says, it threatens to move "to the level of serious art and of involved, committed writing, of moral complexity."[38] And Straub himself, in a recent interview, observes that "every genre," as it matures, "goes in the direction of general literature. It's the only thing it can do."[39]

Pictures in the Fire

This book is not a biography but a series of investigations into his work, occasionally contextualized with aspects of his life and with excerpts from interviews, including those with this author. It fills an important gap in scholarship. Only one other book-length study on him has been written, Bill Sheehan's invaluable *At the Foot of the Story Tree*. Limited to the small readership of a specialty press (Subterranean Books), it was published in 2000 and is out of print and out of date. With his permission, I frequently quote from this volume.

Chapter One, "The Magic Taxi," is a brief survey of Straub's short stories. It begins with an invitation from Straub himself. In one of his earliest stories, "Something about a Death, Something about a Fire," which appears in *Houses Without Doors*, a mysterious character named Bobo, a quiet, ordinary man, whose "painted figure is so akin to ours, and yet so foolish, so theatrical in its grief," one day leaves his house, steps to the curb, and enters a waiting taxi … a *Magic* Taxi. It takes him into wonderful, but terrifying worlds. It transforms him. It is his destiny. This enchanting little fable, along with the other short stories examined here, is representative of that first step that carries us all away from our conventional lives on a trip that is "pregnant with miracle."[40]

Chapter Two, "A Dark Necessity," traces Straub's literary journey from the Gothic influences of the early European masters, such as E.T.A. Hoffmann, Mary Shelley, and Charles Maturin in his first novels, to his forging of an *American* Gothic, inflected by the Americans Charles Brockden Brown, Nathaniel Hawthorne, Herman Melville, Henry James, and H. P. Lovecraft. He is both the Gothic's literary guardian and its critic. He is attentive to its detail, alert to its contexts, and hungry for its larger meanings. We examine the impact that Hawthorne and James, in particular, have had on Straub's first successful novel, *Ghost Story*. Its vision of dark forces underlying the illusory surface of things strikes the essential tone of an *American* Gothic:

> Our literature starts with a vision of blackness [Straub says], and I think that has a lot to do with the fact that our country at first was mostly untameable forest. There were truly bad things out there. Now we don't want to have that. Now in America we want to believe in the surface of things. We put a lot of faith in appearance and spend a lot of money trying to look good according to some rule we have in our minds. But I think daily life is still filled with uncertainty, anxiety and fear. Nobody's life is really safe.[41]

Straub's oft-used Gothic tropes include multi-tiered narrative constructions, buried secrets, ghostly doubles, haunted places, dark magicians, and demonic, vengeful females. "Making creative use of one's personal literary pantheon is not necessarily a bad thing," writes critic Bill Sheehan, "and Straub [builds] a distinguished career writing novels that incorporated within their complex and varied structures affectionate and respectful reflections of, and responses to, the novels, stories, poems and essays that have spoken most directly to his creative consciousness."[42]

Chapter Three, "King of the Cats," examines Straub's connections with and extensions of the rich oral and written tradition of the fairy tale, the "literary fairy tale" (the *Kunstmärchen*), and the *Sagen* of Europe and America. Master literary artificers are invoked, such as The Brothers Grimm, Novalis, Goethe, Washington Irving, and their modern-day acolytes, A.S. Byatt, Walter de la Mare, Philip Pullman, and Straub himself. They are all participants in a kind of storytelling that perpetually alters and expands narratives to suit the contexts and tempers of the times. One archetypal story, "The King of the Cats," winds its way like a black thread through the long and convoluted novel that is the centerpiece of this chapter, *Shadowland*. It and other Straubian narratives, like *The Hellfire Club*, *Floating Dragon*, and *A Dark Matter*, contain stories within stories, tales told, then retold, sometimes contradicted, then told again—of secrets, lost and orphaned children, stolen identities, master magicians, talking animals, imperiled princesses, and rooms locked and forbidden. Straub's own interest in this tradition stems, in part, from the experience of telling stories to his children. However, there are implications here that some fairy tales are decidedly *not* for children. In *Shadowland*, Tom Flanagan discovers a hidden room in the haunted mansion of his magician uncle, where he meets none other than Jacob and Wilhelm Grimm. They are scribbling stories, to "amaze," "terrify," and "delight"—but not for children: "'No child can go the whole way with them.'" Their tale of "The Boy Who Could Not Shiver," for example, "'is full of the most frightening things ever encountered; but many frightening things conceal jokes, and many jokes have ice in their hearts.'"[43]

Chapter Four, "Protean Impostures," is an inquiry into the classic Gothic trope of the *Doppelgänger*. The centerpiece is Straub's *Mr. X*, the "Citizen Kane" of *Doppelgänger* stories. As critic Gary K. Wolfe observes, it exploits, as it transcends, the classic Gothic trope of the Ghostly Double.[44] Straub himself acknowledges that "secret sharers, unknown brothers, and shadow selves, with their inevitable suggestion that the truly dangerous adversary has stepped out of the mirror, had always appealed to me. They had a lovely eeriness combined with great psychological suggestiveness. Poe, Stevenson and Dostoevsky had written *Doppelgänger* stories, and so had Daphne du Maurier, Christopher Priest, Orhan Pamuk and lots of other people. Wilkie Collins, one of my ancestral spirits, had virtually built his career on the conceit."[45]

The figure of H. P. Lovecraft, the Providence master of weird fiction, looms large. His example and his writings, particularly "The Dunwich Horror" and "The Shunned House," ooze through every crack and crevice of *Mr. X*. Straub himself edited Lovecraft's stories for the Library of America and professes a bemused admiration and respect for his work. In sum, the sense of dislocation, fragmentation, and yearning for identity, inherent in *Doppelgänger* narratives—with its attendant risks of self-destruction—is central to *Mr. X* and all of Straub's stories.

Chapter Five, "Datchery's Children," examines Straub's crime and detective fiction. It begins with a detective named "Dick Datchery," who mysteriously appears near the end of Charles Dickens's unfinished *The Mystery of Edwin Drood*. Datchery's example—his elusive presence, disguises, and inconclusive investigation—hovers throughout the works of Peter Straub, particularly the so-called "Blue Rose" trilogy (*Mystery, Koko, The Throat*) and related works, *A Dark Matter, lost boy lost girl,* and *In the Night Room*. Datchery's literary progeny include Straub's collection of amateur sleuths, private detectives, policemen, occult investigators, literary scholars, and, for lack of a better term, interested parties. In common, they all gather clues, take testimonies, make deductions, revise those deductions, and face dangers—all in the quest to reconstruct the buried bones of Straub's Juniper Tree. While their cases resist easy classification, they may be generally categorized as meditations on the variety of the genres of detection—formal puzzles, hard-boiled cases, nightmarish *noirs*, and occult encounters (sometimes all at once)—and the shared affinities between detective and criminal, pursuer and pursued, writer and story that border on identity. Haunting these pages are those archetypes of classic, hard-boiled, and occult investigations that may lay a claim on the evolution of Straub's brand of crime and detection, Conan Doyle's Sherlock Holmes, G.K. Chesterton's Father Brown, Dashiell Hammett's Sam Spade, Raymond Chandler's Philip Marlowe, Ross Macdonald's Lew Archer, and William Hope Hodgson's John Carnacki. Even the real-life psychic investigations of William James claim a place here.

Chapter Six, "The Third Voice: Straub and Stephen King," examines the private and professional relationship between the two most popular and respected novelists of weird fiction working today. Their collaborations on two highly successful novels, *The Talisman* and *Black House*—the first two installments of a projected trilogy—combine a Quest narrative with an apocalyptic vision. Theirs is a collision/conflation of two seeming contradictory temperaments, work habits. As Straub says, not entirely whimsically, he is the lyric, reflective "Raymond Chandler" to King's intuitive, blunt-force "Dashiell Hammett." "Steve has almost instant access to his imagination," Straub says here. "The extraordinary thing was the way I could move through his mind and he could move through my mind. And that's an experience writers never have. And it was very, very moving to have done that."[46] The result is a mutually shared "third voice." Comparisons and contrasts are also offered in a brief examination of how both writers examine the effects of the Vietnam War on America's public and private character. Selections from a new interview with Stephen King conclude the chapter.

The last chapter is "'Invisible Ink." Few writers have more openly shared with readers experiences and insights into the methods, hazards and turmoils of the writer's life. He reveals that an important part of his writing life is conducted *away* from his desk. Like a latter-day *flâneur*, he draws upon observations of the bustling world around him: "To me, a *flâneur* is a gentleman who walks around his city, keeping his eyes open, sitting in cafes watching the parade go by while making mental notes."[47] Central to the discussion are *The Hellfire Club*, "Mrs. God," *A Dark Matter, Shadowland*, and *In the Night Room* which, as metatexts, contain some of Straub's most striking commentaries on the world of writers, writing, publishers, critics, and readers. In *The Hellfire Club* he reveals himself to be a critic and satirist of the academic life he once aspired to. And too often, as we see in *Hellfire* and "Mrs. God," sheer pedantry can have dangerous consequences. His self-criticism has provided some of his most hilarious passages, as he deploys his own *Doppelgänger*, the fictitious academic literary critic "Putney Tyson Ridge," to review his work.[48] Crucial to the chapter is the distinctive nature of his prose. He "speaks" as a novelist, he "paints" as an artist, and he "sings" as a composer and musician. Above all, he dreams as a poet. His background and abiding interest in poetry, particularly his love of the work of William Carlos Williams, Wallace Stevens, Fernando Pessoa, and John Ashbery, are an important part of the discussion. He is preoccupied with rendering in prose those non-verbal art forms of music, particularly improvisatory jazz, and painting, from the Pre-Raphaelites to the Surrealists, that constantly inform his narratives. He is greatly interested in "ear language," the sheer sound of the spoken word. We wonder, at times, is Straub yearning toward a language not yet devised and a book not yet written? He admits he falls short of the ideal: "Given that one always wishes to write a perfect book, and that perfection is impossible to attain, frustration is inevitable."[49]

In an Appendix, "A Magellan of the Interior," Peter Straub meets us at his home. His conversation is full of surprisingly candid comments on his childhood and private life. It is amusing, moreover, that, whereas his literary persona is, by turns, quietly sinister, albeit of a poetic bent, his outward public aspect is nothing if not affable and congenial. Those familiar with the former may be forgiven for momentary bewilderment at confronting the latter. "I've been told I'm not at all what people expect," he admits. "But then again, they are meeting the social person who's out there to be met. They meet the person I'm *willing* for them to meet."[50]

A Note on Straub Page References

For the ease and convenience of the reader (and not to clutter up this book with more chapter notes than is absolutely necessary), this book provides page numbers parenthetically inserted within the text from the Straub stories and novels that are listed in the bibliography. All other sources are included in the chapter notes.

Chapter One

"The Magic Taxi"
The Short Stories

We are separate, lost in our separation.
—Peter Straub, "Something about a Death,
Something about a Fire"

There is no better introduction and approach to the complexities of Peter Straub and his work than his short-story collections, *Houses Without Doors* (1990), *Magic Terror* (2000), *5 Stories* (2008), and, most recently, *Interior Darkness* (2016). More compact and linear in construction—if no less baffling—than the complex narrative structures of his big novels, the stories are either fragments split off from larger narratives, chips from the master's workbench, or stand-alone narratives.[1] "Peter Straub's shorter fictions are like tiny novels you drown in," says Neil Gaiman, "perfectly pitched, terrifyingly smart, big-hearted, dangerous, and even cruel ... and, sometimes, at the edges, allows glimpses of his fierce sense of humour. Straub deploys a host of voices that cajole and whisper and talk to you from the darkness. If you care about the short story, you should read this book, and watch a master at work."[2]

Whereas he has heretofore expressed preference for the longer form of story writing, now, upon the release of *Interior Darkness*, he confesses a change of heart. "When I started writing," he says in a recent interview, "I had no interest at all in novellas; now I love them deeply, and I think I'm right at home with them.... I feel freer when writing short fiction and I'm willing to take tremendous chances.... I know how to handle the length; it suits me to the ground."[3]

Alike defying easy classification, the stories *burn* and *boil* and *sizzle* with buried secrets (to apply several of his favorite verbs) and past traumas. They appear and reappear at intervals throughout these pages, complementing and extending the larger contexts of the novels. If perhaps less celebrated than the novels, they reveal Straub as a master of the short form, the equal of the contemporaries he admires, such as Robert Aickman, Neil Gaiman, John Crowley, and Thomas Tessier.

A "Magic Taxi" appears in an early story, "Something about a Death, Something about a Fire," collected in *Houses Without Doors*. No ordinary conveyance, it carries Straub's characters to transformative worlds, just as it beckons we readers to "ride along," as it were. This enchanting fable vividly compresses into a scant four pages the essential core of his achievement. We meet Bobo the Clown as he enters the circus tent in his Magic Taxi. Who is Bobo and what is a Magic Taxi? Hold on. A performance is about to begin. "At this moment," Straub writes, "the audience falls silent, as if hypnotized. You feel uncertain, slightly on edge, as if you have forgotten something you particularly wished to remember." Bobo wears a funny suit and blats a little horn. "His painted figure is so akin to ours, and yet so foolish, so theatrical in its grief, that we are distracted from our own memories." What does he do? We don't know, or we don't remember. There is just a sense of a beam of light that shines "like a transparent wire" into our eyes. And then there was something about a death, something about a fire.... We awake as if from a trance, "drawn up out of unhappiness by our love for this tinted waif" (215–219). But there are tears in our eyes...

What has happened?

As an observer in the story speculates, Bobo may once have been an "ordinary man with an ordinary job," a man like any of us, trapped in his own separation, his own blank reality. One morning on the way to work Bobo found a Magic Taxi waiting at the curb. "[The Magic Taxi] was his destiny," concludes the observer, "entirely unforeseen, black and purring softly, pregnant with miracle" (219).

Bobo is only one of the many characters in these stories who flee by a back exit from their intolerable private realities. "A lot of experience is unacknowledged," says a Vietnam soldier in "The Ghost Village": "Religion lets us handle some of the unacknowledged stuff in an acceptable way. But suppose, just suppose, that you were forced to confront extreme experience directly, without any mediation?... When a crime is too great to live with, it becomes sacred. Becomes the crime itself" (92). While Bobo is transfigured and disappears in his Magic Taxi into an ever-widening sphere of glory, other characters, in their journeys into madness, find themselves trapped, wedged into an ever-narrowing circle of diminishing options and opportunities. Mr. Bunting in "The Buffalo Hunter" turns inward, like a "Magellan of the interior, where everything important lay" (151–152). Driven by his infantile fantasies, he locks himself in his room, covers the walls with hundreds of baby bottles (from which he sucks large quantities of liquor) and loses himself in the hot-house imagery and fabulous characters of books by Luke Short and Raymond Chandler. The printed page leaps up at him and he plunges head-long into its delicious, seductive world. "Everything you see, touch, feel, smell, everything you notice and everything you think, is organized to take you somewhere," declares Bunting (177). The trip will prove fatal. For all of them, however, there can be no return.

The thirteen short stories in *Houses Without Doors*—six tales inter-spersed with seven brief "interludes," as they are called—effectively sample buried guilts and contemporary horrors—atrocities in Viet Nam ("Blue Rose"), the sexual abuse of children ("The Juniper Tree"), a serial killer ("A Short Guide to the City"), abortion ("Mrs. God") and an assortment of quirky obsessions—like the man who literally buries himself in a room filled with baby bottles ("The Buffalo Hunter") and the business executive who one day goes quietly mad and takes a Magic Taxi into another world ("Something about a Death, Something about a Fire"). The aforementioned "A Short Guide to the City"—in my opinion one of his most important stories, a defin-itive view of his native Milwaukee, Wisconsin, a region that plays a vital role in many of his stories—is a panoramic view of an entire region gone mad, whose "characteristic mode is *denial*" and where "violence is an internal matter, to be resolved within or exercised upon one's own body and soul or those of one's immediate family" (96–100). A serial killer is loose. And once, sev-eral children found a winged man "speaking a strange language none of the children knew" (97). Straub is typically generous in citing the story's origins: "There's a [Gabriel García] Márquez short story that went straight into my bloodstream about children who find this beat-up, tattered old angel in a packing case. And they try to kill him. They throw stones at him until he flies off.

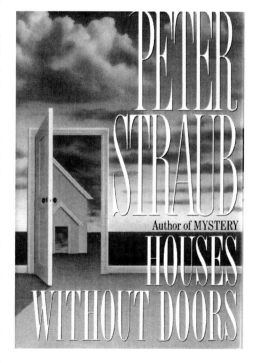

Cover of *Houses Without Doors*, Peter Straub's first story collection (used by per-mission of Peter Straub).

It struck me as though I should have thought of that. And I use it here and there in stories. What it alludes to or what it's about is the presence of the marvelous in a degraded world; and how people respond to it."[4]

As these stories provoke and tantalize, they introduce us to the ambiguity of meanings that is a hallmark of Straub's work. "I've always really liked things I do not understand," he has admitted, "stories that seemed to me to resist, in fact to refuse conventional forms of understanding." Indeed, life itself, he adds, "is riddled with the indeterminate, the unresolved, with the mystery of human motive...."[5]

Readers coming to Straub's work for the first time will be baffled, dismayed, teased and tantalized by the vibrant prose, odd characters, and narrative enigmas. Held in a kind of thrall, we read on and on. The image of the bottle-sucking Bunting is comically pathetic. The incidents of sexual abuse in "The Juniper Tree" are graphic and repulsive. Harry Beevers' sadistic torture of his brother is painfully explicit. And Professor Standish's torturous descent into madness in "Mrs. God" elicits in us a queasy uneasiness that is most disturbing. "Like sweat or semen," writes Straub, "anxiety is a physical substance that pours from a self-replenishing well" (226).

To pursue the implications of the title, *Houses Without Doors*, the partitions between these stories, characters, and incidents are paper-thin—as if these "houses without doors" are also, in effect, houses without walls. For example, the murderer in "Blue Rose," Harry Beevers, reappears as the unnamed serial killer in "A Short Guide to the City." Beevers' wartime atrocities—the slaughter of Vietnamese babies—find a parallel in the abortion of his child that haunts William Standish, the college professor in "Mrs. God." Standish's eventual regression to an infantile state, in turn, is reminiscent of the baby bottle fetish of Mr. Bunting in "The Buffalo Hunter." Everything, in sum, is interrelated, fragments torn away from a greater whole. We perceive this pattern, the figure in the carpet—something akin to recognizing the internal rhyme scheme in a poem. "In violence," Straub writes, "there is often the quality of yearning—the yearning for completion. For closure" (104).

In another story collection, *Magic Terror*, we smell the blood of more of these damaged characters. "Ashputtle" clothes in modern garb the familiar fairytale of Cinderella. Mrs. Asch, an overweight school teacher, herself a victim of a terrible childhood, tells her own story, inviting us down the rabbit hole of her deranged imagination as she victimizes her students. "Hunger, an Introduction" is a ghost story unique in the genre. "Considering that everyone dies sooner or later," the ghostly narrator confides with sardonic understatement, "people know surprisingly little about ghosts" (217). Who but Straub could depict the electrocution of its protagonist as an instant of transcendence, propelling him into the ranks of ghostly: "At that moment, hunger slammed into me, stronger, more forceful, and far more enduring than the river of volts that had separated me from my former self" (245). "Bunny Is Good Bread" is another grim chronicle of the education of a serial killer. We enter the mind of a young boy as he frequents a local movie theater and endures sexual molestation while watching films, whose "characters were turned into smoking ruins, pressed flat, dismembered, broken like twigs, consumed by fires..." (111). "Porkpie Hat," like many of Straub's writings, is about a jazz musician, a legendary saxophonist known, simply, as "Hat." He expresses in his improvisations painful memories of a youth in the racist South: "Hat's sadness seemed to be for the universe, or to be a larger than usual personal share of a sadness already existing in the universe" (8). His mantra could well be that of Straub himself: "You start to grow up," Hat says, "when you understand that the stuff that scares you is part of the air you breathe" (89). "Mr. Clubb and Mr. Cuff" is a gleeful *guignol* that revels in torture and gore as the life of a successful Wall Street banker is taken over by the titular private detectives who subject both him and his enemies to an inventive variety of assaults and tortures. They are "artists" who "instruct" their victims in pain and usher them into transcendence. "There comes a moment when they understand that they are changed for good, they have passed over the border into another realm, from which there is no return" (317). "Ghost Village" is a Vietnam story detached from the main narrative of *The Throat*. A combat platoon on patrol encounters the ghost-haunted village of Bong To, site of recently unearthed atrocities against children. Soldiers and victims alike—and their ghosts—are indistinguishable and inseparable from each other.

In the two other collections, *5 Stories* and *Interior Darkness*, we encounter eight more stories of surpassing ambiguity—"Little Red's Tango," "Why Electricman Lives in New York," "Mr. Aickman's Air Rifle," "The General's Wife," "Mallon the Guru," "Lapland," "The Collected Short Stories of Freddie Prothero," and "The Ballad of Ballard and Sandrine." They seem to detach themselves from normal narrative constraints. They fly free of reason and logic. Consider the *picant* story about the reclusive "Little Red," who lives alone in a ground-floor apartment on West 55th Street in New York City. Insulated from the outside world within the squalor of his crowded shelves of jazz recordings, he receives, as if by papal dispensation, only a few privileged visitors, to whom he dispenses a few Beatitudes ("Accept your imperfections, for they can bring you to Paradise"), performs a miracle or two, and leaves his guests baffled, yet transformed upon their departure. "Being with [Little Red] is sort of like doing the tango," muses one guest. "You might wind up with your head up your ass, but you know you had a hell of a time anyway" (40). "Nobody could tell me exactly what the guy did," recalls another visitor, "or what made him so special.... I felt like something tremendously important had happened to me, but I couldn't have told you what it was" (40–41). In the perversely baffling "Mr. Aickman's Air Rifle," conceived, Straub confesses, in the spirit of the master of the weird tale, Robert Aickman, four writers—a publisher, a critic, a plagiarist, and a popular novelists—find themselves in the cardiac ward of a hospital. They are oddly alike, united in the same illness, the same memories, the same past participation in a mysterious crime.... Did any of this happen at all?—"If we all seem to remember this bizarre story," says one, "then none of us is really remembering it" (110). "The General's Wife" is a tidy little fable about obsession and necrophila. A young lady takes on a job sorting out the memoirs of an elderly General. She meets herself in the manuscript and succumbs to its savagely erotic and obsessive nightmares. "Mallon the Guru" stands in as a preliminary sketch for the novel *A Dark Matter*. The titular Mallon, a guru who plays such an important role in that novel, is here seen as an apprentice, already creating unwonted havoc: "This most peculiar, this most dangerously peculiar man," says the village yogi, to whom he had been introduced, "has awakened disorder within our village" (427). "Lapland" is a witty evocation of the *film noir*, on screen and in the mean streets, a world "characterized by deliberate dislocations, complex and indirect narratives, flawed protagonists, ambiguous motives and resolutions, a fascination with death..." (48).

In the collection of essays, *Sides*, a delightful sketch is appended, hardly more than a comic divertissement, "Why Mr. Electricman Lives in New York." Arthur Groom, otherwise known as the superhero "Electricman," divides his time between writing an advice column and fighting crime in a cool costume, a "skintight outfit of black Spandex emblazoned front and back with a yellow lightning bolt" (200). After being struck by a lightning, Arthur discovers the ability to fight crime in a most unusual way: "[He can] dive into the nearest electrical outlet, fly through an immense network of wires to pop out of a wall or a transformer convenient to a crime scene, and make hay with the perps" (200).

Finally, among the surpassingly strangest of all of Straub's stories are two, "The Collected Short Stories of Freddie Prothero" and "The Ballad of Ballard and Sandrine," that conclude *Interior Darkness*. To say they play with language is like saying that James Joyce tinkered with words. In short, nobody writes like Peter Straub. He is the Merry Prankster of language, of prose that runs headlong into other Realms. For example, little nine-year-old Freddie Prothero is a prodigious literary prodigy who belongs to that gallery of eccentrics in the Pantheon of Straubian mystics that includes Bobo, Little Red, and Pork Pie Hat. His career was cut off short, when he mysteriously died, alone, in a field, leaving behind "the most visionary short stories in the English language." They experimented with the "improvised variant spellings long encouraged by American primary schools." Now, examined by scholars seeking their hidden meanings—"they are difficult to decode"—they seem to tell of a boy mysteriously vanished from the world under the influence of a "Monnuttmon" ("Man not man"?) (469–476). We await further clarification. "The Ballad of Ballard and Sandrine" is a singularly nasty fairy tale which surely must rank among the strangest love stories ever written. As they sail down the Amazon, the two titular lovers listen to the strange, fluting sounds of a race of bird-like creatures along the riverbanks—"miracle people, healers, shamans, warriors"—who sing notes "of the utmost liquid purity," expressing something that has "long since passed through the realm of words and gained again the transparency of music" (92). Is Straub relinquishing the sense of language altogether, in "Freddie Prothero" and the "Ballad"? Is he succumbing to "the weight and the weightlessness of music"? Or is he measuring his meaning against the rhyme scheme of a poem? The *recurrence* of events in *Ballard* is the key, he hints: "I wanted this sense of a piled-reality that was all but invisible to the characters but every now and then they would ask, *Didn't we do this before? Didn't we have this meal before? Wasn't it better before?* It's like an excursion into *déjà vu*, into the experience of living inside a long déjà vu moment."[6]

Meanwhile, Bobo's Magic Taxi waits for us at the curb. It beckons, it invites, it *commands*. Adventures horrific, mysterious, and miraculous lie ahead.

I once asked Peter Straub if somewhere in his past a "Magic Taxi" had waited for *him*, ready to transport him to places "pregnant with miracle"?

"That would have been wonderful!" laughs Straub. "No, I wrote that long before any such thing happened to me! At the time, around 1967–68, I hadn't written anything worth noting at all…. What pleased me about it and the reason I decided to include it in the book, was that it showed me that even way back then, when I had first started to write seriously, that the same kind of duality of the everyday and the miraculous was very much on my mind."

He pauses. It's a bright sunny day in late May 2010. We're having tea in the living room of his townhouse on Manhattan's Upper West Side.

"Actually," he continues, "I guess you could say that that story was my own Magic Taxi! I kept it with me in later years when I went to Dublin and London. God knows how I found it later. It's about wonder and close attention and the way it can widen out into a sense of mystery, of unknowingness; and the sense that glory may not always end that way. Maybe there's a good-sized Magic Taxi somewhere within my own mind and imagination."[7]

CHAPTER TWO

"A Dark Necessity"

Straub's American Gothic

"In old houses like this, you know, dead people are very apt to come back again."
—Hepzibah Pyncheon, *The House of the Seven Gables*

"'The place is haunted, *haunted*!' I exulted in the word as if it stood for all I had ever dreamt of!"
—Henry James, "Sir Edmond Orme"

"Nathaniel Hawthorne turned the key [and] gave me entry to the lost realm."
—Lee Harwell, *A Dark Matter*

Peter Straub's frequent acknowledgment of and implementation in his stories of the works of the great 19th-century Gothic practitioners of England, Europe, and America calls for close attention.[1] He not only draws upon them, but he imaginatively transforms them and gives them fresh breath, in effect. Of particular importance here are those 19th-century literary architects of what is recognized as a distinctively American Gothic, whose forms and expressions were congruent with New World attitudes and ideas. Charles Brockden Brown, Nathaniel Hawthorne, Edgar Allan Poe, Henry James, and Herman Melville claim pride of place. (Here, I will restrict myself primarily to Hawthorne and James.) Yet, it seems that very little criticism has explored in any detail their connections with Straub's work. Clearly, there is a deeply shared kinship that borders on identity. His stories establish him not just as their artistic and spiritual heir, but as their standard bearer toward a modern American Gothic.[2]

Consider as a preliminary example, Straub's "break-out" novel, *Ghost Story*. He had already written two exemplary novels of ghostly obsession, *Julia* (1975) and *If You Could See Me Now* (1977), but their ambition and scope were not to be compared with the extravagance and amplitude of *Ghost Story*.

Published in 1979, it still claims fame as his most popular novel. "With the possible exception of Stephen King's *The Shining*," writes critic Bill Sheehan, "which Straub himself has called 'a masterpiece,' no Gothic novel in recent memory had attempted or achieved as much as *Ghost Story*."[3] It spent almost twenty weeks on the best-seller lists of the *New York Times*, became a Main Selection of the Book of the Month Club, and was reissued in paperback by Pocket Books. Both *Ghost Story* and *Julia* have been adapted to film. *Julia* came first, in 1977, from Cinema International Corporation, starring Mia Farrow and Keir Dullea. *Ghost Story*, from Universal Studios, was released in 1981, with an all-star cast, including Fred Astaire, John Houseman, Douglas Fairbanks, Jr., Melvyn Douglas, and Alice Krige as the demonic Eva Galli. Both are tepid affairs.[4]

The setting of *Ghost Story* is the little upstate New York town of Milburn, currently in the grip of a brutal early winter. Past sins, present recriminations, and their inevitable consequences are at hand. An array of vampires, were-wolves, and ghostly apparitions lurk in the forests, haunt the houses, and glide with impunity about the streets. Of particular interest is the local movie theater, the Milburn Rialto, a "place of dreams," site of the penultimate battle where human and inhuman creatures grapple in a nightmarish tussle while violent images from *Night of the Living Dead* play out on the screen. Movie theaters will prove to be sites of pain and violence in many more of Straub's subsequent stories, including *The Throat* and "Bunny Is Good Bread."

Only a group of elderly storytellers, members of the so-called Chowder Society—Sears James, Ricky Hawthorne, John Jaffrey, and Lewis Benedikt—stands against the horrors. They gather frequently to share "a few bad dreams and a bi-weekly spook story" (47). A young newcomer, Don Wanderley, himself a writer of ghost stories and the nephew of one of their lately-deceased members, joins their ranks; and it is he who foregrounds the realization that everything that is happening is a part of a ghost story he is presently writing, *Nightwatcher*. Together, they provoke the horrors while endeavoring to vanquish them. "'When all of us were joined by Don,'" confesses Ricky, "'the forces, whatever you want to call them, were increased. We invoked them. We by our stories, Don in his book and in his imagination.... We dream horrors...'" (276). Thus, all of *Ghost Story* assumes a meta-narrative quality. These men are both authors and readers, their own stories and storytellers.

Meanwhile, what is the dark secret behind the hauntings in Milburn? We don't learn its nature until well toward the end, and not before Straub entangles us in a complex weave of intertwining narrative lines, buried guilts, mysterious deaths, and unreliable narrators—of ghost stories both told and experienced, of time lines past and present, and characters blended and merged. The revelation, when it finally comes, is both tawdry and terrible: Fifty years earlier, a young actress named Eva Galli attempted to seduce the Chowder men. The sexual frenzy of her advances shocked the young idealists, who had always regarded her as an unattainable goddess. "We were speechless," recalls Sears James. "We had never seen any woman act that way." Ricky Hawthorne adds, "I think what she felt was *hate*, a cyclone of hate.... She *did* seem like a devil; like something possessed. You know how when a woman gets angry, really angry, she can reach way back into herself and find rage enough to blow any man to pieces—how all that feeling comes out and hits you like a truck? It was like that."

Vampire-like, she threatens to "take a bite" out of them. Stripping off her clothes, she literally falls upon Lewis Benedikt, literally devouring him. "It looked like she was eating half his face," adds James. "Imagine that, those hate-filled kisses pouring over you, all that fury biting into your mouth. It must have been like kissing a razor." In retaliation, Benedikt tackles her, pushing her head against the brick fireplace—where she lies still and quite dead. The remaining hours were a nightmare as the men desperately contrived to dispose of her body in a car in a nearby pond. "Her hatred had provoked us to something very like murder, if not murder under the law. And now we were talking about concealing our act—both legally and morally, a damning step. And we agreed to it." The car went down and never came up. But was she really dead? Ricky adds that at the moment the car slid into the water, they saw her face, "starring at us, grinning at us, jeering at us..." (357–360).

Over time, Eva's vengeful spirit, incarnated, variously, in the forms of Alma Mobley, Ann-Veronica Moore, Anna Mostyn, and Angie Maule—and aided by a grotesque collection of shape-shifting creatures—subjects the guilty men and the town at large to a veritable holocaust of murders, savage tortures, necrophilia. As critic Bill Sheehan observes, "She is a master illusionist, and can generate phantasmagorical visions so detailed, so rooted in the psychological predispositions of the viewer, that they achieve their own reality."[5] A key question-and-response mantra is repeatedly voiced throughout: "'Who are you?'" ask the Chowder members of Eva's ghostly manifestations. "'I am *you*,'" she replies. "'*You* are the ghost'" (32).

This "unhappy perception," Don Wanderley realizes, "[is] at the center of every ghost story" (368).

Real, or imagined? The answer is "Yes!" Indeed, *Ghost Story* walks its own tightrope. It is a kind of literary ambigram, as it were, poised between the supernatural and the natural, between the ghostly and the human. As one of the Chowder men admits, "'I do not mean that [Eva] made me believe

in the paraphernalia of the supernatural; but she suggested that such
things might be fluttering invisibly
about us'" (205).

19th-Century American Gothic

Two American masters of the
Gothic tale, Nathaniel Hawthorne
and Henry James, figure among the
prime influences on *Ghost Story*, as
well as on many of Straub's other
novels and stories. Hawthorne and
James had helped forge a distinctively *American* Gothic, derived in
part from the Old World Gothic
example and a New World response.
They followed on the heels of the
late 18th-century and early 19th-
century Europeans writers Ann

Nathaniel Hawthorne

Radcliffe, E.T.A. Hoffmann, Ludwig Tieck, Mary Shelley, Matthew Lewis,
Charles Maturin, who wrought a subversive response to Enlightenment
assumptions about the totality of intellect and reason, and a new generation
of Americans, led by Charles Brockden Brown, who were bringing this political and literary sensibility into a uniquely New World context.[6] Yet another
flowering in Europe and America appeared during the transition to the 20th
century with H.G. Wells, Robert Louis Stevenson, Bram Stoker, Arthur
Machen, G.K. Chesterton, Joseph Conrad, Ambrose Bierce, Stephen Crane,
Henry James, Edith Wharton, and many others.[7]

Meanwhile, Hawthorne and James claim pride of place here. If we fall
back on stereotypical views of the two writers—that Hawthorne's gallery of
witches and ancestral curses and James's company of transplanted Americans
abroad makes for tepid terrors, on the one hand, and hopelessly convoluted
prose on the other—they seem dusty antiques, vapid and unlikely precedents
for the roaring horrors of Peter Straub. Of course, nothing could be further
from the truth. Straub knows better. In Hawthorne, for example, he sees
something much more subtle, and much more terrible—what literary critic
Afred Kazin perceives as the "unreality" and the "doubleness" of his vision:

"He drew shadows and hinted at abysses where there had always been clarity; he strained to find images of the imponderable, the blackness, and the vagueness, even the terror that waits in what he called 'the dim region beyond the daylight of our perfect consciousness.'"[8] This is the Hawthorne who, in the words of the "dark man" in "Young Goodman Brown," "'shall exult to behold the whole earth one stain of guilt, one mighty blood spot.'"[9]

And what fascinates him about James is what the Gothic historian Leslie Fiedler describes as his obsession with the "necrophilia that has always been an essential part of American romance.... It is from the dead that James's truest, richest inspiration comes, from a fascination with and a love for the dead, for death itself...."[10]

On turning to *Ghost Story*, we immediately are greeted with this quotation from Hawthorne's *The Marble Faun*: "'The chasm was merely one of the orifices of that pit of darkness that lies beneath us, everywhere.'"

The quotation is singularly apt. Several American tourists are on a twilight stroll through the ruins of the Roman Coliseum and Forum. They pause before the site of a chasm that, legend has it, had once precipitated Roman armies to their deaths. At that moment, the burden of the past is overwhelming. "'Reality,'" muses Miriam, continuing her thought, "is nothing more than mere 'stage-scenery,'" a "'thin crust'" over which "'we must step very daintily, not to break through the crust at any moment.'"

And that, says Hawthorne, is a subject for a "grim and ghastly story."[11]

Ghost Story

The chasm awaits, ready to open beneath us at the slightest misstep. As we pick our way through this Gothic minefield, we stare into that dangerous chasm—and it stares back. Hawthorne and James appear at every turn of the page. Two of the elderly members of the Chowder Club are appositely named Sears James and Ricky Hawthorne. They carry the narrative and play critical roles in the defeat of the terrors that attack them and beset Milburn. The new arrival to the Chowder Club, Don Wanderley, is a student of Hawthorne. The literature course he teaches includes a lecture on *House of the Seven Gables* and *The Scarlet Letter*. We wonder if those dark tales have bled into his own novel, *Nightwatcher*, and are influencing the terrors besetting Milburn.

Straub has vivid memories of his own first readings "at an impressionable age" in high school and college of James and Hawthorne. His encounters with Hawthorne came early: "I read [poet] Yvor Winters's essay 'Maule's Curse,' about *The House of the Seven Gables*," he remembers. "After that I came across a story that had a great impact on me, 'Young Goodman Brown'": "It made an impression on me, as did few other stories. I liked the idea of all the people and the little communities they inhabited being surrounded by a great dark forest, which they could not but experience as filled with terrors and dangers, but also with desire. At some point, these two emotional responses become the same thing." Straub must have felt an affinity between Goodman Brown's "great dark forest" and the forest that bordered his childhood home (see the interview in the Appendix). Another story, Hawthorne's "My Kinsman, Major Molyneux," also fed directly into *Ghost Story*'s haunted forests and Milburn's dangerous city streets. "It's the story about a young man in some kind of trouble during a time of great political turmoil," Straub explains: "The traveler makes his way to a town through a troubled, very dangerous landscape. And the town itself seems to be going crazy. Here's a hint of sexual danger present. He's trying to find his uncle because he thinks his uncle can give him a job. But when he finds him, he's been tarred and feathered and ridden out of town in terrible humiliation and disgrace. It's a very nightmarish, powerful story."[12] Both Goodman Brown and Robin—for that is the name of the young seeker in "Major Molyneux"—are assailed by wild images of capering figures and violent mirth; and both retire from the scene disillusioned and uncertain if what they have encountered was just a dream, a vision of "fantastic shapes" that had "broken forth from some feverish brain...."[13]

So apparently profound has been this impact, that Straub even co-opts Hawthorne's very *voice* elsewhere in his books.[14]

Likewise, he was profoundly impressed by his readings of James's stories, journals, letters, and the magisterial biography by Leon Edel. The impact on him of *The Turn of the Screw* and *The Jolly Corner*, in particular, has been profound. He recalls, "I saw [James] as a very contemporary human being—that is, contemporary in the honesty of his thought, in the way he understood that joy and pain are never really all that far apart and that one always involves the other."[15] Scenes from *The Turn of the Screw* are invoked in a back story recollected by Chowder member Sears James (appropriately enough) of a terrible event in his youth: As a young country schoolmaster he had fought for the salvation of a young brother and sister, Fenny and Constance Bate, who had been "corrupted" by their wicked elder brother, Gregory, and who are now in danger of being reclaimed by his ghost. Against Bate's "white terrible face" at the window, the schoolmaster fiercely clasps Fenny in his protective embrace—"but [the boy] toppled forward, and I caught him as if he were jumping into the pit of hell itself.... His heart had stopped, and I was holding a dispossessed body" (77). The similarities to the tragic outcome of the battle by the governess in *The Turn of the Screw* against Peter Quint's "white face of damnation" at the window to save the souls of her young charges are unmistakeable: "I caught him [she relates] …—it may be imagined with what passion: but at the end…. I began to feel what it truly was that I held…. [H]is little heart, dispossessed, had stopped."[16] An essential difference between James and Straub is that *The Turn of the Screw* leaves the story—and the reader—suspended in the ambiguity of that moment; but *Ghost Story* propels the moment further forward into the narrative as the spirits of the dead Gregory and Fenny Bate are enlisted by the malevolent Eva Galli in her campaign to destroy the Chowder men and the entire town. "My friends and I will tear the soul from this pathetic town and crush its bare bones between our teeth," she warns (401). What results is a reality and a nightmare that are scarcely distinguishable, explains Wanderley to Ricky Hawthorne: "These beings can convince you that you are losing your mind. We've seen and felt things we argued ourselves out of later. It can't be true, we tell ourselves; such things do not happen. But they do happen and we did see them" (363).

The architect of it all is the shape-shifting, half-human Eva Galli, an incarnation, as we shall presently see, of the many "dark" and vengeful females that haunt the pages of both Hawthorne and James. More broadly, she is a creature of an *American* Gothic. "I have lived," she says, "since the times when your continent was lighted only by small fires in the forest, since Americans dressed in hides and feathers" (401). Straub is openly enthusiastic and indebted to this tradition: "I was moved by the desire to look into, examine, and play with the genre," he says "—to take these 'classic' elements as far as they could go."[17] His engagement is more than that of an enthusiast. Like both a creator and a critic of the American Gothic, he is attentive to its detail, alert to its contexts, and hungry for its larger meanings.

Let's begin with Straub's comparison of Milburn's forests in *Ghost Story* with the "great dark forest" of "Young Goodman Brown." In an extended and complex sequence midway through the novel, Chowder man Lewis Benedikt takes his dog on a ramble through the woods. The Milburn forests seem to be inhabited by the same witches, wild beasts and savage Indians that had encroached upon Salem: "[Benedikt] liked to think of the huge climax forest that had once blanketed nearly all of North America…. Yes, in an endless vault of forest you could believe in spirits. Indian mythology was full of them—they suited the landscape" (90).

Like Goodman Brown, Benedikt soon loses his way. And, like Goodman Brown, he subsequently confronts the reality of his own sin and mortality. What follows is a phantasmagoria, a palimpsest of time-shifting events and characters not unlike the fantasy sequences in a film by Maya Deren or Jean Cocteau. Tucked away among the fir branches, he finds a door—or its illusion.

He enters, only to find himself back in his bedroom, a room flooded with sunshine. His wife enters. Another door, this time to the parsonage of his father. Lewis is now 17 years old. His father instructs him about his cleaning chores and warns him about keeping company with his young friends Hawthorne and James. Cut. Now he's in an empty room beside the sheeted corpse of his wife. She rises, her face broken and torn. There's a horrible vision of Eva Galli. Lewis's father reappears and issues threats of damnation. His ears are assaulted by a cacophony of voices, confessions, recriminations, and accusations, confusions (328–335).

Straub is justifiably proud of this sequence. It would prove to be influential on his subsequent stories, as he has noted in an interview: "In *Ghost Story* a character named Lewis Benedikt walks into the woods and sees a tree coalesce into the shape of a door.... Then he goes through another door.... Now that is the kind of thing that I think I do well, and that, it seems to me, I discovered for myself in *Ghost Story* and tried to extend over the next two books [*Floating Dragon* and *Shadowland*]."[18]

Taking root in the wild forests of New England soil is the pursuit of the unchecked power of imagination and the irrational—one of the many tropes of the literary Gothic of late 18th- century England and Europe. "Our literature starts with a vision of blackness," Straub has said in a recent interview, "and I think that has a lot to do with the fact that our country at first was mostly untameable forest. There were truly bad things out there."[19] At first, this may seem a contradiction. A New Land that lacked the traditional distinctions and fixed conventions of class, history, and gender identities was presumably free, declared Transcendentalists like Emerson, to realize its own destiny of Adamic innocence and hope. Hawthorne himself, in a decidedly disingenuous moment prefacing his last completed novel, *The Marble Faun* (1859), lamented that "no shadow, no iniquity, no mystery, no picturesque and gloomy wrong" existed "in this New Land."[20] It was cry echoed less than two decades later by Henry James in his *Hawthorne* (1879). However, it was an allegation, as will be seen, that both Hawthorne and James roundly overturned, again and again.[21]

If the American Gothic of the 19th century lacked these past traditions, it did operate in its own uniquely *present tense*, suggesting its own "original sin" of a nation that was busily *becoming*, constantly shifting in its dynamics of social, sexual, and cultural life. This was an America, writes cultural historian Camille Paglia, "enamored of the future," which had "rejected the archaic" and was now "a land of transients and transcience, of movement *to* and *across*."[22]

Evil was close as hand. It grew out of the "dangers of *repressing* energies, natural, social, psychic, textual, or sexual," scholar Maggie Kilgour reminds us in her essay "Dr. Frankenstein Meets Dr. Freud," thus offering a means of "*expressing* otherwise taboo forces." It still drew upon "the modern assumption that it is dangerous to bury things (which always return)...."[23]

It found new roots in ancestral and contemporary anxieties peculiar to America. The New England Puritan philosophy, the bedrock of Protestant colonial culture, for more than a century had been treating witches and devils as tangible threats. Moreover, there was a growing distress over the abomination of slavery, the rape of nature, the dispossession and slaughter of Native Americans, the "feminization" of American society, and, later in the century, hostility and paranoia concerning the waves of "alien" immigration. Ghosts glided through the wilderness homes and urban mansions as easily as they did in moldering feudal castles. Ancestral curses emanated from an intolerant Puritan past as effectively as they did from a corrupt Old World aristocracy. The new "sciences" of mesmerism, spiritualism, and psychic research hinted at a kind of supernatural authority that conjured a pre–Freudian awareness of unconscious horrors. And the newly politically and sexually empowered female reformists and writers seemed like a sisterhood of "witches" threatening a paranoid patriarchy.[24]

America's first true architect of the tale of terror, Charles Brockden Brown, was lauded by H.P. Lovecraft, for "contemptuously discarding the external Gothic paraphernalia and properties and choosing modern American scenes" for his mysteries, particularly in the wild forested settings surrounding the action in *Wieland* (1899) and *Edgar Huntly* (1796–1798).[25] Since our institutions, famously wrote Brown in the preface to *Edgar Huntly*, "differ essentially from Europe," the terrors of Gothic castles and chimeras will be replaced by "Indian hostility and the perils of the Western wildernesses." If a "native of America" overlooks these, he concluded, it "would admit of no apology."[26] Thus, we find the titular Edgar Huntly facing the imminent savagery of Native American responses to settlers' encroachments: "I knew that, at this time, some hostilities had been committed on the frontier; that a long course of injuries and encroachments had lately exasperated the Indian tribes; that an implacable and exterminating war was generally expected."[27] All too often, to Lovecraft's dismay, supernatural manifestations in Brown resolve into rational explanations. The ghostly voices assailing Wieland and his sister Clara in Brown's *Wieland* are actually the ventriloquism practiced by the wicked seducer, Carwin. Harold Schechter, author of *The Bosom Serpent: Folklore and Popular Art*, cites *Wieland* as "the first Gothic tale to exploit the creepy potential of 'biloquism' (in Brown's terminology)."

It was also the first American novel to base its plot on an actual, real-life murder case: the family massacre perpetrated by James Yates, a farmer in Tomhannock, upstate New York who ritually slaughtered his wife and four children in December, 1781. It thus stands at the head of a literary tradition that includes Theodore Dreiser's *An American Tragedy*, James M. Cain's *Double Indemnity*, Robert Bloch's *Psycho*, and every other novel, short story, or script "ripped from the headlines."[28]

Brown's *Edgar Huntly*, adds Professor Schechter, "was a pioneering work in which Brown substituted (as he puts it in his preface) "the incidents of Indian hostility and the perils of the Western wilderness" for the "puerile superstition and exploded manners, Gothic castles and chimeras of his predecessors...." He hit upon a theme that turned out to be central to our cultural mythology: the civilized, peace-loving man who makes a journey into the savage wilderness where he is reborn as a stone-cold killer (what the scholar Richard Slotkin calls the theme of "regeneration through violence").[29]

Indeed, Lovecraft nominated Hawthorne as Brown's successor: "The heritage of American weirdness was his to a most intense degree," although the suggestions of supernatural horror and their "force of genius" was "never a primary object."[30] What was lacking in Hawthorne, claimed Lovecraft, was "the violence, the daring, the high colouring, the intense dramatic sense the cosmic malignity" of his contemporary, Edgar Allan Poe. Only the "overshadowing malevolence" of the titular *The House of the Seven Gables* (1851) with its hints of a poisonous Puritan ancestry, rivals Poe's *House of Usher*— yet, "in a subtler way."[31] But it is in that very subtlety, despite Lovecraft's lament that Hawthorne "left no well-defined literary posterity,"[32] that Hawthorne and James, not the more grotesque Poe, would show the way to the modern Gothic horror of Straub and his contemporaries.[33]

Hawthorne and James

Like American Fausts bargaining with the Devil, Hawthorne and James paid a price for their delving into New World anxieties—fear of a boundless new land, a Nature unbridled and poised for attack, the "absence of so-called civilization," and the "terror of human freedom."[34] In particular, as historian and critic S.T. Joshi has recognized, "Hawthorne's mind compelled him to return again and again to what he must have considered a kind of American original sin—the Salem witch trials, the chief black mark on the very town of his birth."[35] When the titular Young Goodman Brown attends and participates in the blasphemous rituals of a witches' coven in the midnight wood, he realizes that everyone there, including the citizenry of his town, bears the mark of the beast. "The fiend in his own shape is less hideous than when he rages in the breast of man."[36] He is condemned to live out his life an outcast from family and community, "with no hopeful verse upon his tombstone."[37]

In Hawthorne's "The Devil in Manuscript" (1834), the protagonist, Oberon, is a writer so horrified by the recognition of evil in his stories that he threatens to burn them: "'I have a horror ... at the manuscripts in which I gave that dark idea a sort of material existence! Would they were out of my sight!'"[38] Hester's Prynne's wearing of the Scarlet Letter lends her a sympathetic knowledge of the hidden sin in the human heart.[39]

Goodman Brown, Oberon, and Prynne speak for other literary Faustian seekers, past and present, whose investigations into evil results in them being branded as outsiders to the world in which they live and write: "'I am surrounding myself with shadows,'" laments Oberon. "'They have drawn me aside from the beaten path of the world, and led me into a strange sort of solitude,—a solitude in the midst of men—where nobody wishes for what I do, nor thinks nor feels as I do....'"[40]

Just as Gothic writers today are haunted by the sins and buried guilts of their native towns—Lovecraft's Providence, Rhode Island; Bradbury's Waukegan, Illinois; King's Bangor, Maine; and Straub's Milwaukee, Wisconsin—Hawthorne's seaport town of Salem, Massachusetts, provided "the weird impression and haunting mystery of Puritan life which [he] drank in during those night rambles in Salem [and] the deep hold in which the beauty and terror of nature had laid upon his soul in those days and nights of solitude...."[41] Biographer Brenda Wineapple adds that "he frequently wrote with a pen dipped in the bloody history, to which he brought his personal angst."[42] As late as his last completed novel, *The Marble Faun* (1859), Hawthorne himself described a heritage that possessed "an odor of guilt and a scent of blood."[43] Among his ancestors on both sides of the family, the Hathornes and Mannings, were judges and interrogators who persecuted Quakers and tortured and executed accused witches in the notorious Witch Trials of the late 1690s. Ashamed of this heritage, Nathaniel changed the spelling of his name and added a "w" to "Hathorne."[44]

We can detect everywhere the heavy burden of his Puritan ancestry. The Pyncheon mansion in *House of the Seven Gables* (1851), the granddaddy of all literary haunted houses to come—applauded by Lovecraft as "New England's greatest contribution to weird literature"[45]—is held in the thrall of an ancient ancestral curse. The mansion has inherited "much of mankind's varied experience"; indeed, "the very timbers were oozy, as with the moisture of a heart. It was itself like a great human heart, with a life of its own, and full of rich and somber reminiscences ... [that] you could not pass without the idea that it had secrets to keep...."[46] In the back story, 17th-century Matthew Maule is executed on a trumped-up charge of witchcraft by the "iron-hearted Puritan," Colonel Pyncheon, who thus clears the way to appropriate his property. On the scaffold,

Maule hurls a curse at Pyncheon: "'God will give him blood to drink!'" Pyncheon tears down Maule's cottage, erects the House over its "unquiet grave," and renames Maule's Lane "Pyncheon Street." The mansion, writes Hawthorne,

> would include the home of the dead and buried wizard, and would thus afford the ghost of the latter a kind of privilege to haunt its new apartments and the chambers into which future bridegrooms were to lead their brides, and where children of the Pyncheon blood were to be born. The terror and ugliness of Maule's crime, and the wretchedness of his punishment, would darken the freshly plastered walls, and infect them early with the scent of an old and melancholy house.[47]

Sure enough, on the day the new Pyncheon home is open to village guests, the old man is found, dead, his face and clothes spattered with blood. The well water, moreover, has turned hard and brackish. Two centuries of subsequent generations of Pyncheons bear the burden of the curse. Hepzibah Pyncheon best sums it up: "'In old houses like this, you know, dead people are very apt to come back again.'"[48]

Building upon this grim foundation, as it were—and perhaps evoking his own homestead, the Old Manse—Hawthorne's spooks are elegantly suggested, rather than overtly manifested. For example,

> the large, dim looking-glass was fabled to contain within its depths all the shapes that had ever been reflected there.... There was a story, for which it is difficult to conceive any foundation, that the posterity of Matthew Maule had some connection with the mystery of the looking-glass, and that, by what appears to have been a sort of mesmeric process, they could make its inner region all alive with the departed Pyncheons; not as they had shown themselves to the world nor in their better and happier hours, but as doing over again some deed of sin."[49]

Meanwhile, generations of Maules are suspected of possessing "mysterious attributes" that include "influencing people's dreams." Hawthorne's narrator is quick to downplay the supernatural implications of all this: "Modern psychology, it may be, will endeavor to reduce these alleged necromancies within a system, instead of rejecting them as altogether fabulous."[50]

This uneasy ambivalence between the actual and imaginary, as already noted in Straub's *Ghost Story*, resides at the heart of the Gothic tradition. Horace Walpole voiced it first in the Preface to the second edition of his *Castle of Otranto* (originally published in 1764), when he attempted to blend two kinds of Romance, "the ancient and the modern." The former relied on "imagination and improbability"; the latter to "copy" nature itself.[51] Clara Reeve, an acolyte of Walpole, confirmed in *The Old English Baron* (1777) her aim to bring together "a sufficient degree of the marvelous, to excite the attention; enough of the manners of real life, to give an air of probability to the work...."[52]

Thus the Gothic tale perilously teeters on this knife-edge of ambiguity. On several occasions Nathaniel Hawthorne echoes Walpole and Reeve, declaring overtly that he suspends his stories between the polarities of waking and dream: "I have sometimes produced a singular and not unpleasing effect, so far as my own mind was concerned, by imagining a train of incidents in which the spiritual mechanism of the faery legend should be combined with the characters and manners of everyday life." Don Wanderley in *Ghost Story* quotes these very words as he prepares his lecture on Hawthorne.[53] Straub has declared, "I wanted to play around with reality, to make the characters confused about what was actually real. So: I built in situations in which they feel they are: (1) Acting out roles in a book; (2) Watching a film; (3) Hallucinating; (4) Dreaming; (5) Transported into a private fantasy." Thus, if the reader tries to hold these separate fragments together, a pattern is revealed.[54] Speaking for all Gothic practitioners, past and present, Hawthorne issues a warning: "A man is always—or always ought to be—careening on the utmost verge of a precipitous absurdity and the skill lies in coming as close as possible, without actually tumbling over."[55] A step away from that balance risks disaster—precisely the dilemma the titular character in Hawthorne's "Wakefield" risks when he returns to the household he had deserted twenty years earlier. His desertion had been the result of an unguarded moment. Now he stands again before the closed door. "We will not follow our friend across the threshold," writes Hawthorne. "Amid the seeming confusion of our mysterious world, individuals are so nicely adjusted to a system, and systems to one another and to a whole, that, by stepping aside for a moment, a man exposes himself to a fearful risk of losing his place forever."[56]

An uncertain equipoise is maintained. Are Goodman Brown's dark visions of the nightly forest revels a reality or a hallucination? Hawthorne inserts a clever note that throws us off balance. When Brown staggers against the "burning" trees, the twigs are cold to the touch. What of the brand of the scarlet "A" that mysteriously appears on the breast of Roger Chillingworth? Hawthorne permits several explanations—that, on the one hand, it is the result of self-mortification, or a drug, or a guilt that has gnawed outward from his inmost heart; and, on the other, that some witnesses dispute it exists at all! In *The Marble Faun* the saintly Hilda gazes with delight on a painting of the Archangel Michael's struggle with his satanic adversary and sees only "'an expression of heavenly severity in the Archangel's face'" and "'a celestial tranquility.'" Her brooding companion, Miriam, offers a counter interpretation: "'A full third of the Archangel's feathers should have been torn from his wings; the rest all ruffled, till they looked like Satan's own!'"[57]

Simple binaries are defeated. Hawthorne's most profound insight—shared by James and Straub—is that in the deepest recesses of the human heart Good and Evil, sin and salvation, pain and pleasure exist in a liminal state. Their boundaries are not fixed, but porous, bleeding one into the other. In *The Scarlet Letter* the narrator wonders "whether hatred and love, good and evil, be not the same thing at bottom.... Each, in its inmost development, supposes a high degree of intimacy and heart knowledge; each renders one individual dependent ... upon another."[58] Again, in *The Marble Faun*, we find Hilda and Miriam at odds. Hilda asserts that "'there is only one right and one wrong,'" to which Miriam protests, "'Ah, Hilda, you do not know ... what a mixture of good there may be in things evil.'" She goes on to say, sin and guilt are "merely an element of human education, through which we struggle to a higher and purer state than we could otherwise have attained? Did Adam fall, that we might ultimately rise to a far loftier paradise than his?"[59] Most remarkably, in another key scene in *The Marble Faun*, after Donatello and Miriam have thrown the body of her mysterious offending pursuer off a precipice to his death, they turn to each other in a conspiratorial embrace that is "closer than a marriage-bond." So intimate is this connection that "it seemed as if their new sympathy annihilated all other ties, and that they were released from the chain of humanity; a new sphere, a special law, had been created for them alone. The world could not come near them...." From their guilt they achieve a "moment of rapture," an ecstatic sense of freedom. Out of "their dark sympathy" is "a bliss, or an insanity, which the unhappy pair imagined to be well worth the sleepy innocence that was forever lost to them."[60]

Meanwhile, disclosures of shared and repressed guilts that are buried in the past don't come easily; and their revelations are murky, to say the least. It takes the entire length of *Ghost Story* to expose the hidden secrets of the Chowder Society—and even then we're not sure if Eva Galli has been vanquished. What is the dark secret that haunts Miriam in *The Marble Faun*? "'There is a secret in my heart that burns me,'" she cries out, "'that tortures me! Sometimes I fear to go mad of it.... Sometimes I hope to die of it; but neither of the two happens. Ah, if I could only whisper it to only one human soul!'"[61] But she never reveals her crime, if that's what it is. Moreover, what is the secret behind Hawthorne's "The Minister's Black Veil" with which the Reverend Hooper conceals his features to the end of his days? To his congregants, that piece of crepe "seemed to hang down before his heart, the symbol of a fearful secret between him and them." He refuses protests that he remove it: "'No mortal eye will see it withdrawn. This dismal shade must separate me from the world. If I hide my face for sorrow, there is cause enough, and if I cover it for secret sin, what mortal might not do the same?'" Meanwhile, children shun him and he is separated from the community, even as he avoids his own mirrored images, lest "he should be affrighted by himself." Ironically, the veil has the desirable effect of "making its wearer a very efficient clergy-man. He becomes a man of awful power over souls that were in agony for sin." On his deathbed, he resists a few desperate attempts to remove the veil. His last words are devastating: "'I look around me, and, lo!, on every visage a Black Veil!'" The truth of the veil and what lies beneath it is never disclosed.[62] Regarding the many other secrets left unresolved at the end of *The Marble Faun*—who was the man stalking Miriam; what was her crime; what happens to Miriam and Donatello; etc.?—Hawthorne keeps his own counsel. Speaking as the "Author" in the novel's conclusion, Hawthorne says that if he brings his secrets "into the actual light of day," his story "becomes nothing better than a grotesque absurdity...."[63] Better "to keep a veil, he confesses, over the mysteries": "The actual experience of even the most ordinary life is full of events that never explain themselves, either as regards their origin or their tendency.... The charm lay partly in their very imperfection; for this is suggestive and sets the imagination at work; whereas, the finished picture, if a good one, leaves the spectator nothing to do, and, if bad, confuses, stupefies, disenchants, and disheartens him."[64] The point here—and we encounter it again and again in Straub—is that the nature and meaning of evil is ultimately unfathomable.

A Female Gothic

Straub's vengeful Eva Galli in *Ghost Story*—just one of the many dangerous females that stalk other stories to be discussed in later chapters, including Alison Greening in *If You Could See Me Now*, Olivia Rudge in *Julia*, Mrs. Asch in "Ashputtle"—inherits the dark legacy of the malevolent females in Hawthorne and James. "Creatures like Eva Galli are behind every ghost story and supernatural tale ever written," says Don Wanderley. "They are the originals of everything that frightens us in the supernatural" (362).[65]

Many of Hawthorne's anxieties and guilts stem from his ambivalence over the emerging generation of American female reformists, popular writers, and spiritualists of the day who were "deviating" from the norms of the Cult of True Womanhood.[66] "The New Woman," as she came to be called, contested in society and sexuality a traditionally dominant masculinity. Men were beginning to feel their agency challenged, even subordinated, to them. Camille Paglia, in her *Sexual Personae*, notes that everywhere in Hawthorne and, later, in Henry James, were the results of "an unsettling caution" and passivity in masculine agency.[67]

In the vanguard of the first American women's rights convention in

Seneca Falls, New York, in 1848 and other conventions in Rochester and Worcester, Massachusetts, powerful spokespersons appeared, contemporary with Hawthorne and James, including the very public Margaret Fuller and her "Conversations for Women"; Victoria Woodhull and her controversial advocacy of women's suffrage, spiritualism, and sexual freedom; and the exceedingly private Emily Dickinson, who, according to Harold Bloom, was a "radical nihilist" who possessed a "daimon" of "archaic ecstasies and shamanistic dislocations."[68] Paglia goes Bloom one better: Emily was "a pioneer among women writers in renouncing genteel good manners," who "had an appetite for murder and mayhem," whose lines are "arenas of extremity" that include "lurid metaphors" and are "crowded with deaths."[69]

Woodhull's mediumship and her séances, in particular—she attributed her oratorical prowess to her spiritual "contacts" and was duly elected president of the American Association of Spiritualists—embodied the supposition that the alleged "finer sensibilities" of women brought them close to the Spirit World and entitled them special privilege to be its spokespersons. At the same time, however, it also implied infernal connections with darker forces. This dichotomy provoked the researches and imaginations of numerous American psychologists and novelists, including William James's founding of the American Society for Psychic Research, Nathaniel Hawthorne's *The Blithedale Romance* and *The Marble Faun*, and Henry James's *The Bostonians* and *The Turn of the Screw*. "As the study of hypnosis, telepathy, apparitions, and dreams states became respectable," writes Howard Kerr in his invaluable overview of the subject, *Mediums and Spirit-Rappers and Roaring Radicals*, psychologists and psychical researchers and writers alike made "increasingly unashamed literary use of such mysteries."[70] Such investigations are an important subject for Straub, as documented in later chapters of this book.

Meanwhile, despite his ambivalence on the matter, and in spite of his own experiences with trance mediums in Italy with the Brownings, Hawthorne regretted that these female spiritual allegories, seduction narratives, and political polemics were invading public spaces and American literary markets—not to mention usurping his own marketable value. "We seldom meet with women nowadays," Hawthorne declares further, "who impress us as being women at all—their sex fades away, and goes for nothing." His own suspicion of this dark "web of femaleness" is a "lingering Puritan suspicion, if not outright hostility to pleasure."[71] Miles Coverdale, in *The Blithedale Romance*, expresses this ambivalence perfectly: "To hold intercourse with spirits of this order, we must stoop and grovel in some element more vile than earthly dust."[72]

Meanwhile, in the mold of their English sisters Mary Elizabeth Braddon

(*Lady Audley's Secret*), Charlotte Brontë (*Jane Eyre*), and George Eliot ("The Lifted Veil"), American female novelists like Fanny Fern bitterly challenged the domestic harmony of the home; Louisa May Alcott, writing under the pseudonym A.M. Barnard, created vengeful females of a decidedly sinister and murderous agency; and Harriet Beecher Stowe, launched her attack on the institution of slavery. They were shaping what critic Ellen Moers dubbed a "female Gothic," examining women from the woman's perspective, as girl, sister, mother, self, and political activist. No longer simply the "Angel of the House," she was regarded suspiciously as the "Madwoman in the Attic."[73]

Thus, according to historian Nancy F. Sweet, many of Hawthorne's females deviated from Puritan norms and "fit the profiles of the kinds of women who most frequently faced witchcraft allegations in the seventeenth century."[74] The witch Mistress Hibbons in *The Scarlet Letter* taunts Puritan beliefs with her talk of forest meetings with the Black Man. The titular "Rappaccini's Daughter" presents literally a poisonous threat to her suitor, Giovanni. "'Thou hast done it!'" he tells her as he expires. "'Thou hast blasted me! Thou hast filled my veins with poison!'"[75] In another story, "The Birthmark," a woman's body is deemed "imperfect" and destroyed by her husband so that, caustically declares biographer Wineapple, "he in some way can remain alone, untrammeled, asexual, and free from responsibility."[76] Hawthorne's attitudes toward Hester Prynne in *The Scarlet Letter* are notably ambivalent: She is both a visionary of women's rights but, in the end, remains voluntarily branded with the punishing scarlet letter.

Consider how his ambivalence toward feminine sexuality also divides his casts of female characters into the kinds of duality so inherent in the Gothic and, as we will see in a later chapter of this book, so marked in Straub. There are the "dark," corrupted women, like the powerful, but doomed feminist Zenobia and the darkly secretive Miriam in *The Blithedale Romance* and *The Marble Faun*, respectively; counterposed by the "ethereal" innocents of the clairvoyant Priscilla and the virginal Hilda in those same books. In *Blithedale* Zenobia's fierce, sexualized feminism—"'If I live another year, I will lift up my own voice in behalf of women's wider liberty!'"[77]—is opposed by Hollingsworth, the man who will reject her love: "'If there were a chance of their attaining the end which these petticoated monstrosities have in view,'" he says, "'I would call upon my own sex to use its physical force, that unmistakable evidence of sovereignty, to scourge them back within their proper bounds!'" The description of her suicide by drowning, by the way, is exceptionally graphic, a startling and stark departure from Hawthorne's otherwise relatively measured, elegant prose (511).

Henry James also responded in his own idiosyncratic way to tensions in the social, sexual, and psychic life he knew growing up in New York and Boston. Like Hawthorne, he was fascinated, perturbed, and baffled by changes in women's social and sexual status. He had actively opposed women's rights and had declared in his book, *Women and the Women's Movement*, that women are not suited to the learned professions.[78] Nonetheless, as he admitted while writing *The Bostonians*, "I asked myself what was the most salient and peculiar point in our social life. The answer was: the situation of women, the decline of the sentiment of sex, the agitation on their behalf."[79]

Henry James

The Civil War had brought these anxieties to a boil. Shunning the conflict, James joined the ranks of non-combatants and survivors who looked rather askance at the women assuming a new dominance in social life: "At a time when the nation's best male element had been destroyed by war," comments Peter Buitenhuis in his book about James's American writings—"a war largely caused, it was supposed in some quarters, by the motive power of female abolitionists, the misdirected energy of a soured Puritanism had driven women to establish a political as well as a numerical and moral superiority over men."[80] James had grown up a "genderless man," alleges biographer Alfred Habegger, "with a dark suspicion that all sexual roles and functions are sinister...."[81]

His was an unusually complicated and dysfunctional family presided over by the brilliant but emotionally and psychologically damaged patriarch, Henry Sr., who was enmeshed in the "gospel" of the Swedish mystic Emanuel Swedenborg. "Original sin"—Swedenborg's term was "vastation"—was implicit in a stern Presbyterian doctrine whose "moral selfhood" had to be abandoned before mankind could achieve "spiritual regeneration."[82] Brother William and sister Alice, like their father, were plagued with lifelong depres-

sive episodes, neurotic tendencies, and illnesses, both psychological and physical.[83]

Ambivalent in his masculinity and subject to severe depressive episodes, Henry Jr., was likewise fascinated with Other Worlds. His kinship with Hawthorne's "feeling for the darker side of life, for the realities of sin and evil"—what he described as Hawthorne's "cat-like faculty of seeing in the dark"—was profound.[84] Moreover, the impact of his elder brother William's involvement with psychic researches cannot be overestimated. "For ghosts who could be taken as either supernatural or psychological, or ambiguously both," writes cultural historian Howard Kerr, "[Henry] needed to look no further than the hallucinatory presences and their 'percipients' studied by his and his brother's friends of the SPR [Society for Psychic Research]."[85] Biographer Deborah Blum confirms: "In James's artful hands the ghosts were hauntingly ambiguous, evocative of all the unknowns that troubled his brother William."[86] Indeed, William would spend his last decades investigating the séances of several female mediums, notably the notorious Leonora Piper. "Those who have the fullest acquaintance with the phenomena," he wrote in his last essay on the subject, "admit that in good mediums *there is a residuum of knowledge displayed* that can only be called supernormal; the medium taps some source of information not open to ordinary people."[87]

The sisters of the manipulative, sometimes dangerous *femmes fatales* found in Hawthorne and later in Straub's Eva Galli, appear everywhere in Henry, Jr.'s novels and stories. These were allegories, reports biographer Lyndall Gordon, that were "filled with evil, renunciation, and the salvation of the soul."[88] In *Roderick Hudson* (1876), the story of an American sculptor in Rome, patterned after Hawthorne's *The Marble Faun*, we find Miriam's counterpart, the rapacious Christina Light, whose seductive lures lead the frustrated Hudson to suicide. In "The Ghostly Rental," a woman impersonates a ghost in order to wreak revenge on her father. In the particularly Hawthornesque story of a family curse, "De Grey," a young woman utters a curse which condemns her betrothed to languish while she "blooms and prospers": "She blindly, remorselessly, drained the life from his being. While she was living for him, he was dying for her."[89] A similar vampiric situation arises in *The Sacred Fount* (1901), one of James's most baffling novels (a particular favorite of Straub's), wherein a wife *apparently* drains her husband of his youth. *The Bostonians* (1886) copies another Hawthornesque device, i.e., the duality of "light" and "dark" females in the actress/feminist Olive Chancellor and the young innocent clairvoyant Verena Tarrant. Chancellor holds Tarrant in the thrall of a distinctly lesbian relationship. The most famous example is the nameless narrator of *The Turn of the Screw*. A cottage industry has grown up around the governess and her consciousness of evil spirits whose status as genuine ghosts or hallucinations is forever in question. Biographer Edel insists that James intended to make the story "the record of the young governess' mind," that her sexual repression made her the victim of hallucinations and the corrupter of the children's innocence.[90]

More Ghostly Matters

A phantom hand bids us stay a moment. As heir to Hawthorne's tales and sympathetic to his brother's psychic researches, Henry James's highly idiosyncratic ghost stories brings us yet closer to the peculiar sort of ghosting we find in Straub. This is to say that the living and the dead are at times interchangeable—there is much that is ghostly in the dead and much that is alive in the ghostly. This is amply demonstrated in the scene late in *Ghost Story* when the surviving members of the Chowder Society witness the death of Eva Galli—now incarnated as Anna Mostyn. The living and the dead intermingle in the expiring body: "They saw a writhing life through the dead woman's skin…. A mouth opened beneath Anna Mostyn's mouth and a body constrained within Anna Mostyn's bloody clothing moved with a ferocious life" (461).

Henry James's ghosting, while perhaps not as gruesome, first brought this striking kind of uncanny balance into the light, as it were. And he did so with a relish all his own. The subtlety of his descriptions of the ghostly—surely a match for any of the ghosts in *The House of the Seven Gables*—are delicious. "There was an alien object in view—a figure whose right of presence I instantly and passionately questioned."[91]

"'The place is haunted, *haunted*!'" cries a character in "Sir Edmond Orme." "'I exulted in the word as if it stood for all I had ever dreamt of!'"[92] There is no mistaking the delight Henry James feels when he takes up the mantle of Hawthorne's haunted characters and haunted places. This kind of enthusiastic declaration, so different from the dread we expect from traditional ghosting, causes concern in commentators like S.T. Joshi, who writes that these stories display a "timidity" to the supernatural; that they are "marginally weird" and "crippled by James's increasingly mincing and affected prose style."[93] I would suggest that is in their very departure from such expectations that they achieve a unique and even elegantly luminous status.

Likewise, James took great care to balance the actual and the imaginary. Nowhere is this more striking than in his ghost stories. "A good ghost story must be connected at a hundred points with the common objects of life," he declared.[94] He echoes, in effect, Zenobia's response in *House of the Seven Gables* when, asked to tell a ghost story, she replies, "'No, not exactly a ghost-story, but something so nearly like it that you shall hardly tell the difference.'"[95]

James was twenty-five when he wrote his first ghost story, "A Romance of Old Clothes" (1868), and sixty-four when he wrote his last, "The Jolly Corner" (1908). These fall within a tradition that Gothic master China Miéville has dubbed with the jaw-breaking sobriquet, the "hauntological." Deriving from Hawthorne and maturing in James, the hauntological, in part, privileges the "traditional stain of the ghostly, the dead-but-unquiet" apparitions that frequently function in a "moral" and "instructional cast."[96] Eighteen in all—including many stories with American subjects, settings, and characters—they exploit a prose style as dense and as measured as Hawthorne and which will find its latter-day expression in the beautifully-crafted prose of Straub. James also drew upon Hawthorne's example of avoiding the standard Gothic props of creaking doors, sheeted specters, and ancient haunted castles in Walpole, Radcliffe, and the Victorian mistress of ghosts, Mrs. Gaskell. The modern country home or a New York townhouse (as in "The Jolly Corner") were suitable dwellings for *his* ghosts. And, emulating Hawthorne, he refused to *specify* the nature of horror and evil, be they supernatural or psychological, playing, as it were, a game of tag with the reader. James was superbly equipped to do this, well aware at close range of the ambivalence with which brother William pursued his psychic and psychiatric researches. "There is either an invoked and embodied ghost or an obsessive image," observes R.P. Blackmur of James, "that is either a hallucinated person or a hallucinated theme, which when we can grasp it gathers up all the meaning in the novel or tale.... They make no surrender of the rational imagination, but constitute rather an extension and enrichment of it."[97]

The blurring of the boundaries between the living and the dead in Hawthorne and James has had a telling effect on Straub. The two worlds are so interwoven that they seem at times scarcely distinguishable from each other; and the meaning we derive from them is up to the reader. "In other words," writes biographer Leon Edel with rare whimsy, "the reader is handed a blank check which may be cashed only at Henry James's bank of fiction."[98]

Excepting his most famous ghost story, *The Turn of the Screw*, wherein the malignant perversion of youth is strongly suggested, and "The Jolly Corner," where a gruesome aspect of an alternate self, is introduced, James's ghosts, as previously noted by S.T. Joshi, are rarely dangerous and almost never terrifying in their appearance. They may appear with no sensational fanfare whatever, even in broad daylight, as in "Sir Edmund Orme." And there's a particularly cunning little moment in *The Turn of the Screw* when the governess, frightened by what she perceives to be a ghostly face at the window, hurries outside to peer through that window back at the children. Their frightened reaction to *her* at the window is—what?—of the living or the dead? Or both. James consistently worked toward what was, for him, a very characteristic theme—the heightening of conscious states. There is a peculiar "delight," as James put it, in these "fine recognitions" of "wonder and terror and curiosity and pity alike."[99] "His ghosts," explains Blackmur, "were invariably the hallucinated apparitions of the obsessions that governed or threatened, or as we say haunted the men and women whose stories he told." Moreover, "the ghost was the projected form of either a felt burden or an inner need…. In one guise or another, they are the meaning that pursues us or is beyond us, drawing their shapes and habits from those parts of our imagination which are not occupied by the consciousness but which rather besiege the consciousness in all its dark environs…."[100]

Only Edith Wharton, James' contemporary, rivals him in these considerations.[101]

Thus the ghosts are "recognized" only by people who suffer extreme guilts or possess a high degree of insight and moral sensitivity. The apparition might be only an "atmosphere" engendered by a packet of letters, as in "Sir Dominick Ferrand," the fatal results of the pressure of a military tradition in the family of "Owen Wingrave," the psychological inability to admit the loss of a loved one, as in "Maud-Evelyn" and "The Altar of the Dead." In "The Third Person" it may be a presence noted solely through the characters' dialogue; a *possibility* that *validates* the lives of insecure people lacking any real identity of their own.[102] Such perceptions are metaphors for the recognition of the interior world of fine moral issues, of identity and justice.

Of especial consequence, when we come to consider Straub's deployment of the multiple identities of Eva Galli, is the example of James's "The Jolly Corner," with its "might-have-been ghost," Spencer Brydon's alternate self. Had he stayed in New York rather than deserting his home for Europe many years before, Brydon might have become the grotesque manifestation he now encounters upon his return to his ancestral home. Like the cousins in the afore-mentioned "The Third Person," Brydon begins to "haunt" the place— to "cultivate his perception"—as he stalks the house for his unseen ghostly double. "People … had been in terror of apparitions, but who had ever before so turned the tables and become himself, in the apparitional world, an incalculable terror?"[103] The confrontation, when it comes, reveals a mutilated figure. Recoiling, Spencer falls backward, literally into the arms of the loving and sympathetic Alice Staverton. His alarming realization that he possesses a *different* self literally hurls him backward from the threshold. Recovering from his collapse, he knows now he is capable of the loving relationship that has so eluded him with his long time friend Staverton. "What he had come back *to* seemed really the great thing, and as if his prodigious journey had been all for the sake of it."[104] Our gaze is shifted from the unknown back upon ourselves, providing us a sense of renewed wonder at our own humanity.[105] Straub will allude to "The Jolly Corner's" ghostly confrontation several times in his stories.

Likewise, by fine-tuning, as it were, his supernatural apparatus, Straub brings some of his own ghosts closer to *human* identity. We recall the question-and-response mantra repeatedly voiced throughout *Ghost Story*: "Who are you?" asks the Chowder members of Eva's ghostly manifestations. "'I am *you*,'" she replies. "'*You* are the ghost.'" The dynamic, as already noted, that had begun in Brown and Hawthorne and extended in James's *Turn of the Screw* and "The Jolly Corner" had been to establish a co-existence of the ghostly and the human in an epiphany that throws us back to the terrible reality *that is ourselves.*

As opposed to the "European Sublime" of Edmond Burke, contends critic Harold Bloom, this is redolent of a so-called "American Sublime" that transcends the human without forsaking humanism. The transcendent here resides not *outside* us so much, but *within*—"an intuition free of morality and beyond ordinary apperception," by which "we go on living and finding our own sense of being."[106]

Ever Hawthorne, Ever James

At last we come to the conclusion of *Ghost Story* and the end to this chapter. In an epilogue that contains some of Straub's noblest pages, Don Wanderley leaves behind a Milburn now purged of its horrors. He is aware, however, that with the vanquishing of each of Eva's incarnations, a tiny creature—a bird, a lynx, an insect—has escaped the scene, waiting to assume a new shape, waiting to kill again. Accordingly, a child he spots one day bears the unmistakeable stamp of yet another Eva. He summons up the courage to kidnap and kill her. On the spot, a tiny wasp appears and repeatedly stings his hand. Wielding his knife, wounding himself in the process, he cuts the insect into little pieces and tosses it into the water. Has Eva been dispatched, utterly and finally, at last? I, for one, have my doubts.[107]

In any event, momentarily released from the nightmare that has clung to him, the town of Milburn, and his brethren in the Chowder Club, Wanderley experiences an epiphany, "a wave of love for everything mortal.... For everything with a brief definite life span—a tenderness for all that could give birth and would die, everything that could live.... He knew it was only relief and adrenalin, but it was all the same a mystical, perhaps a sacred emotion." He silently salutes his friends, living and dead: "Dear brothers, dear humankind" (483).

I wonder if Wanderley's salute is Straub's own tribute to the Gothic tradition and its hallowed masters, especially Nathaniel Hawthorne and Henry James ... and if it is a pledge to enjoin his literary life with theirs. Hawthorne may have doubted that there was a future for his works—as opposed to Henry James, who did everything he could to revise and make available his own stories for generations to come—yet they both find a transformative incarnation in the oeuvre of Peter Straub.[108] Not just in *Ghost Story*, but everywhere in Straub we find more than a *frisson* of Hawthorne's witches and James's ghosts. He seems to be in the thrall of that "grim and ghastly" moment we noted earlier in *The Marble Faun*—when, after committing murder, Miriam and Donatello stand at the edge of that "*pit of darkness that lies beneath us, everywhere*" and embrace in their shared "dark sympathy" and "moment of rapture."

Certainly he has positioned himself as the literary trustee of both writers. In the novel that follows *Ghost Story*, *The Floating Dragon*, we meet the dedicated house restorer Richard Albee. The old houses that Albee restores represent, appropriately enough, the collective Gothic tradition: "He had worked on a dozen large houses in London, starting with his own, and had built a reputation based on care, exactness, and hard work." Once "dismissed as monstrosities," Albee understood precisely "where the beauty in such houses lay and knew how to make it shine again." He took a "deep satisfaction in bringing these absurd Victorian and Edwardian structures back to life" (61–62). Straub has admitted that he sees in Hawthorne's Pyncheon Mansion in *House of the Seven Gables* and James's Bly House in *Turn of the Screw* the very Gothic architectures he honors, restores, and transforms in his stories.

And the ghosts that dwell within.

CHAPTER THREE

"King of the Cats"
The Fairy Tales

The fairy night mirrored itself in [his] soul He felt as though the world lay unlocked within him and was revealing to him as to an intimate friend all its treasures and hidden charms.
> —Novalis, *Heinrich von Ofterdingen*

In waving these mystic utterances into a continuous scene, we undertake a task resembling, in its perplexity, that of gathering up and piecing together the fragments of a letter, which has been torn and scattered to the winds.
> —Nathaniel Hawthorne, *The Marble Faun*

"The ordinary rules don't work—animals will talk, people will turn into animals, the world will turn topsy-turvy."
> —Fitz-Hallen, *Shadowland*

And then there's the story of "The King of the Cats."

On the way to visit a friend, a traveler witnesses a curious sight. A procession of cats is carrying a tiny coffin on their backs on their way to a burial ground. Atop the coffin is a tiny crown. After the coffin is lowered into the ground, the traveler resumes his walk. Upon arriving at his friend's home, he relates the curious sight. He had scarcely finished when his friend's cat, which had been dozing by the fire, leaps up and cries, "Then, *now* I am the King of the Cats!" and disappears in a flash up the chimney.

Where does he go? In the version that begins Peter Straub's *Shadowland*, he goes up the chimney; in another version, he runs out of the house and down the road. There are hazards and adventures, going up or going away. We don't know. The story hasn't ended yet, has it? Maybe it's important that, not knowing, we ask anyway.... Or that we teeter on the threshold of knowing and not knowing, somehow satisfied. We are *inside* the story...

Thrice-Told Tales

The fable of "The King of the Cats" is a story that is so familiar that its title page is missing. Like all the best fairy tales, it belongs to no one. And it belongs to everyone. It numbers among its tale-tellers Washington Irving, Matthew Lewis, Stephen Vincent Benet, and now Peter Straub, who calls it "a novel in miniature."[1] It winds its way like a black thread through the long and convoluted novel that is *Shadowland*, just one of many stories within stories, tales told, then retold, sometimes contradicted, then told again—of secrets, lost and orphaned children, stolen identities, animals that talk, princesses in peril, and rooms locked and forbidden. They don't exist, first of all, as a *text*. A fairy tale, as Philip Pullman reminds us in his exemplary collection of Grimm tales, is not a text of that sort. "It's a transcription made on one or more occasions of the words spoken by one of many people who have told the tale…. The fairy tale is in a perpetual state of becoming and alteration."[2]

Peter Straub's *Shadowland* bids us follow, in effect, the King of the Cats up the chimney *and* down the road. There we find a number of rival magicians contending for the Royal title: Young Tom Flanagan and Del Nightingale are high school students apprenticed to Del's uncle, Coleman Collins, a master magician who lives in a large mansion in the enchanted forest of Shadowland. Uncle Cole is himself the apt pupil of the mysterious conjuror Speckle John. And there is Steve "Skeleton" Ridpath, himself under the sway of Collins. For Tom it is a Bildungsroman, a morality tale that, as Bill Sheehan observes, "is about magic, illusion, and moral responsibility that is rooted in the imagery and ambiance of one of the oldest literary forms: the fairy tale."[3]

Here we have an important contribution to that great tradition of anthologies—of which the Grimm's collections are only the best-known examples—that comingle fairytales of all descriptions from numerous sources into a glorious mashup. It predates by seven years Stephen Sondheim's staging of *Into the Woods* and looks backward to the fairytale music of a song cycle by Robert Schumann (1810–1856) from 1849, *Liederalbum fuer die Jugend*, Op. 79, which brings together tales for children, young and old, from E.T.A. Hoffmann ("The Sandman"), Goethe ("Mignon" and "The Wandering Bell"), and Hoffmann von Fallersleben ("Cloud-Cuckoo Land"), etc.[4]

Fairy tales fuel, parallel, and shape the events and characters in and out of Tom's nightmare-haunted Carson School and Coleman Collins's enchanted forest of Shadowland. It begins with the innocence of young Tom's schoolboy dreams and it ends 20 years later with the bittersweet reality of betrayal and loss. The tone veers wildly from a profound meditation on magic, to the gruesome horrors of a *grand guignol*, to the frantic hilarity of a Tex Avery cartoon. This ambivalence—indeed, the whole purpose of Straub's novel—is nicely captured when Tom discovers a hidden room in Uncle Cole's mansion, where he meets none other than Jacob and Wilhelm Grimm. They sit at their little desks, busily scribbling away. "We are writing down stories," they tell him, "to amaze. To terrify. To delight." But their stories are not for children: "No child can go the whole way with them." The tale of "The Boy Who Could Not Shiver," for example, "is full of the most frightening things ever encountered"; but "'many frightening things conceal jokes, and many jokes have ice in their hearts'" (200–201).[5]

As if to reinforce the idea that fairy tales are not just "twice-told," as in Hawthorne, but told many times over by a variety of speakers, multiple narrators tell Tom Flanagan's story: There is Tom himself; our Storyteller (a nameless former classmate of Tom and Del); and a third "voice," an omniscient observer. It begins with the innocence of young Tom's schoolboy dreams and it ends 20 years later with the bittersweet reality of betrayal and loss.

Once Upon a Time...

Registration Day at Carson School, 1958. Fourteen-year-old Tom Flanagan apprehensively faces his first day. "*Goodbye, freedom,*" he breathes. He remembers a strange dream he had the day before: A menacing figure approaches him. He seeks refuge in a wizard's cottage. He knows it's a wizard's house because it has a thatched roof and a little brown door. "'You are safe here,'" says the wizard. But he warns the boy that ahead there is "'a deep, deep wood'" and several tests to pass. There will be a girl, a wolf, and a fight for his life. "'You'll have your heart broken,'" continues the wizard, "'but you'll never get anything done if you walk around with an unchipped heart. That's the way of it, boy'" (15–16). Many years later we will find Tom practicing stage magic in a shabby Sunset Strip nightclub. He looks back on the boy he was, at the terrible events that befell him and his friend, Del Nightingale, in the enchanted forest known as Shadowland, and at the wizard's prophecy that came true. Or was it *all* a magician's lies and misdirections?

For all its outwardly proper and conventional aspect, there's something very *wrong* about Carson School. Nightmares plague the students. The unchecked, vicious bullying by the deranged upperclassman, Skeleton Ridpath, spreads hate and dissension. The headmaster, Laker Broome, has disturbing notions about student discipline: "'We have to reshape you boys … or you will be doomed, boys'" (48). A sinister stranger in trench coat and low-brimmed hat occasionally appears among the students. Tom and Del, who have become best friends, display unexpected magical talents that include levitation. Moreover, Tom has visions of a jungle-like world lurking behind the school's facades. He senses a "tremendous energy ... humming and buzzing away" beneath his feet (60). Indeed, the weird general tone of the place is best described by the English teacher, Fitz-Hallan, during his lecture on fairy tales: "'The natural world of common sense and social differentiation is set aside, and magic takes charge of things,'" he tells his students. "'It speaks in poetry. It alters the world.... The ordinary rules don't work— animals will talk, people will turn into animals, the world will turn topsy-turvy'" (57). The words prove to be prophetic.

The school term comes to a disastrous end, when a mysterious fire breaks out during a magic show presented to the student body by Tom and Del. It is at this moment that Tom first hears from Del the strange mantra that will be repeated later several times in these pages, the secret of all magic: "'The mind opens, the shoulder opens, the body opens...'" (119). In the ensuing panic a student dies and many others suffer severe smoke inhalation. Under a cloud of scandal, the school limps to semester's end.

With the arrival of summer, Tom and Del set out for the Vermont estate, Shadowland, of Del's Uncle Coleman Collins, a famous magician "'who's full of secrets and information no one else knows about'" (40). "Uncle Cole," who bears an odd resemblance to Headmaster Laker Broom, has promised to apprentice the boys in the practice of magic. Del shares with Tom a message sent from his Uncle Cole. It contains the warning *Know What You Are Getting Into!* and a list of recommended "spells, images & illusions" to learn. "'It's just ordinary stage stuff,'" assures Del, "'all you have to know is how to do it, how the mechanics work'" (135). Tom, meanwhile, feels strangely *drawn* there...

But soon Tom learns that Uncle Cole is anything but "ordinary," his abilities anything but "mechanical," and his intentions far from benign. He lives in a house that is "secretive and mean," whose inhabitants "hated light," and whose presence "implied dispossession" (284). Tom is wary of him at the outset: "There was a sudden, strong resistance to all about him. This man was not his father. His stories would be lies: there was nothing about him that was not dangerous" (157). In events taking up the final two sections of the novel, in a Shadowland compounded of dream and terror, they encounter a kind of alternative Carson School, whose characters and events—including an apocalyptic conflagration—are echoes of the disasters they had thought to have left behind.

Collins confides his own fairy tale to Tom. His magical abilities stemmed from a transformative moment in the Great War, when as "Charles Nightingale" he worked as a medic. One day during an operation on a wounded soldier, he felt a strange power coursing through him: "'My mind began to buzz. My hands tingled. I trembled, knowing what I could do.... I could *heal* him. I put down the instruments and ran my fingers along the torn blood vessel. Radiance—invisible radiance—streamed from me. It was as though I had been raised up to a great eminence and been shown all the things of this world and been told: 'You may have what you like'" (229).

Stories about his miraculous surgical techniques spread. He comes under the influence of a master magician, a imposing black man seated on an Owl's Throne who identifies himself as the King of the Cats, otherwise known as "Speckle John." He abandons medicine and takes up magic under the name "Coleman Collins." Speckle John instructs him in the magical arts and inducts him into a mysterious occult Order that is governed by a mysterious Book (which we eventually learn is a version of the *Gnostic Gospels*). Soon they are performing together. But Collins grows dissatisfied at John's modest and "small conception" of magic, at his unwillingness to use magic to acquire power and instill fear. Drunk with power, greed, and ambition, Collins betrays and overthrows Speckle John. He assumes the rank of King of the Cats.

Once the apprentice, now the mentor, Collins sees in young Tom a possible candidate to succeed him in Shadowland as King of the Cats. He divines "'strange stirrings in him, a boy who does not know who he is'" but who surpasses the abilities Collins had hitherto sensed in his nephew Del. He shows Tom the mysterious Book he had wrested from Speckle John. "'In time it will be yours,'" he promises. It reveals the secrets of Magicians, the real history of the world—"'that gods are only men with superior understanding ... who have found and released the divine within themselves'" (291).

In neither the first nor the last Biblical allusion in *Shadowland*—here, the Book of Luke—he is the Tempter who takes Tom high up into the air: "'Look down,' he says, "that is the world. It can be yours. Everything in the world, every treasure, every satisfaction is there. This is your kingdom too, child, insofar as I make it yours'" (194-196). The pursuit of magic will liberate him from "'ordinary life,'" make him "'a piece of the universe,'" and establish in him "'a *synthesis*, part music and part blood, part thinker and part killer.'" He will learn to fly: "'Spread your hands ... spread your arms ... think of your shoulders opening, opening ... think of them opening out.... Don't wait to be a great man, be a great bird'" (195). But in order to fulfill his latent magical abilities, what Collins calls his "song," he must relinquish his freedom, his "wings."

In short, it's a Faustian bargain. The options are clear: "'You could take the high road.... That way you become master of Shadowland.... The option is open to you. You become stronger and stronger as a magician. Your life is full, varied, and satisfying. Everything you could want comes to you on a high tide of blessings. Or you could take the low road.... You run into trouble almost immediately. You endanger your happiness'" (304). But, in an allusion to the Grimm fairy tale "The Goose Girl," he will be robbed of his identity. He will be bound irrevocably to Collins and his magic and his Book. Unlike what Collins describes as a "'watered down'" *Thomas*, which preaches a Christian morality, Collins's Book dismisses Good and Evil as a "'convenient fiction'" and is founded instead on hate, greed, and power. (291). "'*If you bring forth what is within you,*'" quotes Collins, "'*what you bring forth will save you. If you do not bring forth what is within you, what you do not bring forth will destroy you.*'" Tom is horrified. He realizes what Collins brought forth is only hate and greed, "'a man lost within his own powers, a shadow in a shadow world'" (284). But if Tom denies his own capacity for good, he will be destroyed.

The world turns topsy-turvy. Tom and Del witness bizarre "performances" in Collins's *Théâtre des illusions*. The prankster Peter Straub at his most antic. Collins appears as a mad Master of Ceremonies, a sort of deranged fusion of Penn & Teller—a jointed robot, a mechanical man who dances and capers and turns somersaults. "'Everything you will see here,'" he croons, "'and you will see many odd things—comes from your own mind—from within you.... None of it exists elsewhere'" (186). Like the turning pages of a deranged comic book, scenes and characters from Carson School and Shadowland morph in and out of phase. Rabbits carry parasols and ride bicycles. An oversized doll house swings open, revealing a mad apothecary, whose "sleeping" pills snore, "reducing" tonics shrink, and "vanishing" cream disappears. From a great height—he is suddenly flying—Tom revisits the great fire of Carson School. It's dizzy and it's impossible. In scenes and passages like this—and we recall the precedent of the bizarre Carnival scene in Hawthorne's *The Marble Faun*[6]—Straub's novel has slipped its moorings and is fulfilling, *all by itself*, the injunction earlier uttered by Fitz-Hallen, that "'magic is taking charge of things.'"

Bewildered and disturbed by all this, fearful of the corruption that is tempting him, and afraid for Del, who is passively falling into the clutches of Collins, Tom determines to flee Shadowland. "'You perverted the Book,'" he accuses Collins. "'You perverted magic'" (385). Aiding in the escape plan is a beautiful "guest" in Collins's mansion named Rose Armstrong, with whom Tom has fallen in love. She will presently become an important part of his story. Matters now move quickly to a spectacular climax. When Tom's escape

attempt fails, Collins feels betrayed. "'I had to see if you'd really try to leave.
You don't deserve your talent—but that is academic now, for you won't have
it much longer'" (346). He ties Tom to an X-shaped wooden frame and drives
nails through his hands, another Christ-like allusion. "'I will give you yet
another choice,'" he says. "'The choice of giving up your song ... and leave
magic. Let me have your gifts ... walk out of Shadowland and be the boy you
thought you were when you came here.'" Otherwise, "'pit your powers against
mine, until Shadowland has a undisputed master, the new king or the old'"
(382). Coming to Tom's aid, summoned by his imagination, is none other
than one Bud Copeland, whom we first met as a kindly associate of Del's god-
parents, and who now reveals himself as Collins's former mentor, Speckle
John: "'He took my magic away. He thought that was worse than death'" (353).
In a supreme effort of will, encouraged by Speckle John, Tom wills his mind
"into the swamp of Collins's being, where nothing could hold him now, going
as invincibly as if he wore white armor and feeling Collins melt beneath
him..." (402). The great house, and all of Shadowland, collapses into flames.
At length, Tom and Rose escape the burning scene.

But in the face of his victory Tom suffers his greatest loss. His beloved
Rose is unable—indeed, she cannot—leave Shadowland. She is living in her
own fairy tale. She is the Mermaid who pays a price for living in the world
of mortals, forced to "walk on swords"—her high heels—her every step "a
crucifixion like Tom's" (371). In their last moments, she and Tom lie together
on the beach while in the distance Collins's house collapses into rubble. As
he sleeps, she slips back into the water, from which, after all, she had come.
Left behind is a whispered message, whose words are beyond ordinary "flawed
human speech" (407). Tom is left with the broken, "chipped" heart foretold
in the dream by the Wizard: A struggle against severe difficulties in life is
unavoidable; it is an intrinsic part of human existence.[7]

So concludes Tom Flanagan's story. He has made his choice. Twenty
years later, he will be an itinerant stage magician practicing magic tricks in
a tacky Sunset Strip nightclub, remembering the boy he had been...

And about that story, wonders our nameless narrator—what about the
wicked headmaster at Carson School, Carson Broome; the wild boy, bully
and wannabe magician, Steven Ridpath, known as "Skeleton"; and what about
the magician Coleman Collins and his country mansion known as Shadowland? How much of any of it is true? Our Storyteller decides to investigate.
Of Broome, there appears to be no trace. Skeleton is found in a monastery,
a lowly, silent monk cutting roses and tending a medieval garden. He refuses
to talk with his visitor. We go next to the presumed site of Shadowland, where
Tom's story had concluded with a terrible fire in which rival magicians had

clashed and battles had been waged. There is only a blasted area, revealing little of what perhaps once was a lavish mansion. Yes, it was once the "Collins" place; now owned by Tom Flanagan, who never visits there.

As our Storyteller walks about, he has the uncanny feeling he is accompanied by the characters of Tom's story: "I could almost see them there, Tom and his Rose, curled together on the tiny strip of sand ... could almost see her whispering whatever she had whispered into his ear before she ... what? Slipped into the water and left all that was human behind her, welded into Tom Flanagan's memory?" (417).

The Golden Key

Reducing *Shadowland* to a linear storyline, as I have done here, risks an absurd simplification of Straub's dense, richly complex narrative scheme—rather like stripping a Chopin Mazurka of its underlying harmonic changes and embellishments, exposing only its simple, dance-like motif. *Shadowland* is its own magic box, its lid thrown off, its tales scattered and mixed. It melds the oral folk tradition, magic, the Faust story, the fairy tale, and the Gnostic gospels. It performs riffs on them all, modulating from chord to chord, from event to event, always with the verve and swing Straub always valorizes in jazz. The results constitute one of his most complex, inventive, and challenging novels. We find its visual equivalent in the physical morphings, spatial conflations, and intensity of vision in that amazing fairy-tale painting of the mad painter, Richard Dadd, "Fairy Feller's Master Stroke."[8] *Shadowland* belongs on the same shelf with other modern masterworks in the *Kunstmärchen* tradition, including John Crowley's *Little, Big*, Susanna Clark's *Jonathan Strange and Mr. Norrell*, Elizabeth Hand's *The Waking Moon*, Philip Pullman's *His Dark Materials*, and John Fowles's *The Magus*.[9]

The characters *are* their own stories: Tom Flanagan and Del Nightingale, for example, are representatives of the orphaned, wandering children on a quest through the Great Forest in search of their identity, as in so many tales of the Brothers Grimm.[10] Rose Armstrong is a combination of the Grimm's "The Goose Girl" and Hans Christian Andersen's "The Little Mermaid." Coleman Collins is the deadly Erl King of Goethe's poem. Other tales, including "The King of the Cats," "The Boy Who Would Not Shiver," and "The Golden Key" are prominently featured as metaphors for, respectively, the accession to power, the healing qualities of fear, and the multi-textual nature of fairy tales, in general.

Just as these tales all derive from an oral tradition, so too do many of

Straub's original stories appearing here have their origins in the stories that he told and improvised for his one-year-old son Ben.

> Stories poured out [of] me [he recalls]. I had no idea no idea where they were going when I started them, but along the way they always turned into *real* stories, with beginnings, middles, and ends, complete with hesitations, digressions, puzzles, and climaxes. This was thrilling. My little boy was entranced, and I felt as though I had tapped into the pure, ancient well, the source of narrative, the spring water which nourished me and everyone else like me.[11]

These original tales include "The Mermaid" (a variant on *The Little Mermaid*"), "The King and the Goat," and "The Dead Princess." They are about choices and their sometimes unwonted consequences. For example, in a variant on various "Mermaid" tales, Tom's beloved Rose has sacrificed her voice (song) in return for the legs that will enable her to live in the world and know human love. A condition of that freedom is that walking—a condition of mortality—forces the girl to wound her feet on painful high heels. In "The King and the Goat" an old King asks a wizard to restore his devastated kingdom to its former glory. The wizard offers him a beautiful wife who will love him and bewitch his enemies. In return the king has to agree to sacrifice his gray hair and adopt a beard. Although the king is suspicious of the duplicitous doings of wizards, he agrees. Sure enough the bride is beautiful and passionate on the wedding night. She does indeed bewitch the rival armies. But when the wizard reappears he claims his part of the bargain and transforms the King into a creature with grey fur and chin whiskers—a goat.

In what is perhaps the most important of these original tales, "The Dead Princess," a kingdom has fallen silent and its people plunged into sleep because of the death of their beloved Princess Rose. A flock of helpful sparrows overhead seeks the assistance of a wizard. He tells them they must first choose between sacrificing their wings or their songs. They give up their songs. Upon returning, the sparrows find the kingdom restored and the Princess come back to life. But they are now no longer birds but earthbound frogs. "They are still trying to sing and still trying to fly. But they can only croak and hop" (180). What once was is now gone forever, vaguely remembered and only imperfectly recaptured.

This is an allegory of the human condition, after all. Coleman Collins himself says we were all once birds who were tricked by a great wizard and selfishly chose our "song," our art, over our "wings," our freedom. Indeed, birds and flight are the foundational metaphors of Straub's book. Bird-motifs can be found everywhere in fairy tales. "You have heard how magical birds aid their masters in quests and divinations," he says. "You know how they roam widely and freely in the world, bringing rumors of goodness here and there, soaring above what holds us to our earthly existence—ladies and gentlemen, aren't birds our very image of the magical?" (396).

Birds of all kinds—benign white doves, savage black vultures, gentle sparrows flutter and swoop throughout these pages. They are there from the very moment Tom and Del enter Carson School, whose motto is *alis volat pripriis* ("He flies by his own wings"). And in Shadowland Coleman Collins welcomes them as "birds come home" (146). Moreover, the owl of wisdom and power is carved on the chair of the King of the Cats. The appearance of a vulture signifies the death of Tom's father. The savage bird screaming for admittance to Skeleton's room foretells the violence of Collins's seductive powers. And Del's final transformation into a defenseless little sparrow at the end signals his inability to withstand Collin's power.

Shadowland soundly rebukes those who insist that fairy tales are fixed narratives, beyond revision. For example, Charles Dickens had condemned George Cruikshank's rewriting of fairy tales in *The Fairy Library* in an article entitled "Frauds on the Fairies": Whoever "alters [the traditional tales] to suit his own opinions, whatever they are, is guilty, to our thinking, of an act of presumption, and appropriates to himself what does not belong to him."[12] "Guilty as charged," then, are not just Straub, but the Brothers Grimm themselves, who, according to Maria Tatar, in her *The Hard Facts of the Grimm's Fairy Tales*, "played a role in shaping the plots of the tales they heard" during a span of forty years.[13] They are endlessly mutable. Recent retellings have included "literary" volumes by Walter de la Mare (*Told Again*, 1927) and Philip Pullman (*Fairy Tales from the Brothers Grimm*, 2012); modernist versions from Angela Carter (*The Bloody Chamber*, 2011); A.S. Byatt (*The Djinn and the Nightingale's Eye*, 1998); and Roald Dahl (*Roald Dahl's Revolting Rhymes*, 1982)—with their gutsy heroines and satiric *guignol*—and a variety of transgressive and queered readings privileged by the academic community, notably Cristina Bacchilega's *Postmodern Fairy Tales: Gender and Narrative Strategies*, 1997). Angela Carter has defended her intentions in her own highly sexualized versions in *The Bloody Chamber*: "I was taking the latent image—the latent content of those traditional stories and using that; and the latent content is violently sexual. And because I am a woman, I read it that way."[14]

Sometimes, admittedly, perversities have resulted. Tatar reports, for example, that during the years of the Nazi Reich, Red Riding Hood was rescued by an SS officer![15]

Straub's own strategy of Tale-telling can be seen in his treatment of the familiar Grimm story, "The Golden Key." A boy discovers a golden key and an iron casket. He turns the key and then—

And then—nothing. That's where the tale ends.

In many editions of the Grimm's Tales "The Golden Key" is the last story. It positions us on the threshold of speculation, leaving us to savor the marvelous quality of all fairy tales, i.e., that they are *never-ending*...

Now, Peter Straub is no stranger to ambiguity, to the indeterminate. "I've always really liked things I do not understand," he has admitted, "stories that seemed to me to resist, in fact to refuse, conventional forms of understanding." Indeed, life itself "is riddled with the indeterminate, the unresolved, with the mystery of human motive...." He valorizes the poetry of John Ashbery and writer Robert Aickman for precisely these reasons. In their ambiguity he finds their "actual richness and, dare I say it?—meaning."[16]

Now back to *Shadowland* and "The Golden Key." In Straub's version of "The Golden Key," the boy *opens the box*. But resolving one ambiguity only releases others. And what follows elicits some of Straub's most beautiful prose: "Every story in the world, every story ever told, blew up out of the box. Princes and princesses, wizards, foxes and trolls and witches and wolves and woodsmen and kings and elves and dwarves and a beautiful girl in a red cape.... Then the wind caught them and sent them blowing away, some this way and some that..." (159). Like the parallel worlds of Carson School and Shadowland that morph in and out of each other, these Tales have been shaken and stirred, "until they cohere into a story that is neither one nor the other—but 'as smooth as a stone from a river.'"[17] We find a precedent in Nathaniel Hawthorne. (Do we not always turn to Hawthorne in talking about Straub?) In *The Marble Faun*, in a chapter called "Fragmentary Sentences," the narrator declares: "In waving these mystic utterances into a continuous scene, we undertake a task resembling, in its perplexity, that of gathering up and piecing together the fragments of a letter, which has been torn and scattered to the winds."[18]

As a result, stories are torn apart, then reconfigured, like the scattered bones in Straub's favorite working metaphor, the fairy tale of the "Juniper Tree." "The fairy tales had *blown into each other*" (my italics), writes Straub with marvelous whimsy, "and got mixed up so that the old king had a wolf's head under his crown, and the young prince in love with the maiden fluttered and gasped in a sparrow's body, and Little Red Riding Hood walked forever on knives and sword blades, and the wise magician who enters at the end to set everything right was only a fifteen-year-old boy kneeling on bloodied floorboards..." (383).

Similarly, the mundane worlds of Carson School and the magical realms of Shadowland are interchangeable, their characters and incidents mixed, blended, and reconfigured. "Insofar as I had a general scheme," confides Straub, "mine was to have everything happen twice—what took place at the school would be repeated, in a more dreamlike and dramatic, therefore more unreliable, fashion, at the magician's Vermont estate, Shadowland. Realism, perhaps even the idea of reality itself, would dissolve into a hallucinatory field of possibility."[19] Co-existing in a suspension, they resist our attempts to separate them. The resulting ambiguity should hover, much like the suspensions between harmonic and enharmonic changes in a Schubert sonata, resulting, says Bettelheim, "an eerie, dreamlike emotive state close to the classic definition of 'the uncanny.'"[20]

The Kunstmärchen

The comingling of alternate worlds.... Thus the Gothic tale in Europe and America reveals its kinship with the German tradition of the *Kunstmärchen*, a term that roughly means "literary fairy tale." The form first came to prominence early in the 19th century in the work of the master German storytellers, Goethe, Novalis, Ludwig Tieck and E.T.A. Hoffmann, and subsequently exerted a profound influence in America in the stories of a writer who we know had a considerable impact on Straub, Nathaniel Hawthorne. As Robyn Schiffman asserts, Novalis, in particular, "demands careful reexamination in the history of nineteenth-century American literary culture."[21] Together, they forged a narrative invention, explains Gordon Birrell in *German Fairy Tales*, that, for the most part, takes considerable liberties with fairy tales, reestablishes them in contemporary settings, and invests them with authorial self-consciousness and ironic quotation.[22]

A significant feature of the *Kunstmärchen* is its sophisticated juxtaposition of alternate worlds. In his study of Ludwig Tieck, for example, William J. Lillyman makes a key point: "The supernatural realm of each tale intrudes into the everyday human world *as an actual part of reality*, not as an hallucinatory experience.... The fairy-tale realm is an actual part of the reality portrayed in the story and is not the phantasy of a deranged mind..." (italics added).[23] They lie so close to each other. Neither is *outside* the other, but each is *within* the other. Thus, Tom's dizzying conflation of the worlds of Carson School and Shadowland recall that archetypal, E.T.A. Hoffmann classic "The Golden Pot." The Faery and the Real co-exist and interchange: "While you are in this region that is revealed to us in dreams," writes Hoffmann, "try, gentle reader, to recognize the familiar shapes that hover around you in the ordinary world. Then you will discover that this glorious kingdom is much closer to you than you ever imagined."[24]

A heightened attention—what Straub repeatedly describes as *clarity*—

to worlds both real and unreal attends these juxtapositions. In *Heinrich von Ofterdingen*, Novalis had described this super-sensual state: "A thousand recollections were alive, and every stone, every tree, every hill invited recognition, each one the symbol of an old tale."[25] G. K. Chesterton calls this recognition "the silent witchery that lies in common things. Corn and stones and apple trees and fire" are revealed "as magic stones and magic apple trees..." Stare steadily at them at twilight and you "will be unable to assert that they are not magic."[26] Parenthetically, contrast this with the perverse perceptions of the character of the deranged Skeleton Ridpath in *Shadowland*, who finds that "every leaf, every grain of sand, had a killer in it." In everything he touched he felt only "a wave of blackness pumping through it, drawn up from the ground and breathed out through the bark" (55).

Tom Flanagan and his Rose find their parallels in the protagonists of Novalis's seminal , the story-fragment known as *Heinrich von Ofterdingen* (*The Blue Flower*, 1798–99). Novalis's novel of travel and experience follows the quest of a young man for the "extravagant gaze," to open himself up to the wonders of the phenomenal world around him: "The fairy night mirrored itself in Henry's soul. He felt as though the world lay unlocked within him and was revealing to him as to an intimate friend all its treasures and hidden charms."[27] In a dream, Heinrich finds a Book, which tells the story of his own life—but which is unfinished. He falls in love with a young woman named Mathilde, who embodies his ideal of a mysterious "Blue Flower." Her parting words to him, like those of Rose to Tom, convey a "secret" he is unable to understand: "With her lips to his she spoke a wonderful secret word which echoed through his whole being.... He would have given his life to know what that word was."[28] In sum, a Quest, a mysterious Book, a feminine ideal, and a language that is incomprehensible—unite the worlds of Straub and Novalis, Tom Flanagan and Heinrich von Ofterdingen, Rose and Mathilde.

And about Heinrich's mysterious Book... Could it be the same book that Coleman Collins has stolen from Speckle John and which now belongs to Tom? Perhaps its revelations, albeit in a secret language, hint at the "divine truth" of the Gnostic Gospels. As critic Bill Sheehan observes, the "self," like the world it inhabits, strives toward the condition of revelation.[29] Magic is just another name for that revelation. "My notions of the meaning of magic had developed," Straub recalls. "I had no idea why this should be important to me, but magic, real magic, which could be expressed in stage magic but was not confined to it, was connected by the internal resources of the magician to the unseen, subtle, powerful internal structures of the world itself."[30]

Gnostic Revelations

Even before Straub began writing *Shadowland*, he had been interested in Gnostic writings and their connections with the meaning of magic. While searching for "a kind of alternative to standard Christian belief," he discovered the work of the 16th-century monk Giordano Bruno.[31] "Gnosticism, which I didn't understand at all at the time, seemed to offer a kind of way in to a realm that I had perceived only at certain very privileged moments." Later, he came across the Gospel of Thomas, "which I found very, very moving and kind of explanatory." Straub was beginning to regard the world and the self as "a Gnostic structure," the possibility that the divine can be released within the self. Even the act of writing could become a form of magic when, performed daily, can lead into revelation.[32]

References to the writings of the Gnostics, such as the *Gospel of Thomas*, first surface in *Shadowland* and are explicitly referenced in the search for identity and meaning in the protagonists of many of Straub's later stories, as we shall see. The quest for transcendence, reveals what is within, not imposed from without. This is contrary to a major premise of Christianity, explains Elaine Pagels in her book, *The Gnostic Gospels*. Only through Gnosticism, it was presumed, will we gain the secret knowledge that allows us to see the real world and save our souls. As opposed to the Christian doctrines that God is "wholly other," self-knowledge is knowledge of God; the self and the divine are identical. We share a common being with the realms above. Instead of coming to save us from sin, "[Jesus] comes as a guide who opens access to spiritual understanding. But when the disciple attains enlightenment the two have become equal—even identical."[33] Such statements, attributed to Jesus, appeal to Straub. This is a spiritual guide "I want to believe in," he has said, they seemed so "authentic" that "I was compelled to write them down and insert them into fiction."[34]

In sum, Tom Flanagan's education in magic achieves what Bruno Bettelheim says is the "central theme of the wide variety of fairy tales," a rebirth to a higher plane, or awareness of his selfhood. "Children (and adults too) must be able to believe that reaching a higher form of existence is possible if they master the developmental steps this requires."[35] One of those lessons learned is contained in the fairy tale the Brothers Grimm told Tom about the "Boy Who Could Not Shiver." Here, again turning to Bettelheim, the moral lesson is that to realize one's humanity, "feelings must become accessible ... to feel fear is human, not being able to feel it is inhuman." Repressions "must be undone." It is the "last transition needed for achieving mature humanity."[36] Just as the wizard in his dream had foretold, Tom must endure a painful, bittersweet "chipped" heart.

By contrast, in becoming his own God, in effect, the magician Collins turned away from Gnostic truth. "You perverted the Book," Tom says. "You perverted magic" (385). A mere pretender to the King of the Cats, he had forsaken the "light within" while pursuing the "secret of hating." In quoting one of the sayings the Gnostics attributed to Jesus—"If you bring forth what is within you, what you bring forth will save you. If you do not bring forth what is within you, what you do not bring forth will destroy you"—he was predicting his own fate. He is the Demiurge of the Gnostics, who falsely claims to be the ultimate authority in the universe. His repression of his true spiritual potential left a void that left him open to destruction at Tom's hand.

Pied Pipers

Collins is Straub's contribution to the literature of the charismatic con man, in folk lore, in literature, in life. In the fairy tale tradition we find his archetype in the Pied Piper of legend, that motley-clad, flute-playing figure who enticed more than a hundred children out of the town of Hamelin to an undisclosed fate.[37] In Chaucer's "The Pardoner's Tale," he is a trickster, a combination of itinerant preacher and salesman of salvation, whose sermon topic always remains the same: *Radix malorum est Cupiditas*, or "greed is the root of all evil." He confesses his own corruption and takes a perverse pride in it. He carries a bag of "relics," which, he readily admits to the listening pilgrims, are fake. He will take a sheep's bone and claim it has miraculous healing powers for all kinds of ailments. The parishioners always believe him and make their offerings to the relics, which the Pardoner quickly pockets. He readily admits that he preaches solely to get money, not to correct sin, that his sermons are the product of evil intentions.[38]

American 19th-century Gothic literature provides a carnivalesque gallery of Collins's ancestors, all of them Serpents in the New World Eden. Since the appearance of the conniving ventriloquist Carwin in Charles Brockden Brown's *Wieland*, he (or she) has appeared and reappeared in a variety of guises. To cite just a few outstanding examples, he is the capering devil and the fake spiritualist in Hawthorne's "Young Goodman Brown" and *House of the Seven Gables*, respectively. In Mark Twain's "The Mysterious Stranger" he is Philip Traum, a magician who claims supernatural attributes and turns the whole world into a sideshow. In Henry James' *The Bostonians*, Basil Ransom claims a supernatural authority that claims for his own use the soul of a helpless girl, who has been deluded into thinking herself a medium of spiritual communication. In a reversal of this dynamic, the preacher Theron Ware, in

Harold Frederic's *The Damnation of Theron Ware* (1896) is seduced and corrupted by the free-thinking "aesthete," Celia Ware. Not the Snake in the Edenic Garden, she is the tempting Eve: Her "absolute freedom from moral bugbears" and rejection of conventional gender roles ("I am not related to them") leads to Ware's utter decline and collapse. She mocks his delusion of enlightenment: "'What you took to be improvement was degeneration.'"[39]

One of the finest, even sympathetic portraits of this character type, is found in William Dean Howells's *The Leatherwood God* (1916). The titular character, the preacher Dylks, is a rural prophet, a chronic liar, whose misguided promises of spiritual salvation bilk his congregation to the point where they angrily rise up against him. He commits suicide. Howells brings the magician/trickster into a particularly American context: "'You see, life is hard in a new country, and anybody that promises salvation on easy terms has got a strong hold at the very start,'" says the atheist Squire Braile: "'People will accept anything from him. Somewhere, tucked away in us, is the longing to know whether we'll live again, and the hope that we'll live happy.... We want to be good, and we want to be safe, even if we are not good; and the first fellow that comes along and tells us to have faith in him, and he'll make it all right, why, we have faith in him, that's all.'"[40] What these seductive figures have in common, writes Susan Kuhlmann in *Knave, Fool, and Genius*, "is their charismatic quality, their success as the focal point of crowd interest and even of crowd hysteria. [They are] physically attractive; they use as their 'weapon' the communicative organs, the burning eye and the thrilling tongue. Their 'skill' is in the mastery of religious jargon, and their 'game' is the manipulation of a primitive soul hunger."[41]

Straub finds his own model of the magician/trickster in the real-life figure of Henry Cornelius Agrippa. "He was *the man*," he says, "a Renaissance magician who had a very turbulent life. He wrote four great books of magic, including *Magical Ceremonies* [1565]. He died too young in a monastery, watched over by a bunch of priests who thought he was a heretic, even satanic character. He's inexplicable. He described spirits conjured up that were beautiful and dangerous. I sucked them into my book [*A Dark Matter*]. But this also seems dubious—where did Agrippa *get* this stuff? He's describing stuff that would alter our own understanding of the world. Even if we're not sure what that meaning is!"[42]

And of course, characters like this pop up everywhere in Straub, in a variety of names, guises and genders. They pipe their victims into the enchanted forests of nightmare and transformation. Eva Galli in *Ghost Story* and Coleman Collins in *Shadowland* are joined by Gideon Winter in *Floating Dragon*, Heinz Stenmetz in *Throat* and "Bunny Is Good Bread," Manny Dengler in *Throat*, Tillman Hayward in "A Special Place," the nameless molester in "The Juniper Tree," Joseph Kalendar in *In the Night Room*, the Crimson King and his dreaded minions in *The Talisman* and *Black House*, and Spencer Mallon in *A Dark Matter*. A few of their victims, Underhill in "The Juniper Tree," Eel in *A Dark Matter*, Mark Underhill and Lily Kalendar in *In the Night Room*, eventually recover buried and repressed memories and move on to productive lives. On the other hand, Fee Bandolier in *Throat*, Manny Dengler in *Koko*, Keith Hayward in "A Special Place," Skeleton Ridpath in *Shadowland*, Mrs. Asch in "Ashputtle" are so "darkened" by these experiences that they grow up to perform their own fairy tales about child abusers.

Straub's most recent novel, *A Dark Matter*, provides a particularly pertinent demonstration of these trickster magicians. Spencer Mallon is a creature of the sixties, a charismatic guru aflame with a kind of "spiritual greediness." Told in a series of flashbacks, he had gathered his acolytes, four high school students, in Madison, Wisconsin, in 1966 to venture into a Meadow outside of town to indulge in a series of occult rituals: "'He held his 'chosen few' together, recalls one of the students, years later: "'He got them to do what he wanted … never thinking that he was being pushed by forces he did not understand and could not control…'" (227). He implied that his final goal involved using a "sacred violence" as a means of destroying the earth and transforming it in a fiery rebirth. "'We are very close to that reality,'" Mallon had said, in words that recall those of the magician Coleman Collins: "'Usually, the closest you get is the feeling that something *almost* happened— that the veil trembled for a second, and you came close to seeing what was on the other side. Or that some extraordinary force was hovering just out of sight, almost close enough to touch, but you weren't good enough to hold it there, or strong enough, or concentrated enough, or that something else in the room screwed things up'" (68).

"'He actually wanted to change the world,'" recalls one of his acolytes, "'and in a way … he actually did!'" It lasted no more than a couple of seconds, but something went horribly wrong in that dark meadow of strange rituals and secrets—but what? The four, meanwhile, traumatized and withdrawn from the world, have repressed the memory. Now, decades later, the group reunites, each attempting to make sense of their experience, telling the story, over and over—but in various and contradictory versions. In the end, Straub writes, Mallon had "peeled back the material of [their] world at least far enough for a horde of spirits and demons to come tumbling out" (389). Finally, what is revealed is the Great Mystery and the Final Secret—"Nothing on earth means anything, or can mean anything, but what it is" (240).

And Then There Were Two

Apart from *Shadowland* we find elsewhere in Straub a number of additional fairy tales pertinent to this discussion. "Night Journey" is a story-within-a-story. It is enclosed within the novel *The Hellfire Club*. "Ashputtle" dwells as a stand-alone short story. Both are sourced in the Brothers Grimm. The first is generic, the tale of a boy wandering alone in the forest in search of the secret of his identity. The second is loosely based on "Cinderella," or, as the Grimms titled it in their 1812 volume, "Aschenputtel."

The true authorship of "Night Journey" is unknown, or at least in dispute. This is as it should be. Several claimants are considered, then dismissed. Meanwhile, we get the story in bits and pieces at various times throughout *The Hellfire Club*. Our hero, Pippin Little, awakens from a mysterious illness and finds himself in a death-haunted landscape, which he must traverse in search of the truth of his identity. On his way to the Mountain Glade, "an unhallowed haunt of baleful spirits," he fords the Field of Steam and encounters the mysterious Stones of Toon. He meets many strange and wonderful characters, including "The Cup Bearer"; "Lord Night"; and a hero-figure, "The Green Knight." His journey is described in terms that perfectly capture the narrative strategy of Straub himself:

> [He] wandered from character to character, hearing stories. Some of these characters were human and some were monsters, but they were fine storytellers one and all. Their tales were colorful and involved, full of danger, heroism, and betrayal. Some told the truth and others lied. Some wanted to help Pippin Little, but even they were not always truthful. Some of the others wanted to cut him up into pieces and turn him into tasty meat loaf…

Vital to his search is a Golden Key, which will open the door and reveal an undisclosed Secret—"what he most feared, yet most desired to see…" (317–318). Straub is having a great time here, tossing into the air bits and pieces of classic fairy tales, watching them assume their own shape, tantalizing us with their parallels to the characters and adventures of *Hellfire Club*—its protagonist, Nora Chancel (Pippin), her Quest for identity (the true authorship of *Night Journey*), the villain of the novel, Dick Dart (Lord Night), and its central location, the Shorelands' Writers' Colony, located in a remote forested region of Massachusetts (the Mountain Glade).

Straub is up to less whimsical business with his version of the Grimm Brothers' "Ashputtel." A brief review of the Grimm tale is necessary: A girl is abused at the hands of her wicked stepmother and two stepsisters. She is stripped of her fine clothes and jewels, forced to wear rags, banished into the kitchen, and given the nickname "Aschenputtel" ("Ashfool"). When the King of the land invites all the beautiful maidens in the land to a castle Ball to vie for the hand of the Crown Prince, Aschenputtel is forbidden by her step-mother to attend. But when a kindly bird comes to her rescue and gives her a silver gown and silk shoes, she slips away and captures the eye of the Prince. Later, returning home, she leaves behind one of her slippers. The Prince promises to marry the maiden whose foot fits the golden slipper. The two stepsisters mutilate their feet in trying to make them fit. But when the slipper fits Ashenputtel, the Prince marries her. The stepsisters, meanwhile, are pun-ished for their treachery when Aschenputtel's bird friends peck out their eyes.[43]

Straub's version is told in the first person by the titular Aschenputtel, a grossly overweight, middle-aged kindergarten teacher known only as "Mrs. Asch." As she tells her own story, we realize we are trapped in the mind of a mad woman, a serial killer, who goes from job to job, school to school, slaying and mutilating her young pupils. All unknowing, parents and teachers alike admire her dedication and stern discipline. "People think that teaching little children has something to do with helping other people," she says, "something to do with service. People think that if you teach little children, you must love them. People get what they need from thoughts like this" (1). Of her own childhood, she recalls a "golden time" when her parents were alive, when "all of nature echoed and repeated the awareness of perfection in my mind" (3). But after losing her father and acquiring an abusive stepmother and stepsis-ters, it all changed. She began to feel isolated. She took refuge in food bingeing and bizarre behavior. Sometimes she would stand in her room, strip off her clothes, and smear her feces over her body and the wallpaper. At the culmi-nation of these self-displays, she experiences what she calls "a nameless joy." Meanwhile, her "figments," her stepsisters, are coming to her and asking, "*Is there is anything wrong?*"

Now, as a teacher, she wields power over her young charges. Looming over them, she imagines that "darkness pours out of me." From time to time, some of her children mysteriously disappear. "A lost child lies deep within the ashes," she says, "her hands and feet mutilated, her face destroyed by fire. She has partaken of the great adventure, and now she is the same as all nature. [She] will have the opportunity to learn that nature never gives you a chance to rest. Every animal on earth is hungry" (13–14). For each of these "lost" children, she sends "sympathetic notes," joins "volunteer groups to search for bodies," and "attends the funerals" (12). Soon, she knows she will leave her job for another school. "My record is spotless," she boasts. "I never left a school except by my own choice" (12). She is confident her principal will write her a recommendation, although "he has never quite been able to con-ceal the unease I arouse within him" (17).

Peter Straub at his ease (courtesy Fales Archive).

Mrs. Asch dwells inside the fairy tale of "Aschenputtle." Her story and Aschenputtel's mix, blend, and break apart again. In living one she *performs* the other. A classic Straubian serial killer, she thinks of herself as a "work of art," detached from her atrocities. Like her namesake, she "waters" her mother's grave with tears. She bestows "smiles" everywhere, "like a queen riding through her kingdom in a carriage, like a little girl who just got a gold and silver dress from a turtledove up in a magic tree." Her birds stream out of her body "in a rapture of power, activity and rage"; they return with "diamond rings and emerald tiaras." She survives her abused childhood in the only way she knows: "I have always known that I could save myself by looking into my own mind" (15).

Who Is Telling This Story?

What is the difference between the magician and the magic, between the teller and the tale? And should we place our trust in either? Perhaps in all these tales Peter Straub is telling his own story. "[The magician] is the storyteller whose only story is himself," says his spokesperson, Coleman Collins (155). Like the writer in Borges's "Pierre Menard," he recreates texts, *not* so much by entering into their sources and authors, but by continuing to *be himself* and by coming to them *through his own experiences*. His traces, "faint but not indecipherable[,] … must shine through."[44]

Indeed, while writing these stories, Straub says he began to wonder if there was more to them than just fiction—if he had been describing something he had forgotten." Indeed, it is the condition under which so many of his characters labor. "Every man has forgotten who he is," wrote G.K. Chesterton. "We have forgotten our names…. [Moreover] we forget that we have forgotten. All that we call spirit and art and ecstasy only means that for one awful instant we remember that we forgot."[45] Straub has acknowledged several times that he had also been "describing something I had forgotten" and inserted into his stories.

In an essay entitled "Fearful Places," Straub writes candidly about his experiences on the psychotherapist's couch, wherein he recovered repressed memories of a dysfunctional family, disturbing incidents in a local movie theater, and a devastating auto accident that had left him partially paralyzed for weeks. "I don't remember it," he says enigmatically, "but I know it happened." Any chance to grow up in an envelope of innocence, feeling protected and safe, was "an illusion denied me." He became a writer of horror stories, because, he continues, his recovered memories were "of such a force and such a power, [they] inclined me always to look for the tragic and (because I was a kid) the grotesque, the morbid, the ghastly, because those conditions matched my experience." Later, as a writer, he brought a deep compassion and empathy to these unfortunate children: "Whatever power [my books] came from [they are] a reflection of what was alive and boiling in its author…. Once I started writing, I realized I could put my hands on the levers of my own problems. I could manipulate them, play with then, spin them out and make them mine."[46]

Peter Straub is his own King of the Cats, whose Book, *Shadowland*—identified variously as a fairy tale, a Gnostic text, and a *Kunstmärchen*—is written in a secret language of his own. It is unfinished. It leaves us with Rose's last words to Tom, which, like those Mathilde whispered to Heinrich, are "impossible to reconstruct into ordinary flawed human speech" (470).

Maybe it is a language understood only in the realm of all fairy tales.

But we must go there to hear it for ourselves.

CHAPTER FOUR

"Protean Impostures"
Straub and the Doppelgänger

I soon became aware, flocked the infinitude
Of passions, loves and hates, man pampers till his mood
Becomes himself, the whole sole face we name him by...
　　　　　—Robert Browning, *Fifine at the Fair* (XCV-XCVI)

I think these masks open a mine of the most delicious humor, of the
most striking irony, of the freest—I might almost say the most impu-
dent—whimsy...
　　　　　　　　　　　　　　　　　　—Robert Schumann (1835)

　　　　　I wanted to wear my own blood.
　　　　　　　　　　　　　　　　　　—Peter Straub

One day a young man in a "deplorable state of mind" encounters a
stranger "of a mysterious appearance" walking toward him. In a moment
"fraught with the most tremendous consequences," he is drawn by an "invisible power" to the stranger, whom he knows to be his Double. Soon, his every
move, his every ambition, is anticipated and thwarted by the man. He is followed. He is harassed. He loses control of his own identity. Under the
stranger's baleful influence, he turns to a life of crime. As he declines into
despair and madness, suicide is his only recourse. "There is some miserable
comfort in the idea that my tormentor shall fall with me," he realizes. As he
sets the hangman's noose, he concludes, "I will now seal up my little book
and conceal it; and cursed be he who trieth to alter or amend."[1]

James Hogg's *The Private Memoirs and Confessions of a Justified Sinner*
(1824) is one of the first in a long succession of Gothic *Doppelgänger* stories.
The story of Robert Wringham's struggle with his Double, Gil-Martin, for
power and domination has been told and re-told countless times in the history of the Gothic narrative. Notwithstanding his warning curse against writers who follow him, Heinrich Heine, Edgar Allan Poe, Nathaniel Hawthorne,

Dostoyevsky, Robert Louis Stevenson, Henry James—and including such recent classics as Stephen King's *The Dark Half* (1989) and Joyce Carol Oates's *Jack of Spades* (2015)—have all pursued the mysteries of fractured identities and divided souls.[2] What they all have in common, moreover, is that the appearance of the Double prefigures *danger* to the normative Self, whose life will be appropriated and, in many cases, destroyed.

After the relatively straightforward crime narratives of *Koko*, *Mystery*, *The Throat*, and *The Hellfire Club*, Peter Straub returned with a vengeance to supernatural horror in his *Doppelgaenger* tale, *Mr. X*. A mad counterpoint of Gothic doublings, dual narrators, ghostly doubles, twins, and multiple personalities abound. They are around every corner, down every dark street, within every character and situation, and within Straub himself, as we shall see. Pagan Gods are paired with a corrupt American family dynasty. Legend-haunted Providence, Rhode Island is shadowed by the modern town of Edgerton, Illinois. Edgerton itself has its dark side, the slum of Hatchtown. Horror master H. P. Lovecraft (1890–1937) finds a modern counterpart in the deranged "Mr. X" (and his stories are parodied in the effusions of the latter). And we're just getting started.

Enter "Mr. X"

Mr. X is the "Citizen Kane" of *Doppelgänger* stories. As critic Gary K. Wolfe observes, it exploits, as it transcends, the classic Gothic trope of the Ghostly Double.[3] Straub himself acknowledges that secret sharers, unknown brothers, and shadow selves, with their inevitable suggestion that the truly dangerous adversary has stepped out of the mirror, had always appealed to me.

> They had a lovely eeriness combined with great psychological suggestiveness. Poe, Stevenson and Dostoevsky had written doppelgänger stories, and so had Daphne du Maurier, Christopher Priest, Orhan Pamuck and lots of other people. Wilkie Collins, one of my ancestral spirits, had virtually built his career on the conceit.[4]

It comes as no surprise that *Mr. X* is a very complex narrative, even by Straub's standards. Impelled by a mysterious premonition of the impending death of his mother, 35-year old Ned Dunstan returns to his home town of Edgerton, Illinois, and hastens to her bedside. Having grown up in a series of foster homes, Ned knows relatively little about his parents and the Dunstan family legacy. Since the age of three, when his father had abandoned the family, every birthday has been marked by a series of disturbing visions of horrific murders committed by a diabolical figure he knows only as "Mr. X." Now, as he prepares for his mother's funeral, and as he goes in search of his long-lost father, someone—or something—is stalking him. A serial killer is loose, and the body count is piling up. The local police have reason to suspect him of a series of recent crimes. Unexpectedly, his long-lost twin brother shows up, a mocking, shadowy, half-human figure who may not have his best interests at heart. And there is the Dunstan family legacy to contend with, as we shall see…

A peculiar legacy indeed. There are hints that the Dunstans are descended from pagan gods. Once rulers over Earthly dominions, their supernatural powers have since been degraded and debased by generations of inbreeding, corruption, and criminal excess. In 18th-century Providence, Rhode Island, a black magic practitioner named Omar Dunstan had grown wealthy plying the slave trade. By the time the aroused citizenry raided his house, Omar had mysteriously disappeared. Only the empty house, dubbed the Shunned House, remained to crumble into ruins. More than a hundred years later, two Dunstan brothers, Omar and Sylvan, former grave robbers, shipped the stones of the original Providence house to the town of Edgerton. Rumors of unspeakable practices soon spread throughout the town. The family collapses in violence. Omar is murdered by Sylvan, who in turn kills his son, Howard, who subsequently dies in a fire in 1935. The bones that were found were not recognizably human.

Fragments of this dark past are revealed to Ned over time, piece by piece, as, armed only with his father's name, which he now knows to be "Edward Rinehart," he takes to the streets of Edgerton and Hatchtown in his search for him and for his own identity: "'Sometimes I think,'" he observes, "'that everyone I've ever known has had the feeling of missing a mysterious but essential quantity'" (317). What transpires, as critic Bill Sheehan observes, is essentially a *Bildungsroman*, "with Ned moving from place to place and encounter to encounter, gradually assembling a coherent portrait of the city and its scandals, past and present; and of the hidden, infinitely strange history of the Dunstans."[5] It combines the poetry-inflected violence of Raymond Chandler, the corrupt and tangled family histories of Ross Macdonald, and the Occult Mysteries of a psychic investigation.

A composite image of Ned's elusive father emerges, described, variously, as a gangster with a sordid past, a sinister figure with deadly, uncanny gifts, and a failed writer with a demented obsession with the stories of the horror writer, H.P. Lovecraft. Reputed to have died in prison, Rinehart seems to be very much alive, now cloaked in a series of disguises, and leaving a trail of brutal murders. He might be one of several suspects—perhaps Wilbur Whately or Charles Dexter Ward, the two men who earlier had leased two cottages on the far side of town where Rinehart keeps his hoard of Lovecraft books and papers; or Earl Sawyer, caretaker of the cottages; or Cordwainer Hatch, a member of an Edgerton family incestuously connected with the Dunstans. And he might be linked somehow to that mysterious dark man Ned knows only from his dreams, the sinister "Mr. X."

Indeed, it is possible, no matter how improbable, that *all of them* are his father, united in a dream state, the sort of condition August Strindberg describes, where "time and space do not exist," where "imagination sings and weaves new patterns made up of memories, experiences, unfettered fancies and improvisations," and where the various personae "split, double, and multiply, evaporate, crystallize, scatter and converge."[6] As if this weren't confusing enough, Ned is finding *within himself* the dark Dunstan legacy, of which he has had bewildering presentiments since boyhood—invisibility, the ability to pass through solid walls, the capacity to travel through space and time, etc. At crucial moments he is able to "flip"—to borrow a term from the Straub-King *The Talisman*—into another reality to escape whatever dangers befall him during his investigation.

Who could blame Ned—or this novel's hapless reader—if he pauses at one point and confesses, "'I feel so *baffled*. Every time I think I finally understand something, I have to start all over again at the beginning'" (330).

Meanwhile, in a parallel narrative, unbeknownst to Ned, Mr. X, who (spoiler alert!) is indeed his father, is disclosing in a series of journal entries aspects of his own past life. As a young man in school, already emboldened by hints of the strange powers of the Dunstan line, he began his "'impersonation of an ordinary child with passable success'" (23). Since discovering the "Sacred Books" of H.P. Lovecraft, he had already begun to assume the manner and mood of the solitary Providence master. "'I drift down the narrow lanes and look up at shuttered windows I could pass through in a second,'" he writes in his diary, "'but I do not: part of my happiness is in the weighing and measuring of the lives about me'" (7). On his rambles, "'invisible to all but a deeply unfortunate few,'" he leaves behind a trail of broken and mutilated victims. His journal also reveals that he is possessed by what he believes are Lovecraft's Elder Gods empowering him on a "'Sacred Mission ... adumbrated by the Providence Master.'" Enormous forces are coming into play, he writes: "'The ancient Gods, my true ancestors, congregate with rustlings of leathery wings and rattlings of filthy claws to witness what their great-grandson shall accomplish'" (7–9). As the "Opener of the Way," his task is revealed to be more than just the destruction of his son Ned Dunstan: "'O Great Old Ones, read these words inscribed within this stout journal by the hand of Your Devoted Servant and rejoice!... My role is clear, after me, the Apocalypse ...

the Destruction of mankind, Your long-awaited repossession of the earthly realm'" (58).

The source of Mr. X's delusions (if that is truly what they are)—his "Elder God"—is, of course, not really Lovecraft but his grandfather, Howard Dunstan. Since perishing in the fire in 1935, Howard's spirit is pursuing a deadly mission to destroy the remaining male heirs of the debased Dunstan line. "'What wretched lives we were given,'" Howard laments. "'I'm sick of it…. We should be gone from the earth'" (258).

Meanwhile, as we catch our breath, Ned is assisted in his quest by two unlikely allies, one the very material Captain Mullen, Edgerton's one honest cop, and the other, insubstantial Robert, Ned's own shadow-twin. Oh, yes … about Robert…. This long-lost brother has literally been shadowing him all his life. "'You are me, and I am you, yes,'" says Robert, "'but only in the sense that we each have qualities the other lacks'" (15). Robert is one of Straub's most imaginative and moving creations, a liminal, mocking figure seen mostly in the half-light. At birth, he had also been torn from his mother's side, separated Ned, forced to live as an Outsider, "'like a starving Wolf'" (339) in a series of foster homes. He possesses a "dark and destructive beauty, with eyes clear and lustrous, his nose so perfect it might have been shaped by a godlike chisel." His whole aspect bespeaks "quickness, assurance, grace, vitality" and a "pure hunger that made him rejoice in destruction." He scarcely seems human, at times. Like one of those "pod-people" in the classic Jack Finney novel, *The Body Snatchers* (1955), he is *unfinished*, without fingerprints and lacking a final polish. "Imported in every particular from an actual dream," he passes in and out of visibility, through solid walls, through space" (153). In short, he is a kind of Peter Pan, an anarchic wild child, the *puer eternus* of myth. He is "forever trapped within childhood … imprisoned in a half—life," unable to achieve full maturity and materiality. "'I hardly knew our mother,'" he tells Ned resentfully, "'you got to *live* with her, at least off and on….'"

In a series of serio-comic episodes, Robert intrudes into Ned's affairs as, alternately, a protector, a dangerous threat, and a sardonic presence. He leaves behind a trail of thefts, conflagrations, even killings that leave a bewildered Ned to take the rap from a very suspicious Edgerton police department eager to arrest and incarcerate him. At times, Robert exists apart from Ned; at others he *flows* into Ned's body, the two selves fusing temporarily. At such times, Robert achieves a materiality and substance *at Ned's expense* (269). "'I knew the powers I had discovered and those [Robert] had known all his life shared a common root,'" reports Ned at the moment of their psychic union. "'There came again a breathtaking expansion into unguessed-at wholeness and resolution that in no way erased our separate individuality. We knew what the other knew, felt what the other felt, but within this symbiosis remained a Robert and a Ned'" (403). Meanwhile, we, dear reader, begin to wonder, finally, is Robert the doppelgänger of Ned, or is it the other way around? Who's in charge here?

An answer—sort of—is disclosed in the final pages of the story.

Together, they find that the twin cottages belonging to Rinehart, now called Cordwainer, contain incriminating volumes of Lovecraft's works and a book of Lovecraftian pastiches. Traveling through time with Ned and Robert, Cordwainer is forced to confront his scheming grandfather, Howard Dunstan. He now realizes that his identity as a Lovecraftian Elder God was nothing but a delusion. "'Howard Dunstan manipulated you,'" accuses Ned. "'He *showed* you things. He made sure you came across a certain book and primed you with fantasies about H.P. Lovecraft. All along, he was just amusing himself. It was a game.'" Cordwainer protests, "'All nature spoke.'" But Ned persists: "'Haven't you ever had doubts? Weren't there times when you realized that everything you believed came from short stories written by a man who never pretended they were anything but fiction?'" At last, echoing the ending of Cordwainer's own Lovecraftian story, "Blue Fire," Ned summons up "'the forces and powers I had never known I possessed and never to command'" and hurls him to a fiery death inside the burning Dunstan ancestral house (418–419).

But Ned's quest is not finished. He and members of the Edgerton police department, including the sympathetic Captain Mullan, have been implicated in the crimes of Rinehart-Cordwainer-Mr. X. They find Cordwainer's lair, a squalid pit of trash and unspeakable filth, where, as "Mr. X," he had written his journal and prophesied global holocaust. Evidence everywhere mutely attests to his complicity in recent crimes and murders in the city. By now, fully aware of the Dunstan clan's supernatural powers, Mullan shakes his head in dismay. "'What happens if *that* goes public? A thousand reporters start digging into these murders. The whole town turns into the *National Enquirer*. The chief is out, and I'm out, spending the rest of my life running from people who want to write books about the Edgerton monster'" (448). Therefore, in an amazing feat of crime reconstruction, Mullan spins out, in a mind-bending example of Gothic rationalization of supernatural terrors, a preposterous but convincing explanation of the terrible events. "What I do know," says the admiring Ned, "is that Mullan reached into his imagination and instantly, without hesitation, unfurled the story that rescued us both" (450).

In a moving epilogue, a pathetic footnote to the main story, Ned discovers final evidence of the debased legacy of the Dunstan line. Hidden away in the attic of a great-aunt, is a distant relative, a monstrously deformed child, who is scarcely human. On a compassionate impulse, he smothers to death in a mercy killing the poor creature. He leaves Edgerton at last, still haunted by his family legacy.

And what of the shadowy Robert? Peter Straub has prepared for us one of those "falling beams"—what we call "Datchery Moments"—characteristic of hardboiled narratives. In other words, a real switcheroo is waiting for us. Ned says the "ticking footsteps" of his phantom brother continue to sound in his ear. He then addresses the reader with an earth-shattering question: "'Are you sure—*really* sure—you know who told you this story'" (482).

Has Robert, in true *Doppelgänger* fashion, finally consumed his normative Self?

Split Images

"*Mr. X* is classic Straub," writes Gary K. Wolfe, "a hugely assured narrative that recapitulates its author's traditional virtues and familiar concerns. As in the best of Straub's fiction, its extravagance—and it really is an extravagant creation—is rooted at all times in the closely observed reality of the American Midwest and in a Dickensian flair for characterization."[7]

Not so much a *Bildungsroman*, *Mr. X* may be more properly considered, appropriately enough, a *twin Bildungsroman*.[8] Ned's story is paralleled and countered by the fractured, self-destructive history of Mr. X, whose narrative is itself broken and incoherent. Traditionally, the *Bildungsroman*, from Goethe's *Wilhelm Meister's Apprenticeship* (1795–1796) to Saul Bellow's *Augie March* (1953), centers on the story of a life, usually mapped from adolescence to adulthood, from troubled beginnings to a fulfilled maturity. As critic Ronald R. Thomas has observed in his study of Gothic doublings, "it stresses the processes of growth, education, judgment, and progress that enable that movement and leads to the individual's accession to power in the world by the forging of a will, the articulation of a voice." However, Mr. X's story, as revealed in the scattered journal entries throughout the book, counters the process. Essentially a modernist *Bildungsroman*, "it is no longer the scene of self-possession"; it becomes "a sign of self-dissolution."[9]

We see this in the feverish pages of Mr. X's journal. Mr. X concocts a literary Double in the persona and stories of H. P. Lovecraft. This Dark Messiah is "'my Genesis, my Gospels, my gnosis'" (67). He entrusts to Lovecraft and his Great Beings "'these words penned by Your Devoted Servant'" for the benefits of "'aeons to come'" (8). At first, Mr. X feels newly empowered, "'god-like and fearful'": "'My pen flew across the page, and for the first and only time in my life I wrote what I knew not that I knew until it was written—I knocked at the door of the Temple and was admitted—my life became *a dark wood,* a *maze,* a *mystery*'" (206). In His name he thrives on a career as a serial killer. But subsequent entries finds him beginning to have doubts about his Sacred Mission, even about the authority of Lovecraft himself: "'I told myself He may have been incapable of distinguishing between truth and fiction in His own work'" (117). Finally, the journal stumbles as Mr. X faces the rejection of his stories by *Weird Tales* publisher and, ultimately, their destruction by fire at the hands of his enemy, Ned: "'Crucifixion is no picnic,'" he despairs. "'let me say that. Let me add that a half-human wretch and Outcast can only take so much! I scream—my Scream shall reach the Heavens—they have Destroyed my Work.'" As if reiterating the last words of the aforementioned James Hogg's *Private Memoirs and Confessions of a Justified Sinner,* there will be no more words: "'I set down the Pen—& close the Book....'" (402). The fires that await him will end his story.

Mr. X's Lovecraftian Double first enthralls, possesses, then finally consumes him. The aforementioned pattern is familiar, as we know from James Hogg's *Private Memoirs,* and including Hawthorne's "Young Goodman Brown" (1835), Poe's "William Wilson" (1843), Dostoyevsky's *The Double* (1846), Stevenson's *Dr. Jekyll and Mr. Hyde* (1886), and Henry James's *The Jolly Corner* (1908)—respectively, Goodman Brown's Mephistophelian double inducts him into the horrors of satanic revels; Wilson's second self thwarts his ambitions, leads him to insanity and death; Mr. Golyadkin's Double usurps his lodgings, his friends, his job, and ultimately drives him into an insane asylum; Henry Jekyll's Hyde performs the sins that Jekyll has repressed and which, ultimately, fatally consumes him; and Spencer Brydon's confrontation with his Double in his New York mansion nearly destroys him. Thus, in all of them, the arousal and creation of the Double—either by a satanic revelation (Hawthorne), neurotic aberration (Poe), the banality of the stifled self (Dostoyevsky), the repression of sexuality (Stevenson), and the "might-have-been alternative" (James)—results in the assumption of the Double's autonomous existence and the eventual obliteration, or near-obliteration, of the self.

These ritualized acts of self-estrangement contest the authority of the creator. The writer ultimately disappears into his own story and, in effect, is eradicated by the very thing he has written. The story told finally denies the existence of the teller. How many of Lovecraft's stories end in the writer's own demise at the hands of his Double, at the very instant *as he writes it!* The last journal entry of the doomed Robert Blake in "The Haunter of the

Dark," for example, reads as follows, degenerating into an outré language, complete with the requisite ellipses: "... the thing is stirring and fumbling in the tower—I am it and it is I—I want to get out.... It knows where I am.... There is a monstrous odor ... senses transfigured ... boarding at that tower window cracking and giving way.... Ia ... ngai ... ygg.... I see it—coming here—hell wind—titan blur—black wings—Yog-Sothoth save me—the three-lobed burning eye...."[10] The Thing shambles up the steps and through the door of the writer's study, the words on the pages deteriorate into a nonsensical jumble. How many times, as cited in the chapter on Straub's crime and detective stories, have we seen Straub's storytellers likewise dissolving into their own narratives, literally losing weight, substance, visibility? Even Straub's own literary Double, the durable and enduring Tim Underhill, is continually threatened with his own dissolution. Not altogether whimsically, we note how on many occasions we see an iconic work of fiction, music, theater, painting, poetry eclipsing the artist, reducing him to relative anonymity—respectively, Straub's own *Ghost Story*, Edward Elgar's *Pomp and Circumstance* music, Samuel Beckett's *Waiting for Godot* play, Grant Wood's *American Gothic* painting, etc., etc. Rather than the creative act conferring immortality on the artist, it threatens to usurp him.

"If we wish to know the writer in our day," Michel Foucault has noted

Peter Straub with bust of H.P. Lovecraft (photograph by John C. Tibbetts).

about modern and postmodern literature, "it will be through the singularity of his *absence* and in his link to death, which has transformed him into a victim of his own writing" (italics added).[11] We are perhaps not accustomed to noting this sort of thing in the works of popular storytellers like Peter Straub; rather, it seems more at home in the abstruse and experimental writings of theorist Roland Barthes's "Death of the Author," and the prose work of Samuel Beckett, whose trilogy of *Molloy*, *Malone Dies*, and *The Unnameable* (1947–1950) roughly parallels what Straub and his Gothic brethren are doing.[12] These modernists, popular and avant-garde, are all "concerned with the loss of personal authority in a character (and narrative) divided against itself. In each case, the denial of a repressed, hidden self leads to the formation of a destructive, monstrous version of it."[13] These and related topics are further discussed in the "Datchery" and "Invisible Ink" chapters of this book.

A Providential Affair

If we whimsically suggest that, in this case at least, Straub and his writings are in the thrall of H.P. Lovecraft himself—and without question he admits the influence of the Providence Master on him as well as his enduring respect and bemusement he feels toward his stories—we also can happily report that both Straub and HPL have survived to each other's mutual satisfaction. The same can be said for Lovecraft's other real-life acolytes, notably Ramsey Campbell, who began in his orbit and has since successfully ventured out into his own distinctive styles and themes.[14] However, that has not always been the case of certain other Lovecraft disciples. There is the notable instance of August Derleth, who has been instrumental in furthering Lovecraft's career through the agency of Arkham House, but whose adoption of the Lovecraftian "Mythos" in his own stories has threatened to usurp his own identity as a promising American Regionalist and master in his own right of the Gothic tale.[15] Appositely, in his "Author's Note" appended to the first edition of *Mr X*, Straub cites a letter Lovecraft wrote in 1933 to acolyte Clark Ashton Smith regarding an individual named William Lumley, who believed literally in the writings of Lovecraft and his Circle of Elder Gods and the Great Old Ones: "He is firmly convinced that all our gang," wrote Lovecraft, "are genuine agents of unseen Powers in distributing hints too dark and profound for human conception or comprehension. We may *think* we're writing fiction, and may even (absurd thought!) disbelieve what we write, but at bottom we are telling the truth in spite of ourselves—serving unwittingly as mouthpieces of Tsathoggua, Crom, Cthulhu, and other pleasant Outside gentry" (483).[16]

Lovecraft's example and his writings ooze through every crack and crevice of *Mr. X*. Readers today readily know him from the last two decades of critical notice and public acclaim. It was not always so. It takes but a moment to remember that at his death in 1937, Lovecraft was revered by only a small but fervent body of specialists, who regarded him as the greatest American practitioner of the weird and the macabre since Edgar Allan Poe. Today, book shelves groan under a growing body of literary and biographical studies. New generations are discovering that in the novels *The Shadow Out of Time*, *The Dunwich Horror*, and *At the Mountains of Madness* and in many short stories, including "The Call of Cthulhu," "The Colour out

H. P. Lovecraft

of Space," "The Shunned House," and "The Dunwich Horror"—many of which derived their atmosphere and place names from his native Providence, Rhode Island—Lovecraft wrought a distinctive combination of science fiction, spectral, and gothic horror. He was most famous for his so-called "Cthulhu Mythos," about which he explained: "All my stories, unconnected as they may be, are based on the fundamental lore or legend that this world was inhabited at one time by another race who, in practicing black magic, lost their foothold and were expelled, yet live on outside ever ready to take possession of this earth again."[17]

A portrait emerges here of a gaunt and impoverished New England revisionist whose tales of "eldritch" horrors (to use his favorite adjective) and unnameable cosmic entities drew upon the Gothic extrapolations of 18th-century writers Edmund Burke and Horace Walpole, 19th- century writers

Edgar Allan Poe and Charles Brockden Brown, and the early 20th-century masters of cosmic horror, Arthur Machen and William Hope Hodgson. Lovecraft's own unique alchemy brought them into our modern age of science and psychology. Through his example, elements of the Gothic storytelling tradition, with its spectral terrors, haunted spaces, guilt-ridden dark secrets, harassed maidens, and over-reaching "mad scientists," combined with the extraterrestrial terrors of science fiction, flourish to this day as symbolic modes to exploit the longings and anxieties of modern western civilization as in no other fictional medium.

As might be expected, opinions of the man and his work are wildly disparate. The most notorious negative view was voiced by Edmund Wilson in 1945, who stated that "the only real horror in most of these fictions is the horror of bad taste and bad art."[18] More recently, Joyce Carol Oates takes a more measured view. She acknowledges his "monomaniacal passion out of a gothic tradition" and dubs him " the American writer of the twentieth century most frequently compared with Poe, in the quality of his art (bizarre, brilliant, inspired, and original) … and its thematic preoccupations (the obsessive depiction of psychic disintegration in the face of cosmic horror)." How rare, she continues, "to encounter, in life or literature, a person for whom the mental life, the *thinking* life, is so suffused with drama as Lovecraft."[19] In his own appreciation, Stephen King has written, "The best of [Lovecraft's] stories packed an incredible wallop. They make us feel the size of the universe we hang suspended in, and suggest shadowy forces that could destroy us all if they so much as grunted in their sleep."[20] Most recently, Lovecraft's indefatigable biographer, S. T. Joshi, declared in a recent interview with this writer that in the entire range of "weird fiction," Poe and Lovecraft stand out radically over every other Gothic practitioner. Comparison is futile:

> Lovecraft's fiction is a distinctive fusion of intellectual substance with enormous technical skill. This latter quality is often overlooked: Lovecraft, adopting Poe's strictures on the "unity of effect," made every word count—and did so even when he was at his most picturesquely florid. His stories are constructed meticulously to proceed inexorably from beginning to end. And his ability to use the supernatural (or supernormal) as a metaphor for truths about humanity and its place in the cosmos is exceptional.[21]

Parenthetically, regarding the undeniable racism that surfaces in the stories, Joshi acknowledges, "It was the one area of his thought where he failed to exhibit the flexibility of mind and openness to new evidence that characterized the rest of his thought. How satisfying this approach is, I shall have to leave to others to decide."[22]

Straub talked affectionately about Lovecraft during a Writers Forum at the International Center for the Fantastic in the Arts (ICFA) on 18 March

2005, moderated by Gary K. Wolfe. It had been five years since he had published *Mr. X*, and he had just edited *Lovecraft: Tales* for the Library of America. He took on the task, he admitted, not because he had any particular affinity with Lovecraft—"he hadn't really been much of an influence upon me, not specifically"—and certainly not because he brought to the subject an unabashed enthusiasm, but because he could bring to the task a "measured" admiration for the subject.

The following remarks are from a transcript of that talk.[23]

Initially, Straub offered to write an Introduction for a two-volume set of stories. It was quickly rejected. No Introduction. One volume only. "I didn't scream and yell," he says. "I just said, 'OK, I'll give you 800 pages of the best stories, the most typical stories, the most achieved stories I can find.'"

He began the project on a personally sympathetic note.

> When the Library of America asked me to make a selection of stories, I discovered that he was much better than I had acknowledged.... The poor guy had two nervous breakdowns in high school. His father died of syphilis and was transferred to the hospital, where he died. His mother was nuts. He was raised by two old ladies. He was frail. He was really smart. He was shy. He fell in love with astronomy obviously because it allowed him to escape into a vast, distant immensity, which he quickly populated with monsters because in his world monsters were always present.

Straub went on to confess that he had first read him "with great affection" at the age of twelve or thirteen. It was not until he was in his early thirties, when, "at the urgings of some friends," he returned to the stories "and I read them in a sort of delirious and giddy way." He found himself "taken up by the sort of crazy power that inhabits some of those stories.... I discovered that much of what I had taken for Lovecraft's deepest faults were in fact wished upon him by August Derleth in rewriting or concluding wisps of stories that he published under both their names."[24] Yes, the notoriously extravagant prose is problematic, but

> it occurred to me that to object to his essential manner was to take a very strict constructionist view about writing, an essentially ungenerous one.... It is true Lovecraft used adjectives in the ripest, in fact most purple [manner], and he never met an adjective he didn't like ... but it has to be accepted on its own terms. You have to look for what it expresses and see how it pans out. He was a more deliberate, leisurely, atmospheric writer than I had remembered. And I wound up feeling very affectionate about Lovecraft.

Upon the publication of the Library of America volume, Straub says, most reviewers were pleased, although a few thought the stories frankly "ridiculous." One critic, added Straub, objected: "'I read these things where everything's liquid, everything squishes, everything has tentacles. Give me a break, now.... This isn't scary.'"

Meanwhile, to return to the Lovecraft-obsessed Mr. X, whose pen all this time has been impatiently poised over his feverish scribblings.... His short-story collection, *From Beyond*, as noted, was inspired by Lovecraft's *The Dunwich Horror*.[25] Stories like "Professor Pendant's Inheritance," "Recent Events in Rural Massachusetts," "Darknesss over Ephraim's Landing," and "Blue Fire" are Doubles of Lovecraftian themes and overheated prose: A scholar stumbles a library of arcane occult lore. A family member returns to an ancestral home. They stumble across monstrous horrors—ancient gods returned to wreak havoc on Earth; half-human creatures the progeny of inbreeding or congress with cosmic entities. The conclusion of one story is typically swamped in italics: "*I burst into the sacrosanct chamber and by the flickering light of my upraised candle glimpsed the frothing monstrosity which once had been Fulton Chambers crawl, with hideous alacrity, into the drain*" (204).

One of Mr. X's stories, "Blue Fire," is clearly inspired by Lovecraft's 1928 story, "The Dunwich Horror." The Lovecraft original is set in a tiny village near Arkham, Massachusetts.[26] The place is blighted, and "the natives are repellently decadent." They constitute "a race by themselves, with the well-defined mental and physical stigmata of degeneracy and in-breeding" (157). Wilbur Whateley and his grandfather, "of scarcely human aspect," live a reclusive life in a house within whose walls is sheltered a monstrous presence. The Whateleys call upon a race of Elder Gods to "wipe out the human race and drag the earth off to some nameless place for some nameless purpose" (198). Upon Wilbur's death, the creature breaks loose and rampages through the village. After it is defeated by the chanting of an ancient spell, it is revealed to be Wilbur's twin brother. Kingsley Amis applauded the story as achieving "a memorable nastiness."[27] Purple passages abound, like this description of Whateley's creature: "'Oh, oh, my Gawd, that haff [sic] face—that haff face.... It was a octopus, centipede, spider kind o' thing, but they was a haff-shaped man's face on top of it ... only it was yards an yards acrost...'" (197).[28]

Mr. X's "Blue Fire" traces a similar plot trajectory (and significantly, parallels the twin narratives of Ned Dunstan and Mr. X). As a child, Godfrey Demmiman is summoned to an "ancient wood" where an "inhuman" voice informs him that he is half human, the offspring of an Elder God, who shall bring about the Apocalypse by granting entry to his unearthly fathers. By the agency of a mysterious "blue fire" and a "sacred text," he goes mad and commits a series of crimes. Years later, he is drawn to the New England village of Markham, the ancestral home of his Master. He senses a strange presence, an Other, who searches for him but flees at his approach. Increasingly aware the figure is his Double, he stalks the house's rooms and corridors. Finally, his search takes him to the library on the top floor, where—

Here, after deploying the requisite Lovecraftian device of the ellipse....
We quote at some length from the "Blue Fire" manuscript:

> Demmiman entered the old library and eased the door shut behind him.... The Other's
> presence etched itself upon the endings of his nerves.... It awaited his arrival with an equal
> terror.... Slowly, with dragging step, an indistinct figure emerged from the shadows. Dem-
> miman found himself unable to breathe. Here was what for either release or surrender he
> knew he must confront at last.... He saw, upon a forward step, that what had made the face
> indistinct was the pair of raised hands concealing it.... *[Then] the figure lifted its head and*
> *spread its fingers, seeming to sense his shift of mood. Then, as if in a sudden moment of*
> *decision, it dropped its hands and bared its face with an aggression Demmiman knew beyond*
> *his capabilities. Horror held him fast* [italics added]. A thousand sins, a thousand excesses
> had printed themselves upon that face. It was the record of his secret life, hideous and
> inescapable, and yet, however coarsened and inflamed, the Other's features were hideously,
> inescapably Demmiman's own.... Had all his efforts been designed but to bring him face
> to face with this monstrous version of himself?

Aware that the creature's strength surpasses his own, Demmiman shrinks
back and sets the house on fire. He tries to flee, but again, drawn inexorably
toward an "unforeseen fate to which Demmiman's suddenly exalted spirit
gave its full assent," he plunges into the flames, where he finds his "ecstatic
release" (221–222).

If these incendiary passages seem familiar, they are the literary Doubles
of yet another story familiar to us by now in our readings of Straub—that of
a man who has returned to his New York ancestral home seeking his own
Double, the "self" who remained behind during his many years abroad. Yes,
Henry James's "The Jolly Corner," to which Straub alludes in several of his
works, comes to the fore once again.[29] Compare the italicized passages quoted
above from "The Blue Fire" to this moment near the end of James's story
when Spencer Brydon confronts his Double: "Rigid and conscious, spectral
yet human, a man of his own substance and stature waited there to measure
himself with his power to dismay.... The hands, as he looked, began to move,
to open; then, as if deciding in a flash, dropped from the face and left it
uncovered and presented. Horror, with the sight, had leaped into Brydon's
throat, gasping there in a sound he couldn't utter."[30]

The resemblance between the two passages is not accidental. "I love that
part of 'The Jolly Corner,'" confesses Straub, "where the man returns from
England, is in his ancestral house in New York, and begins to be aware that
there's probably somebody else in there with him, and there are hints of closed
doors or the lights that go on and off or just the hint of movement. I was in
love with that moment, and so I repeated it in *Mr. X*."

Admittedly, adds Straub, Henry James and H.P. Lovecraft make for an
odd trifecta. But, he adds, "You can do it!"[31]

The Gnostic Split

"The concept of the *Doppelgänger*," observes critic Bill Sheehan, "is itself simply a metaphor for a more fundamental condition: the sense that our lives are somehow out of joint: that we are waiting, always, for that vital connection that will lead to the restoration of a lost harmony."[32] Certainly this sense of dislocation and yearning for identity—with its attendant risks of self-destruction—is central to *Mr. X* and all of Straub's stories. We repeat the mantra that dominated *Shadowland* and which is singularly apposite here: "*The mind opens, the shoulder opens, the body opens...*" (119).

Straub's doublings provide another example of his abiding interest in Gnosticism. The doublings in *Mr. X* are essentially Gnostic doublings, the Kantian division of the phenomenal and the noumenal. We recall that as early as *Shadowland*, in the pairing of the "True" magician, Tom Flanagan," with the corrupt magician, Coleman Collins, Straub presented an example of Gnostic Doubling, ie., that there is not one Creator but *two*; that the True God is concealed in his Realm of light; and that the secondary Creator God, the Demiurge, handles the affairs of the material world. Not just the world, but the Self, is a Gnostic structure. Interiors are related to interiors, the one embodied in the other. In his essay on the subject in *Sides*, Straub finds in the practice of magic this pairing of the sublime and the material. Magic is not confined to the mere artifice of the stage magician, for example, but to "the unseen, subtle, powerful internal structures of the world itself." There is an awareness of doubling—"As above, so below"—of how the individual soul reflects the nature of the surrounding world; and that both strive toward the condition of revelation.[33]

The dream of a unified identity, the fusion of the divided self, may be only a dream—or is it a carnival? *Mr. X* can be construed as an elaborate, even extravagant exercise in the Carnivalesque. It is a play of masks in which Straub deploys a series of performative gestures that explore shifts in mood and identity. We are reminded that the question of multiple and slippery identities was the lifelong inspiration of one of Straub's favorite poets, the Portuguese writer Fernando Pessoa, who adopted the multiple and slippery identities of the fictitious "Alberto Caeiro," "Ricardo Reis," and "Alvaro de Campos," and others in his works. Acknowledging his enthusiasm—"I am sort of crazy about Pessoa"—Straub holds in special regard Pessoa's *The Book of Disquiet*, from which he appends the line, "To live is to be someone else" at the start of his collection of stories and essay, *Sides*.[34] Indeed, this Carnivalesque mode, which we have identified in the aggregates of horrors on display in *The Floating Dragon* and *Black House*, is the ideal vehicle for Straub's free play of identification:

Carnival festivity temporarily frees its participants from the demand that they organize their physical and emotional lives into a coherent, restrained totality. This normative self splinters amid the general outbreak of buffoonery, playacting, and masquerade; its component parts assume the guise of separate characters, or, more exactly, caricatures, personifications of excess or impulse. Caught up in the anarchic scene, the reveler is free to identity with any, or all of these figures.

These words are not by Straub, nor do we find them in any critical discussions of *Mr. X*. Rather, they are from the eminent musicologist, Lawrence Kramer, of Fordham University. And they refer not to a book but to a piece of music, the *Carnaval* of Robert Schumann.[35] About which more presently.

Thus, multiples of settings and characters spill out onto the pages of all Straub's novels and stories. Space doesn't permit an exhaustive (and exhausting) litany, but a few examples confirm what we already know: The books written in collaboration with Stephen King, for example, are fraught with doublings, from the pairing of the Territories with the "real world," to the "twinners," or counterparts of characters inhabiting those worlds. We saw varieties of "twins" in *Shadowland*, from pairings of Tom Flanagan's Carson School and Coleman Collin's Vermont estate, to alternates of Grimm fairytale characters personified in the real world's Rose Armstrong ("The Little Mermaid") and Collins ("The Erl-King"). Characters good and evil come in matched pairs: In *Ghost Story* Don Wanderley finds his Double in the aforementioned repeated exchanges with the wicked Eva Galli ("Who are you?" "I am You" [368.]) In *Julia* we find two blond girls; the ghostly presence of little Kate is benign, that of Olivia is wholly evil. In *If You Could See Me Now*, paired opposites are the malevolent Alison Greening and the benign Alison Updahl—together locked in a sexual coupling with Miles Teagarden. The scene is gruesomely erotic: Miles makes love to them both—the one living, the other very dead—*at the same time*. Both writhe in his embrace. The touch of warm flesh shifts into something cold and spectral: "The experience seemed at times during the night [to be] double-exposed, shifting imperceptibly in shape so that in one half of a second it was that body [of Alison Greening] I had seen flashing in the water and in the other half, it was fuller. The breasts against my chest were small, then heavy, then small; the waist, slim, then sturdy ... both were present at once ... a flickering between the two halves of a second..." (344–345). Which Alison is it? Alison Greening or Alison Updahl? Or both at once? A loving presence or a succubus? Is it love or necrophilia? When Miles wakes up, it is Alison Updahl who lies beside him. But her body is scratched and bleeding. A handful of sharp twigs is found in the bed. And there is that smell of cold water.... We find a similar moment in "The General's Wife," when Andy Rivers in finds herself in a complex instance of erotic doubling when she—and her Double—make love to the ageing General Leck, and *his* younger Double, in one ferociously erotic and bloody moment.

The novels and their characters find their Doubles in the stories embedded within them: We recall *Ghost Story* is doubled by author Don Wanderley's *Nightwatcher*; *The Hellfire Club*'s odyssey of Nora Chancel is doubled in the adventures of Pippin Little in Hugo Driver's *The Night Journey*; the tragic horrors of *The Throat* are doubled in Manny Dengler's childhood obsession with the story of "Babar the Elephant"; the meta-hijinks of *In the Night Room* are doubled in the embedded novel by Willy Patrick of that name; the horrors catalogued in *The Floating Dragon* parallel novelist Graham Williams's book of that name; and books and stories featuring Tim Underhill contain narratives written by—Tim Underhill. This is also true of the many books and motion pictures cited in the narratives. In "Bunny Is Good Bread," Fee Bandolier merges his real world into the film noir, *From Dangerous Depths*. The protagonist of "The Buffalo Hunter" projects himself into the hardboiled narrative of Raymond Chandler's *Lady in the Lake*. Keith Hayward in *A Special Place* finds his alternate life in Alfred Hitchcock's *Shadow of a Doubt*. Novelist Lee Harwell in *A Dark Matter* finds his birthright in the stories of Nathaniel Hawthorne. And Professor William Standish in "Mrs. God" invites, entertains, protects, and nurtures the themes and tropes of the literary guests, past and present in Esswood House—including Nathaniel Hawthorne, Henry James, Robert Aickman, Shirley Jackson; the poetry of Emily Dickinson, Wallace Stevens, John Ashbery, and the fictitious Isobel Standish.

Straub's oft-noted passion for music provides other examples of Doubling. Not since E.T.A. Hoffmann early in the 19th century and Charles Beaumont and Richard Powers in our own time, has a writer more persistently invested his writings with music and musicians. One is tempted to think that, like the American visionary composer, Charles Ives, and the Australian film director Peter Weir, Straub is a ready conduit for musics popular, classical, and vernacular appropriate to every plot and thematic occasion. Ives has stacks of Tin Pan Alley sheet music and Baptist church hymns at his beck; Weir has his boom box on the set of every film; and while writing, Straub has his LPs and turntable cranking out favorite jazz improvisations of Coleman Hawkins and Charlie Parker, and the operas of Benjamin Britten and Frederick Delius to provide musical correlatives and tonal analogues, to his characters, story structures, and moods.

"At the end of *Mr. X*," explains Straub, by way of example, "I tried my best to provide a musical analogue to its general plot layout by describing an alto sax solo by Paul Desmond of 'These Foolish Things' in *Mr. X*...."[36] "He fastened his mouth to his horn and repeated the fragment of melody just played as if it were newly minted.... The melody expanded, and the alto player said, *We are on a journey*. As he settled into his story, it opened into interior stories, and variations led to other, completely unexpected, variations" (483). Another passage is an attempt to replicate in musical terms the plot convolutions of one of Straub's most complex novels, *The Hellfire Club*: "On the other side of the meadow, high-pitched voices swooped and skirled, climbing through chromatic intervals, introducing dissonances, ascending into resolution, shattering apart, uniting into harmony again, dividing and joining in an endless song without pauses or repeats" (432).

Koko has many passages wherein the horrors of Vietnam find musical correlatives. In a striking sequence, set in 1968, members of the combat platoon huddle together in a tent and listen to renditions of "Ko-Ko" by Duke Ellington and Charlie Parker. The Ellington is described as "the music of threat," with "nightmarish chords which are half-submerged in the cacophony of the band"; and the classic 1945 Parker recording is "as unsentimental as a Picasso portrait of Dora Maar or a paragraph by Gertrude Stein." Then comes the moment in *Koko* when the scene of pain and suffering is transmuted by music into ecstatic beauty:

> When Parker reaches the bridge of the song, all that open-throated singing against threat is resolved in a dazzle of imaginative glory. Parker changes the beat around so that he actually seems to accelerate, and all the urgency is engulfed in the grace of this thoughts, which have become Mozartean.... From different parts of the room Poole heard snatches of unmelodic wordless song, the music of nothing on earth, the music of no-place. Sometimes it sounded as if children were speaking or crying out a great distance away. These were the dead children painted on the walls [559].

Another Vietnam novel, *The Throat*, evokes the music of Frederick Delius's *Walk to the Paradise Garden* in the scene when Tim Underhill enters a village hut and encounters evidence of the torture and mutilation of children. "For a second, music from my old life, music too beautiful to be endurable, started playing in my head.... Tears filled my eyes.... Some part of my mind as detached as a crime reporter reminded me that 'The Walk to the Paradise Garden' was about two children who were about to die and that in a sense the music *was* their death." In a flash of recognition, realizes Underhill, "the unhinged thought came to me with absolute conviction that *this* was the Paradise Garden" (62).[37]

Permit me a brief digression on one aspect of music that in many ways directly parallels Straub's use of Doublings. The name of the German Romantic composer, Robert Schumann (1810–1856) may not be readily linked to Straub. Admittedly, you will find no references to Schumann in Straub's work. My own allusions to him here may seem willful on my part; but inasmuch as Straub constantly turns to music and literature for effect and analogy, I feel empowered to likewise rope Schumann, the most "literary" of composers, into the discussion. I have devoted a lifetime to the study of Schumann; and as I have become more and more acquainted with Peter Straub, his affinities with the composer, it seems to me, are striking, and profound. Although separated by time and space, Straub and Schumann seem to share a "voice" that resonates between them, like a sound from two harps in a room, one vibrating sympathetically to the plucked string of the other. It is a complicated, mysterious Doubling we find here, as if Schumann and Straub, unbeknownst to each other, are inhabiting the same skin. Space prohibits a detailed speculation about this, and I will touch again on the importance of music in Straub in the last chapter of this book. But for now, oblige me with a few observations.

Straub and Schumann—a writer fascinated by music, and a composer involved with literature—are profoundly intertextual. They "double" music as words and words as music. The saxophone improvisations by Paul Desmond parallel and inform Straub's stories. Jean Paul Richter's novel *Flegeljahre* (1804–1805), the story of two contending twins, finds its tonal analogue in Schumann's piano cycle *Carnaval*, Op, 9, itself a musical projection of the composer's contrasting alter-egos, the manic "Florestan" and the melancholy "Eusebius."[38] The Carnivalesque scenes in Straub and the carnival masquerade in *Carnaval* enact a free play of identification, a pageant of masks and identity transferences and reversals. Moreover, just as the Doubles in Straub's many stories first appear at a time of turmoil, Schumann's Doubles likewise emerged at a time of great emotional stress in his early life. That's how it is with this Doubling business. They express and *perform* conflicts and erotic impulses. They offer critiques of the normative Self. Characters like Tim Underhill survive by keeping life's terrors and beauties in a balance. Schumann, however, led a sane and healthy life only as long as his Doubles were kept in check through the device of yet a third persona, an arbitrator he named "Master Raro." But in his last years, when order eroded into chaos, Schumann descended into ill health and madness, ending his life in an institution for the insane. Again, the classic paradigm of the *Doppelgaenger* that we have seen in Straub and his literary brethren also presents itself in Schumann—creation of the Double, its usurpation of the Self, and the eventual possibility of destruction of the Self.

The Shadow Within

Under what circumstances, to what degree, and when, does the Self split, and when is it subsequently subsumed by its Double? For Schumann, the precise nature of his bi-polar affective disorder and the circumstances of his physical and mental collapse continue to be endlessly debated.[39] But in Straub, we can find this splitting in key moments in stories like "Bunny Is Good Bread" and "The Buffalo Hunter." The first is a grim account of the education of a serial killer, young Fee Bandolier. He begins a process of dissociation after enduring the horrors of child molestation in a movie theater and upon witnessing the sight of his dying mother: "Fee observed that he had left his body and could see himself standing by the bed." He begins to ignore the reality around him and live in the images on the movie screen: "If you forgot you were in a movie, your own feelings would tear you into bloody rags." Looking out his window he sees himself—his *former* self—on the street: "He saw the boy growing fainter and fainter, like a drawing being erased. Traces of the lawn and sidewalk shone through him. All at once it seemed to Fee that something vastly important, an absolutely precious quantity, was fading from his world. Once this quantity was gone, it would be lost forever" (150). A serial killer is born. "The Buffalo Hunter" describes a young man's splitting from reality as he reads the fictions of Luke Short and Raymond Chandler: "What had happened to him was both deeply disturbing and powerfully, seductively pleasurable. It was as if he had traveled backward in time, gone into a different body and a different life, and there lived at a pitch of responsiveness and openness not available to him in his real, daily life. In fact, it had felt far more real than his 'real' life" (144).

The Shadow Within

We might rightly inquire, at this point, to what degree these doublings might counterpoint Straub's own life. Do they constitute something in the nature of an autobiography? To be sure, unlike his characters, Straub has neither suffered a mental collapse nor has he turned to serial killing! Instead, he admits, he has "learned much" from the character of Tim Underhill: "Tim has been useful to me. He is able to do all kinds of things that are beyond me. He's been very convenient, like a kind of Familiar, a handy presence always nearby. I've learned a lot from him, a lot of history and emotion."[40] But Straub has hinted at moments in his own life when he suffered experiences that have both fractured and divided him from his normative sense of self. In other words, Straub is *himself* his own true Double. During childhood moments of pain and abuse, he began, as he puts it, "impersonating" himself:

When I was a kid, I was a fictional character, but the fictional character was *myself*, the self my parents wanted me to be, the self I would have been perhaps had I not been injured and abused as a small boy. I didn't want to be the person who was injured and abused. It didn't fit my *idea* of myself. I always experienced myself as a person of some integrity and wholeness; and also of a certain mental or spiritual force of some kind. I didn't see myself as being victimized. It was a horrible insult; it made me angry and humiliated and ashamed. So I had to pretend it wasn't true.[41]

In "Inside Story," a memoir published in 2011, he adds more details. "I once told an audience ... that I had a seven-year-old twin, and he lived in eternity. 'Every now and then,' I said ... 'he grabs the pen.'" Straub was recounting a horrible accident in which at age seven he had been severely damaged in a car accident and left broken and bleeding on the street, "a bloody rag and a smear on a four-lane thoroughfare." It was then, he told his mother, in words too terrifying to truly comprehend, that he wanted to retrieve his bloodied clothes: "*I wanted to wear my own blood*" (my italics). He continues: "The child I had been died, and a twitchy, fearful, furious, embittered, larval-stage sociopath in a perpetual state of denial now bore his name." He began writing horror stories, and the event surfaces in two novels, *Mystery* and *Throat*. "I was trying to fit it into me, me into it, with as much truth as I could find, remember, or invent. But the buried trauma subsequently "began to bubble up, and I went off the rails." Years of psychiatric therapy explored the "terrible deathly darkness" within him. When the reality of his suppressed near-death experience—the momentary sense of leaving his body and hurtling through a void, in the grip of "an immanent, absolute transformation that involved the utter loss of everything earthly"—came back to him, he realized: "What I had undergone, one had to die to see."

The epiphany lasted scant seconds, but that "seven-year-old twin" that lived in "eternity," which wore the bloodied shirt, and which lay buried deep within, was gone. "I was going to live," Straub concludes, "I could go no further. Death would elude me until it eluded me no longer."[42] Meanwhile, he has continued to write....

In conclusion, on a somewhat lighter note, meet Straub's most vocal and testy critic, Professor Putney Tyson Ridge, Ph.D., of Popham College. Although "Putney," as Straub calls him, represents the academic life that Straub abjured long ago, he displays a most peculiar empathy with Straub. Indeed, it borders on identity. Yes, they are colleagues, in a way, and Straub has even generously allowed many of his critical notices, no matter how negative, to appear in the pages of his book, *Sides*. He even alludes to him in the novella "Mrs. God." "Over the years," writes Bill Sheehan, "Putney has provided extensive commentaries on virtually all of Straub's books. Although he does find some kind things to say about a couple of Straub's novels, *Julia* and

If You Could See Me Now (which he views as sensible, seemly entertainments, Novels That Know Their Place), most of his assessments are outraged, virulent, and very, very funny" (334).[43]

Putney's critical attacks, always couched in high-flown academic rhetoric, have continued apace, even increased in their ferocity. His disappointment in *Mr. X* is all too typical: "I innocently imagined a means by which my old pal might rediscover the first principles of his modest art," he writes, "and cleanse himself of those excrescences that have disfigured his work since the disastrously over-praised *Ghost Story*." Putney goes on to pronounce the book a "catastrophe":

> "Narrative back-hoes and earth-movers, narrative chainsaws, narrative wood-chippers, nail guns and chisels came into play. Painted backdrops and artificial scenery came into play. So did pointless flashbacks, whimsical sub-plots, and the intrusions of colorfully instructive dreams, a sure sign of desperation on the part of a hard-pressed novelizer. He waded into [it] like an invading army and devastated it, utterly. When he had finished, air-castles of his own devise hovered unconvincingly over the smoking ruins" [*Sides*, 297].

Do enthusiasts of Straub wince at this? Behind the paraphrastic effusions, dare we recognize insights into some of the very real challenges in Straub's books—that Straub pointedly acknowledges himself?

So what does Straub think of all this? I broached the question during an interview in 2011.

What about these scurrilous attacks on Mr. X. *Who is this guy?*

Oh yes. Putney was an academic who taught at Popham College, in Ohio.

Hmm, the same college you refer to in "Mrs. God"...

Poor Putney! When my daughter, Emma, first read this guy, she wailed, "Dad, why is he saying these awful things about you?!" I had to tell her I *invented* Putney. Over the years, I had read a number of reviews of my work by somebody who really *hated* my work. What he wanted was me to be Stephen King 24/7. He wanted really *direct* things, language that sounded like the guy on the porch, for the action to start in the second paragraph. I was all wrong for him. I thought to myself, he's complaining that I'm not *stupid* enough! So I invented an academic character at Popham College who looked down on my work because I was writing above myself, and if I had any sense about me, I would *try* to write like a sub-par, inferior Steve King and settle for the little effects that I'm capable of, that were within my range.

You even write about Putney coming to stay with you at your house!

That's especially uncomfortable for my wife! She's never liked the guy at all. I used to spend weeks writing about Putney and his critiques. Finally I had enough of insulting myself, so I dispatched Putney. He had a very sad ending. At Popham College, Iowa, the chairman of the college, Bob Liddy ("Old Bob") was involved in a certain scandal we never speak of and was forced out. His replacement had no use for Putney, so when Putney got in trouble (again), he was forced out of his digs in Bluebell Lane. He had been doing research into erotic journalism. And he had an archive in Bluebell Lane of erotic materials. While he was moving them out of his apartment, he was felled by a stroke. And he was found lying beside a huge pile of pornographic magazines—

Doubtless with maybe an ecstatic light in his eyes?

[laughs] Putney left behind a few graduate students who cherish the memory of his greatness and who are still pissed at me. Anyway, that was fun. I suppose Putney represented both my confidence in my writing to confront critical attacks; but at the same time, those reservations I have about myself. Putney was very hard on some things that were happening to me, and I have to admit that I wasn't happy about them, either.

In a later interview, Straub relates some disturbing news about his old friend, who seems to have fallen on hard times:

> Putney died when his creator got tired of him writing all these nasty things about me. He didn't die quietly. If you look at my new website, you can find him. Putney was always being charged with sexual harassment at his college. But when the president was fired and went to jail for mishandling of funds, Putney lost his protection. Now, complaints made him move out of his faculty housing into the Black Flag Motel in the nearby town of Granite; and he had a journal in his basement, erotic journals. He was carrying them up the stairs from his basement and he fell backwards and he died on the floor of his basement, surrounded by big boobs and gigantic butts. I'm not sure where Putney is buried. I leave it up to you if we mourn his loss.

Perhaps Peter Straub has reversed the direction of those Doubles we have seen who have haunted, confounded, and eventually usurped their normative Selves. Putney Tyson Ridge is defeated, gone. Maybe.

"I'm not sure where Putney is buried," concludes Straub. "I leave it up to you if we mourn his loss."

CHAPTER FIVE

"Datchery's Children"
Stories of Crime and Detection

When once we take leave of the lie that shines like a glittering surface on the world and no longer see the world as the mirror of our desires—when we want to know *who* we are—ah, that's the beginning of the end, the Fall of Man…. Don't sink into your soul, or into anyone else's, but stay on the blue surface of the mirror, like the gnats above the water."
—Max Frisch, *Don Juan and the Love of Geometry*[1]

The criminal is the artist; the detective is the critic.
—G. K. Chesterton

The smile of Alan Ladd is both tough and wounded, an effect akin to that of headlights reflected on a dark, rain-wet street…
—Peter Straub, "Lapland"

Who is Dick Datchery?

Late in the unfinished pages of Charles Dickens's *The Mystery of Edwin Drood*, a mysterious, white-haired stranger appears on the scene. He declares himself to be one "Dick Datchery." A self-described "idle buffer," he displays a certain military bearing and the energy of a much younger man. No incidental bystander, he is making inquiries into the recent disappearance of young Edwin Drood.

In this, the novel Dickens left incomplete at his death, we have several mysteries shrouded in a fine Gothic nightmare of violence, obsession, and, possibly, murder. Behind Drood's disappearance there is reason to suspect foul play. Datchery's suspicions fasten on orphan twins Neville and Helena Landless, lately arrived from Ceylon; and John Jasper, Drood's uncle, opium addict, and frustrated rival of Edwin for the hand of the fair Rosa Bud.

"'There is said to be a hidden skeleton in every house,'" says Jasper.[2]

Datchery is a liminal character. Half-seen, ultimately mysterious, he may be either an outside private investigator or one of the story's characters in disguise, conducting an amateur investigation of his own. Perhaps he is Drood himself (not dead but returned to avenge an attempt on his life); Neville Landless (Drood's former enemy); or Helena attempting to "clear" her brother of any suspicion)? In his essay on the subject, G.K. Chesterton inclines toward the option that Drood has been murdered and that Jasper is the culprit.[3] As to Datchery's identity…? Indeed, just what *is* the "mystery" here? We'll never know, of course, because at his death in 1870 Dickens left no trace of his intentions. Datchery remains an enigma and the Drood case will be forever unresolved.[4] Maybe, as Chesterton suggests, not altogether whimsically, the book really should be titled, *The Mystery of Datchery*! "[It] is the only one of Dickens's novels which he did not finish, [but] the only one that really needed finishing…."[5] We are left suspended, listening, as it were, to a musical discord left unresolved.

The example of Datchery's elusive presence, his disguises, and his unsolved investigation hovers over Peter Straub's crime and detective stories. A gallery of private detectives, amateur sleuths, policemen, occult investigators, and, for lack of a better term, interested parties, flit in and out of the shadows, chasing elusive suspects, taking testimonies, pounding the streets, eluding dangers, drawing and revising conclusions, etc.—all in the attempt to reassemble the buried bones of Straub's Juniper Tree. Among the mysteries involved, the greatest may be, as with Datchery, not so much the identity of the criminal but that of the detective—not to "catch a thief," as it were, but to *catch a detective*. Moreover, as metatexts, they examine the relationships between characters and stories, readers and writers. Be warned: As in *Drood*, everything is inconclusive: "These books," declares amateur sleuth Tim Underhill in *The Throat*, "are about the way the known story is not the right or the real story" (46).

Almost all of Straub's books and stories are procedural investigations of one sort or another. Some of them, like detective Jack Sawyer's pursuit of the serial killings of *Black House*, are examined elsewhere in these pages. Others—*If You Could See Me Now*, *Julia*, *Ghost Story*, *The Floating Dragon*, "Mrs. God," *Mr. X*, *A Dark Matter*—are Gothic stories inflected with secondary elements of crime and detection and are of relatively secondary interest here. Another book, *The Hellfire Club*, features a different kind of detective, a *literary* detective on the trail of a mystery surrounding the authorship of a book. It, too, will be considered briefly in due course.

My primary purpose here, however, is to confine my own investigations to the cases of amateur sleuth Tim Underhill, and his friend and associate, the private detective Tom Pasmore. Their "game is afoot" in five books, the so-called "Blue Rose" trilogy of *Koko*, *Mystery*, and *The Throat*, and the related pair of novels, *lost boy lost girl* and *In the Night Room*. Their Gothic tropes and implications of supernatural horror, are, in the words of Gary K. Wolfe, "subsumed to the effects of personal traumas ranging from a violent childhood event to the experience of the Vietnam War, and to his characters' quests to transcend, or at least accommodate, these powerful events."[6] Critic Bill Sheehan argues that they constitute "what is arguably the most significant—and underrated—body of popular fiction published in America in recent years."[7] Inexplicably, no serious studies have yet been written about this particular aspect of Straub's oeuvre. It is time to make a start, although my findings may prove as inconclusive as Datchery's investigations.

Peter Straub in his study, New York City (photograph by John C. Tibbetts).

"Blue Rose"—The Facts in the Case

As recounted in three loosely connected novels—*Koko* (1988), *Mystery* (1990), and *The Throat* (1993)—the term "Blue Rose" refers to a series of unsolved murders that transpired in 1950. Left behind at the scene of the crimes was the killer's "signature," the words "Blue Rose." During the next thirty years, several detectives get involved, directly or indirectly, in the case, including the legendary private eye, Lamont von Heilitz; his protégé, Tom Pasmore; and Pasmore's friend, Tim Underhill.

Koko refers to the "Blue Rose" killings only briefly: We recognize one of the characters, a Vietnam combat soldier named Harry Beevers, as the young boy who had appeared earlier in the short story "The Blue Rose." Young Harry had used the words "Blue Rose" in the tortures he inflicted on his younger brother (which subsequently led to his later career as a serial killer). The term also occurs in passing as the subject of a novel being written by Beever's soldier buddy, Tim Underhill. In the second novel, *Mystery*, we find several more references to a series of unsolved murders that had transpired in and around the St. Alwyn's Hotel on the Caribbean island of Mill Walk. The words "Blue Rose" had been left behind at the scene. In the third novel, *The Throat*, the Blue Rose murders now assume center stage. The scene shifts to Millhaven, Wisconsin, now identified, as it turns out, to be the true location of the Blue Rose murders. Tim Underhilll's true-crime book about them is now correctly identified as *The Divided Man*.

This so-called "trilogy" is a decidedly complicated business told by multiple narrators in which characters, crimes, and locations shift and change in time and space, moving from the overseas locations of an exotic island in the Caribbean, to the urban horrors of Bangkok, to the atrocities of the jungles of Vietnam, and to the mean streets of New York and Wisconsin. As metatexts, they reflect Straub's own considerations and reconsiderations about just what the term "Blue Rose" is all about; what kind of investigation is being conducted; and what is the identity of the killer, or killers.[8] He is a "shapeshifter," as Tim Underhill observers in *The Throat*, someone who has spent "a lifetime of pretending to be someone else" (547). Considered together, they constitute one of the most complex bodies of work in all of Straub's oeuvre.

In sum, like Dick Datchery, we readers must conduct an investigation of our own into a bewildering collective of half-seen characters and unresolved crimes. We cannot even be certain, at times, *who* is telling these stories. The narrative ground shifts constantly under our feet.

MYSTERY

Rather than begin our investigation with the first book in the series, *Koko*, I have decided to begin with the second, *Mystery*. As critic Bill Sheehan observes, it is a novel that is both a mystery, in the classical sense, and a contemplation of those larger mysteries that have occupied a place in virtually all of Straub's mature fiction" (191).[9] Tom Pasmore's education as a detective is linked to his maturing as a man and an artist. He grows up in a tiny island in the Caribbean, Mill Walk. This "mythical" place has its American counterpart in the exclusive resort of Eagle Lake, Wisconsin, a playground for the idle and wealthy. Tom is connected to the two powerful ruling dynasties of both locations. His mother is Gloria Upshaw, daughter of the wealthy and thoroughly corrupt Glendenning Upshaw, patriarch of a powerful family of construction contractors. Tom's Father, Victor Pasmore, works for the Redwing clan, whose island business interests have "devoured morality, honesty, scruples" (410).

Forty years before the opening of the novel, the body of Jeanine Thielman, wife of a wealthy Mill Walk contractor, had been found drowned under suspicious circumstances in the waters of Eagle Lake—the same waters that had claimed Glendenning's wife a year before. More killings may have transpired in the Shady Mount hospital on the island, "where the people who ran Mill Walk put its embarrassments when they wanted them to die. It was the most respectable hospital on the island, the safest place on Mill Walk for a discreet little murder..." (389). And there had been a number of unsolved killings in and around the St. Alwyn Hotel, where the victims—a prostitute, a gay piano player, a doctor, and a butcher—had been found with the words "Blue Rose" scrawled at the scene. The case had been fictionalized in a book by a young writer named Tim Underhill. More recently, the body of Marita Hasselgard, sister of Mill Walk's finance minister Felix Hasselgard, was found in the trunk of a car in Mill Walk.

The mounting toll of bodies attracted a number of private and professional investigators, including Lamont Von Heilitz, a retired private investigator; Captain Fulton Bishop a corrupt Mill Walk police chief; Detective David Natchez, an honest Mill Walk cop. How all these plots, murders, and character threads in both locations prove to be interrelated, how they involve the two corrupt families, the Upshaws and the Redwings, and how the investigations profoundly transform the lives of young Tom Pasmore makes for a byzantine, typically Straubian tangle of events, characters, and embedded stories. As a narrative relatively close to the classic procedural, there are suspects to find and interrogate, buried secrets to disclose, and assumptions to prove and disprove.

Now, in the present, amidst the violence, and trauma haunting Mill Walk and Eagle Lake, the preternaturally sensitive youngster, Tom Pasmore, is about to begin his education as a detective. At age ten, he witnesses an ugly incident that seems to incriminate his grandfather, Glendenning Upshaw, in criminal activities. He is disturbed by a presentiment of something underlying the moment, "an essential scene, every particle of which overflowed with an intense unbearable beauty. It was as if great engines had kicked into life beneath the surface of what he could see" (7–8). And then occurs the incident that will change his life and define his destiny: An altercation with some street toughs from the Redwing clan hurls him into the path of an oncoming truck. He suffers a "near-death" vision and an enforced incarceration in the hospital.

The accident inoculates Tom into the terrors of the adult world to come. He is transfixed in a kind of still point. Events freeze in place, the moment is expanded. He experiences a moment of invisibility and feels a "lightness and harmony" at the instant of the collision, a "freedom from gravity" that gently pulls him upward. The grip that holds him down to earth relaxes: "The membrane released him with a final, soft, nearly impalpable *pop* and his love for all earthly things doubled and overflowed and he knew, having lost the earth, that love was identical to grief and loss" (29). He sees himself and the street chaos below: "Tom looked down at the person he had been with some surprise, as well as with love and pity." His senses preternaturally accelerate and he has glimpses of incidents to come. "A delicious feeling of *absolute rightness*," comes over him, "of all worry having been thrown off, never again to be met.… They were the feelings caused by the sense of a real radiance existing at the center of life…" (31–33).

Tom's "invisibility" is no mere conceit. It's a key trope in Straub, and we encounter it again and again in many of his stories. Moments of vanishing, of the loss of physical substance, may connote a passage from one reality to another, of transcendence, as in the *Talisman* books; or a moment of suspension between life and death, as in *Mystery*. Be it a metaphor or a preternatural moment, Straub takes it quite seriously: "[Tom] was vanishing, becoming nothing. His body continued to disappear as he moved down the stairs. In seconds his hands and feet, his whole body, was only a shimmer in the air, then only an outline. When he reached the bottom step, he had disappeared altogether. He was dead. He was free" (149). As critic Bill Sheehan puts it, Tom realizes for the first time that "the world is filled with strange corners and unresolved mysteries.… Any attempt to convey the essential reality of the world must take into account the tangential, periodic presence of the numinous and extraordinary.…"[10] Indeed, he is a "Datchery" character, a liminal presence, veering in and out of visibility, in and out of the prosaic narrative.[11]

Tom wakes up in the Shady Mount hospital to a pain that "would obliterate the world." Kindly Nurse Vetiver observes that "Tom had this special thing inside him. He *saw* things.…" She tells him, "'You had this way of looking at things, like you could see parts of them nobody else could. Sometimes, it looked like the world could just make you glow. Or tear you apart inside…'" (209). Indeed, ever since the accident (or because of it), he seems somehow not quite of this world. Wheelchair bound, he loses himself deep in the pages of mystery stories. He devours detective stories of every stripe, from Sherlock Holmes to Dashiel Hammett and Raymond Chandler.

One of the books he reads is *The Mystery of Edwin Drood*…

Where books like this had once been mere "escape" for him, now they were "life itself." He suffers an epiphany: "At times, deep in a book, he felt his body begin to glow: an invisible but potent glory seemed to hover just behind the characters, and it seemed that they were on the verge of making some great discovery that would also be his—the discovery of a vast realm of radiant meaning that lay hidden just within the world of ordinary appearances" (56).

His education as a detective has begun.

At times like these, "he left behind his body and his useless anger and roamed through forest and cities in close company with men and women who plotted for money, love, and revenge." Tom's parents begin to realize that their "oddly unknowable boy … seemed to have chosen shadows, passivity, unreality…. It seemed to him that he had stepped into the real stream of life" (55).

Tom is not the only "invisible" character. His whole world now seems at times strangely insubstantial. Tom's mother, traumatized by sexual abuse as a child, has withdrawn from the world. His father is a passive figure, largely absent from family affairs. Across the street lives the reclusive Lamont von Heilitz, a legendary private detective who once allegedly was the inspiration for the famous radio detective "The Shadow." He is something of a dandy who affects old-fashioned suits and matching gloves. He first appears to Tom in a preternatural aspect, as "a slim, fantastic figure … with webs of shadowy darkness dripping from his shoulders" (39). His only interests are crime and murder. The epitome of the armchair detective, he solves many of his cases through deductions drawn from the data he finds in the newspapers and legal documents that clutter up his rooms.

During his recuperation, like a moth drawn to the flame, Tom grows obsessed with the history of crimes on Mill Walk and Eagle Lake. He apprentices himself to the eccentric von Heilitz. When a detective investigates a crime, von Heilitz tells him, he becomes more alert, more alive to the terrors and beauty of their world: "'Every leaf, every pine needle, every path through the woods, every bird call, had come alive, was vibrant, full of meaning. Everything *promised*. Everything *chimed*. I knew more than I knew. There was a secret beating away beneath the surface of everything I saw."' Von Heilitz goes on to scoff at fictional sleuths like Hercule Poirot, who never conveyed these deeper meanings:

> They were abstraction machines, and you never had any idea at all of what it felt like to be like them, but by the last chapter they could certainly tell you who had left the footprint beneath the Colonel's window, and who had found the pistol on the bloody pillow and tossed it into the gorse bush. They were walking crossword puzzles, but at least they could do that. A book like that was comfortable: It made you feel better, like a fuzzy blanket and a glass of warm milk. A kind of simple clarity shone through everything and everybody, and the obstacles to that clarity were only screens that could be rolled away by the famous little grey cells [307–308].

Von Heilitz complains, "'You never got the feeling that a real darkness surrounded anyone, not even murderers'" (344).

Events now move steadily forward. Von Heilitz confides to Tom that recent murders in Mill Walk are connected to the Thielman case at Eagle Lake, which he had investigated years before in 1925. At that time, he had implicated a man named Anton Goetz. When Goetz's body was subsequently found hanging from a crossbeam, it was judged a suicide. Now, von Heilitz has reason to doubt Goetz' guilt and suspects Glendenning Upshaw had something to do with his death. He asks Tom to go to Eagle Lake for a fresh investigation of both the Thielman and Goetz murders. Tom runs into all kinds of trouble, some of it involving an erotic relationship with Sarah Spence, whose fiancée is Buddy Redwing, and whose stooges are harassing him. Alone, he spends his nights on his deck gazing out onto the lake, attempting an empathic connection with events of forty summers past: "He decided to throw out everything he had been told about these people's motives and experiment with new ones. He saw gaps and holes in what he had been told, and prowled through them, following his instincts and his imagination...." He has visions of "bodies rising like smoke from the lake, raising their arms above their dripping heads and hovering in place with open eyes and mouths..." (366). And at times he hallucinates that Jeanine Thielman is rising up from the lake in a dripping white dress—"her face dead and heavy—walking toward him through feathers of smoke—her moth gaping open like a trap and her white tongue flapping as she struggled to speak..." (425).

Tom discovers a series of notes which appear to have been written by Jeanine Thielman to her killer: "'*I know what you are and you must be stopped*,'" and "'*This has gone on too long. You will pay for your sin.*'" Then he is almost killed when a mysterious fire engulfs his lodge. He is too late to save a former resident who has loaned him the place, and whose charred body is found in the ruins. The remains are mistakenly identified as his. He returns incognito to Mill Walk and von Heilitz to continue his investigation.

It is revealed at this point, to no one's surprise, that von Heilitz is in actuality Tom's real father. Father and son together reexamine the 40-year old murders and now conclude the culprit to be Glendenning Upshaw. Tom and von Heilitz decide to draw out Upshaw by sending him duplicates of the incriminating notes that had been sent him by Thielman years before. It becomes clear that their veiled threats had alluded to Upshaw's incestuous union with his daughter (Tom's mother). Upshaw had murdered Thielman to cover up the truth of her allegations.

During their deliberations, von Heilitz decides to recruit Tom as his partner. "'I'm not sure I really want to be like you,'" declares Tom in confusion. "'I wonder what I am. I wonder who I am.'" Nonplused, von Heilitz replies, "'We're going to accomplish something great. It's been a long time coming, but we're going to do it—together'" (487–488). It's at this point that in a passing reference, von Heilitz tells Tom about a series of unsolved murders years ago that had fascinated him but which he never had the time to investigate. The victims were found in and around the St. Alwyn Hotel, and the only clues to the killer were the words "Blue Rose" left behind at the scene. A young writer named Tim Underhill had recently written a semi-fictitious account, *The Divided Man*, and relocated the crimes to a "gritty Midwestern industrial city of chain-link fences, inhuman winters, foundries, and a thousand bars" (472). Unsolved to this day, the "Blue Rose" murders may or may not be related to Mill Walk's recent crimes.

But von Heilitz's dream of a collaboration with Tom goes unrealized. He is murdered by Upshaw's thugs, led by the corrupt policeman, Captain Fulton Bishop. Tom finds his savagely beaten body in a house that has been turned upside down, its files and papers scattered. Suddenly fatherless, Tom takes the old man into his arms and suffers his second out-of-body experience: "It seemed to him that he left his body: part of him separated cleanly out of himself and floated and saw the whole room, the ripped bed and the bloody prints..." (509).

In desperation, Tom turns to the only person he now can trust, Detective David Natchez. The tough, by-the-book policeman had always thought von Heilitz' and his methods "too whimsical, intuitive, and theatrical to be taken seriously" (515). But now he regrets the loss of the old man, who had helped him in past cases. Convinced now that his grandfather, Glendenning Upshaw, had indeed engineered von Heilitz' death, Tom and Natchez confront Upshaw and taunt him with Thielman's words, "*I know who you are; you must be stopped.*" Natchez kills Upshaw. He and Tom contrive to make the scene of Upshaw's death look like a suicide.

After the subsequent court proceedings, Tom inherits a lot of money from the dead von Heilitz. But many of the Redwing clan go free and have fled to Switzerland: "'They'll all have plenty of money,' says Tom. "'They'll always have enormous houses and lots of paintings and cars and people who work for them, and they'll never think it's enough. They just won't have their own island anymore'" (545).

In a telling scene in the concluding pages, Tom now fully realizes that his destiny is to be a detective. "Tom meets Sarah Spence at the zoo," Straub explains in an interview: "He has inherited all of von Heilitz' papers, his money, and his house. As they talk, Tom notices that a panther has fixed its eyes on him. It's a big, beautiful, but dangerous animal. Sarah says, *"The panther's looking at* you!'" At that moment, Tom realizes he shares identity with this animal: He *is* what he *does*. He is *who he is supposed to be*. The torch is passed. He's a detective now."[12] As Bill Sheehan has observed, "Both Tom and von Heilitz have yielded to the most compelling of their inner voices, and have, in their idiosyncratic fashion, become artists, just as anyone—whether poet, novelist, magician, or musician—whose work is intimately involved with the process of discovery is, in a sense, an artist."[13]

Straub admits he was torn about continuing a series of novels with this father-son duo, rather in the manner of the Ellery Queen-Inspector Queen pairing. "I was tempted to continue with a series of books about them," he says. "But I thought, no, the very idea was *nauseating*. It made my skin crawl! I can't imagine anything worse, taking both these guys around the Midwest, solving crimes. So I killed off von Heilitz. But, I admit, I miss him, now and then...."[14]

Although *Mystery*, in its general outlines and procedural investigation is Straub's "purest" story of detection, it is, nonetheless, like Datchery's *Drood*, open-ended and inconclusive. The references to the "Blue Rose" are broken off. We will have to wait for *The Throat* to learn more about them.

Koko

Enter Tom's friend, Tim Underhill. He steps forward into the light—or is it *half*-light? The "Blue Rose" murders recede into the background for the moment, and Tim's authorship of *The Divided Man* is left dangling, as it were. For now, he is caught up in a convoluted narrative about a series of crimes that have been committed by a mysterious character known only as "Koko." The action spans a back story about past events in the jungles of Vietnam, continues in the present day in Singapore and Bangkok, and concludes in the streets of New York's Chinatown. We begin in 1982 with news of a series of killings and mutilations in the Far East, committed by a maniac who identifies himself as "Koko." He has left behind in the mouths of his victims playing cards bearing that signature. Evidence points to his identity as a member of a combat platoon that had committed similar atrocities in the Vietnamese village of Ia Thuc fourteen years earlier. Tim Underhill was a member of that platoon. Now, in the present, he and his buddies are struggling to put their lives back together. Back in the States, Conor Linklater is a solitary alcoholic; Tina Pumo is a failed restaurateur; Michael Poole is a physician whose dead child was the victim of the Agent Orange he had suffered during the war. And Tim is living in Singapore. After achieving initial moderate success with his novel *The Divided Man*, he is now barely eking out a living. None of them is able to repress the nightmares and guilts of the war. For them, "deep down, the things that happened ... never *stop* happening" (175).

In a startling development, accumulating evidence left behind by Koko throws suspicion on none other than Underhill himself! Fearful that they will be his next victims, Tim's Army buddies leave for the Far East to intercept him. After searching through Singapore and Bangkok, they finally locate him. What become clear, however, is that Koko has appropriated Tim's identity and forged his name on incriminating documents. Tim, Poole, and Linklater return to New York, only to find Koko has preceded them and murdered Tina Pumo. A desperate investigation continues. Suspects are considered, then rejected, one by one. Finally, a former platoon member named Manny Dengler, a participant in the Ia Thuc atrocities and thought to have been killed in Vietnam, is identified as Koko.

What manner of monster is this Dengler? Does his killing have anything to do with the atrocities he participated in in Vietnam? Underhill discovers that Dengler himself had been abused as a child and had suffered "a catalog of large and small cruelties, among them beatings, confinement, sexual abuse..." (473). Straub explains,

> He had survived a hideous childhood, and he was only holding it together in his adult life, and then the incident happened in the cave—something he saw—triggered this deep time bomb and then off he went. Every time I tried to describe a serial killer, I always went back to that same conception that some people are made out of other people who have a great potential for good that was by cruelty and ignorance pounded out of them, their lives turn into retribution. Unfortunately, the retribution is wreaked upon the innocent.[15]

Imagery surrounding Dengler now snaps into focus: The playing cards he had left with his victims featured the image of a rearing elephant. Elephant imagery pervades his subjective view of events. A "sacred text" of his childhood had been the story, *Babar the Elephant*, about an elephant whose mother is shot and killed by a hunter, and who is rescued by flying elephants (the word "Koko" appears in their "Song of the Elephants"[16]). Perhaps, it is suggested, Dengler has perverted the story, committing terrible acts in order to banish all the terrible things that had happened to him in his childhood and exorcise the acts he himself had committed against children in Vietnam (490). "It is true that Koko must have yearned for death," realizes Underhill. "I think he thought of himself as giving his victims the gift of freedom from the fearful eternity he perceived all about him...." Indeed, he and all the killers in Vietnam are all "dirty angels, agents of release from one kind of eternity into another." Dengler is in a cage of his own devising, trapped "in an eternity which has become intolerable to the man" (553–554).

Underhill, Poole, and the others corner Dengler in an underground room in Chinatown. The man, with a strangely childlike aspect and manner, is surrounded by images of dying children on the walls, their bodies "only partially painted in.... Some held their hands upraised, others reached out with sticklike arms. Red paint wound through them like a skein" (532). A strange, wordless music, "the music of no-place," fills the air: "Sometimes it sounded as if children were speaking or crying out as if from a great distance. These were the dead children painted on the walls" (535).

In the ensuing struggle, Dengler escapes. The case remains unresolved. He is last seen fleeing to the jungles of Honduras. Tim Underhill goes in pursuit, not of Dengler so much as of the novel he wants to write about him.

There is a disturbing affinity between Underhill and Dengler. This becomes a key consideration when we later discuss the so-called "hard-boiled" detective story. We recall that Dengler had called himself "Underhill" and had identified himself to others by that name. "Sometimes I think I must have an evil twin," Underhill muses (321). Criminal and detective share a resemblance that borders on identity. There is nothing comfortable about this realization: "Nothing is sane," Tim realizes. "That's what I saw, nothing is safe, terror and pain are beneath everything—I think God sees things that way, only most of the time He doesn't want us to see it too" (243). Its not just that everyone in his platoon had committed atrocities; everyone also *could have been guilty* of Koko's murders. However, unlike Dengler, who had ushered his victims out of their world of pain, Underhill had chosen another course: "I went home and wrote. Then I wrote some more ... which I called 'Blue Rose' (243)."

The Throat

In the third novel of the trilogy, *The Throat*, we are once again with Tim Underhill. He is living as a successful novelist in New York. His book, *The Divided Man*, we recall, had been a thinly fictionalized version of the Blue

Rose murders committed at the St. Alwyn's Hotel in his hometown of Mill-haven, Illinois. Now, in a burst of metatextual indulgence, Tim reveals that he and his drinking buddy, Peter Straub, are the authors of *Mystery* and *Koko*! Events in *Mystery*, he reveals, had actually transpired in Millhaven, not Mill Walk.

The narrative ground is shifting. Like Datchery, we have been cast adrift in a liminal world, a metatextual limbo of real and fictional worlds.

"After *Mystery*," Tim Muses, "I thought I was done with Millhaven, and with the Blue Rose murders" (5). But word reaches him about the attack on the wife of an old friend, John Ransom, a former Vietnam buddy. After beating her into a coma, her attacker had scrawled the words, "Blue Rose" on the wall above her body. This triggers Underhill's memories of the murder of his seven-year-old sister, April, forty years earlier in the shadow of the St. Alwyn Hotel. Are the Blue Rose killings being repeated now?

The facts in the original Blue Rose case bear repeating: The mutilated body of a young prostitute had been found in the alley behind the St. Alwyn Hotel. Above the body were two words chalked on the wall: "Blue Rose." A week later, another body, that of a jazz piano player is found in a room at the hotel. Again, the words "Blue Rose" are inscribed on the wall above his bed. Perhaps the pianist had witnessed the girl's murder and was subsequently killed. A detective named Damrosch—fictionalized in Tim's book as Hal Esterhaz—was given the case. He had links to the two victims. He knew the girl and had had a brief homosexual affair with the pianist. When yet another body is found, Damrosch kills himself and leaves a note on his desk with the "Blue Rose" signature. Was he the murderer, or was he the victim of blackouts which led him to believe he was?

And so it is that Tim Underhill returns to a thoroughly corrupt Mill-haven, where not one but several killers wait for their victims in the shadows of St. Alwyn's Hotel. Facts are not to be trusted. Solutions are tentative and soon to be discarded. Suspects are practically falling out of trees. Events are ambigrams, which can be viewed differently from different angles. Is it possible, he wonders, that they may be related to the atrocities in Vietnam that had been chronicled in *Koko*?

Tim joins forces with Tom Pasmore. Since his appearance in *Mystery*, Tom has become a highly successful private detective. He lives alone in the home formerly owned by his late mentor, Lamont von Heilitz. In their new partnership, Tom processes information with his computers and newspaper files at home, while Tim hits the streets, collecting clues and tracking down suspects. One particularly promising suspect is one Walter Dragonette, whose home is discovered to be a charnel house of grim souvenirs. He is apprehended. But his complicity in the Blue Rose murders, past and present is in doubt. Reasoning the killer must have had some intimate connection with the St. Alwyn Hotel, Underhill and Pasmore stumble across the former hotel manager, Bob Bandelier, who had reasons to want to impugn the hotel's reputation. And there is his son, Fielding, survivor of an abusive childhood and traumas in Vietnam (as recounted in Tim's story, "The Blue Rose"). But "Fee," as he is known, slips in and out of the narrative under several names, including Vietnam veteran "Franklin Bachelor" and Millhaven cops Fontaine and Hogan. A trap is set: The suspects are all lured to the Beldame Oriental movie theater, where Mike Hogan is revealed as the killer. The moment is deliberately anti-climactic: "When we do learn the identity of the Blue Rose murderer," says Straub in an interview, "the information comes in a muted, nearly off-hand manner.... Previous depictions of reality expressed in newspaper stories and fictional accounts have been discredited, and the surest, most accurate tool for the apprehension of the ever-shifting, multi-layered enigma called 'truth' seems to be imagination—the creation of mere fiction."[17] Tim shoots him dead and arranges the scene to look as if it were another Blue Rose murder. Incriminating diaries and letters are found and sent to the newspapers.

Tim is increasingly disturbed at what he realizes is his affinity, even empathy, for the man known variously as Fee/Bachelor/Hogan. Tom, who knows all about the strange sympathies that exist between the hunter and the hunted, explains: "You've been obsessed with Fee Bandolier even before you really knew he existed. You almost made him up out of your own history.... You love the child he was, and that child is still recent enough to make himself visible to you, and he makes himself visible to your imagination because you love him" (636).

But the investigations are not over. In a last revelation, Tim's friend, John Ransom, who had brought Tim back to Millhaven in the first place, is now identified as the murderer of his wife, April. It was Ransom who had revived the whole "Blue Rose" business in the first place to make it look as if her death was part of the St. Alwyn pattern.

At this point, the hapless reader is prepared to believe anything. The collection of suspects and culprits has only proven one thing: *Everyone* is complicit in one way or another. Straub, in a monumental understatement, admits he "didn't want to write a neat, contained, classic detective novel. I wanted much more room, more color, more light, more orchestration." Indeed, *The Throat* emerges as one of his most complex, even convoluted novels.[18]

Meanwhile, rather than experience the closure and exhilaration of a job well done, Tim returns to New York extremely depressed. The Millhaven murders will never really be behind him. Only by writing another novel can he find some sort of release: "I was mourning the disappearance of that entranced, magical state. To find it again, if it could be found without the disturbance that had surrounded it I'd have to write another book." Tim has his explanation—but will someone now *explain the explanation!*

Tim's investigations have been dual in nature—not just into external events but into the truth of his own repressed memories from his Millhaven boyhood and his later service in Vietnam: "It is as though some old part of yourself wakes up in you, terrified, useless in the life you have, its skills and habits destructive but intact; and what is left of the present you, the person you have become, wilts and shrivels in sadness or despair: the person you have become is only a thin shell over this other, more electric and endangered self" (51). The evils of the former were preparations to confront the events of the latter. Like the villages of Bong To and Ia Thuc in Vietnam, the St. Alwyn Hotel and the Beldame Oriental Theater constitute the dark heart of the story. Indeed, he refers to his childhood as a "Vietnam" before the real Vietnam. They "were oddly interchangeable, fragments of some greater whole, some larger story" (79).

In yet another "Datchery-esque" complication, Straub pulls the narrative rug out from under us *again* as we learn that the traumatic auto accident that we thought had befallen and transformed young Tom Passmore into an "invisible man" in *Mystery*, was just a fiction devised by the partnership of Tim Underhill and Peter Straub! In reality, if that is the word, the accident had befallen *him*. Moreover, Tim recalls being molested in Millhaven's Beldame Oriental Theater (an incident he recounts in the short stories "The Juniper Tree" and "Bunny Is Good Bread"). The repressed memory is threatening to surface: "The child that had been trapped in the movie theater, the buried child that was Tim," appears at times in his dreams, hand outstretched, the palm inscribed with "a word no one can read, a word that cannot be spoken" (419).

Indeed, ghosts have been waiting for Tim in Millhaven, visitations of guilts and recriminations demanding recognition. "'They still want things,'" says one of the suspects in the case. "'They look at us all the time, and they miss being alive. We have taste and color and smells and feelings, and they don't have any of those things.'" *They are like detectives*: "'They stare at us, they don't miss *anything*. They really see what's going on and we hardly ever really see that'" (175).

"I wonder if I would ever know the truth about anything at all," wails Tim (611).

"Falling Beams": Classic, Hard-Boiled, Noir, Occult

Classical Problems

The narrative trajectory that began with *Mystery*, perhaps Straub's "purest" piece of classical procedural detection, and continued with the more *noirish*, psychologically troubled nightmares of *Koko* and *The Throat*, now threatens to leap into the void of the Occult. Pasmore and Underhill's next two cases, *lost boy lost girl* and *In the Night Room* leave behind Blue Roses and enter into case studies fraught with more metatextual narratives that include haunted houses, ghosts, and a cosmic Realm of nameless terrors.

It is not such a step from Blue Rose to psychic terrors. In teasing out elements of the preternatural and the irrational in those cases—what we will define presently as aspects of the "hard-boiled" school of detection—Straub has already delivered what, in the words of Ross Macdonald, is "an unstable balance between reason and more primitive human qualities [that] is characteristic of the detective story. For both writer and reader it is an imaginative arena where such conflicts can be worked out safely, under artistic controls."[19]

Those "controls" are now about to be tested.

But before we venture timidly into the horrific Realm of *lost boy lost girl* and *In the Night Room*, we must first retrace our steps and remember that Pasmore and Underhill are inheritors of a rich tradition of crime and detection that has always possessed, to varying degrees, elements of the hardboiled narrative and the Occult investigation. This must seem a strange thing to say, inasmuch as the modern detective story is customarily consigned to the classical "ratiocinations" in the 1840s by Edgar Allan Poe's Chevalier Dupin and his successors, Arthur Conan Doyle's Sherlock Holmes, Chesterton's Father Brown, S.S. Van Dine's Philo Vance, Ellery Queen's titular sleuth, Agatha Christie's Hercule Poirot, and John Dickson Carr's Dr. Gideon Fell. It is true, admittedly, that central to this tradition, as cultural historian Jacques Barzun stipulates, "that the world must yield to a sense of reality based on the persuasiveness of things.... The main interest of the story should consist in finding out, from circumstances largely physical, the true order and meaning of events that have been part disclosed and part concealed." Order must resolve confusion. Clues are "scanned for what they imply, studied as signs of past action and dark purpose." Barzun concludes, "This search for history in things is anything but trivial. It reflects the way our civilization thinks about law and evidence, nature and knowledge."[20] Unerringly, the truth of the matter, the solution to the crime, must be the *only* possible resolution. Lamont von Heilitz had said as much to Tom in *Mystery*: The true detective "could certainly tell you who had left the footprint beneath the Colonel's window, and who had found the pistol on the bloody pillow and tossed it into the gorse bush'" (307–308).[21]

Yet, however vigorously these super-sleuths explained away the possibilities of the irrational and the infernal with their ingenious deductions, disguises, tricked-up murder weapons, the smoky incense of the inexplicable still stings the nostrils. Someone, or *something* keeps tugging at the locks of the sealed rooms. Even John Dickson Carr, that master juggler of fancy and fraud, disclosed a tandem of solutions, one rational, one supernatural, in one of his greatest puzzle crimes, *The Burning Court*

Sir Arthur Conan Doyle

(1937).[22] Distinctions between innocence and guilt, moreover, grew clouded and ambiguous. Beware of "ascending the tower of reason," warns a detective in Chesterton's classic *The Man Who Was Thursday*, "[you will find] a thing more hideous than unreason itself."[23] Even the creator of Dupin, Poe himself, admitted as much.[24]

Indeed, as early as the transition years of the Gothic tales of Ann Radcliffe and E.T.A. Hoffmann between the 18th and 19th centuries, the stable balance of the rational and irrational—what has been described as "The Janus Resolution"—was clearly in dire jeopardy.[25] In Hoffmann's "Mademoiselle de Scuderi" (1821), the thief Rene Cardillac eludes the police by passing through an apparently solid wall. "'It must be the Devil himself who is mystifying us,'" says the investigating policeman, M. Desgrais. The revelation that a hidden door effected his escape was weak and unsatisfying. If the reader, quite rightly, felt cheated, it is because, as Hoffmann himself noted in his novel *Kater Murr* (1822), "a terrible fright pleases a man more than the natural explanation of what seems to be ghostlike."[26] Surely Peter Straub whole-heartedly endorses this view!

Charles Brockden Brown and Edgar Allan Poe were taking the same risks in America. They teased their readers with the possibility of an ultimately inexplicable, even supernatural agency. Were we really satisfied that the bizarre murder in a locked room in "Murders in the Rue Morgue" was accomplished by a wall-climbing orangutan? Were we content that in Brown's *Wieland* (1799) the "voices" heard by Theodore Wieland directing him in the name of God to slaughter his family came from the ventriloquism practiced by the sinister Carwin, the "biloquist"? Although the narrator of the story, Theodore's sister, Clara, flatly states that the dreams of superstition are worthy only of contempt—"Witchcraft, its instruments and miracles, the compact ratified by a bloody signature, the apparatus of sulphurous smells and thundering explosions, are monstrous and chimerical. They have no part in the scene"—we're unconvinced. And how about the strange death by conflagration of Wieland's father, carefully ascribed by Brown to an action of "spontaneous combustion" (a phenomenon he proceeds to document as verified fact)? Wieland's slaughter of his family is a trenchant satire on Biblical sacrifice, which he believes are God's dictates. Forces of good and evil are indistinguishable. He tells his accusing jury: "I will not accept evil at [your] hand, when I am entitled to good; I will suffer only when I cannot elude suffering."[27] In another novel, *Edgar Huntley* (1796), there are two characters, Huntley and Clithero, who frequently wander about it in trance-like states. Maybe this is sleepwalking, a condition due to inner psychological tensions and repressed guilts. Or are there Otherworldly forces in play?

Any explanations that purported to explain miracles, wrote Chesterton, had to be worthy of those miracles: "It is not only necessary to hide a secret; it is also necessary to *have* a secret; and to have a secret worth hiding.... It is useless for as thing to be unexpected if it was not worth expecting.... The climax must not be only the bursting of a bubble but rather the breaking of a dawn."[28]

I'm impelled to stay with Chesterton, for the moment. Predating by decades the "hard-boiled" and Occult schools of detection, Chesterton's detectives, including Father Brown, Judge Basil Grant, and detective Horne Fisher were—like Datchery—liminal figures positioned uncertainly on the threshold between the "light" of classical deduction and the "dark" of irrational mystification. It might seem strange to thus single out Chesterton, staunch Catholic and herald of orthodoxy. Yet, while his detectives are generally lauded as among the finest sleuths in the classical school—in a class with Poe's Chevalier Dupin and Ellery Queen's titular sleuth—their pronounced distrust of deductions based on the mere accumulation of facts is significant; moreover, their knowledge of the "crooked track of man" is profoundly empathic. For example, Judge Grant in Chesterton's early story "The Tremendous Adventures of Major Brown" scoffs, "Facts, how facts obscure the truth I never could believe in that man—what's his name, in those capital storied?—Sherlock Holmes. Every detail points to something, certainly; but generally to the wrong thing."[29] Recall the fatal errors in deduction that led Straub's von Heilitz astray in his investigation of the Thielman murder in *Mystery*. It is rather an intuitive, self-appointed agenda, even if it lies outside codes of civil justice that enables them to probe at what Jorge Borges has described as the limits of "that precarious subjection of a demoniacal will...." It was apparent, con-

G. K. Chesterton and "Father Brown"

cludes Borges, that "something in the makeup of [Chesterton's] personality leaned toward the nightmarish, something secret, and blind and central."[30]

Empathy borders on identity. Consider how Chesterton's celebrated detective Adrian Hyde's investigation of a murder reveals the guilty party to be—himself! "'[Detectives] get to know about criminals by being half criminals themselves,'" explains Hyde's assistant, "'by being of the same rotten world, by belonging to it and by betraying it, by setting a thief to catch a thief.'"[31] Even mild little Father Brown confesses, "'Has it never struck you,'" he explains to the thief Flambeau in his first case, The Blue Cross, "'that a man who does next to nothing but hear men's real sins is not likely to be wholly unaware of human evil?'"[32] In "The Secret of Father Brown," he explains how he intuits a killer's identity: "'I wait until I know I am inside a murderer, thinking his thoughts, wrestling with his passions; till I have bent myself into the posture of his hunched and peering hatred.... Till I am really a murderer.'"[33] And on "The Chief Mourner of Marne," he compares himself to a "vampire of the night," who feeds off the confessions of "the men who commit the mean and revolting and real crimes."[34] "An intuitive faith in the benignity of paradox or the law of contraries," writes Chesterton scholar William J. Scheick, "may enable Father Brown to live in 'the impossible,' but it is not a belief which comforts the reader nor, I suspect ever fully satisfied Chesterton, who has a character in one of the stories wonder, 'Was it possible that the priest was a little mad?'"[35] Further, "it is not the Gothic elements, not the riddles or paradoxes, not even the murders that intimidate; these Father Brown can explain away, however arbitrarily. What lingers are the darker implications beneath these features ... the threat that in spite of the faith of Father Brown, life may be in fact "a maze with *no* centre."[36] Chesterton scholar Garry Wills sums up the peculiar quality of these stories in words that well apply to our consideration to come of the connections between the Hard-boiled and Occult schools of detective fiction in *lost boy lost girl* and *In the Night Room*: "All is a chase, an evasion, and dream ... prolonged, page by page, beyond our waking. [Here is] the compelling inconsequence of nightmare, its tangle of mutually chasing loves and hates, where the impossible becomes inevitable and each wish comes partnered with its own frustrations.... A dream mood leads us on, linking all its incidents."[37]

Hard-Boiled Problems

Which brings us by an admittedly tortuous route to elements of the so-called hard-boiled school of detective fiction that surface in Straub's Blue Rose books and other stories. It is entirely to the point, as we shall see, that Straub is profoundly influenced by his favorite writers in the genre, Dashiell Hammett, Raymond Chandler, and Ross Macdonald. Hammett and Chandler had first brought to the pages of pulp magazines like *Black Mask* magazine a tough-minded reaction to the tensions and anxieties of 1920s and 1930s America. Disillusionment, cynicism, and big-city loneliness were key themes. A compulsion toward action, told in laconic wit and imagistic poetry, took over. "Hammett took murder out of the Venetian vase and dropped it into the alley," wrote Chandler in his seminal essay, "The Simple Art of Murder": "He wrote at first (and almost to the end) for people with a sharp aggressive attitude to life. They were not afraid of the seamy side of things; they lived there. Violence did not dismay them; it was right down their street."[38] Moreover, Chandler wrote in a letter, "It is just possible that the tensions in a novel of murder are the simplest and yet most complete pattern of the tensions in which we live in this generation."[39]

As we have already seen in the cases of Pasmore and Underhill, Straub is profoundly dissatisfied with the formal detective story. He once declared he was "Chandler" to Stephen King's "Hammett." In a recent interview, he explained, "Yes, I think my comparison of myself and Steve [King] to Chandler and Hammett does apply, although I think Steve prefers to be regarded as a bit more like Chandler! As for me, I admit that I really prefer Chandler and Macdonald to Hammett. Everything in Hammett is too much on the surface."[40]

Perhaps, as Chandler had suggested, the formal detective story had never really existed in the first place: "What did exist was an elaborate scheme for gulling the public into thinking it was getting something it never really did get; and after awhile the fraud was found out. The tricks became known and there was nothing behind the tricks. They were fun for a while but human ingenuity could only go so far."[41] The hard-boiled mode, by contrast, provided a corrective to the pretensions of the classic detective story, portraying, as Gary K. Wolfe has pointed out, "a complex and corrupt world in which the solution of a single murder fails to restore order to an otherwise innocent society...."[42]

Dashiell Hammett

Hammett led the way in the mid-to-late 1920s with his Continental Op and Sam Spade, followed after 1933 by Raymond Chandler's Philip Marlowe.[43] Ross Macdonald's Lew Archer—a particular favorite of Straub's—would appear in the early 1950s. "The *Black Mask* revolution was a real one," writes Macdonald: "From it emerged a new kind of detective hero, the classless, restless man of American democracy, who spoke the language of the street.... Thrust for his sins into the urban inferno, he pits his courage and cunning against its denizens, plays for the highest stakes available, love and money, and loses nearly everything in the end." They faced criminal behavior that was real, implacable, and deadly. "There is no rational counterstatement," says Macdonald. "We are left with a residue of terror and understanding pity … which can't be explained away."[44] In *The Long Goodbye*, Chandler catalogued the array of killers slouching through the "mean streets": "A murderer is always unreal once you know he is a murderer. There are people who kill out of hate or fear or greed. There are the cunning killers who plan and expect to get away with it. There are the angry killers who do not think at all. *And there are the killers who are in love with death, to whom murder is a remote kind of suicide*" (my italics).[45] Compare this with Tim Underhill's description of the serial killer in *The Throat*: "It is true that Koko must have yearned for death—I think he thought of himself as giving his victims the gift of freedom from the fearful eternity he perceived all about him…" (553–554). In short, evil was a human quality, generated from *within* rather than from some inhuman, or Satanic impulse from outside.

The concept of "evil" does not obtain here, says Straub. "[It] seems to me to be a convenient theological category that is not actually found in life. I don't believe in supernatural evil at all, and I believe that human evil is a sort of misnomer for ignorance and stupidity and brutality…. I believe a lot of what is called evil has been sponsored by bad treatment. It can be created by abuse and by unimaginative, unsympathetic, brutal treatment."[46]

Raymond Chandler

Straub locates his "mean streets" away from Hammett's San Francisco, Chandler's Los Angeles, and Macdonald's fictive Santa Teresa (Santa Barbara, CA). The upper Midwest region of Wisconsin, which is depicted in the Blue Rose novels and many short stories— definitively in "A Short Guide to the City"—is his "beat." His native Milwaukee, frequently re-cast in a variety of names, like "Millhaven" and "Milburn," is a frigid frontier of deviance and corruption, where inexplicably gruesome things happen, where serial killers such as Ed Gein and Jeffrey Dahmer ply their trade.[47] "I wanted to have total imaginative freedom over the city," Straub has explained in an interview.

> I could heighten [Milwaukee]. I could darken it. I could stretch it out like taffy or like Play-Doh and mold it in any shape I like…. A great many serial killers seem to have originated in the version I call Millhaven. [These] are the places in which I came alive and what I saw was of immense importance to me. I was trying to understand things; I was trying to work things out. When I was five years old, I thought everything had a meaning….[48]

Here is a region in decline, in *denial*, where "violence is the physical form of sensitivity," he observes in "Short Guide," and where "an odd fabulousness permeates every quarter of the city, a receptiveness to fable, to the unrecorded." A serial killer, the Viaduct Killer, lurks here, and the trail of mutilated bodies "makes us breathless with outrage…" (104–105).

Random violence is the order of the day. We recall the "Flitcraft" anecdote in Hammett's *The Maltese Falcon*. Like Nathaniel Hawthorne's short story "Wakefield," to which it bears a striking resemblance, "Flitcraft" is about a successful businessman and good husband and father, who one day suddenly leaves his wife and children and years later resumes his life with a second family. What has happened? On the day he disappeared he had narrowly missed death from a falling beam on a construction site. At that moment Flitcraft "felt like somebody had taken the lid off life and let him look at the works…. The life he knew was a clean orderly sane responsible affair." But now, "the falling beam had shown him that life was fundamentally none of these things…. He knew then that men died at haphazard like that, and lived only while blind chance spared them. He left his old life on the spot, for he knew now that only 'blind chance' had spared him." Flitcraft must now change his life "at random" and walk away. When, years later, he meets another woman similar to his first wife, he marries her and has another family. "He wasn't sorry for what he had done…. He adjusted himself to beams falling, and then no more of them fell, and he adjusted himself to them not falling."[49]

Indeed, "falling beams" are a constant threat in the hard-boiled worlds of Hammett, Chandler, Macdonald—and Straub. Consider the sudden catastrophes of firefights in the Vietnam jungles of *Koko* and *The Throat*, the auto accidents that befall young Tom Pasmore and Tim Underhill in the city streets of *Mystery* and *The Throat*—not to mention the crippling incident that afflicted Straub as a young boy (see the *Doppegänger* chapter). Even the quietest and most subtle of moments might trigger catastrophe. "'Let's say you're just walking down the street,'" explains Bobby Bunting in Straub's long story "The Buffalo Hunter": "Let's say you're not thinking about anything in particular.... You're absolutely, completely, inside the normal world. And then something happens—a car backfires, or a woman with a gorgeous voice starts to sing behind you—and suddenly you see what's really there—that everything, absolutely everything is alive ... like you don't really exist anymore in the old way at all..." (175).

Underhill and Pasmore—and yes, their creators Straub, Chandler, and Macdonald—have been tested, torn apart, and transformed by such moments. Their subsequent epiphanies, their moments of *clarity*, either traumatize them or inoculate them against worldly hazards. One way or another, to paraphrase Straub, we *learn to wear our own blood.*[50]

Like Straub, Chandler emerged from a restless and troubled, even dysfunctional background of aborted career choices. He has been described as a "devious, self-pitying man" who worked from a "self-punishing conscience" and a "persecution from within."[51] Macdonald says his detective, Lew Archer, was created "from the inside out. I wasn't Archer exactly, but Archer was me" (Nevins, 295). Hinting that Archer "was a means of exorcizing or controlling [personal] guilt," he wrote in the Foreword to a volume of his novels, that he also came from a background that left him with "my sense of self and my sense of territory [that] were both askew." Further, "the inner shape of a man's life, if he is a man of action, plots the curve of his movements. If he is a writer, it is what he writes from and about. But it remains as personal and hidden as his skeleton, just as intricate, almost as unchangeable."[52] Underhill and Pasmore become amateur detectives who, like the dicks in Hammett, Chandler, and Macdonald, "hedge themselves so thoroughly against betrayal that they live in self-imposed isolation and loneliness."[53] Their empathy with the violent and disordered minds of Glendenning Upshaw, Manny Dangler, and the others suggests their own complicity with them.

Having said all that, it should be noted that the closest Straub comes to Hammett's tough, two-fisted detective is Milwaukee homicide detective George Cooper, who appears in *A Dark Matter* and, in a spin-off of that novel, "A Special Place," one of Straub's most disturbing tales about the apprenticeship of a serial killer. Like Sam Spade, George Cooper is as dangerous as the criminals he pursues. In *A Dark Matter* he is described as "not a man to be lightly swayed, he did not yield to whims, he had no fancies or daydreams. His version of guesswork rode upon endless slogging and a cop's finely tuned instinct" (137). On the trail of Milwaukee's serial killer—the "Ladykiller"—Cooper approaches young Keith Hayward, nephew of the chief suspect, Tillman Hayward. "'We're the good guys, Keith,'" he says, in "A Dark Place," with scarcely a trace of irony, "'we keep people like yourself and your family safe from the scum of society that might hurt them if we weren't around"' (27). Ironically, young Keith is already on his way to a killing career of his own, under the tutelage of his Uncle Till. In the end, all Cooper has to show for his efforts are frustration and an inconclusive case. Cooper resigns from the department and drinks himself to death. Among the scribbled writings he leaves behind is a note worthy of Hammett: "'*The way I live wears reality down.... It has taken me nearly sixty years to learn that in this life, if it ain't shit, it ain't nothing at all*'" (172–173).

In a related vein, it should be noted that two other "tough" detectives appear on the scene in Straub's hilariously John Collier-esque, grand-guignol story, "Mr. Clubb and Mr. Cuff." Based loosely on Herman Melville's "Bartleby the Scrivener," a Wall Street banker hires these two "Private Detectives Extraordinaire" to wreak vengeance on his unfaithful wife and her lover. As perversions of Chandler's knights of the Mean Streets, they display a peculiar *relish* in inflicting tortures upon the woman. "'A subject who can render you one magnificent scream after another,'" they explain, "'while maintaining a basic self-possession and not breaking down is a subject highly attuned to her own pain, sir, and one to be cherished.'" They are proud of their peculiar talents: "'We are artists, and we know how to set our feelings aside and address our chosen medium of expression with as pure and patient attention.... We do not assault. We induce, we instruct, we instill. Properly speaking, these cannot be crimes, and those who do them cannot be criminals.'"[54] Having then burned down their client's house, they proceed to take the narrator under their "care" and continue what they call their "grand design," and what the narrator refers to as "the meaning of tragedy." Finally, our hero, dispossessed of everything, including his bank book and parts of his anatomy, returns to the little humble village from whence he came, where he ministers to the poor (always keeping his headgear in place to conceal his injuries) and keeps in a little box the relics of his late wife and lover.

Straub singles out Chandler's *The Long Goodbye* and *The Lady in the Lake* and Macdonald's *The Galton Case* as his favorite hardboiled novels. A brief examination of them throws light on Straub's own themes and methods. Although they may be categorized as "hard-boiled" narratives, yet in their sensitivity and psychological subtlety they stand apart from the more tough-minded surface narratives of the Hammett style.

Like Straub, Chandler and Macdonald consciously attempt to confer literary distinction upon a marginalized genre.[55] They deal with profound psychological studies of criminal behavior and feature literate and sensitive detectives who bespeak their authors' own experiences and sensibilities— but which find little purchase in a cynical and corrupt world. They pursue characters like Terry Lennox and John Galton, orphans who are products of childhood trauma and wartime atrocities, respectively—damaged people who betray Marlowe and Archer, while, Datchery-like, remaining hidden behind shifting names, identities, and masks. And in both we find a flair for a graceful, yet pungent prose style, terse dialogue, and intricate plotlines that frequently double back on themselves.[56]

"Everything [Chandler] thought about the emotional depth available within the genre of crime fiction blossomed under his hand," wrote Straub.[57] Direct allusions to *The Lady in the Lake* gets a real workout in Straub's long story, "The Buffalo Hunter," one of Straub's finest, most disturbing portraits of mental disintegration. The troubled and solitary Bobby Bunting immerses himself in *The Lady in the Lake* and finds himself pulled into the Los Angeles of 1944, where he now *is* Philip Marlowe and, as Marlowe, undergoes the search for the missing, estranged wife of wealthy businessman Derace Kingsley. Events, characters and dialogue are lifted right out of the novel and pour through him. The excitement of the chase. Chandler's world engulfs Bobby in all its hallucinatory clarity. "*This is why I'm a detective!*" he enthuses: "'Everything means something, because it was all chosen. Everything you see, touch, feel, smell, everything you notice and everything you think, is organized to take you somewhere, do you see? Everything *glows!*'" (177).

"It was not just Bobby's excitement," Straub explains, with a touch of nostalgic regret, "it's the sense he has of *imminent discovery*."[58]

The Long Goodbye, says Straub, "was the last good book [Chandler] would ever write, and it was his best his richest and most fully achieved."[59] He acknowledges it was the model for *The Throat*. "Both are about the betrayal of a friend," he says—"by Philip Marlowe's friend Terry Lennox and by Tim Underhill's Army buddy, John Ransom. And you'll notice that early on there is a reference to *The Long Goodbye* when Ransom recommends it to his future wife."[60] Elsewhere Straub quotes with particular pleasure the "aria" of a soliloquy of Marlowe's, as he gazes out a window at "the night of a thousand crimes" where "twenty-four hours a day somebody is running, somebody else is trying to catch him."[61] Chandler critic Peter Wolfe confirms the generally high esteem in which *The Long Goodbye* is held: "It gave the American murder mystery a resonance it had never enjoyed before. Taking fictional crime away from the mob and dropping it into the family, it also anticipated the best work of Ross Macdonald."[62] Macdonald himself applauds "Chandler's highly charged blend of laconic wit and imagistic poetry" and its "passion for our new language."[63]

There is no mistaking the affinities Straub also shares with Macdonald. They both came from academic backgrounds. Straub wrote a Masters thesis about the poet Wallace Stevens, and Macdonald wrote a Ph.D. dissertation on Samuel Taylor Coleridge. Both have been vocal in their ambitions for the "legitimate" consideration of their work: "Maybe we can find a better label than hardboiled [declared Macdonald], better sponsors than Hammett and Chandler. They're my masters, sure, but in ways that count to me and a lot of good readers I'd like to sell my books to, I'm beginning to trace concentric rings around these fine old primitives."[64] Both underwent psychoanalysis at various stages in their lives, and their thematic concerns are consequently similar, witness the mistaken identities, familial dysfunctions, and subtle psychological examinations of lost and orphaned children in Macdonald's *The Galton Case* and in the Kalen-

Ross Macdonald

dar and Underhill families in Straub's *lost boy lost girl* and *In the Night Room.*

"You know," muses Straub, in a rueful aside, "whenever I write about the sort of detective investigation where characters get into a car to go somewhere, or go around ringing doorbells, I think of the way Lew Archer conducts his investigations. These days, you can't have that sort of thing anymore!"[65]

The Film Noir

It comes as no surprise that Straub is drawn to the series of *films noirs* that brought the hard-boiled stories to the screen in the 1940s and 1950s. Hollywood, always a decade late in reflecting trends in fiction, waited until the war years of the 1940s to catch up. A spate of detective, mystery, and suspense films captured wartime anxieties, disillusion, and paranoia, including Hammett's screenplay for a proto-noir, *City Streets* (1931), and Chandler's work on screenplays for *Double Indemnity, Shadow of a Doubt, The Blue Dahlia,* and *The Big Sleep.* His *Farewell, My Lovely* was the basis for one of the very finest *noirs, Murder, My Sweet,* although he did not work on the screenplay.[66] (One shudders at Chandler's reaction, had he lived, to the deconstruction in 1973 of *The Long Goodbye* by director Robert Altman and screenwriter Leigh Brackett.[67]) Yet, Chandler's years in Hollywood were unhappy and, for him, unsatisfactory. Although well paid, he regarded the film colony as "a degraded community whose idealism even is largely fake. The pretentiousness, the bogus enthusiasm, the constant drinking and drabbing, the incessant squabbling over money, the all-pervasive agent ... the whole damn mess is out of this world."[68]

"As a group, these movies seem bottomless to me," Straub says. He cites *Criss Cross, The Hitchhiker, Pickup on South Street, Night and the City, Macao* as "the kind of movies I sat through as a small child who had wandered away from whatever he was supposed to be doing and used his allowance to gain entrance to the Sherman Theater." In his short story, "A Special Place," there is a striking scene where serial killer Tillman Hayward recommends *Shadow of a Doubt* to his nephew and protégé, Keith Hayward. He complains that censorship forced Hitchcock into altering the "real" ending of the film, in which the character of Uncle Charlie, instead of perishing beneath the wheels of an oncoming locomotive, would escape with his niece to become together "partners in crime."[69] Straub, moreover, particularly liked the Alan Ladd movies, like *The Blue Dahlia* and *Chicago Deadline*.[70] These and other classics, like *On Dangerous Ground* (Nicholas Ray, 1951), *Murder, My Sweet* (Edward Dmytryk, 1943), and *The Glass Key* (Stuart Heisler, 1942)—almost anything starring Alan Ladd—find their way, altered and transformed, into the pages of his stories.

His story, "Lapland, or Film Noir," is his definitive dissection of the *film noir* style. He could also be describing the world of *Mystery* and the contemporary scenes in *The Throat*:

> In Lapland, one always finds gambling clubs; also, drunken or corrupt night watchmen; a negligee; a ditch; a running man; a number of raincoats and hats; a man named "Johnny"; a man named "Doc," sometimes varied to "Dad"; an alcoholic; a penthouse; a beach shack; tavern full of dumbells; an armored car; a racetrack; a shadowy staircase ... the effect of headlights reflected on wet urban streets" (46).... Once you turn away from the sunny pieties and forced optimism of the Hollywood mindset during World War II, there opens before you a kind of stunning emotional truth, the truth of disillusion and loss which grants the kind of liberation rooted in actual honesty—to face it, all you need is the heart of a spelunker and the rage of a cornered wolverine.

Here is a world where most non-criminal adult males are either policemen, who "accept bribes and arrest the innocent," or private investigators, who discover bodies, wear trench coats, and "rebuff sexual invitations from females with charming lisps and hair that hangs, fetchingly, over one eye" (46–50).

"It occurred to me," Straub says, "that I could approach this lovely material from a mock-scholarly angle and puree the noir films themselves into a series of exaggerations and highlights.... And if I aim to be honest, evasion deepens as we encounter Alan Ladd, he who attracts the light and whispers to a traumatized child that whatever happened back there during the ellipses was not his fault."[71] It is a world that bleeds into Straubian crime and detective narratives, characterized by "deliberate dislocations, complex and indirect narratives, flawed protagonists, ambiguous motives and resolutions, a fascination with death" (48). Although Straub concocts *noir* pastiches, one of the films is real. "I remember one day while writing my story, 'The Juniper Tree,' that *Chicago Deadline* came on the television, with Alan Ladd and Donna Reed. I thought, this is terrific! And I decided to insert it into the story."[72]

We recall in *The Throat* that young Tim Underhill is victimized by a child molester in Millhaven's Beldame Oriental Theater—a fictionalization of the Sherman Theater in Milwaukee—while watching *Chicago Deadline* and the *faux*-noir called *From Dangerous Depths*. In these nightmarish scenes, conveyed in a kind of stream-of-consciousness prose, his molester is described as a "Minotaur" lurking at the center of a maze, a monster hidden in the dark of the theater waiting to "yank him into a movie about treachery and arousal." "Under the Minotaur's instruction," Tim's sense of reality is distorted: "[It was] flattened out under the Minotaur's instruction—the real feelings aroused by the things he did would tear you into bloody rags, so you forgot it all. You cut up the memory, you buried it in a million different holes. The Minotaur was happy with you, he held you close and his hands crushed against you and the world died" (217–218).

Similarly, in another, related story, "Bunny Is Good Bread," young Fee Bandolier, a serial killer in the making, seeks refuge from the terrible realities of his home life inside the same movie theater watching the same movie, *From Dangerous Depths*. Awash in scenes of murderous violence, illicit love, and betrayal, Fee endures the abuse of the fat butcher, Heinz Steinmetz. In a remarkable passage of prose, Fee loses himself in the events on the screen while submitting to oral sex with the child molester. The two worlds intertwine, blend, and unite, until—his mouth has the "taste of bread, warm and silky" (134). Outside the theater, memories of what had happened are clouded and uncertain. Fee realizes, "Nothing around him was real. The moon had been painted, and the houses had no backs, and everything he saw was a fraction of an inch thick, like paint" (116). In self-defense, the traumatized child retreats from the terrors at home into the *film noir* world of movie sex and violence. "If you forgot you were in a movie, your own feelings would tear you into bloody rags" (150). Fee will soon embark on a series of killings and mutilation, a campaign that he will continue into his adulthood.[73]

Tim Underhill escapes the quagmire that claims Fee Bandolier and pursues a career as a writer-investigator. Fee descends into the serial killings documented in *Koko* and *The Throat*. Gary Wolfe notes, "The movies that the boys watch become entangled with their own stories."[74]

Before moving on to the Occult investigations of Pasmore and Underhill, it should be noted that among Straub's gallery of detectives is a detective unique to his own literary interests. In *The Hellfire Club*—which is discussed in greater detail in a later chapter—he gives us a *literary* detective in the person of Nora Chancel. She is investigating allegations that a legendary writer, Hugo Driver, is not the rightful author of the phenomenally popular novel *Night Journey* and its two sequels. Since its publication fifty years before, *Night Journey* has acquired cult status and brought millions into the coffers of Chancel House publishers. Now, a half century later, any question of Driver's authorship could mean disaster for the publisher.

Nora is a peculiar kind of detective, part textual scholar and part amateur criminal investigator. The original manuscript of *Night Journey* has disappeared. Only scattered lines and fragments exist. She is forced to sift through the two sequels, looking for telltale consistencies of diction, structure, and thematic usage that would identity the rightful author. At the same time, she uncovers what might have been a series of murders of those who either had participated in the writing of the book or had been in a position to expose Driver as a fraud.

There is nothing "academic" about Nora's quest. She uncovers a labyrinth of buried secrets, many of them dangerous and potentially homicidal, in the forested location of the Shorelands Writers Colony, where the *Night Journey* saga had started a half century earlier. "Don't you think all this Shorelands business is like some huge plot that you can't quite see?" is the question that haunts Nora (77). Those attending the Colony in 1938 had vied for a contract from businessman/publisher Lincoln Chancel. Only Hugo Driver had emerged with the coveted commission. *Night* Journey was the result. The other writers had been subsequently murdered, one by one. The only female in the group, poet Katherine Mannheim, had vanished without a trace. She shares the unknown fate of another poet, Isobel Standish, in "Mrs. God," who came to Esswood House, but never left. The comment that "Shorelands didn't bring much luck to these people" is an understatement (75).

Now, 55 years later, Nora encounters a new series of killings. Someone is preventing the descendents and friends of the original group of Shorelands writers from coming forward with new findings that would dispute Driver's authorship. And this is where the charismatic and decidedly villainous Dick Dart—one of Straub's most successfully realized creations—comes in. As the son of the law firm representing Chancel House, Dart must protect their copyright and block any other claims. If it is proven that Hugo Driver was nothing more than a hack and opportunist, and that Chancel House cooperated in the fraud, all of its profits, in the millions, must go to the true heirs. If he has to commit murder in the process, well.... For her efforts, Nora faces rape and torture at Dart's hands. Battered and bruised and confused, at times, she wails the lament of every hardboiled investigator caught up in the nightmarish tangle: "People keep grabbing me and moving me from one place to another without ever telling me the truth.... People lie to me, they just want to use me, and I'm sick of all these secrets and all these plots" (288).

In the end, nothing is conclusive. Even the person likely most responsible for *Night Journey*, Katherine Mannheim, remains a liminal figure. At the center of *Night Journey*—and of *Hellfire*—she is never more than a shadowy figure, a fugitive from a *film noir*, her presence only suggested by a variety of contradictory testimonies, by turns "rude," "a saint," "evasive" and "truthful," "completely crazy" and "completely sane" (342). And just as in typical hardboiled narratives, everyone is complicit of crime or guilty of *something*, all of Nora's suspects of crimes, past and present, and all of the suspected participants in the writing of *Night Journey*, are involved to a degree in fraud and murder. If guilt is shared, so is authorship. Indeed, the search for a killer can be as fruitless and inconclusive as search for the *urtext* and the true author of any book.

The Occult Problems: Investigations and Metafictions

And now, at last, we are ready to take the plunge into the Abyss as Tom Pasmore and Tim Underhill prepare to confront the occult horrors of *lost boy lost girl* and *In the Night Room*. Both, as we have seen, possess preternatural sensibilities. Datchery-like, Tom and Tim are liminal figures, half-in and out of their fictional realities. They are worthy inheritors of the legacy of more than a century of occult investigators. It's a dangerous business. Supernatural forces are the criminals here, and at stake is not just a life, but a soul.[75]

As we have seen previously in the "Dark Necessities" chapter, the subjects of Spiritualism, séances, and ghost hunting, so prevalent in the novels and stories of Nathaniel Hawthorne and Henry James, have had a profound impact on Peter Straub. And we know that the history of occult sciences, in general, constitute an important element in his ongoing interests, from Renaissance mage Henry Cornelius Agrippa to a member of the Golden Dawn, Aleister Crowley.

Although Sherlock Holmes scorned the type, the psychic sleuth came into his own around the middle of the 19th century. Hard on the heels of the advent of modern Spiritualism, their models were real-life psychic investigators, such as scientists Sir William Crookes and Charles Richet, philosopher William James, poet Robert Browning, and professional magicians J.N. Maskelyn and Harry Houdini. They devoted their energies and risked their reputations inquiring into the alleged psychic phenomena produced by the mediums the Fox Sisters, the Davenport Brothers, D.D. Home, and Mrs. Piper.[76]

Their literary counterparts soon appeared in the stories of J. Sheridan LeFanu, Algernon Blackwood, William Hope Hodgson, and Seabury Quinn.[77] Some of them worked with law enforcement agencies, some did not. Some were psychically empowered, some were not. Some of their cases proved to have rational explanations, some did not. As Quinn's Jules de Grandin, a veteran of many psychic investigations, declared, "'The wisest man today cannot say where the powers and possibilities of nature begin or end. We say, "thus and so is beyond the bounds of our experience" but does that therefore put it beyond the bounds of nature? I think not.'" And as John Carnacki, a psychic investigator in stories by Hodgson, noted: "'I am as big a skeptic concerning the truth of ghost-tale as any you are like to meet—only I am what I might term an unprejudiced skeptic. I am not given to either believing or disbelieving things "on principle," as I have found so many idiots prone to be…. I view all reported "haunting" as unproven until I have examined into them.'"[78]

Many of Peter Straub's stories have featured amateur investigators, many of whom were, significantly, writers who confronted the world of the Occult in *If You Could See Me Now, Julia, Ghost Story, Floating Dragon, Mr. X*, "Mrs. God," and *A Dark Matter*. For example, as we have already reported in the "Dark Necessity" chapter of this book, *If You Could See Me Now* pits writer Miles Teagarden against the malignant spirit of Alison Greening, a woman who had drowned under mysterious circumstances, years before. Haunted by guilts in his past, he suffers in the course of his investigation into the serial murders in the rural Wisconsin community of Arden, a "psychic rape" by the ghostly Alison: "She wanted me dead," says Miles. "She wanted me with her. I had awakened Alison's spirit … and I knew now that spirit was rancid with jealousy of life" (349). She is vanquished in a fire … but … the climax is inconclusive. "[Alison] would be back—as a gesture seen on a crowded street, or as a snatch of music heard from an open window, as the curve of a neck and the pressure of a pair of hands, or as a child. Who would always be with us, now" (387).

In *Julia* the eponymous young woman battles forces both real and ghostly in a seriously haunted London house. Her husband, Magnus, is a threatening figure—"Sometimes I think Magnus is not from this world at all, or that he is thousands of years old, preserved by some black magic" (303). And there is the likewise menacing presence of a rampaging demon child, Olivia Rudge, who had been murdered 25 years before. Another ghostly visitation is her own dead child, nine-year-old Kate, whose recent death had been due to a bungled tracheotomy by Julia. In her attempts to unearth buried secrets, past sins, and exorcise her own past guilts, Julia learns that Kate and Olivia were half sisters, fathered by Magnus. Olivia had died in the very house Julia now occupies. Bewildered, distraught, and fearing for her own sanity, Julia undergoes a desperate investigation, attending séances, researching old newspapers, talking to informed parties: "She felt, more than ever, that she was living inside a comprehensive error, the mistake that her life had become: bigger forces lay without, waiting" (60). In a climactic rooftop battle, she falls in defeat to Olivia: "Strong arms embraced her, and Olivia's smoldering odor invaded her nostrils and the white column of air whirled her into it…" (172). She leaps to her death. But in a suggestion of Datchery-esque ambivalence, the epilogue implies that all is not over. Julia's death might be cynically construed by her husband Magnus as a "suicide." Outside his window, however, unbeknownst to him, waits a blond-headed child bearing a resemblance to the malignant and deadly Olivia.

The central "investigator," if you will, in *Ghost Story* is aspiring occult novelist Don Wanderley, newest and youngest member of the guilt-haunted Chowder Club. As we know, he and his brethren must confront the spirit of the wicked Eva Galli—incarnated variously in the forms of Alma Mobley, Ann-Veronica Moore, Anna Mostyn, and Angie Maule—and her grotesque host of shape-shifting creatures in the little town of Milburn, New York. At the end, bursting in the door of her latest incarnation, Anna Mostyn, they witness her "death," if that's what it is: "[They] saw a writhing life through the dead woman's skin…. A mouth opened opened beneath Anna Mostyn's mouth and a body constrained within Anna Mostyn's bloody clothing moved with ferocious life: it was as swirling and varied as an oil slick, and it angrily flashed out at them for the moment it was visible; then it blackened and faded, and only the dead woman lay on the floor" (461). In another inconclusive moment, however, we have reason to believe that she is not yet at rest. In the Epilogue, a tiny wasp bearing her spirit appears to Don. He kills it and severs its limbs, yet, it still moves. "'That thing ain't *ever* gonna give up the ghost,'" he is told. Don replies, "'Doesn't look like it'" (483).

Another novelist, Graham Williams, in *Floating Dragon*, investigates the evil spirit of The Dragon, a cosmic entity laying waste to the little town of

Hampstead. Graham is more familiar than anyone with the history of this recurring malignancy. Years before, in an unexpected discovery of inner psychic powers, he had defeated its earlier incarnation. Now, Graham and his three brothers-in-arms track down the Dragon to the site where it had been buried more than three hundred years before. In a spectacular confrontation they destroy it in a rain of fire. "First they saw its face … like a roadmap to vice. A long and meaty tongue licked out of the curling lips … and an odor of shit and sweat and filthy skin drifted off it. At its waist began muscular goat legs and hindquarters" (483). Afterward, Graham muses in a startling moment of clarity, "'Had that scene actually played itself out, in that place and in that way?'" (504) Meanwhile, his new novel, *Floating Dragon*, like *Drood*, remains unfinished. We remember that his defeat of the Dragon years before had not been final. Why would it be, now?

Ned Dunstan's investigation into the identity of his father and the source of the killings in *Mr. X*, already examined in detail in an earlier chapter, plunged him the thickets and brambles of multiple narrative threads and fractured family identities. Like any hard-boiled detective, Ned confessed that he "felt as though I were a kind of Russian doll, hiding secrets inside secrets that led to an unknowable mystery" (232). And in one of those Datchery-esque, inconclusive switcheroos, we learned in the last paragraph that the story we have just heard might not be from Ned's viewpoint at all, but from his shadow-twin, Robert….

Further, the maddeningly enigmatic and open-ended "Mrs. God" finds failed academic William Standish traveling to the English country home of Esswood House, a past haven of other writers, including Henry James and D.H. Lawrence. As a self-appointed *literary detective*, he's investigating the identity and work of the late obscure poet Isobel Standish, his grandfather's first wife. Walking the deserted halls, dining alone, reading in the lonely library, his reality quickly breaks down. His researches are fraught with dreams and nasty hallucinations of lost children and damaged babies. They disclose a past history of violence and ritual murder, both in the house and in his own past. The manuscripts he reads are couched in a language that seems to be some sort of Occult "code." Inexorably, inevitably, he falls victim to Esswood House. "Essentially," writes Bill Sheehan, 'Mrs. God' is a story about hunger, about people sacrificed to the endless hunger of whatever entity animates Esswood … and its guardian family…." The theme of "supernatural hunger" manifests itself everywhere in Straub, particularly in the short story, "Hunger, an Introduction" (232).[79] Curious, isn't it, that in Straub sometimes it's the *ghost* that is investigating the *living*…?

Finally, novelist Lee Harwell is conducting a dual investigation in a novel already cited several times, *A Dark Matter*. On the one hand, he is on the trail of the perpetrator of the "Lady Killer" murders, a series of crimes from decades before. The chief suspect, Keith Hayward, seems to have disappeared during an occult ritual held in a Meadow outside of Madison, Wisconsin, in 1966. In a related investigation, on the other hand, Lee seeks the truth about the Horrors witnessed during that mysterious night in the Meadow. During the course of strange occult rituals led by the charismatic guru, Spencer Mallon, a group of high school students witnessed monstrous visions that so damaged them that they subsequently tried to erase them from their memories. The disclosures are couched in the highest "Weird" manner of Peter Straub:

> These scenes were like dioramas in front of them [reveals one of the witnesses], only the dioramas were alive, and the things in them moved ... a crazy world like a wild party. A king was riding on a bear, waving his arms and thrashing every which way, and a queen, an angry queen, was shouting and pointing here and there with a long stick—the Bear King and the Roaring queen, Meredith called them. They had a big dog, like a hound of some kind, and all of them were made of shiny silver, or something like that, and none of them had faces, just these smooth shiny liquid surfaces [234–235].

They reflect, moreover, Straub's readings of the aforementioned Renaissance magician, Henry Cornelius Agrippa:

> I came to this chapter [Straub reports in an interview] about the spirits of Mercury, and it was just completely delightful, this king and queen made of mercury or some shiny surface, and the red giant gesticulating, and an old man and an old woman on a white landscape—all sounded really colorful and startling, and I thought if put that on the page, it would make people stop and take it in. Because nobody had ever really seen pictures of things like that, depictions of such things, in novels before, I don't think.[80]

Lee sifts through the clues relating to both cases and seeks the testimonies of everyone involved. But each account is different. Such is the fate of every hard-boiled investigator, private or professional: "The central characters have all denied or forgotten something crucial and determining about the event in the Meadow. It boils and smokes inside them.... You can only approach truth in *A Dark Matter* in a sidelong way, from many angles.... Everybody shapes and shaves experience while describing it.... We can't help doing this; it's how we are built."[81] "No story is justified," wrote Albert Camus, "until it can be read from another point of view."[82] And when the final testimony comes, from Lee's wife, the truth of what happened that night is disclosed in perhaps Straub's wildest phantasmagoric flight of fancy. Did the kids in the meadow really witness "a horde of spirits and demons come tumbling out?" (389). We are left with this conclusion: "If the only place where it actually happened was her imagination, then it still really did happen" (389).

lost boy lost girl

But we are keeping Tim Underhill and Tom Pasmore poised on the brink of their own occult investigations in *lost boy lost girl* and *In the Night Room*. In the first, Tim Underhill once again returns to his hometown haunts of Millhaven upon learning of the death of his younger brother's wife, Nancy. The sites are familiar by now from the Blue Rose books, including the Beldame Oriental movie theater and the St. Alwyn Hotel. His old friend, Tom Pasmore, still conducts his solitary investigations in the house of his former mentor, Lamont von Heilitz. Surrounded by computers and file cabinets, he works only when the occasion—or his own conscience—dictates.

Told by an omniscient narrator, interspersed with entries from Tim's diary entries, the story unfolds…. Shortly after his arrival, Tim learns that his sister-in-law had committed suicide, and his nephew, Mark, had discovered the body, wrists slashed, in the bathtub. Behind one of both of these events are the disappearances of a number of young boys at the hands of a madman dubbed the Sherman Park Killer, the "Dark Man." Possibly related to all this is the mysterious house next door to his brother, at 3323 North Michigan Street, which had once been inhabited by the alleged killer.

At first, Tim is only concerned with the welfare of Mark, whose grief over the loss of his mother has turned into an obsessive interest in the abandoned old house on the other side of the alley from his father's house. Now young Mark assumes the mantle of amateur sleuth and pursues an investigation of his own. After keeping the house under surveillance, he finally gains entry and finds evidence of mutilation and torture. The house itself is riddled with hidden passages and chambers, which has enabled the killer to roam freely about the house, unseen and unsuspected by the victims he has confined there.

Mark also learns that the house was once inhabited by a notorious serial killer, Joseph Kalender, who was his mother's cousin. Kalender, who had been convicted of numerous tortures and killings, including his own wife and son, had been convicted and sent to prison, where he had been killed by a fellow inmate. Meanwhile, Mark sense the presence of an elusive, black-clad figure in the neighborhood and inside the house. His back is turned, and his face is always averted. Could it be that the malevolent spirit of Kalender, who had also had the habit of always turning his back to photographers, has somehow returned? Or is there a "copy-cat" killer now on the loose?

Mark senses yet another presence, a young girl, in the house. We eventually learn she was the "secret" child of Kalender. Under the pretence of a miscarriage, Kalender had spirited the girl away to his house, only to torture and kill her.

The Kalendar house is one of Straub's most remarkable "Old Dark Houses." It "looks like a clenched fist": "It was a little house, nondescript in every way, "except for the lifeless, almost hollowed-out look of a building that had long stood empty" (59–60). It bears the scars of a fire—"The place had assimilated the dead fire into its being.... It was a madman's house, and it resembled the workings of his mind, being riddled with unseen, unseeable passageways" (178). It's a veritable killing machine crafted by master carpenter Joseph Kalendar, modeled after murder palace of serial killer H.H. Holmes during the Chicago Columbian Exposition in 1893, an apparatus serving the Dark Man's every whim and device.[83] In the finest Gothic tradition, it is riddled with passages behind the walls, secret panels, and hidden rooms. Slipping through its interior, Kalendar is described "as a great spider speeding across his web and he was capable of appearing anywhere" (179). And it's hardly empty. Mark notices immediately a strange kinship that both attracts and repels: "A hesitation, some delicacy of feeling, kept Mark from going up the walkway.... He felt that the house's very emptiness and abandonment made up a force field that extended to the edge of the sidewalk. The air itself would reject his presence and push him back.... The house seemed to vacuum his ordinary concerns out of his mind and replace them with itself.... It felt as much an active partner in his obsession as himself. Present from the first moment the place revealed itself to him, the sense that it possessed a will, even the capacity for desire, had taken hold in him..." (71). As he prowls the interior, seeking whatever lurked there, one is reminded the man who haunts his own house in Henry James's *The Jolly Corner.*

The house discloses its occupants subtly, as "a faint change in the texture of an area of darkness beyond the right front window" (80). One of those occupants is a girl, seen through the windows. She also suddenly appears before Mark's mother, a silent reminder of her mother's guilt at averting her eyes to the abuse suffered at the hands of Kalendar: There she stands, a six-year-old girl in dirty overalls, her bare, filthy feet on the outmost edge of the faded rag rug, her small, slim, baleful back turned to Nancy. "Anger boiled from her and hung in the dead air between them.... Lily had come through the rip in the fabric to cast judgment on her weak traitorous aunt. She had come for Mark, his mother saw. Mark was half hers already" (123–124).

Mark declares to his friend, Jimbo Monaghan, that whatever—or *who*ever—is in the house is "'like something left behind. Something real enough so sometimes you can see it.'" A lot of people see dead people—the part left behind. Don't you think? A friend of yours dies, and one day you're walking down the street and you look in a window and just for a second you see him in there. The next day, maybe you see him getting on a

bus, or walking across as bridge. That's the part of him that's left behind"'
(205). And it's to Mark alone that the presence is vouchsafed. "'It cheered you
up!" Jimbo observes: "'It did, didn't it? You're all, like electrified about something'" (207).

Straub, as is his wont, sometimes takes the viewpoint, as it were, *of the
ghost*—if that's what it is. Pausing before the house, Mark feels a suspension
of his worlds: "He felt a numb, suspended clarity that, he thought, *must be
similar to what ghosts and dead people experienced*, watching the living go
through their paces" (126; italics added). Mark has a sighting late one night
outside on the fence: "Out in the night, something *happened*: a bloated, dark
shape melted through the barbed wire at the top of the wall and—he thought,
dropped into the alley" (74).

Mark claims to an incredulous Jimbo that he is having an affair with the
mysterious inhabitant. She had been waiting for him, he says; he had "called
her into being." At first he could hear her moving around behind the walls.
Hiding from him. Running away whenever he got close. "'[T]hen she came out
through the secret door under the stairs … and took his hand.'" She said her
name was Lucy Cleveland and she was nineteen years old. She was so beautiful
"'it almost hurt to look at her.'" Lucy is not an *ordinary* person—"'[Mark] wasn't
really sure what she was. But she had been waiting for him; he had called her
into being'" (219–220). She had been hiding from her father, who had subjected
her to torture on an enormous bed in the basement, the "night room," to which
he had bound her with clamps and handcuffs. But now she was having sex
with Mark on that same "giant's bed." She "'had a way of finding the comfortable
places on that ugly bed'" and taught him how to bound her to it, which "'made
the sex even more incredible.'" Jimbo determines to see for himself. But Mark
forestalls him, explaining Lucy doesn't want to know anyone but him, and she
doesn't want to leave the house. But one day Jimbo sees Mark through the window talking to someone who isn't there. By now Jimbo is convinced his friend
is crazy. What is certain is that lately Mark is exhausted, he looks older, he has
stopped eating. The obsession with Lily is draining him.

He seems on the verge of a decision….

It's then that Mark goes to Sherman Park, where the children had been
abducted, in search of the Dark Man. A man with his face averted and his
back turned has been seen in the area.

Soon after that, Mark disappears.

"'Everybody knows what happened to Mark,'" Jimbo tells Tim. "'He
walked into Sherman Park, and the Sherman Park Killer, or the Dark Man,
or whatever you call him, grabbed him. Mark wasn't even thinking about his
own safety…. He was in his own little world'" (224).

Tim turns to a neighbor, Omar Hillyard, who remembers recently seeing a figure resembling the late Joseph Kalendar going in and out of the house at night. Like Kalendar, he had always averted his face. "'He was always turning his back on you'" (228), Hillyard remembers. His presence is palpably evil: "Joseph Kalendar made rooms feel smaller and darker than they were. He had that power: He removed all the extra air from wherever he was. When you were with him, you felt like you were carrying a tremendous weight.... Hostility. It was like a black cloud [that] surrounded him. When you were with him, it surrounded you too.... I've often thought that's what evil feels like" (229). If this is not Kalendar, who is dead, after all, then who is the figure seen around the house and in Sherman Park?

Tim consults with Pasmore. The normally pragmatic detective is confused. While he doesn't believe Mark is really dead, he lamely concedes, "He's just elsewhere" (236). Pasmore's own investigation, in the meantime, has revealed that Kalendar had had a second child, a daughter, whom he had concealed in an annex he had built to the house and where he had committed atrocities on her and the other children in the neighborhood. Mark's mother had had suspicions about Kalendar, and when Mark became obsessed with the house, she killed herself. Kalendar had been arrested and imprisoned, where he was slain by another prisoner.

Pasmore, meanwhile has consulted city records and learned that a man named Ronald Lloyd-Jones had recently purchased the house visits it occasionally in secret. His description matches the "dark man" seen in the area. After a long search he and Underhill locate and confront him. Convinced he's their man, they turn their findings over to the local police. Like the serial killer Dengler in *Koko*, "Ronald Lloyd-Jones had appointed himself the escort to the next world, and he loved his work" (245–246). And now, says Pasmore, "'he's going to get arrested, booked, and charged with at least a couple of murders, depending on what and how much they find in his house.... Sooner or later the police will uncover human remains...'" (245).

And what about Mark and Lucy? There is no trace of either. However, in the following weeks, Tim receives what he calls "a gift." He inadvertently catches the sight of the shining faces of a young man and girl in a Starbuck's café. He is convinced they are "what remains" of Mark and Lucy. It's a magical moment, captured in Straub's most compelling prose:

> [They] had exited their *elsewhere*, long enough to display themselves before me in all the fullness of their new lives.... A share of that blazing joy resided in me now, and I thought it would be mine for eternity. *It partook of eternity.* What I had seen, that glory, burned in my memory. *God bless Mark Underhill*, I say within the resounding chambers of my heart and mind, *God bless Lucy Cleveland, too, though already they are so blessed, they have the power to bless me* [247].

Just as remarkable are several emails that Tim had received several days *after* Mark's disappearance. "we r 2gether/ in this other world/ rite next door," reads one of them (251). Later, when Tim investigates Mark's laptop computer, he finds a note directing him to a web site, where a brief video shows a boy and a girl happily running onto the sand, before an oncoming thunderstorm. "Tim could not see the faces turned from him, but he knew them. They were unforgettable" (277).

The police, meanwhile, are excavating the grounds around the Kalendar house. A body is found. Then more bodies. None are Mark's.

What is real, and what is not, remains unresolved. What happened to Mark? Did he indeed have a ghostly relationship with a young girl? Was Ronnie Lloyd Jones merely a deranged copy-cat, imitative of Joseph Kalendar, or had he been truly possessed by the man's malevolent spirit? Tom Pasmore and Jimbo Monaghan are dubious, of course, but Tim Underhill has made up his mind.

We are left with a genuinely haunting incident. Or is it merely the projection of Mark's disordered mind? Shortly before Mark had disappeared, he was sitting alone in the house, waiting … waiting, *for what*? It's a humid, sunny afternoon in June. He is sitting at the bottom of the stairs in an empty house that "he knew not to be empty." He knows that a "presence" inhabits it, and "she had come for him…. She had whispered to his mind, to his heart, and without hearing he had heard." Mark senses "a light footstep" on the stair.

> A great tuning fork had been struck. This was what he had been called to witness, Mark thought—this enormous thing that had already passed from view…. When she at last showed herself, if this time she did, she would emerge through the closet door ten feet to his left. The footsteps chimed like brush strokes…. [The house] contracted, and he felt himself contract around his excitement…. He had put himself here, and now he would have to accept what occurred…. It had been waiting for him ever since the house had risen up before him like a castle rising from a plain….

That day, she told him her name.

The next, she threw off the simple things she had been wearing, then undressed him, and led him to the sheet-covered sofa. "After that, Mark felt as if branded. She brought him hand in hand to the giant's terrible bed and taught him to arrange his limbs in its grooves and hollows, which received her as well as him, so that they seemed almost to make the giant's bed beneath them as they moved" (253–254).

In the Night Room

On the heels of *lost boy lost girl* Tim Underhill pitches headlong into the mysteries of the otherworldly Realm in *In the Night Room*, where he awaits instructions from the godlike WCHWHLLDN and his minions; and where an array of apparitions ranging from the fictitious spectre of Willy Patrick to the ghosts of Lily Kalendar and Mark Underhill are ready to receive him or destroy him. Another Realm awaits. And metafictional antics are just beginning.

Mark and Lucy are revealed now to be merely characters in a fiction written by Tim Underhill, the book we know as *lost boy lost girl*. In this, Peter Straub's most overt, postmodern meta-narrative, reality and fantasy, whimsy and horror are tussling for dear life. The hints of supernatural horror in the books examined earlier now emerge full blown into an occult investigation into the Weird, fraught with ghosts, angels, and monstrous cosmic entities. At stake, moreover, is not just the "reality" of fiction but the very nature of Straub's own authorial agency. Narrative reliability is everywhere in question. *In the Night Room* stands on its head, as it were, like Lewis Carroll's "Father William." And, if we are to sort things out, it would be wise to execute the same posture. As Gary K. Wolfe has observed, *In the Night Room* is a virtual deconstruction of *lost boy lost girl*. In effect, it seeks to move its "emotional devastation of serial murders and a suicide" toward "some sort of accommodation, possibly even toward some version of grace."[84] There are ghosts to be confronted and angry spirits to be exorcised.

Consider *In the Night Room* as a "reverse angle" on *lost boy lost girl*. Straub is himself reconsidering what he has written, weighing his options. A writer has his priorities, after all. Just one way to regard his ghosts is not enough; we now see them front to back, as it were. Words in Tim's diary now achieve a very real possibility: "'You write your journal like it was fiction,'" Tim is told. He replies: "'What makes you think it isn't?'" (240).

At the novel's open, Tim is living and writing in New York. But his sense of normalcy is proving to be fragile: "In the hitherto semi-peaceable kingdom of Timothy Underhill, things appeared to be falling apart. Yesterday he had hallucinated seeing his [dead] sister and a gigantic, pissed-off angel; yesterday he had been rattle by a crazed stalker posing as a fan; today aa dead man had sent him an e-mail. Down on the street, cars and trucks crawled eastward through rain as vertical as a plumb line" (68).

Still grieving over the disappearance of his nephew, Mark returns to his hometown of Millhaven, Illinois, on a singularly strange mission He is no longer your standard amateur sleuth, apprehending serial killers Joseph Kalendar and his protégé, Lloyd-Jones, but an occult investigator prying into a crime he may have committed against them *in his books*.

Yes, Tim is writing a new book (or rewriting an earlier one). He has already published *The Divided Man* and has finished *Blood Orchid* and *A*

Beast in View.[85] In a few weeks his newest, *lost boy lost girl*, will reach the book stores. In that book, as we have seen, Tim had given Mark Underhill and Lucy Kalendar the continued life that the serial killer, Lloyd-Jones, had stolen from them: "Mark Underhill slipped away into an 'Elsewhere' with a beautiful phantom named 'Lucy Cleveland,' in reality Lily Kalendar, the daughter of Joseph Kalendar.... *She* had almost certainly died at her father's hands sometime in her fifth or sixth year, although as with Mark no remains were ever found" (15). Tim's book left them hand-in-hand, running before a darkening sky.

As if triggered by his new project, e-mails begin appearing on his computer screen from friends and former platoon members long since dead. The strangled words and inarticulate sentences are relayed by an inhabitant of a parallel world who identifies himself as "Cyrax," "a citizen of Byzantium who had been dead for six hundred years" (268). Cyrax "speaks" in a weird half-language appropriate to the sequences of letters on a keyboard. He reminds us of "Mr. X" in the book of that title, the Lovecraftian figure who sits at his desk churning out otherworldly tales in a language all his own. "'Of course, it isn't a real language,'" Cyrax explains to Tom, "'merely a system of jokes and substitution'" (103). No longer of the Earth, Cyrax is a citizen of a parallel world called The Realm. What Tim writes and does in his world affects conditions in the Realm.

Specifically, when a copy of *lost boy lost girl* reached the Realm, Joseph Kalendar's ghost, called a "sasha" (otherworld lingo for the recently deceased), was outraged at Tim's accusations that Kalendar had raped and killed his daughter. From the series of garbled e-mails in his computer, Tom learns that Kalendar was abusive, yes, but from his otherworldly perch, he insists now that he loved his daughter, in his own twisted way. He had not killed her, but had given her over to orphanage to save her life: "Maybe it was the only way he could stop abusing her" (277). Now, Tim is told, in a curiously garbled message that "winds of disorder, tides of resentment, waves of confusion" are disturbing the Realm: "You have created a DIFFICULTY & TROUBLE! You have given a **WEDGE** to **CHAOS**" (104).

Tim is summoned to Millhaven, where a "Higher Being," a "cleresyte" named WCHWHLLDN, waits for him to revisit the Kalendar home and CLEANSE the contaminations of the angry Kalendar.

"Yrs wuzs the crime, yrs will be the punishment" (109).

No detective, amateur or otherwise, had ever been given a stranger assignment!

Accompanying him on his mission, and bound up in its purpose, is a writer of Young Adult books named Willy Patrick. There are hints that there is something *strange* about this young woman and her world. Her similarities to Tim are striking. Like him, she is a writer. They share the same nightmares. She has total recall of Underhill and his books. Like Tim's character of Lily Kalendar, she had been given over to a foundling home as a child. Her new book bears the title—wait for it!—*In the Night Room*. She sometimes appears to him illuminated "in a sudden shaft of brightness" (4). She frequently lapses into a "trance," or a "daze charged with a purpose" she is unaware of (5). She is not in control of her life, and there are inexplicable gaps in her sense of time. "Sometimes it feels as though I am being *made* to do things," she says, "'like I'm a marionette, and someone else is pulling the strings'" (125).

In short, Willy is not real, although she can move freely about Tim's world. She is a creature born of his imagination, an alternate version of Lily Kalendar that didn't exist until Tim began writing about her in the new book. Her name, "Willy," was her childlike mangling of her real name, "Lily." Now, fleeing from violent events in the world of Tim's new novel, she comes face to face with her creator during Tim's book signing in a New York bookstore. Strangely drawn to him, she feels that Timothy Underhill "had something to give her; he had something to tell her; he would draw a map that she alone could read.... Without this man, she would be lost" (175). She is shocked to earn that her books, which have won numerous prizes, including a Newberry for *In the Night Room*, are not in the bookstore, not online, and don't seem to exist at all!

Tim already feels a peculiarly intimate contact with her. He says he has been "living with her for months," i.e., writing about her in his new novel about Lily Kalendar. "'I fear I'm on the verge of letting the crazy events in my life lead into my fiction,'" he writes in his diary" (137). Does her entry now into his waking world mean that their histories are now intertwined? "'Can fictional characters live out ordinary human lives, or does their existence have a term of some kind? What happens when they die?'" (183).

Similarly, the characters in *Willy's* books slip in and out of substance and visibility, subject to the "mortality" their creators endure. In a mind-boggling exercise in metafiction, the same fate threatens the fictive characters in *her own* books. Boxes within boxes. When Willy's writer friend, Tom Hartwell, is "killed" in Tim's book, his boy detective hero, Teddy Barton, begins to *disappear*. In some of the most touching pages in the book, Teddy "awakens to a world that has been altered in some subtle yet unmistakable fashion ... everything in his neighborhood seems slightly drained of color and energy. In some sense the world around him just died" (149). Tragically, he realizes "nothing new is ever going to happen to him again. His fate is uncertain. From now on, he can only go backward, through older worlds,

solving mysteries that have already been solve, and as if for the first time"
(150–151).

Straub presents some amusing consequences to these mind-boggling
interfaces of fictive and real worlds. The money that Willy has in her purse
has Tim's picture on it! When he and Willy are menaced on the road by some
thugs, Willy reminds them they are not real: "'The secret is, you're in a book.
You used to be in a book, and I did too, but something happened, and now
were here. Where we don't belong'" (249). There's an amusing and revealing
exchange with a hotel bellhop, who recognizes him. Tim tells him not to read
his latest book, since hardly anyone gets killed in it. "'You must he outta your
mind,'" the kid replies, "'who wants to read something like that?'" (257). Willy
joins in, telling Tim: "'You should write books [like that] or your career's
down the drain'" (259).

They both sense that her destiny is bound up in the return to the Kalendar house in Millhaven. However, Tim has a dark presentiment that once he
takes her inside the house, she will not come out again. He reminds her that
the tortures Lily had endured had also happened to her, but she had repressed
those events with false memories of a happy childhood: "'That is a fantasy, a
false memory you use to conceal what your life was actually like in those
years'" (229). She in turn delares, in words echoing Cyrax, that he had never
understood Lily Kalendar. She, Willy-Kalendar, "'was so much better, so much
stronger, than you thought'" (223). Unwittingly, she is defining her part in
Tim's mission to Millhaven. *"Find the real Lily Kalendar!"* [Cyrax had said].
*"See what she is! Understand the deep complexity of her self & her position, so
u know that u got WRONG! Payment must be made!"* (221).

So there they are, on the road to Millhaven, where the Kalendar house
still stands and where the ghost—or "what remains"—of an angry Kalendar
must be confronted. During their journey, a mutual erotic attraction springs
up and soon evolves into sexual intimacy—surely one of the oddest, most
unsettling couplings in literature. Autoeroticism? Literary incest! Every time
Tim makes love to her, "his invention," he becomes "more attached and more
involved, deepening the process that had started when he had placed her [in
his novel] like a figure on a chessboard" (200). One of Cyrax's weirdly garbled
messages is proving to be prophetic: *"u will have a chance of achieving something extraordinary & incestuous & ravishing unto heart melt & impossible for
every crack-brain author but u!"*

But now that Willy has emerged from Tim's book, and is in his waking
world, she is in constant danger of losing her substance, becoming transparent, flickering in and out of existence, constantly fading away. "'I don't belong
in this world, which is the reason I feel this way—the reason I'm in danger

of fading away. *Fading out.* Put me back in the world where I belong, crummy as it was. In that world I was a person, at least'" (233). Amusingly, only massive intakes of candy bars tether her to the ground. "'My whole boy feels too *light*,'" she wails (198).

Immediately on arrival in Millhaven, Tim is greeted with a disturbing vision: A large man, "built like a plow horse and wearing a long black coat that fell past his knees," is standing with his back turned before the Kalendar house. "He was the sort of man who looks like an assault weapon, and he appeared to be holding his hands over his face..." (261).

Kalendar? Ronald Lloyd-Jones? But both are dead.

"'Kalendar is playing his new book back to me,'" Tim realizes. "'*Make haste, make haste.... The Dark Man cometh....*'"

Minutes later, when Tim reaches his brother's house, he introduces Willy.

"'I'm one of your brother's fictional characters,'" she says sarcastically. "'It's a wonderful job, full of excitement, but the money's no good!'" (263).

Philip, not quite realizing what he's heard, asks, "'Is this book fact or fiction?'"

Willy interrupts: "'That's the question I always want to ask him!'" (267).

But what about Willy's counterpart, the "real" Lily Kalendar, who had survived her father's tortures and who had been turned over to an orphanage? Tim and Willy locate Lily's foster mother, Diane Huntress, who relates the terrible details about Joseph Kalendar's terrible treatment of Lily: "'He kept that child as his toy ... and he beat her and starved her, because that was his version of love'" (289). She goes on to disclose that Lily had emerged from the experience greatly damaged, physically and psychologically. Miraculously, she recovered and went on to a distinguished academic career. As a successful pediatrician, she now lives alone in Millhaven under the name of "Lily Huntress" and practices out of her home. She "'helps children, that's her life. I think she thought of it as the most beautiful thing she could do. That's the way her mind works'" (195).

Tim seeks her out. He and Willy find her at home in a modest little house located at the far end of a cul-de-sac. Unbeknownst to her, they gaze at her through a window. The moment is frozen in time:

> A woman with bright blond hair that fell to within two inches of her shoulders walked past the window holding an open book in one hand and a cup of tea in the other.... The tumult I had experienced when we came upon Lily Kalendar's street reawakened, amplified to an internal earthquake. The woman's face was turned from us, and all I could glimpse was the side and back of her head.... A moment later, we were looking at an empty window [302].

Tim notices a curious detail in her manner: "'Like her father, she hid her face whenever she could; certainly, she wanted no one to look in and see that face.

Tim is overwhelmed at the sight, at the rush of emotion that engulfs him. "It was only by a closely monitored borderline," he knows, "that she restrained herself from going out hunting exactly as [Kalendar] had…" (303). Lily has established her own uncertain accommodation with the world. The conviction and sincerity with which Straub handles this episode is, as Gary K. Wolfe declares, "one of the few moments of irreducible reality given to Underhill in either *lost boy lost boy* or *In the Night Room*."[86]

"The cruelty and wickedness she had absorbed," says Straub in a recent interview, "and for which she paid with service to her patients, still lived in her:

> Yes, I do make a point of that. Joseph Kalendar keeps his back turned. Lily does not. I took the idea from a painting by Magritte, which shows a man facing a mirror, but reflection is of *the back of his head*.[87] But Lily only averts her face. She has survived and as a doctor helps people. In *In the Night Room*, Tim and Willy find Lily in her home off in a cul-de-sac. They look through the window and see her although she doesn't see them. And she keeps her face turned away. But she doesn't turn her back, like her father does. I want the reader to know she has coped with her demons, *contracted* with them, you could say. But it's important that she realizes that she *still* has these awful impulses. She *just barely* able to control them. But she can't let people get close. That moment when she is seen through the window is, I think, the most moving moment in the book.[88]

What still lies before Tim and Willy is the visit to the Kalendar house. It is Willy, not Tim, who now seems to know what she is to do. "'I'm going to be turned back in like a counterfeit bill,'" she tells him. "'I'm some kind of *prize*. You made this mistake, and I am how you pay for it'" (309).

The Kalendar house awaits. "'We knew we had to be there,'" reflects Tim. "'We knew that 3323 North Michigan had been our goal from the moment we'd left the bookstore'" (310). The house glares at them with the "multiple eyes" of its ghostly inhabitants, while "it gathered its breath, its heartbeat pulsed, and all the while it pretended to be no more than an empty, unappealing building." You could walk by it without noticing it—"a building the eyes slid over too fast to see" (310).

Willy conquers her reluctance to enter. Ill-defined shadows fade in and out, indistinct. "'This is what I was created for,'" she whispers to Tim. "'I came into your life exactly at the moment in the book when the girl shows herself in that house. Anyway, my whole life is a sacrifice'" (313). Tim admits he doesn't know if he can go into the "night room" of tortures. He just hopes that Willy "'was going to a place I had already established for her; in a sense I had already placed her there'" (313).

Looking on is the "Clerestyle," the unpronounceable WCHWHLLDN, ready for the cleansing.

Inside, a small boy "with Willy's face" appears and takes her hand. "They were instantly in the roles Tim had given them; and he could not follow.... His Lily had joined his Mark. Perhaps one day Tim would see them again, as he had glimpsed the world's glorious, disastrous Lily Kalendar, through a car window. On these glimpses he would live; on the hope of them he would do the work of the rest of his career" (319).

It remains now for Kalendar himself to appear. "An insane fury" steams from his body.

Tim addresses him: "'I made a mistake. I thought she was dead. I didn't know you had saved her.'" Further: "'I made a lot of mistakes. I'm still making them. It's almost impossible to write the real book, the perfect book'" (321).

The menacing angel that is WCHWHLLDN brushes past Tim and enters. A great concussion shakes the house. All the pain of Kalendar's victims goes up on a colossal column of flame. Again the again the creature reappears, each time bearing away the "scraps and residue of that stinking darkness," until the house is cleansed.

WCHWHLLDN is the cosmic night crew. "He" does the cleaning. "His job, his task throughout eternity," realizes Tim, "had been purification, and he had been assigned this case. He cured infection and eliminated pollution. In his eyes, I, along with every other human being, represented a vast irritant. We carried pollution and contamination wherever we went, and we were far too imperfect to be immortal" (324).

And now Tim must write a book.

This book.

Oh, yes, there is a last scrambled e-mail from Cyrax: "*those 2 u love r in yr ELSEWHERE, which is our EDEN, from whence they began so long ago. We watch ovr them in their EDEN, self-created & beautiful to behold, u gave them that!*" (326).

The final words are a consolation, if that is what they are, that Tim very human failings, his mistakes, even his flawed books, are his strength, lodestone, and compass.

In the Night Room confirms what was already apparent in the Blue Rose books, i.e., Straub's detective stories are primarily metafictions, meditations on the writer's life, on the purposes, methods, and limits of fiction. Indeed, this is true of almost all of Straub's novels and stories. Tim is a latter-day Scheherazade, telling his stories in an attempt to bring control to his life. Fiction gives him "entry into the worst and darkest places of his life, and that entry put the pain and fear and anger right in his own hands, where he could transform them into pleasure." He had always told stories during a life of pain and violence, in and out of Vietnam, and "bit by bit fiction let him straighten out his life. It allowed him to live many lives at once, all in the peace and seclusion of his little apartment" (38). In *Ghost Story*, for example, Don Wanderley is writing *Nightwatcher* and declares, "I was just getting the feeling that everything happening has a direct relationship to my writing" (275). Similarly, Graham Williams is writing *Floating Dragon* in the novel of that name. A novel called *Night Journey* describes, fuels, and controls events in *The Hellfire Club*. Fairy tales interpenetrate and fuel the action of *Shadowland*. And we have seen how the *films noirs* in story after story both reflect and influence characters and actions.

Yet, these stories, like Tim's world—like Datchery's *Drood*—are necessarily imperfect and unfinished. They hint at a mystery story that has not yet been written. Just as his character Willy Patrick fades away when closest to Tim's reality, so Tim suffers states of invisibility at the moments when the border between him and author Peter Straub is at its thinnest.

Years before, Nathaniel Hawthorne had been haunted by this sense of his stories's inevitable *incompleteness*: "A better book than I shall ever write was there," he wrote in the prefatory pages to *The Scarlet Letter*—"leaf after leaf presenting itself to me, just as it was written out by the reality of the flitting hour, and vanishing as fast as written, only because my brain wanted the insight and my hand the cunning to transcribe it."[89] And we recall Tim's singularly apt confession to Kalendar: "'I made a lot of mistakes. I'm still making them. It's almost impossible to write the real book, the perfect book.'" Is there, perhaps, another plane of existence, some alternate location in Cyrax's Realm, where books have an ideal, perfect existence and criminal cases are neatly tidied up: "*Each volume is as its Author wisht it to be & dreamed it might be, in its Perfect State. Unflawed, Uncorrupted, Undamaged by the fevers & intoxications & hastes & forgetfulnesses of the human Author*" (106).

We had gotten hints of this early in *In the Night Room*. A mysterious character named Jasper Kohle had accosted Tim. He seems at first like one of those self-professed "fans" that persist in annoying writers with incessant demands for autographs. But there's more to Kohle than that: In one such encounter, Kohle produces *unpublished* copies of Tim's forthcoming book, *lost boy lost girl*, and declares he is searching for more. "'*One of them might be the real book*,'" he says enigmatically. "'What, you ask,'" explains Kohle, "'is the real book? The one you were supposed to write, only you screwed it up. Authors think every copy of a book is the same, but they're not.'" Every time a book goes to the presses, he explains, "'two, three, copies of the *real* book come out. *That's* the one you wanted to write when you started out, with everything perfect, no mistakes, nothing dumb, and all the dialogue and the details exactly right'" (30).

Paradoxically, the lure of the Ideal, the perfect novel, is not only unattainable but to be avoided. It's HUMANITY, not the IDEAL that the novelist must accept and celebrate. Tim wonders if he can ever write a "true" book about the ghostly and the real that inhabit both Kalendar's house and his own books. It's a seductive thought: "'It might be the 'real' book of my best book—I realized first how beautiful it must be, then how much I can learn from it. What powers would be mine, were I to read it. I could, it occurred to me, learn the real book, which was the perfect book, every time. I could be the best novelist in the world!'" But the image of April appears and with a glance reproves him. And Tim remembers that Cyrax had told him to "'pass by'" the "'IDEEL.'" He realizes, finally, "'I want no part of the ideal, I want nothing to do with it. I've seen what it does to people. Give me the messy, un-perfect world any day'" (330).

The investigations in Straub's detective stories takes us into his confidence, in effect, and reveals the limitations and frustrations of the writer's life. He admits in an interview that neither *lost boy lost girl* nor *In the Night Room* were ever "seen as a whole." Devising their strategies to balance the reality and fantasy of the existence of Tim Underhill and his character cost him endless hours of writing and rewriting:

> It took me long months to realize they should be able to be read in two different and opposed ways, to work out how to tell the reader that Tim is imagining things, inventing stuff based on details he has seen and actually telling outright lies of the hopeful variety. The reader should hold both versions of the facts at the same time: Mark is dead; Markhas been stolen away to a realm beyond death. [The whole book] can be seen as a compensatory fantasy should make it more beautiful—because of the great and moving beauty of imagined things.[90]

And so we see Tim Underhill occasionally stepping forward in the pages of *In the Night Room* voicing Straub himself, attending to his own authorial Muse, his own concerns—his own Cyrax, in effect—strategizing how to construct "the scene of the crime," how to insert characters, how far to push improbabilities, how to strategize plot manipulations, when to kill off a character, etc. He is his own muse, critic, and guide, calculating how the reader of this work will react. He confesses uncertainty about how to manipulate the character of Willy: "'When I look again at the chapter I finished last week,'" he confesses in his journal, "'its information seems to come out in too great a rush.... We have to get this information, it sets up [Willy's] flight from the villain & her discovery of the truth behind what she imagines to have been her life....'" How far can he push narrative conventions without risking generic stereotypes: "'Drag in too much exterior stuff and you've got a soap opera on your hands.'" When does he have Tim reveal to Willy her fictional identity? When does he allow the story to take control over the author? He realizes Tom and Willy, for example, are sometimes *dictating their story to him*: "'We've established the love between Willy and Tom (and, in fact, for some reason I found myself noticing a little sexual attraction between them, a kind of spark that surprises the two of them only a little more than it surprised me'" (137–138). Tim caps one of these confessional diary entries with this revealing sentence: "'I have to go back and insert some of this. It belongs in the book, not my journal'" (137–139).

Straub subjects himself to some self-criticism here. An exchange recorded in Tim's journal has Willy accusing Tim of writing fictions unduly preoccupied with pain and suffering. Tim's response is Straub's own testament: "'Willy, other people's pain does not make me feel good. It's that I don't want to overlook it or pretend it doesn't exist. I want to do it justice'" (281). When visiting Lily Kalendar's foster mother, Diane Huntress, Tim is asked about the nature of his book about Lily. He admits in the following exchange that it is a combination of fact and fiction:

> "Excuse me, Mr. Underhill [responds Huntress], but what is the point of mixing genres? Doesn't combining fiction with fact merely give you license to be sloppy with the facts?"
>
> "I think it's the other way around. [says Tim]. Fiction lets me really get the facts right. It's a way of reaching a kind of truth I wouldn't otherwise be able to discover. I like the space between. The space between dreaming and wakefulness. Between imagination and reality. Between no and yes. Between is and is not. That's where the interesting stuff is. That's where you are. You are completely a product of the space between."
>
> "Between *is* and *is not*?"
>
> "Where they both hold true, where they become one thing" [281].

Straub also takes time to take satiric jabs at his own status as a writer of dark fantasy and his penchant for damaged lives and abused children. Witness the following dialogue between Tim and his brother:

> "You never give up, do you?."
>
> "What do you mean by that?" [asks Tim].
>
> "Childhood, healing, childhood trauma ... sound familiar?"
>
> "I'm not writing about myself, Philip."
>
> "You're not *not* writing about yourself, either, are you?" [268].

And there's this wicked aside by Diane Huntress: "'Maybe I should not admit this, but I'm a big fan of your work. *I love those books you wrote with your collaborator*'" (my italics) (277)—a sly reference to Straub and King's *The Talisman* and *Black House*.

Like the fragment that is *The Mystery of Edwin Drood*, all of Straub's fiction seems *unfinished*, ultimately, a suggestive of a larger vision, of bones forever buried beneath the Juniper Tree. "The closer we think we are to understanding the shape of the dark forces that often surround his characters," writes Gary K. Wolfe, "the more we learn that we've only glimpsed a portion of the whole picture. Like a fractal coastline that at first seems to be a clear border but upon closer inspection reveals a near-infinite complex of inlets, bays, and outcroppings, the nature of evil in Straub's world is forever receding from any definitive view: There's always another story, and behind that, yet another...."[91]

Thus, the detectives in Straub are the children of Datchery. Like that disguised gentleman, they wear the masks of the stories and the criminals they pursue. And like him, their tragedy is that they exist in *half-told* tales. Their investigations are forever unfinished and inconclusive. "Fiction wants to replace life because fiction wants to be written," explains Straub. "Potential books demand to be expressed. I live by making a sort of imitation of life, but if I make it right, it has distinct reality of its own.... I get to inhabit three or four different people on any given day. I don't have a single life at all. In fact, I'm hardly there...."[92] As a wandering soul, Peter Straub himself is a child of Datchery, lost in his story, and looking for a body."[93]

Indeed, perhaps his true identity and purpose exists there ... *elsewhere*— In the Realm.

CHAPTER SIX

"The Third Voice"
Straub and Stephen King

There is some kind of third voice there that isn't Steve's and isn't mine,
but is just the voice of *The Talisman*.

—Peter Straub[1]

When Peter Straub first met Stephen King in London in 1970, he suggested that they were the "Hammett and Chandler" of the horror genre. King's blunt, tough-minded prose and propulsive narrative drive suggest the Dashiell Hammett of *The Maltese Falcon*; and Straub's "poetic" diction and "literary" pretensions provoke comparisons with the Raymond Chandler of *The Long Goodbye* (a novel Straub openly admires and frequently quotes in his own stories). Like Hammett and Chandler, Straub and King had encountered marginalization at the hands of the literary establishment. "[Stephen] knew what I meant," remembers Straub in an early essay, "that our genre had to live in the wider world of literature or it was merely a warped species of children's novel, that it had to be as well written as any other sort of novel to be worth anything.... We wanted to take our chances in the world outside the ghetto of horror-fantasy...."[2]

We will remember, and perhaps contest, this comparison/contrast as we plunge into the epic novels they wrote together, *The Talisman* (1984) and *Black House* (1999); and in their Vietnam-related novels written separately, Straub's *Koko* (1988) and King's *Hearts in Atlantis* (1999). A brief interview with King, conducted especially for this book, is appended at the end.

Flying Men

Early in *The Talisman*, as young Jack Sawyer rambles along the Western Road in search of adventure, he witnesses a bizarre scene. Winged men launch

146

themselves off a high tower and soar high above him (are the wings real or manmade?). Their flight seems easy and graceful—until a closer look reveals how hard the men must work to defy gravity. "That such a reversal should demand so much and last such a short time was terrible," Jack realizes, "but

Peter Straub and his son Ben with Stephen King, London, 1978 (courtesy Fales Archive).

that people would go for it anyway was both terrible and wonderful" (280). It's an epiphany of transcendence, like the "rainbow, rainbow, rainbow" of Elizabeth Bishop's celebrated poem. (281).[3] "*These people live in a mystery,*" marvels Jack. "*It's joy that holds them up*" (280).

The vision of the Flying Men sustains Jack on his own "flight," his epic trek westward, from coast to coast, toward terrors as yet unknown and a confrontation that may alter the fate of this and *other* worlds. With the "wings" of his innocence and enduring faith, he contends with his own "gravity," the weight of experience, cynicism, and doubt. On the road behind him his father has died and his mother lies dying of cancer; up ahead is a mysterious Black Hotel that houses a magical Talisman, whose healing powers can heal his mother.

But Jack's journey is not finished. In the sequel, *Black House*, a still greater cosmic horror awaits, a climax of apocalyptic proportions from which he will emerge transformed and transfigured, no longer a part of this world.

Published in 1984 and 1999, respectively, *The Talisman* and *Black House* seem, at first, to be greatly different from each other in ambition, tone, and diction. And to a degree, this indeed, is the case. "[*The Talisman*] was a novel that did not seem to demand a sequel," wrote critic Gary K. Wolfe, "even though the Territories, like many evocative fantasy worlds, looked like an eminently franchisable arena for more of the same."[4] Moreover, *The Talisman's* rambling, episodic, brightly illumined quest narrative contrasts with *Black House's* more tightly-focused, *noirish* detective story. Both Straub and King are themselves studies in contrasting attitudes and techniques. Yet, I would argue that both books ultimately display similar thematic concerns and possess in common a unified narrative "voice." Indeed, Straub and King have insisted these two books offer not a collection of different voices and attitudes, but a *conflation* of narrative concerns and authorial identities. Putting it another way, says Straub, the books "speak" neither as Straub nor King—nor Hammett and Chandler—but in "a *third* voice" that is neither. That assertion bears scrutiny.

A brief overview is in order. The first book, *The Talisman*, is a loose-limbed tale about rambling—and sometimes flying—creatures and people. We nip at Jack's heels on the way to the Black Hotel, letting the narrative take us where it will. Dubbed "Travellin Jack" by his friend and mentor, Speedy Parker, Jack has the rare ability to "flip" back and forth from the waking world to its dream-like alternate reality, the Territories. This is a largely agrarian, medieval world that is devoid of technology and ruled by magic. "'[It] might be a somewhere a fellow could get to,'" says Speedy, "'get to anytime he liked, that is, if he wanted to see it bad enough'" (42). This world *glows* with an "incredible clarity of the air," a clarity of morality and compassion, that stimulates Jack's harmony of mind and body in a way "that in an adult would have been a dangerous overload" of madness and hallucination (69). It lends him in his travels a peculiar aspect. A farmer encountered along the journey gazes upon him in wonder: "This unwashed boy sitting beside him was beautiful ... [and possessed] a kind of straightforward goodness that had only been dented by a host of unusual experiences" (290). Indeed, others are noticing that Jack is "gaining some sort of power, almost like an electrical charge" (305). He will need it in his final confrontation in the Black Hotel.

Populating the Territories are "twinners," people who are *Doppelgänger*, if you will, counterparts of their selves in the "real" world. The twinner of Jack's ailing mother, a faded movie actress named Lily Cavanaugh (who was billed in her time as the "Queen of the B Movies"), is Laura DeLoessian, Queen of the Territories, likewise lying sick and languishing near death. The twinner of his wicked and scheming Uncle Morgan Sloat, a Hollywood agent and former business partner of his father, and who contrives to wrest control of the family holdings from his mother, is a despot named Morgan of Orris. He seeks to control the Territories by introducing the pollutants of modern atomic weapons technology. And Speedy Parker's twinner is a mysterious character named Parkus, whose true identity and purpose are yet to be revealed. As for Jack's twinner, Jason DeLoessian was killed at a young age as the result of the machinations of Morgan of Orris.

As all of them commingle and stray from place to place, from world to world, so the storylines in both worlds intertwine as they move from subject to subject. The boundaries everywhere are permeable. Events in the Territories trigger changes in the real world, sometimes with catastrophic consequences. Even the very act of Jack's "flipping" can create unwonted disturbances. As Jack traverses the lushly beautiful Territories and beyond to the sterile terrain of the Blasted Lands, where he battles grotesque monstrosities spawned by atomic experiments in the real world, he arrives at last at the Black Hotel. Facing still greater terrors, he seizes the Talisman, which blazes and sings in his hands. It opens "a hole between worlds" and releases a blaze of light that destroys the villainous Morgan (885–887). The joy of the Flying men is his again.

Rainbow, rainbow, rainbow...

We can regard *The Talisman* itself as a kind of "twinner" of other classic quest narratives, including Tolkien's "Ring" Trilogy and Mark Twain's *Tom Sawyer* and *Huckleberry Finn* (to which there are overt allusions). In his commentary on the book, Bill Sheehan reveals significant parallels with Twain, particularly in *The Talisman's* subtext of slavery, which will be extended and amplified in *Black House*.[5] I would suggest in addition perhaps a less obvious, but likewise useful, comparison to another classic serio-comic novel of picaresque adventures and high villainy, Charles Dickens's *Nicholas Nickleby* (1839).[6] Straub himself frequently cites Dickens and his writings as important influences on his work.[7] Like poor young, fatherless Nicholas, walking the High Road while striving to extricate his mother from the machinations of his uncle, the monstrous Ralph Nickleby, fatherless Travellin' Jack treads both worlds to save his dying mother from the clutches of *his* uncle, Morgan Sloat. Jack's encounters with Queen Laura's colorfully theatrical Summer Pavilion has its counterpart in Nicholas's recruitment in "Vincent Crummles's Theatrical Company," and his destruction of both Sunlight Gardener's Scripture Home for Wayward Boys and the Thayer School—both fronts for the exploitation and abuse of children in the Territories—recall Nicholas's overthrow of Dotheboys Hall and the brutal headmaster, Wackford Squeers. Moreover, just as Nicholas is aided in the end by a gallery of supportive characters, including a lowly boy named Smike, who sacrifices himself for his friend, Jack wins the day with the help of his new friend, a shape-changer named Wolf, who is also martyred for the cause.

As we turn to *Black House*, we are reminded of yet another novel by Dickens, *Bleak House* (1853), which Straub on several occasions has cited as his favorite Dickens novel), whose title bears more than a coincidental similarity to *Black House*, and whose text Jack reads to the blind Henry Leyden in the early chapters. Whereas *The Talisman* and *Nicholas Nickleby* are examples of the picaresque narrative of travel, of going from place to place, *Black House* and *Bleak House* are nightmares of moody atmosphere and cyclic construction, revolving around a fixed center. Their stories and characters are anchored to their domestic structures. They are permanent addresses. No matter when and where events and characters may occur and stray, they keep coming back to the titular Black House. As G.K. Chesterton says, this is a kind of story formula "with a recurrent melody and poetic justice," possessing "artistic constancy and artistic revenge."[8]

"Travellin' Jack" is now "Hollywood Jack," a retired Los Angeles police detective, grown disillusioned and cynical. He no longer rambles along the Western Road. His "glow" has greatly diminished, just as the Talisman has dwindled away to a faded memory. As the story opens, he has decided to reverse his direction and travel eastward, where he comes to ground in the little Wisconsin town of French Landing. A serial killer is loose. Three children have already been murdered, and a fourth is currently missing. Jack is reluctant at first to take up the case. Yet, a vestige of the glory that was his at the end of *The Talisman* remains. The lure of the Talisman, like an addictive drug, had aroused in him a "hunger" and "a need without a name" (69). Now, in *Black House*, this yearning impels him to take up the case.

As Jack goes in pursuit of the missing boy and the killer known as "The Fisherman"—so-called because his killings seem to be imitating the methods of the notorious serial killer and cannibal, Albert Fish.[9] He enlists the help of a gallery of vividly realized characters, including a group of disaffected bikers, the "Thunder Five"; a blind radio personality named Henry Leyden; and, eventually, his old mentor Speedy Parker. His quarry is elusive. In the course of the story The Fisherman shifts in and out of a variety of identities and names, including "Burnside," "Bierstone," and "Munshun." We first encounter him as an Alzheimer's patient in an Elder Care Unit, who mysteriously disappears from time to time to conduct his killing sprees. He is "something not human," the ultimate Outsider: "Here is a true American loner, an internal vagrant, a creature of shabby rooms and cheap diners, of aimless journeys resentfully taken, a collector of wounds and injuries lovingly fingered and refingered" (33). Jack fears The Fisherman is planning a particularly horrible fate for the missing boy, Tyler Marshall. Indeed, it develops that Jack shares a kinship with the child and will eventually forge a common bond with him.

Meanwhile, Jack pursues another investigation, one that takes him *inward*, into the repressed memories of past events in the Territories. Recovery of them will enable him to retrieve vestiges of the strange powers once afforded him by the magical Talisman. Even if he no longer feels the intoxicating, innocent joy he shared with the Flying Men, he retrieves in this new case at least a vestige of that "joy," an inner compulsion toward "something vital" he needs to detect" (383). The consequences of his investigation, which climaxes inside the cosmic portal that is known as Black House, exact a great personal cost.

Journey's Ends

In both books, Jack's rescue missions take him beyond the Territories into terrible regions of surpassing corruption and evil. In *The Talisman*, he has to venture through the gauntlet of the nightmarish Blasted Lands—a sterile terrain populated with grotesque monstrosities that are the result of nuclear experiments in the real world of the American West—to a final confrontation with the twinner of his villainous Uncle Morgan at the Black Hotel. In that battle, the Talisman "blazed and sung in his hands," "opened a hole between worlds" granted Jack a vision of many worlds, and released a blaze

of light that destroyed Morgan. The joy Jack had felt at the Flying Men—
"rainbow, rainbow, rainbow"—returns to him then (885–887).

His destination in *Black House* is another of those haunted dwellings
that are literally the foundation of the Gothic tale. The titular structure is
introduced as a "Castle of Terrors" that would not be out of place in an amuse-
ment park. Not just any spooky place, it is a tesseract house, an "insane"
structure not entirely of this world. "[It is] a house that won't keep its shape
but whirls and wavers in a most distressing way." At times it is no bigger than
a humble shack, but, "a blink, and it seems to be a ragged monolith that blots
out the entire sky." It is, in fact, "almost infinite," disclosing worlds upon
worlds (616). Herein is the gateway to the malevolent presence known only
as the Crimson King, who controls a vast enterprise of slave labor. A towering
machine of belts and gears, known as the Big Combination, enslaves a million
children, some of this world, some not, who labor and perish beneath the
wheel under the cruel whips and lashes of the grotesque Overseers. These
are the "lost" children of every world, "[whose] faces we have seen on milk
cartons and flyers headed MISSING and on child-find Web sites, faces from
the dreams of heartbroken mothers and desolate fathers" (803). Not even the
Dickens of *Nicholas Nickleby*'s Dotheboys Hall and *Bleak House*'s Chancery
could have envisioned such horrors.

As noted, the moral concern over slavery and the exploitation of children
are important binding elements in both *The Talisman* and *Black House*. Jack's
wanderings in *The Talisman* had already introduced the subject and brought
him into contact with the realities of slavery (160). There, the exploitation of
the children in the aforementioned Sunlight Home had its analogue in the
slave pits of the Territories, a perversion introduced into those otherwise
benign lands by the twinner of Morgan Sloat. Jack wonders if these horrors
had somehow inspired the grotesque gargoyles of Medieval cathedrals: Had
an artisan from the Middle Ages somehow "flipped over, saw this place, and
thought he'd had a vision of hell?" (492). Now, with *Black House*, the enslave-
ment of children is amplified into literally cosmic proportions.

He encounters a monstrous plot by an elusive, numinous figure known
only as "The Crimson King," who is bent on annihilating all of existence.
Jack realizes that the Blasted Lands, through which he had traveled as a boy
on his way to the climactic battle in the Black Hotel, were evidence of a con-
tagion corrupting the Territories. That corruption has now grown worse. A
great burning Tower, the reverse image of the benign structure from which
the Flying Men took flight in *The Talisman* (497), is dominating the land. It
is like a great, cosmic axle around which many wheels—many worlds—
revolve. Criss-crossing force beams hold the Tower in place like guy wires.

But most of the Beams are down and only one is still holding it in place. Plotting the overthrow of the Tower by breaking that Beam are the Crimson King and his minions, who are known as Breakers. Arrayed against them are figures of special powers known as Gunslingers. And in the battle against the Crimson King, Jack finds an ally in young Tyler Marshall. Tyler, whom we remember as the missing fourth victim of the Fisherman, is unaware that he possesses great latent powers as a Breaker. It is Jack Sawyer's task to rescue the boy from the clutches of the Crimson King in the Black House, release his powers as a Breaker, turn those powers against the Crimson King, and free the millions of enslaved children toiling on the great wheels of the aforementioned Big Combination.

We recognize Tyler as the counterpart of Jack's former youthful innocence. Just as his adopted father, Speedy, had taught Jack how to locate and exploit his inner powers, so now Jack performs the same mentorship for Tyler. Once the son, Jack is now the father. Together, with the help of the residual magic of the Talisman, they will destroy the Crimson King and his dreadful deputies. What ensues is a veritable apocalypse of carnivalesque horrors spanning numberless worlds: "Evils shrivel and disperse; despots choke to death on chicken bones; tyrants fall before assassins' bullets before the poisoned sweetmeats arrayed by their treacherous mistresses; hooded torturers collapse dying on bloody stone floors ... on and on, worlds upon worlds collapsing" (802).

Jack has regained at last that simple clarity of joy he first felt as a boy while watching the Flying Men. In short, he is *travelling* again. He *is* Travelin Jack: "Everything seems touched by a higher meaning.... His blood sings in his veins.... Beauty and terror, beauty and pain—there is no way out of the conundrum." Jack is fully aware "of the world's essential fragility, its constant, unstoppable movement toward death, of the deeper awareness that in that movement lies the source of all its meaning" (679).

No longer a mere visitor, he is now a *citizen* of the Territories. Although in the end he is killed by an assassin's bullet, thanks to the residual protection of the Talisman he will still live—but only henceforth in the Territories. They had been his "wellspring" as a child; and now they claim him as an adult, never relinquishing him again to his former world. In a nod toward what surely will be a third book in this series, Jack's friend Speedy (whose name is "Parkus" in the Territories) observes, "'He's a creature of the Territories now. And God the Carpenter knows there's work for him over here. The business of the Tower is moving toward its climax. I believe Jack Sawyer may have a part to play in that...'" (830).

A Dark Tower?

Those readers of *Black House* who may be bewildered by the many references to a Dark Tower, a Crimson King, Gunslingers, and Breakers, etc., will, upon due reflection, recognize allusions to that great cycle of stories by Stephen King, collectively known as the *Dark Tower* books. Taken together, *The Talisman* and *The Black House* lay a claim to belong to that series.[10] We recall that in the first book Jack's removal of the Talisman from the Black Hotel—which may have been an analogue of the Dark Tower itself—released a flux of realities, among which may have been a glimpse of the Tower. *Black House* suggests that as a consequence of Jack's actions in *The Talisman*, the Dark Tower had become vulnerable to the Crimson King and his Breakers. The Territories were polluted, and time and space began to unravel. It needed the efforts of Jack Sawyer—not "Travellin Jack," not "Hollywood Jack," but "*Gunslinger Jack*"—and young Tyler Marshall, a nascent Breaker, to bring down the Crimson King and the Big Combination.

Worlds within worlds … novels within novels … the works of King and Straub themselves, merged…

Regarding the promise already held out, that Jack may have a part to play in a projected third volume to follow *Black House*, we can only speculate. As critic Bill Sheehan reports, Jack Sawyer has had no other role in King's stand-alone subsequent *Dark Tower* books. Perhaps this will force the two collaborators to reconsider the direction a third book will take.[11]

Consider *The Talisman* and *Black House*, collectively, as the Aleph in the Borges short story, a point in space that contains all other points—in this case, not only all the characters, tropes, and effects of the Gothic and Quest genres but those of the stories of Straub and King, in particular.[12] The devices of the Talisman and the Black House are themselves Alephs. When young Jack first lays eyes on the floating globe of the Talisman, he gazes entranced upon a sphere of unbearable brilliance that contains "all possible worlds," a "universe of worlds," where characters and places keep flipping back and forth, "jammed up like a triple exposure on film" (763), and whose unbearable whiteness is "true goodness" (829). By contrast, the Black House encountered by the adult Jack is a perversion of the Talisman, an infernal Funhouse of whirling vortexes of all things perverse and corrupt.

The striking narrative "voice," of *Black House*, Aleph-like, speaks in past-present-future tense. It freely ranges across the geographical and social space of French Landing, visits the houses and introduces the characters figuring in the narrative—all the while commenting and speculating about unfolding events, even issuing cautionary advisories to the reader—"If you choose to go on, never say you weren't warned" (807). Early in our tour, a mysterious bee appears at the scene of one of the Fisherman's victims, its aspect mysteriously radiant. There is a hint that its presence, too, will figure in future events. There are even moments when the narrator slyly makes a metatextual reference to the "other storytellers," namely King and Straub. And at one point, it even seems to echo the tone and atmosphere of the opening pages of Dickens's *Bleak House*: "Let us slip through the fog, then, silent as a dream…" (398). But for most of the time, like the omniscient eye of a television camera, it holds itself at a remove from the story, an ironically detached omniscient presence. "We are not here to weep," proclaims the opening pages of *Black House*. "We have come to observe, register, and record the impressions, the afterimages, left in the comet trail of the mystery." But then again, it becomes a voice of tender compassion. Pulling back at one point from a scene of gruesome horror, the voice gently comforts us: "A deep, deep gravity flows outward from the scene, and this gravity humbles us.… We must honor this scene…" (47).

It remains to be said that the device of alternate worlds is a tradition as old as another, related genre, the Fairy Tale. As we discussed earlier in these pages in our examination of Peter Straub's *Shadowland*, it began in the tradition of oral storytelling, developed in the Tales of the Brothers Grimm and the *Kunstmärchen* of Novalis and E.T.A. Hoffmann; came to America in the stories of Nathaniel Hawthorne; matured in latter-day storytellers Lord Dunsany and Arthur Machen; and reached its modernist apotheosis with storytellers Straub, A.S. Byatt, Neil Gaiman, Philip Pullman, Angela Carter, and others. Here, suffice to say, Jack's epiphany, his awareness "of the world's essential fragility," his realization, as Speedy says, that the Territories "might be a somewhere a fellow could get to … if he wanted to see it bad enough," echoes the words of that quintessential fairy tale, Hoffmann's classic, "The Golden Pot": "While you are in this [fairy] region that is revealed to us in dreams at least, try … to recognize the famil-

Stephen King

iar shapes that hover around you in the ordinary world. Then you will discover that this glorious kingdom is much closer to you than you ever imagined."[13]

Twin-Speak

When Peter Straub and Stephen King decided to collaborate on *The Talisman* and, later, its sequel, *Black House*, they sought to take the books, as mentioned, "outside the ghetto of horror-fantasy...."

Let Straub and King define each other. To begin with, nobody writes better *about* Stephen King, and with more obvious affection, than Peter Straub. While working with King on *The Talisman*, Straub took time to write an engaging essay, "Meeting Stevie," in appreciation of his partner. "He possesses all the virtues of the ideal Boy Scout," he wrote, "possibly excepting reverence, if the ideal Boy Scout drinks a lot of beer and has a taste for fancy cars." There is more than a touch of respectful envy of King's drive and production: "If he were locked in an elevator overnight, he'd tell stories to himself until the janitor got him out in the morning. Really, you know—and this is easy to say—I love him and don't know what I'd do without him."[14] Similarly, no one writes more perceptively about Straub than Stephen King. As early as 1981, he was praising at length Straub's early novels, *Julia, You Could See Me Now*, and *Ghost Story*: "Straub seems aware that he is carrying a basket dangerously filled with horrors, and turns the fact splendidly to his own advantage."[15] A little later, with the publication of *The Talisman*, King added, "He is, simply, the best writer of supernatural tales that I know." His books "smack neither of tired academic ennui or foolish self-indulgence. Instead there is the clean enthusiasm of the authentically crazy human being—the sort of dudes who staggered back from the wilderness with the skin around their eyes blasted black by the sun of visions and a scorpion or two crawling in their hair."[16]

Before their first face-to-face encounter, in 1977, Straub reports that King for him was just "a name on a blurb" that had been written in support of Straub's early novel *Julia*. King's comment "was easily the most insightful" of the various responses the book received. "Stephen King showed in a few sentences that he understood what I was trying to do—he had a sort of immediate perception of my goals. So I filed the name away...." Months later, while browsing in a London bookstore, Straub bought 'Salem's Lot "with no expectations." The book immediately "claimed him." "King was not fooling around" with the trappings of the vampire formula, enthused Straub—"he was just slapping the cards on the table." Most impressive, continued Straub, "was the way [King] had cleared a high fence without even breathing hard. Stephen King became one of my favorite writers on the spot." After another insightful blurb from King about Straub's *If You Could See Me Now*, "it was clear that if I had an ideal reader anywhere in the world, it was probably Stephen King." Not only did King's aims and ambitions seem very close to his own, but Straub responded to the "seriousness, to the driven nature of his writing," to a fellow writer who "was serious about the shape and tone of his writing, and he wanted to work with the real stuff of the world…. He invested his characters with feeling; he was tender toward them." At the same time, Straub recognized some fundamental differences between them. "Good taste has no role in his thinking: he was unafraid of being loud and vulgar, of presenting his horrors head-on … into the garish beauty of the gaudy." For Straub this spelled a personal release: "He armored my ambition."[17]

After exchanging some letters, they met at last in a London bar in 1976. King had come to London on vacation. Straub was living there at the time. This was followed by a visit to Straub's house for dinner, where the whole King family "burst in full of energy, on a torrent of talk"; and later a "raucous, riotous" Thanksgiving dinner at King's rented house. According to critic Bill Sheehan, it was King who first suggested to Straub that they collaborate on a novel..[18] He was just coming off *Pet Sematary* and Straub from *Floating Dragon*. When the paperback rights to King's *Danse Macabre* was sold to Berkeley Books, he and Straub now had in common two major publishers, G. P. Putnam and Viking Press, and the promise of a healthy advance. The possibility of a film deal even loomed on the horizon.

When Straub returned to America in 1982 from his prolonged London stay, he set to work with King on a storyline for what became *The Talisman*. It was a hectic time. He was still working on *The Floating Dragon* and Stephen King had three books about to hit the market, *Pet Sematary*, *Christine*, and *Cycle of the Werewolf*. "Some people tried to warn us off the project," Straub remembers, "on the basis that doing this would destroy our friendship, and at times, it was kind of a strain. We're still good friends, though."[19]

After a protracted delay working out publishing logistics for their respective separate projects, and after batting around ideas with each other, they set to work long distance via word processors. Straub documented the process in an interview in 1985 in an interview in *Writer's Digest*, just a year and a half after *The Talisman* was published. He bought an IBM DisplayWriter and learned quickly that it offered special features and mechanical shortcuts unavailable on standard typewriters. Straub in Connecticut and King in Maine hooked up their word processors long-distance on a Wang System 3 via telephone modem. "The IBM is a very adaptable machine," explained Straub; "and by fooling around with the codes on mine, I could make it possible for 99% of our stuff to go through without a hitch. There were only a few little problems, most of which had to do with the disparity in the codes for underlining. For some reason, the codes for italicizing didn't match, and we had to put in other symbols to replace the symbols for italicizing."

At other times, they worked shoulder-to-shoulder:

> Steve came down from Maine to my house in Westport. We both had big yellow pads and pens, and we jointly worked out an outline for the first 400 or 500 pages. Then Steve started to type up these notes that we made. I noticed that he added his imagination to these notes, making them more specific and details.... Steve and I actually wrote the beginning couple of chapters together on my word processor. We were in my office at my house in Connecticut. He'd sit down for a little bit and write something, and then I'd sit down. He'd look over my shoulder. Now that was a great way to start.... Then he drove back to Maine.

For the next few days, Straub typed up the rest of the outline, elaborating on it and "making it more concrete": "By the time I was done, we had about a 30–35-page outline that was very specific, even with dialogue. Then we assigned each other parts of the outline.... It was more like he'd do about 100 pages, and I'd do 75 pages, and then he'd do about 200 pages. He does write a lot more than I do...."

They were very much aware that there was a difference in their styles. Straub had already consciously assumed the mantle of Raymond Chandler. "This is extremely pretentious," he confessed, looking back from the standpoint of 1985, "but I thought that, in a way, I was trying to improve, to raise the standards of, the horror genre a little bit.... I did try to do in horror something of what Chandler had done." While admitting that he "did not succeed in writing Raymond Chandlerish horror novels," he did admit to "some interesting things" and "created some effects" that might not have been possible otherwise." To try to get around stylish inconsistencies, he and King agreed to write the book in "as simple and flat a style as possible, because the material itself was so strong that we didn't want to undermine it by having style call attention to itself...." Upon completion, they went through it separately, "taking big chunks out of it and trying to change things around." While Straub says he loves cutting, King "loathes" it. "He doesn't want to give up a thing. But every book is improved by pruning, I think, and Steve bit the bullet a couple of times."[20]

From the beginning, both Straub and King discount any distinct authorial voice, neither specifically Chandler nor Hammett, Straub nor King, but a *third* voice, a "peculiar voice, which isn't the voice of either of us."[21] And in 2001 we find Straub qualifying the "Chandler-Hammett" comparison: "No,

Steve is as literary as he has to be," he said in a typically tongue-in-cheek interview for the *Hellfire* journal, "and I'm fed up with being described as some kind of embalmed mandarin who thinks in polysyllabic, orotund sentences. If I were that guy, nobody would buy my books."[22] At the same time, *Talisman* had been greeted by critic Gary K. Wolfe as "oddly uncharacteristic of the work of either author," belonging "more to Tolkien."[23]

Both men appeared at a World Fantasy Convention in 1984 on the heels of the publication of *The Talisman* and addressed the issue. King declared it was not a "horror" novel but a "fantasy," that it was "gross in places" and "horrifying" in places—"but on the whole it has a tone that is a little bit delirious and sort of crackbrained, and I think it's a lot of fun!"[24] Which is a pretty fair assessment. King compared the process to "making a coat," where the pieces had to be carefully dyed and joined: "I can point out a number of places in the book," he said, "where it looks as though you might sense that I had written it, and yet I know damn well that Peter wrote it." Straub playfully took up the subject: "In fact, the book is full of little tricks between us where we're trying to fool the reader into thinking that the other guy wrote it. And if you come along something you think is a dead giveaway, the thing with a dead giveaway is a trick...." In sum, Straub concludes, "[It] isn't Steve's and isn't mine, but is just the voice of *The Talisman*. In fact, my wife can't tell what parts I wrote and what parts Steve wrote, and Steve's wife can't tell."

Further complicating things are admissions by Straub and King that working together influenced their own approaches to writing. "I learned a lot about style," confessed King, noting Straub's notoriously precise diction and careful prose rhythms. "I can't remember ever writing anything and being so conscious about what I was writing." Straub revealed a new emphasis on pure "narrative"; he has learned to "revise" more and his "instincts about storytelling were broadened up, as if some rough spots were knocked off."[25]

The Name Game

Where does that leave us? With rhetorical questions, mostly. Is it relevant to anything in particular to play the game of "Spot the Author"? Doubtless, Straub and King would pull a "Mission Impossible" strategy and disavow all knowledge of our speculations. Yet, undaunted, we forge ahead.... It might first be supposed that certain incidents, characters, and prose passages might reveal more of Straub than King, and vice-versa. The material concerning the "Dark Tower," for example, might be presumed to belong only to King. That is true, but only to a degree. In a recent interview, Straub reveals that he, not King, is primarily responsible for the inclusion of the "Dark Tower" mythos:

> I had been reading Steve's *Hearts in Atlantis* and was struck by the character of Ted Brautigan in the first story, "Low Men in Yellow Coats." I already knew something about Steve's "Dark Tower" ideas, but I didn't know about what he called "Breakers." He had not yet explained anything about that. I wanted to learn more about that on my own. Then I contacted him and suggested we work those materials into the end of *Black House*. It was my idea. Yes, I think you can find implications of that in *The Talisman*, too—but that's more just because we find ourselves thinking along the same lines sometimes. Anyway, I remember Steve calling me on the phone, all excited about having just come up with the idea of the "Big Combination." He was running with it. It's how we have learned to work together. The amazing thing about Steve is that he can start from "zero" and reach "100" in a short time. Like a sprinter off the blocks, or a race car. So he wrote the Dark Tower stuff and the Big Combination in the last part of *Black House*.

Straub is happy with these inclusions, although, he adds, "I don't think they'll be developed further in the third book."

In addition to the Dark Tower-related material, Straub acknowledges that King was responsible for passages at the end of the book about Jack's transfiguration into a new incarnation in the Territories: "It was better than I could do. I credit him for that."[26]

Serial killers and damaged children are, of course, ongoing preoccupations with Straub, but they are not his exclusive province alone. Of course not. They are just as important in King's fiction, as well. Perhaps we're on firmer ground with the prolonged sequence in *Black House*, when Jack Sawyer makes his way down the Rabbit Hole of the House's grotesquely haunted interior. We are reminded of Straub's penchant for the carnivalesque sideshows in books written before the *Talisman* and *Black House*, already noted in the circus performance in "Magic Taxi," Dr. Rabbitfoot's carnival in *Ghost Story*, and the "Theater of Illusions" in *Shadowland*. Is this not the "voice" of Straub? "In a long, narrow room like a Pullman car, living cartoons—two rabbits, a fox, a stoned-looking frog wearing white gloves—sit around a table catching and eating what appear to be fleas. They are *cartoons*, 1940s-era black-and-white *cartoons*.... The rabbit tips Jack a knowing wink as the Sawyer Gang goes by..." (779). Everywhere there are Straubian descriptions of the "glow" and the "incredible clarity" of the light in the Territories, such as this description early in *The Talisman* of a sunny day, with all the painterly qualities that illumine so much of Straub's prose: "The next day the sun was back—a hard bright sun that layered itself like paint over the fat beach and the slanting, re-tiled strip of roof Jack could see from his bedroom window. A long, low wave far out in the water seemed to harden in the light and sent a spear of brightness straight toward his eyes" (31).

Another device typical of Straub is his description of an epiphany experienced by Jack. As he begins to recover the preternatural abilities he had temporarily lost at the end of *The Talisman*, he suffers one of those transformative moments we find in so many of his stories, wherein the character's extreme emotional state of mingled beauty, terror, and pain reveals the essential "fragility" of the world—rendering him *transparent*, vanishing before our eyes...

And what about the "Red, Red Robin" song that we recall used earlier in *Floating Dragon* as a kind of magical protection mantra? And there is that "travellin'" narrative voice that sets the opening scenes in *Black House*. We feel a compassion toward his characters and the sympathy and empathy for the horrors they endure: "We must honor this scene—the flies, the dog worrying the severed foot, the poor, pale body of Irma Freneau, the magnitude of what befell Irama Freneau—by acknowledging our littleness" (47). Our suspicions of Straub's authorship here are confirmed. During a recent interview I suggested the narrative voice was not unlike the Stage Manager in Thornton Wilder's *Our Town* (1938): "I wrote the beginning of *Black House*, that long introduction to the scene. It took me a long time. As you say, I did feel like a tour guide, a little like the Stage Manager in Wilder's play. I didn't know at the time that Wilder had also written that dark picture of smalltown life in Hitchcock's *Shadow of a Doubt*. How about that?! It is like my portrait of a Midwestern town in *Houses Without Doors*" ("A Short Guide to the City"). Straub adds, ruefully, "Some people *hate* that long introduction to *Black House*. They say it slows down getting into the story. But Steve loved it. And so do I."[27]

Add to that the citation of the poetry of Elizabeth Bishop, the gallery of damaged and victimized children, and the depredations of the serial killer, the Fisherman.

On the other hand, as critic Bill Sheehan has pointed out, do we not sense a certain blunt, "Hammett-esque" straightforward prose style in the long section in *Black House* called "The Taking of Tyler Marshall"? Here the action crosscuts from The Fisherman in the Elder Care Ward to the kidnapping of the boy. It is also in this section that allusions to the Crimson King of the *Dark Tower* saga are first introduced. Some of the characters in both books also suggest King's penchant for bizarre creatures and brutal violence: In *The Talisman* there is the memorable characterization of Jack's shape-changing friend, Wolf (vide *Cycle of the Werewolf*), who single-handedly destroys the Sunlight Home. In *Black House* we have the broadly-sketched heroics of the members of the motorcycle gang called The Thunder Five. Tyler Marshall's killing of The Fisherman/Burnside is a guignol exercise in visceral horror. And there is the manifestation of the Crimson King himself as an unexpectedly absurd, comic figure wearing a vest festooned with bones: "[He is] a shuffling, busy figure in a black suit and a flowing red tie ... with a vast white face dominated by a red mouth and a single blurry eye ... like Humpty-Dumpty gone bad" (788).

But what do we make of other, aspects of the story that seem to elude ready identification? I refer specifically to the weird "bee" motif introduced in the opening pages of *Black House*. Indeed, bees are everywhere, buzzing singly, swarming constantly. At first, a single bee mysteriously appears, rising above the mutilated body of the Fisherman's third victim: "It has ceased to be a welcome distraction and has been absorbed into the surrounding mystery.... The speaking bee circles back to the window and passes into another world, and, following its lead, we move on..." (47–48). Then, bees appear in greater number at critical moments as a magical protective shield against the evil forces arrayed against Jack. They impart a spiritual quality to the otherwise disturbing events: They appear "almost *illuminated*, like the radiant pages of a sacred text," and their "massed buzzing is low and harmonious, as peaceable as a Protestant hymn" (672–673). They settle protectively about his body, "like a blessing" (672–673). And they lead the way through the Black House in the concluding chapters. Not since Samuel Beckett have there been such raptures about the secret life of bees.[28]

What is going on? A moment's reflection suggests an answer: We recall that Jack's mother, now dead, was once dubbed the "Queen of the B Movies"— the "*Queen of the Bs.*" Are we are prepared to make the leap and see the "bees" as the manifestation of the protective presence of his mother, the moral center of his life? It's a strangely beautiful touch and seemingly wholly out of the provinces of both Straub and King. Unless ... unless we remember that in other Straub stories we find many references to bees and other insects—like this tiny detail from *Ghost Story*, whose climactic moments depict the defeat of the wicked Eva Galli: Her death is not final—a tiny insect appears...

What's important is the *commonality* achieved by the two men, a quality, or presence that is not easily detectable, but conveyed in a kind of literary counterpoint. It finds painterly analogues in the work of artist Paul Klee, who theorizes that "invisible lines" are suggested by the sporadic intersections of two or more lines running roughly parallel with each other. And in music, composer Robert Schumann seems to echo John Keats's "music heard is sweet, music *unheard* is sweeter" in a contrapuntal episode in his great *Humoreske* piano cycle: Three staves of music were employed—the top and bottom staves corresponding to musical lines played by right and left hands, but whose middle stave contained a musical line he explicitly directed in the score "*not to be played....*"

In sum, while critic Gary K. Wolfe hails *Black House* as a "better" novel than *The Talisman*—"one that is more wholly and comfortably what it is, and some kind of dark masterpiece"—he concludes that it "couldn't really exist without the fantasy-novel template that *Talisman* provided."[29]

In Country

Finally, additionally useful points of comparison and contrast between the two men can be gleaned in other contexts, such as the novels King and Straub wrote separately about a common subject—Vietnam. King's *Hearts in Atlantis* (1999) and Straub's *Koko* (1988) alike dwell in the long shadows of the 1968 My Lai Massacre, when American soldiers killed more than 400 unarmed civilians. Both their novels deal with combat soldiers who return to civilian life haunted by memories of their involvement in wartime atrocities. King eulogizes an America that has lost its way, leaving behind an entire generation awash in recriminations and regrets. Straub burrows deeply into the damaged psyches of individuals who brought the war back home with them. Violence is subsumed in mourning in the first. It continues to rage in the second. Both define what "Vietnam" means to them—a public tragedy on the one hand, a transformative, public agony on the other. Either way, as Straub writes, in *Koko*, "the things that happened to you never stop happening" (143).[30]

Hearts in Atlantis consists of five interrelated stories that span the early 1960s to the last years of the century—"Low Men in Yellow Coats" is set in 1960; "Hearts in Atlantis" in 1966; "Blind Willie" in 1983; and "Why We're in Vietnam" and "Heavenly Shades of Night Are Failing" in 1999. The first and last stories properly belong to King's *Dark Tower* cycle, and should be considered in that context. The other interrelated stories more directly recount almost forty years in the lives of several friends—beginning with their college years, and continuing with the Draft, the Vietnam jungles, and the return to America—as political apathy yields to a growing social-conscience wartime trauma, and eventually a grief-stricken, traumatized aftermath. Documentary-like inserts detail the progress of the ongoing war—quotes from LBJ, statistics of downed helicopters, body counts, peace marches, etc.

In the episode "Blind Willie," we learn that there had been an incident involving atrocities in a little village in Dong Ha Province. A number of soldiers, had gone berserk and threatened to kill all the villagers. The slaughter was interrupted only when the unit's second lieutenant, Dieffenbaker, ordered one of his own men to shoot the culprits. Looking on at the carnage, helpless to intervene, was one of the school friends, Willie Shearman. "In the bush you sometimes had to do something wrong to prevent an even greater wrong," Willie muses years later. "Behavior like that shows that you're in the wrong place to start with, no doubt, but once you're in the soup, you just have to swim." He now lives out his later years, haunted by the ghost of an old woman he saw bayoneted in the village. He walks the streets, victim of a psychosomatic blindness, practicing a kind of ritualized penance for the war. He stands in, comments the narrative voice, "for all those who can only stand in the shadows, watching while the damage is done." When Willie's friend, Sully, visits the lieutenant who ordered the killing of the American soldier, he speaks for his whole generation: "'We never got out of the green. Our generation died there.'" He is scornful of what has since happened to them, growing fat in front of their computer screens and watching *Jerry Springer*. The lieutenant replies, "'But there was a time, when it was really all in our hands. Do you know that? I loathe and despise my generation, Sully. What have we done since Nam? Those of us who went, those of us who marched and protested, those of us who just sat home watching the Dallas Cowboys and drinking beer and farting into the sofa cushions? We had an opportunity to change everything.... Instead we settled for designer jeans and retirement portfolios and rock concerts. Man, we suck.'"[31]

Straub's *Koko* has been discussed earlier in these pages as an example of Straub's stories of crime and detection. Here, we will consider it in a different context. A brief summary is in order: *Koko* introduces us to the surviving members of a combat platoon that had seen action in Vietnam. Interspersed with flashbacks of their time in country, we meet Poole, a pediatrician, his buddies, Conor Linklater a carpenter, Tina Pumo the owner of a New York restaurant, and Harry Beevers their former platoon leader. The recent machinations of a serial killer in the Far East—the handwritten word, "Koko," is found stuffed into the mouths of the mutilated victims—point them back to their own experiences in the small village of Ia Thuc.

Believing Ia Thuc to be sympathetic to the Viet Cong, the soldiers were ordered to destroy the village, which resulted in the slaughter of several children. In an adjacent cave, there is evidence that one of the soldiers executed an estimated thirty children. (We won't know what really happened there until Straub revisits the scene in another Vietnam-inflected novel, *Throat*.[32]) But in the absence of crucial evidence, Poole realizes they will incur no consequences for their actions. "Unless the entire platoon was court-martialed nothing was going to happen.... Actions that took place in a void were eternal actions, and that was terrible" (331).

Suspecting that the killer is one of several former platoon mates who had "snapped" and gone on a rampage against anyone involved in the atrocities, including themselves, they embark on a mission to Singapore and Bangkok to track him down. The killer, meanwhile, whom we know only as "Koko," reverses his trajectory and returns to New York to continue his killing spree. He is described as "the embodiment of death who stands at the center of his own delusional universe" (126). Before the killer is unmasked, several culprits are considered, then dismissed. The implications are clear: They *all* are capable of these killings, just as they all are their victims.

Ultimately, Koko is revealed to be a former comrade named M.O. Dengler, a seemingly mild and sane person who had served with distinction in the war; but who, it is revealed, had been violently and sexually abused as a child by his father. In a horrific episode, Dengler is confronted in an underground room, whose walls are covered with images of dying children: "Their bodies had only partially been painted in. Some held their hands upraised, others reached out with sticklike arms" (532). The victimization of children here, as always with Straub, is of paramount concern. *Koko* scatters throughout its text images of abused and abandoned children, brutalized by forces both random and deliberate. As Poole surveys these disturbing images, he has an equally disturbing insight into Dengler's motivations: "'I think he thought of himself as giving his victims the gift of freedom from the fearful eternity he perceived all about him'" (553–554). But there is no real escape for him: He is caged within an eternity of cycled and recycled past events, no matter how often he kills to make them stop.

Straub has only compassion for the plight of these damaged men and their victims: "I could see them open themselves to an enormous grief, part of which was grief for themselves. The magnitude of what they felt healed them or was helping them to heal—they were forced to inhabit the incredible pain at the center of their lives, in the face of which almost everything else was shallow, superficial, in a way trivial."[33]

These incidents and their attendant mysteries are at the heart of one of Straub's longest, most complex, and most violent novels. Through a tangle of interrelated, winding narratives, multiple viewpoints, frequent shifts in time and space, fragmented scenes, and numerous secondary characters and incidents, we catch glimpses of the atrocities. It's almost as if Straub can't bring himself to confront directly the horrors of the scene.

Although he had not served in the war, Straub has said he understands "Vietnam" as a metaphor for the evil, for the traumas, for the victimizations that afflict him and all of us, each in our own separate ways. (This is confirmed in the later *The Throat*, in which writer Tim Underhill refers to his childhood home of Millhaven as a "Vietnam" before the real Vietnam.) "Millhaven and Vietnam were oddly interchangeable, fragments of some greater whole, some larger story..." (79). We are prepared to admit that *Koko*, in the final analysis, hardly seems about the Vietnam War at all. Unlike King, Straub offers no political commentary or anti-war rhetoric; rather, he is concerned about the human condition in the face of war and childhood trauma alike, about the private hells that afflict characters like Dengler, in and out of war. And unlike the Vietnam vets in King, several of the men, we learn in the final pages, do survive and enter into productive lives.

If there is a single word, or mood, or attitude that best sums up these two writers and their books, I would suggest that in King it is "elegy," a public lament for a lost world, the lost "Atlantis" of the title. For Straub it is "compassion" for his characters, for those who ultimately embrace their humanity and for those who lose it.

"I agree that, from my point of view, Vietnam was a *personal* tragedy," Straub confirms. "And yes, that Steve King sees it more in terms of a *national* tragedy. I spent a lot of time traveling through the countries I wrote about in *Koko*. I wanted to get the right feel of the places. But not Vietnam. I got letters from veterans after the book was published. I remember one man, a returned veteran, who was angry at me for what he called 'violating' the veterans. I wrote him back, saying that he should *drop his pose; that it's not working*. I said, *You don't own Vietnam. I have free access to it in my imagination.* But I also got another letter from the wife of a veteran, who told me that my book had helped her and her husband talk about his experience."[34]

Interview with Stephen King

(The following is from this author's interview with Stephen King, conducted via email, 9 February 2016.)

JOHN C. TIBBETTS: Please recall your first meeting with Peter Straub in London.

STEPHEN KING: I thought he seemed very British for an American! And full of good humor. He had the world's most infectious laugh. Also, he introduced me to my very first gyro! We sat on a park bench, ate, and talked about books while we wiped sauce off our mouths. It was as very good first meeting. We saw eye to eye.

Which of you first suggested teaming up on The Talisman?

I can't remember who brought it up first, possibly because it seemed like such a natural idea. I was thrilled at the prospect of working with him.

Has there been progress on a third book in the series?

Right now, I'm working on what has turned out to be a very long book with my son, Owen. The plan is to write the final book in the *Talisman* trilogy once the book with Owen is done. So ... two collaborations in a row!

How did elements in your "Dark Tower" mythos come to be embedded in Black House?

Peter knew the Dark Tower books, and we both felt that the *Talisman* world and Mid-World were pretty much the same place. Having a number of fantasy elements firmly in place eased some of the heavy lifting. Also, Peter knew by then that all my work was revolving around the Tower stories.

How do you react to Straub's not altogether whimsical description of you guys as the "Dash Hammett and Raymond Chandler" of horror fiction? Or, is there a lot of Chandler in King and a lot of Hammett in Straub?

It's a fair assessment. Although he and I have been more prolific!

You and Straub have both written about Vietnam. How do you regard your respective treatments in Koko *and* Hearts in Atlantis?

We dealt with it in different ways, and—frankly—Peter did a far superior job. *Koko* and *The Throat* are novels that only grow in my estimation over the years, and *Koko* should have been considered for a National Book Award. The bottom line is that everyone in my generation was scarred by Vietnam in some way, and in writers that always shows up. I repeat, those books Peter wrote after *The Talisman* are giants. *Hearts in Atlantis* tried to get a grip on the home front, and while I like the book, it isn't in the same league.

In your opinion, how is Peter's work unique in the field of weird fiction?

He brought a poet's sensibility to the field, creating a synthesis of horror and beauty. There's always the feeling of growing dislocation in Peter's books, They begin with deceptive simplicity, and become steadily weirder—this is especially clear in stories like "The Buffalo Hunter." He writes a beautiful prose line that features narrative clarity, sterling characterization, and surprising bursts of humor. He's particularly good with characters and places from his native Midwest.

CHAPTER SEVEN

"Invisible Ink"

On Writers and Writing

Through all the tones in this colorful, earthly dream, a quietly drawn out tone sounds for one who listens furtively.

—Friedrich Schlegel, *Die Gebüsche*

With her lips to his she spoke a wonderful secret word which echoed through his whole being…. He would have given his life to know what that word was.

—Novalis, *Henry von Ofterdingen*

She would have spoken to him, I think, whispered a message into his sleeper's ear, but … it would have been impossible to reconstruct into ordinary flawed human speech.

—Peter Straub, *Shadowland*

In *The Hellfire Club*, serial killer Dick Dart and his captive, Nora Chancel, infiltrate the venerable Shorelands Writers Colony. It is a haven and refuge for writers, their scandals, and their ghosts. Dart feels quite at home. Masquerading under the name of the avant-garde poet, "Norman Desmond," and possessing no literary credentials whatever, save an eidetic memory that allows him to quote at length Thoreau, Emily Dickinson, and Shelley, the irrepressible Dart takes time off from his homicidal activities to opine on all matters poetic. "'Every now and then,'" he boasts, "'I could reel off some verse to impress the shit out of the guardians of culture. Wouldn't have to be Emily, I can quote lots of other idiots, too. Keats, Shelley, Gray—all the greats'" (355). He scorns Dickinson and labels her poems "'this gibberish language she made up'" (190). He practices his "gifts" with Shelley, retaining only every third word of the poem:

> Thee, bird wert—
> Heaven it full profuse unpremeditated
> Still from thou a fire.
> Deep and still and singest.

He can recite *Pride and Prejudice* backwards, in the same fashion: "'Austen Jane by? Almost as bad as the forward version'" (423).

Now, to his startled Shoreland hosts he brands former resident, T.S. Eliot, as "'that stuffed shirt'" who "'stayed here exactly two days, and all he did was complain about indigestion.'" He enthusiastically endorses Ezra Pound's fascist politics: "'Let's call a jackboot a jackboot, okay?'" He recites snatches from his own poetry which, it must be admitted, possesses a distinctly, er, derivative flair. He deletes every two words from the beginning of "The Waste Land" and, with "'adjustments for poetic effect,'" produces a wildly avant-garde masterpiece that wows his hosts: "'Us, the shower; we went sunlight. Hofgarten Coffee.'" He smiles, "'Heck of a lot punchier, don't you think? My "Prufrock" is even better.'" How appropriate, as we shall see, that as the words *vanish*, so their meanings elude us.

Dart, meanwhile, boasts he can do that with everything by Eliot. How about: "'Go, and the spread, the patient upon; Let through muttering, restless hotels, restaurants, shells insidious.... Oh, ask it'" (363).

Later, during a wild dinner party scene, Dart delivers the following lines:

> Farewell, bliss—world is, are,
> Lustful death them but none
> His can I, sick, must—
> Lord, mercy us!

Dart's listeners are wowed. Unaware that Dart has "adapted" Thomas Nashe's "In Time of Pestilence"—with every two words deleted—a listener responds, "'What I find really remarkable is that even though this is the first time I've heard the poem, it seems oddly familiar!'"[1] To which Dart's companion, Nora, slyly adds, "'Norman's work often has that effect.'" Another listener. With more insight than she knows, she confides to Nora: "'To hear your husband talk, you'd think he didn't know anything about poetry at all!'" Convinced now they have a celebrity poet in their midst, they shower him with hospitality (362–387).

Peter Straub, at times the Merry Prankster of Gothic writers, views such antics with bemusement: "I am only attacking the most pretentious aspects of such poets and such places," he says. "Dart invents a perfectly acceptable avant-garde poetry by reciting conventional masterpieces by leaving out every third word, turning sentences into more interesting ones that require more involvement from the listener and reader."[2] In other words, as foolish as Dart's impulse, the more dazzling his presentation! Dart accepts, even celebrates— with Straub's approval—the contradictions between the banal and the sublime, the plagiarist practice and the poetic declamation, privileging both at times, disavowing them at others. The fact that Dart is a psychotic narcissist in no ways invalidates his achievement. Perhaps it confirms them. He might be compared to Straub's alter-ego, the pompous academic critic Putney Tyson Ridge, Ph.D., whom we met in the *Doppelgaenger* chapter, another narcissist plowing critical pastures, whose deadly critiques cannot be entirely dismissed.

Writers and Readers

Tucked away in a forested region of Massachusetts, the Shorelands Colony is the "Hellfire Club" of the book's title. We may have been misled near the beginning of the story, thinking the "Club" an enclave of sin tucked away in New York at 9th and Second Avenue, frequented by dissolute figures like Nora's husband, Davey Chancel. "'There was no Hellfire Club,'" says Davey, "'not really. That was just what we called it…. It's just these guys who get together to mess around. They do hire a good chef now and then, or they used to…. There was a bar, and you could take girls to the rooms upstairs. I only went there a couple of times…'" (331).

No, the *real* deal is the Shorelands Colony, every bit as exotic and treacherous as its New York counterpart. To review the backstory: During the summer of 1938 an assortment of visionary poets and hack writers convene at Shorelands, where they opportunistically court the attention of a wealthy publisher, Lincoln Chancel. What results is the disappearance of its one authentic poet, Katherine Mannheim, the publication of a masterpiece, the legendary *Night Journey*, and an unholy liaison between the Colony's matriarch, Georgina Weatherall, and Chancel's publisher, Lincoln Chancel, in support of Chancel's Fascist cause. Georgina in turn blackmails him for the murder of Katherine Mannheim. It is a match made in hell: He gains the box office prestige of *Night Journey*, his chief moneymaker, and she gets the money she needs to keep Shorelands going. As for Hugo Driver, the nominal author of *Night Journey*, his authorship is disputed and he is suspected to be nothing more than a hack, a sell-out to Lincoln Chancel.

In the present, when Nora and Dart come to Shorelands, they find the Colony gone to seed. Duped by Dart's pretensions as a poet and Nora's claim that she is writing of a puff piece about the place, a young Shorelands staff member, Marian Cullinan, seizes the opportunity to dream of a "restoration," of converting the Colony to a kind of literary Theme Park with Hugo Driver's *Night Journey* as its center of attraction. "'We could put on Hugo Driver weekends,'" she gushes. "'To tell you the truth, attendance has been suffering lately, and this could turn things around for us'" (367). Her boss, Margaret, adds,

"'I see more than that. I see a *Driver Week*. I see Hugo Driver T-shirts flying out of the gift shop.... Give me three weeks and I can turn [Driver's cottage] into a shrine to him.... Every single thing [we] remember about him is worth its weight in gold'" No matter that a few survivors from Driver's time remember him as a nasty thief and "a plague" in the Colony: "'We're going to polish this fellow up until he shines like gold. Was he untidy? We can drop some socks and balled up typing paper around the room. 'Historical accuracy'" would be "'too raw for the public'" (388).

Shoreland's "natural" state is only disclosed when Nora is granted a view of one of the untouched rooms; its "real history was still visible." Here it was when the original matriarch of the Colony reigned supreme: "Georgina Weatherall, whose greatest advantages had been wealth, vanity, and illusion, had risen day after day to admire herself in her mirrors, brushed her hair without ever managing to push it into shape, painted on layers of makeup until the mirrors told her that she was as commanding as a queen in a fairy tale. If she noticed a flaw, she submerged it beneath rouge and kohl, just as she buried the stains on her walls and the rents in her lace beneath layers of fabric" (390).

Elsewhere in *Hellfire*, Nora Chancel has her own opportunities to weigh in on the Literary Scene. She is the reluctant Reader of an unpublished manuscript, the sort of amateurish product that all too often floods the popular market. Her mother-in-law, Daisy Chancel, has thrust into her keep an unpublished manuscript, an "unwieldy epic" fraught with a sketches, notes, unfinished sentence, digressive episodes, wildly erratic tonal shifts and repetitive passages. It bears a startling epigraph attributed to one "Wolf J. Flywheel": "The world is populated by ingrates, morons, assholes, and those beneath them" (118). From there on, Nora is off and running—or is it stumbling?—into a plot following the adventures of Clementine and Adelbert Poison, secret Nazi sympathizers. Immediately, Nora recognizes a thinly veiled chronicle of the infamous Chancel family and its fascist sympathies. With growing dismay, she plunges on:

> After another hour she decided that if this story was going anywhere, it was in some Daisyish direction unknown to the normal world. Scenes concluded, and then, as if an earlier draft had not been removed, repeated themselves with slight variations. The tone swung from dry to hysterical and back. At times Daisy had broken up a straightforward scene to interpolate handwritten passages of disjointed words and phrases. Some scenes broke off unfinished in midsentence, as if Daisy had intended but forgotten to return to them later. There was nothing faintly like a conventional plot. One chapter read in its entirety: *"The author wants to have another drink and go to bed. You idiots should do the same"* [122].

By this time, Nora is dazed. Daisy grows impatient for her reaction. The following dialogue is quoted at length:

"You got through the whole thing [asks Daisy]? You couldn't have, you must have *skimmed*."

"No, I didn't" [Nora replies]. It isn't the kind of book you can skim, is it."

"What do you mean by that?"

"For one thing, it's so intense…. You have to pay attention when you're reading."

"It's a real experience."

"What kind of experience? Be more specific."

"Confusing? Irritating?"

"An intense experience."

"Ah. I think you already said that, though [protests Daisy]. What *kind* of intense experience?"

"Well … intellectual."

"*Intellectual?*"

"You have to think when you're reading it…. Some of it is very funny."

"Goody goody. I meant for parts to be *ecstatically* funny. Not all of it, though."

"Of course not. There's a lot of anger in it."

"You bet. Anger upon anger. Grr."

"So it seemed very experimental to me."

"Experimental [wails Daisy]? What could possibly seem *experimental* to you?"

"The way you repeat certain scenes."

"You're talking about the times when the same things happen all over again after they happened the first time, but differently, so the real meaning comes out. And the other thing you're talking about is when anyone with half a brain can see what's going to happen, so there's no point in setting it all down. My God, it's a novel, not journalism."

"Well, a lot of books start in one place and tell you a story, and that's that. I guess what I mean is, you're willing not to be linear."

"It's as linear as a clothesline. If you don't see that, you don't see anything at all" [125].

After this exchange, poor Daisy explodes in a rage and orders her daughter-in-law out of the house.

Who Dun It?

Nora Chancel is involved in another, far more serious literary matter. In dispute is the authorship of *Night Journey*, nominally ascribed to Hugo Driver. As a "literary detective," her search for the true author and the solution to the murders subsequent to its creation have already been discussed in the "Datchery" chapter of this book. For our purposes here, her engagement with the text itself, the process by which she *reads* it and how it begins to reflect and influence her life is entirely to the point. Nora has not yet read the book when the action of *Hellfire* begins. As she takes up *Night Journey*, she reads sporadically at first, over an extended period of time, quoting passages at intervals—sometimes a sentence or two, sometimes whole paragraphs and pages. She is interrupted at times. She goes back to it at others. She skips ahead, then looks back. Events, characters, and meanings, come at her, seemingly in no particular order, until, gradually, they accumulate and coalesce into hints at a meaning. What she thought at first were mere "cardboard" landscapes, "flat" characters, and "stilted" dialogue, begin to take her over: "The hateful book had enough narrative power to draw her in," until the story no longer seems "artificial" (265–266). The story is a *living* experience. It captures her rhythms and moods and arouses her passions. Word by word, sentence by sentence, chapter by chapter, it reveals the truth of the larger narrative that is her *own* life. Her processing of *Night Journey*, moreover, is how *we* process *The Hellfire Club*. Her experience is our experience. Earlier, we saw how Straub's *In the Night Room* is a metatext about the *writing* of a book; now, *Hellfire* is a meta-text about the *reading* of a book.

Straub well understands how books can come into our lives, capture our attention, and influence our behavior—sometimes with dubious results. Some of his favorite writers themselves understand this. Henry James understands this, when his nameless protagonist in *The Aspern Papers* obsessively pursues his search for the lost papers of a dead poet. H. P. Lovecraft understands it when his protagonists endure unspeakable horrors in their quest for the infernal *Necronomicon*. And perhaps Peter Straub understands it, as he grapples with his fascination with poets John Ashbery and writers Nathaniel Hawthorne and Henry James. Certainly today's "fanboy" culture gets it as it falls under the sway of the *Harry Potter* and *Star Wars* franchises. "A lot of [people] never read anything else," observes Dick Dart, who well understands the nature of obsession.

> They love *Night Journey* so much they want to read it all over again. Then they think they missed something, and they read it a third time. By now they're making notes. Then they compare discoveries with other Driverites. If they're tied into computer discussion groups, that's it; they're gone. The really sick ones give up on everything else and move into those crazy houses where everybody pretends to be a different Driver character [265].

A House of Books

The Hellfire Club, along with "Mrs. God," *A Dark Matter*, and *Shadowland*, contains some of Straub's most striking commentaries on the world of writers and writing. They populate his House of Books, his own Writer's Place, if you will. He presides there, like Georgina Weatherall at Shorelands, Edith Seneschel in Esswood House, Coleman Collins in Shadowland—and perhaps even like August Derleth in his House of Books, known as Arkham.... Gothic edifices all, they are haunted by desperate visionaries in the attics, failed poets in the basement, and hapless critics and publishers wandering the corridors looking for a quick buck. They are an unruly lot. They shout and argue and vent their satisfactions and their frustrations at the unholy calling to which they are committed.

We readers have come to call at this House. We ignore the commotion at the doorway and mount the winding stair and edge past the Shorelands Reading Room, the Esswood Library, and Mr. X's Lovecraft Room. Behind an unmarked door we claim our own comfy nook. We settle back and peruse the books spilling out of the shelves. They are all by Peter Straub. The pages seem to turn by themselves. The prose *boils*, the words *blaze*, the world *sizzles*. People are burning. The world is "a picture over the face of a terrible fire." "Smoke and fire billow beneath the street." A bloodstain "moves toward the drain like a living thing." People die and ghosts live (they are *hungry*). Cats talk and silver boots fill with blood. It is odd; it is fabulous. Everything has already happened. *"In violence there is often the quality of yearning."* The ink disappears... And a little clown figure named Bobo *blats* his horn and rides away in his Magic Taxi...

By now we know that Peter Straub and his stories elude easy classification. Like the works of other masters of imaginative prose that we have referenced throughout these pages—the finely-crafted fables of Nathaniel Hawthorne, the densely textured social studies of Henry James, the exquisite lyricism of Lord Dunsany, the sonorous hymns of Arthur Machen, the eldritch archaicisms of H. P. Lovecraft, the paradoxical cadences of G.K. Chesterton, the metaphor-rich psalms of Ray Bradbury—his stories find their own distinctive, synaesthetic, albeit elusive, identity. He "speaks" as a novelist, he "paints" as an artist, and he "sings" as a composer and musician. Above all, he dreams as a poet. "Do you see what excites me in this?" declares the writer Kai Glauber in *Under Venus*, as he describes in paradoxical terms his passionate interest in the German master Goethe: "He was a genius at manipulating his own language.... He outgrew poetry even as he became a greater and greater poet" (440).

Indeed, Straub began as an aspiring poet. In high school he was fascinated by the carefully observed surface details of the poetry of William Carlos Williams (1883–1963). He chose Williams's *Desert Music* as the subject of his Masters Degree at Columbia University, which was completed in the spring of 1966.[3] "Williams remained unsatisfied," Straub wrote in his thesis (perhaps expressing his own struggles with poetry writing), "with a formal organization of structure which was a poem-by-poem matter; he desired a formal organization of language that would order his poetry as a whole, and yet allow greater freedom and flexibility than conventional prosody."[4] He must have felt a deep affinity with the poet's struggle for the synergy of prose and poetry, for what one critic has described as "the poetic line [that] is organically welded to American speech as muscle to bone."[5] He also recognized

Williams as a kindred spirit who expressed a *verbal* response to both music and the visual arts. Williams's Pulitzer-Prize-winning *Pictures from Breughel* (1962), for example, were careful, descriptions of the painterly surfaces of the mid–16th-century Dutch master. And in *The Desert Music*, an ambitious account of a trip to Mexico in search of the restorative powers of colorful indigenous musics, Williams celebrated the "wonders of the brain" that enables our hearing of musical sounds. Straub must have been especially piqued when Williams writes of the mystery of sounds that may be "addressed not wholly to the ear." In sum, the "strange directness of his poems" appealed to Straub, "the way they sounded so personal without sounding at all like me. The slight formality in the language elevated it into a realm where matters of great beauty, meaning, seriousness could be laid down on the page. All of this might have played into my later interest in prose-poetry."[6]

Meanwhile he was making another poetic discovery of a somewhat different nature. John Ashbery's second volume of poems, *The Tennis Court Oath*, published in 1962 to largely negative reviews, had a "revelatory effect on Straub," reports Bill Sheehan, "forcing him to reexamine his most fundamental notions about the nature of literature, and freeing him, eventually, to pursue his own writing."[7] Ashbery's influence played a crucial role in Straub's decision to leave a teaching position and depart, with wife Susan, for Ireland, where he enrolled in the Ph.D. program at Dublin's University College. Straub admits that "it really is hard to pin down the actual *meaning* of his work, but he clearly means *something*":

Ashbery for me and for a lot of other people is the greatest living American poet. He was part of a brilliant generation. His work was always unlike anybody else's, except certain sides of Wallace Stevens. Ashbery's poems were as much about the *act* of writing and what goes through your mind while writing as what he was actually writing about what he calls "the divine sepulcher of life." He talks, for example, of "hands that are always writing on mirrors." He's writing about all the other things that occur to him while writing.... The unfortunate thing. was for a long time I imitated Ashbery and wrote Ashbery-ish poems. My whole generation was dominated by him. You find some Ashbery in my "Open Air" poems [1973], which were published by Irish University Press. They're now very hard to find.[8]

While in Dublin Straub made a third discovery, one that has had a longtime effect on him, personally and professionally: During a 1970 poetry reading in the cellar of a Dublin pub called Sinnot's, Straub first met aspiring poet and playwright Thomas Tessier. "Thom," as he prefers to be called, was not yet the distinguished writer of weird fiction he was to become. Soon he would move to London, where he would become the Managing Director of Millington Books, a publishing house located on the western fringes of Bloomsbury near the British Museum.

Tessier takes up the story:

> I was a student in Dublin and I loved the city. It had a lively literary scene and a certain raffish, seedy charm –poets going from pub to pub, selling badly printed broadsheets for a half crown, other writers who carried typescripts of every single thing they'd ever written (so far) around with them in plastic laundry bags. It wasn't the Paris of the 1920s, but it was the Dublin of Yeats, Joyce and J.P. Donleavy, and the written word was sacred... [Someone] drew my attention to a tall, bearded feller seated on the other side of the room and told me I ought to meet him: "He's another Yank poet living here, like yerself."

Later, near closing time, as folks were herded out into the foggy night.

> I noticed the Yank again later, at closing time, as we were all leaving the premises, and I introduced myself to him. His name was Peter Straub and he was from Milwaukee, by way of Columbia University. It turned out we were neighbors, living just a couple of streets apart. We became fast friends, and in the weeks and months that followed, the best of friends. We would get together once or twice a week, sometimes more often, showing each other the latest we had written, praising, criticizing, analyzing, celebrating when one of us had something accepted for publication or commiserating over rejections, or just talking about books, jazz, Nixon, jazz, and life its ownself....[9]

Straub remembers the freewheeling exhilaration of these exchanges: "Our literary conversations were taking an unusual course. We talked about Geoffrey Hill (a modernist English poet), Derek Mahon (a not very modernist but anyhow wonderful Irish poet who was a friend of Thom's), Wallace Stevens, John Berryman, John Ashbery and Yeats."[10]

Today, we scarcely know Straub as a poet. His three volumes, *Ishmael* (1971), *Open Air* (1972), and *Leeson Park and Belsize Square* (1983), are very rare and, in Straub's view, of limited interest. There is a line in "Tracking," from *Open Air*, a series of lyrics loosely organized around animal motifs, that nicely typifies his efforts:

> Black and white: the map of branches.
> (But the self can slide through, thinking.)[11]

Black scratches on the white page? The lattice of words through which creeps the poet's identity...?

Over the years, he has said in an interview in 1999, the poetic impulse gradually yielded to prose writing: "After I wrote prose day after day after day for a couple of years I couldn't write short lines anymore."[12] Yet he honors those years of struggle: "My brief career as a poet was of far more value to me than to the world of poetry and its readers. For one thing, I enjoyed myself tremendously during that period. It was hugely pleasurable to work on poems and try to get them right. Also, it demanded that I pay great attention to individual words, the weight and duration of phrases, and the rhythms and cadences of the lines. All of this concentration leads to an increased awareness of verbal texture and verbal possibility, valuable to any writer."[13]

Poetry in prose, or prose in poetry? No better attempt at a definition can be found than in Charles Baudelaire, a writer with whom Straub surely feels a kinship. "Who among us," wrote Baudelaire, "has not dreamed, in his ambitious moments, of the miracle of a poetic prose, musical, yet without rhythm and without rhyme, supple and darting enough to adapt to the lyrical stirrings of the soul, the undulations of reverie, and the sudden leaps of consciousness?"[14] Straub's prose is up to the task. I submit, almost at random, this moment from his early novel, *If You Could See Me Now*, whose poetry and prose seems to respond to Baudelaire's challenge. Miles Teagarden is rambling through his beloved Wisconsin forests:

> I set out into the full rustling night. My mud-laden boots felt the knotted roots of trees thrusting up through the earth.... I was out from under the dense ceiling of branches, and the narrow road unrolled before me, through tall fields lighter than the indigo sky. When it traversed the creek, I once again heard frogs announcing their territory.... I walked quickly, resisting the impulse to glance over my shoulder. If I felt that someone or something was watching me, it was only the single bright star in the sky, Venus, sending me light already thousands of years old [273].

A step or two, then a pause. Another. Sights, sounds, textures and touch. A vagrant thought, a momentary doubt, a leap into the imagination.... A microcosm of searching, memory and betrayal. "Every sentence," says Straub, "is to be an arrow into the secret center of the book. To find my way into the secret center I must hold the entire book, every detail and rhythm, in my memory. This comprehensive act of memory is the most crucial task of my life."[15]

To be sure, the *spirit* of poets and poetry suffuse his stories. Ashbery is everywhere, of course. A copy of *The Tennis Court Oath* even turns up in the library at Esswood House in "Mrs. God"! A handy guide can be useful to readers wishing to pin down some of the more obscure poetic references on the wing. For example, there are references to Elizabeth Bishop's "The Fish" in *The Talisman*; the sonnets of Ted Berrigan in *The Hellfire Club*; Charles Bernstein's "Content's Dream" in "Mrs. God"; Theodore Roethke's "The Waking" in *Under Venus*; etc., etc.

Although he now regards his vocation primarily as a prose writer, he continues to be attentive to a new generation of poets. Rebecca Wolff, an editor of *Fence* publications, told him that a young poet named Laura Sims had been influenced by his work.[16] Her interest in the confessions of serial killers particularly intrigued him.[17] Straub says, "Her work goes very deep. It draws water from thousands of feet under the surface of the earth.... 'Would I like to have one of her books?' they asked me? 'Sure,' I said, and not long afterward I received one of Sims's *Fence* books in the mail. It turned out to be a specific poem, and that poem had in some way not obvious to me been influenced by my *If You Could See Me Now*.[18] Very nice, I thought." A couple of months later Rebecca wrote to say that she was publishing a new book of Laura's and wondered if I would give it a blurb. The book came, and it was *my god is this a man*. These lines particularly moved me:

> *They wanted their bodies to be handled boldly, as they'd boldly handled the bodies on water or land. They carried their fear of the living, assured into crawl spaces lighted with singular bulbs.*

I was really stunned, thrilled, almost startled by the book. It really did seem to be about a set of things that had long been of interest to me. I kept it on my desk and looked through it, not daily but pretty often, for months. After a while I came across a very strange passage that I thought would make an excellent epigraph for one section of my work in progress. Later on, I wanted to use another set on lines in the epigraph for another passage. I wrote Laura to ask her permission to use her poetry in this way, and she quickly wrote back to assent.[19]

For her part, Laura Sims appreciates special qualities in Straub's writing.

> His attention to language has always made his fiction stand out to me—it's clear he has a musical ear, and I wasn't surprised to read that he'd been influenced by Ashbery's work, or that he'd written poetry himself early on. They "make sense" but also remain stubbornly mysterious, just as the best poetry does. I'm very drawn to this quality in his work; I think that's what has prompted me to respond to his fiction in verse.

Her first exposure to Straub's work was *Ghost Story*, after which she went on to read his later books. The underrated *If You Could See Me Now*, one of Straub's most lyric and atmospheric ghost stories, became a favorite:

> I'm not sure why that one in particular spoke to me so strongly, but I fixated on it (even the title—I love that title!) and stole directly from it for two of the poems in my first collection, *Practice, Restraint*! My poem, "Restaurants, the Howling Alley, Fields," comes from my mis-reading of a line in *IYCSMN* that read "restaurants, the bowling alley, fields." I'm ashamed to say I didn't even acknowledge the stealing—in the poem or at the end of the book—because I didn't know one was supposed to do that at the time. Now I know better, and properly acknowledge when I steal. The other poem, "Former Quarry Song," is a kind of précis of the novel—I think Straub is a master of atmosphere (among other things), and I was seeking to recapture or pay homage to the haunted, haunting atmosphere of the book in that poem.

Sims is also intrigued by that special quality in Straub we have identified throughout this book—for want of a better term, *transcendence*—of the trauma of horror and terror as a gateway to "transformation":

> I was focused on that idea in writing *My God Is This a man*, drawn to the voices of those serial killer who had, in one way or other, traveled to the outer limits of human experi-

ence—either by doing something awful, or by having something awful done to them. I was interested in the way these two groups of people—"victims" and "perpetrators"—usually so stringently divided in our minds and in real life—could overlap, speak to each other, speak together of pain and suffering and even transcendence. Straub's work seems to express that same understanding of the complexity of human nature. He and I also seem to appreciate that *traveling deeper into darkness, rather than moving toward sunshine and ease, can heal whatever wounds you have. Sometimes you have to go deep into the darkest place before you can emerge into light* Straub's work has allowed me to experience that as a reader—and has inspired me again and again, in that way and many others, through the years since I began reading his work.[20]

The Poetry of Prose

Straub's experiences in poetry were influencing how he wrote and structured his novels. "Well, my books are like these poems," he explained in an interview: "Events repeat themselves like words that rhyme with each other. Rhymes are repetitions, too. In *Shadowland* I wanted every event in the first part of the book to be echoed— or *rhymed*—later in the latter part. And if you look through the book carefully, I think you'll find everything is repeated in that way. In "Mrs. God" that's about the only kind of organization there is, how one event *rhymes* with the others."[21]

Moreover, he was learning how to render prose that, in the words of Stephen King, was "almost always structurally correct ... [with] each sentence as tight as a time-lock, as unobtrusively strong as the good (but hidden) joists in a fine Victorian house that will last for three hundred years."[22]

Straub was also learning that language is not just a tool

Peter Straub at a book signing (courtesy Fales Archive).

of description but has its own inherent meaning. In the first instance, his mastery of descriptive prose and his close attention to detail is everywhere apparent. Even in a collaboration with Stephen King, *The Talisman*, where the individual "voice" of each can be difficult to detect, passages like this reveal Straub's distinctive, peculiarly *painterly* prose: "The next day the sun was back—a hard bright sun that layered itself like paint over the fat beach and the slanting, red-tiled strip of roof Jack could see from his bedroom window. A long wave far out in the water seemed to harden in the light and sent a speak of brightness straight toward his eyes" (31). Compare this with the forest imagery in *Ghost Story*, wherein "the woods looked like an illustration in a book—not the real woods, but a drawing on a page. It was a fairytale woods, looking too perfect, too composed—drawn in black ink—to be real.... It was the clarity which gave it mystery. Each bare and spiky branch, each tangle of wiry stalks, stood out separately, shining with its own life. Some wry magic hovered just out of sight" (157).

And in the story "Bunny Is Good Bread," where the world appears like a flat, painted canvas to a sexually abused boy: "Nothing around him was real. The moon had been painted, and the houses had no backs, and everything he saw was a fraction of an inch thick, like paint" (116).

To apply the word "painterly" to prose like this is quite intentional. No reading of Straub is without numerous references to painters and painting, from the Pre-Raphaelites to the Surrealists and Abstract Expressionists. It's all about what he calls "the mystery of representation." In stories like "The Juniper Tree," "The Veteran," and *Shadowland* he will have characters gazing at a screen, or at a wall, on which are inscribed the images of his imagination. "What I have in mind is a painter in front of a canvas," he explains, "and if the writer puts his hand on the screen, something springs to life: You see trees, a road, and fairly soon a whole landscape is visible before you—complete with human beings moving through it. This image suggests itself because of what seems the magical nature of creation."[23] The challenge is to render in prose what is an inherently *visual* medium. He applies a sensibility that is just as attentive to "the weight of a line, the gradations of color, the accumulation or rejection of detail," of a painting as to the careful selection of diction, phrasing and sentence structure in his prose. The results can "hum and glow" with meaning—"the sacred meaning we would always be able to see if we had the eyes of Constable, Hobbema, Magritte, or Cezanne."[24] We savor another example of painting-in-prose in this night scene from *Julia*: "Across the street the lights of the pub burned softly red through the windows; glasses hung upside down, bat-fashion, gleamed like Christmas, points and blurs of red. Rain jumped in the street and ran in rivulets toward the drain. The streetlamps produced a shining streak along the pavement, a harsh acid yellow, a color which eats the skin" (148).

A subtly different kind of descriptive prose unites his characters and events with the material reality that surrounds them. This is readily apparent in that most beautifully lyrical of his novels, *If You Could See Me Now*, which resonates powerfully with sense memories of his own youth.[25] Writer Miles Teagarden has returned to his native village of Arden, in rural northeast Wisconsin, to complete his dissertation on D.H. Lawrence. He surrenders to the area's seductive embrace and confronts his long-buried secrets and guilts. During a walk through the surrounding forests, he responds to its nocturnal beauty and senses the ghostly presence of Alison haunting the landscape: "She was printed deeply into every scrabble of rock, every tick of leaf.... The moon, as medallion-like as Alison's face, shimmered and glowed from the water's center.... That flat pane of water with its glowing center drew me on, brought me down toward it..." (374).

Thus, the prose attends closely to the surfaces and textures of the material world, which yield up their own meanings, their solace, their mystery. "I've tried to notice things," says Professor Alan Brookner in *The Throat*, "to pay *attention*.... There is another world, and it's *this* world" (235–237). Like a modern-day John Ruskin, Straub and his characters recover the surfaces of reality in all their texture and detail.[26] "'Every leaf, every pine needle, every path through the woods, every bird call,'" says detective Von Heilitz in *Mystery*, "'had come alive, was vibrant, full of meaning. Everything *promised*. Everything *chimed*. I knew more than I knew. There was a secret beating away beneath the surface of everything I saw'" (98). In yet another striking passage in *If You Could See Me Now*, young Miles Teagarden strives to recover his emotional balance after a series of highly-charged revelations of murderous events in the little town. He turns to the physical world around him. "I was aware of the force with which sensory impressions were packing into my mind, and I clung to them for sanity" (320).

This palpable *hunger* for the details and surfaces of the immanent world is not just felt by the living. Ghosts feel it too. Straub's ghosts, shriven from the world, fix their hungry, "ravenous" gaze upon what was left behind. Ironically, they perceive more than the living, as in this passage from *The Throat*: "[The dead] still want things. They look at us all the time, and they miss being alive. We have taste and color and smells and feelings, and they don't have any of those things. They stare at us, they don't miss anything. They really see what's going on, and we hardly ever really see that" (175). In one of the most striking passages in "Hunger, an Introduction," the ghostly Frank Wardwell, newly executed in the electric chair for murder, returns to gaze raptly through a window at "this little miracle" of a five-year-old child. As she enters the room and sits before the television, he drinks in the details scene, the room, the child's "inward-looking little face," her every motion, unstudied and natural, her every emotion rendered "*instantly visible*—written in subtle but powerful runes on the blank page that is [her] face" (247–248). A mysterious identification, a shared "deep-diving rapture" is forged between the watcher and the watcher, the living and the dead. The reader, embraced and encompassed by the prose, shares in the moment. And we recall that *In the Night Room* has a magical moment, described in detail elsewhere in these pages, when Tim Underhill gazes through a window upon Lucy Cleveland in her kitchen—her very *reality* is palpable, the fleet glimpse of her averted gaze "amplified to an internal earthquake" (302).

The prose frequently yearns toward a Straubian synaesthesia, a fusion of scene, sound, tactility, and music, as in this passage from *Black House*: "[The hordes of buzzing bees] seem almost *illuminated*, like the radiant pages of a sacred text … the touch of their many bodies is surpassingly smooth and soft; their massed buzzing is low and harmonious, as peaceable as a Protestant hymn" (672–673). In "Mrs. God," the poetry of the vanished poet Isobel Standish is evoked as a riot of sight, sound, and touch: "The long pond *simmered*.… The library was an *oven, a volcano*, and poetry was *lava*. Every surface *shimmered* and *gleamed*, and everything *trembled* with the pressure and force beneath it" (136). And sometimes poetry itself is cited as a correlative to events, as when Jack Sawyer's epiphany while watching the Flying Men in *The Talisman* is described as akin to Elizabeth Bishop's poem "The Fish."

In the second instance, as with other prose stylists, like Dickens, Machen, Dunsany, and Bradbury, we find that Straub's prose is the most important character, the "real" story, beyond structure, description, and theme, possessing a sense and significance all its own. In a remarkable passage in *A Dark Matter*, the monstrous forces that appear to Hootie Bly in The Meadow are essentially *verbal* and *syntactical*:

> [There were] many, many words: *hot* words, *boiling* sentences, many, many thousands of sentences, thrashing and coiling like monstrous, endless, interconnected snakes. And he knew all those sentences; they were within him.… He slipped out of his body, which was consumed, and threaded into a comforting subject-verb-object sequence; thence into a concatenation of independent clauses that scattered him amongst a hive of semicolons.… Several complex sentences took him up, carried him into winter, and dumped him on the back of a wagon pursued by wolves [271–272].

Like Charles Dickens, Straub bestows playful, inventive names upon his characters. The sinister killer in *Koko* acquires his name from the mysterious

"Song of the Elephants" heard in *Babar the King*, from which Straub borrows these lines:

> Patali Di Rapata
> Cromda Cromda Ripalo
> Pata Pata
> Ko Ko Ko [516].

There are other character names, like Bob Bunting, Fee Bandolier, Bob Squadron, Lamont von Heilitz, and the superbly unpronounceable (and upper case) cosmic entity, WCHWHLLDN, to cite just a few; and names derived from literary characters, like Sears James, Ricky Hawthorne; and others from jazz musicians, Miles Teagarden and Tom Flanagan.[27] Straub sometimes devises strange dialects and dictions for other characters—languages sometimes merely garbled, sometimes possessing a wholly different vocabulary and syntax altogether. In "A Short Guide to the City," several children find "a winged man huddled in a packing case" who speaks "a strange language none of the children knew" (96–97). Voices from the Dead appear on Tim Underhill's computer screen in *In the Night Room*; and an otherworldly entity named Cyrax "speaks" to him in a weird half-language born of computer/text speak: "'Of course, it isn't a real language,'" Cyrax "writes," "'merely a system of jokes and substitutions'" (103). In "Mrs. God" a landscape "speaks" its own language: The stars crowning the roofs of Esswood House present "a vast, unreadable pattern" extending "far back into the vault of the sky, like a sentence in a foreign language that went on and on until first the letters and then the whole becomes too small to read" (186). And a nine-year-old boy's innocent, but oddly disturbing mangling of language appears in "The Collected Short Stories of Freddie Prothero." Straub explains in a recent interview that for "Prothero" he wanted "to mess around in a little linguistic world I invented for myself. I wanted to write a story that used nonsense, childhood garble, the kinds of crazy stories my kids when in first grade and in kindergarten would bring home that have nothing spelled right at all.... I thought I could get somewhere if I tried to do something serious and with emotional depth in that language...."

He loves to read the story aloud, moreover, "because I get to make all these weird noises and sounds that ordinarily aren't part of my linguistic pattern at all."[28]

Such unusual language systems construct a fictional space of their own, a liminal condition that "hovers a little distance off the ground," as Straub puts it, where a kind of generous, exploratory receptiveness allows for inconclusiveness, ambiguity, and a general, accommodating recognition that in this particular universe no valid position can be final.... It is the space between the received and the as yet unknown that will never really be known, except as it is glimpsed there.... In fact, anything like conclusions, answers, and finalities no longer exist, because in the fictional space these blunt conditions instructively dissolve before their own rigidity.[29]

Perhaps, as has been noted, Straub is yearning toward a condition, a reality, not yet perceived, a book not yet written, a story inevitably unrealized. "I'm not really interested in writing any story from which I'm not going to learn something," he explains. "I'm not interested in writing a formulaic tale that arrives to me flags flying, fully buttoned down, and fully present.... I already know that story. I don't care a damn about it. What I want is to be led somewhere where I don't know where I am. I want to be led in to unexpected, slightly alarming, disorienting territory from which I must find my way back out."

Accordingly, he continues, the use of ellipses—as in his *film noir* story "Lapland"—"speaks of what cannot be seen...." Shades of H. P. Lovecraft[30] "help express the unexpressible."

In *If You Could See Me Now*, writer Miles Teagarden is asked: "Why don't you write a book about something fantastic and important that other people can't even see, about what's really going down?" (234). Straub admits he falls short of the ideal: "Given that one always wishes to write a perfect book, and that perfection is impossible to attain, frustration is inevitable."[31] As suggested by the baffling search for the writer of *Night Journey* that fuels events in *The Hellfire Club*, the true authorship of a book—and its *urtext*—must at best remain obscure. Nathaniel Hawthorne had admitted this in his introductory chapter to *The Scarlet Letter*: "A better book than I shall ever write was there; leaf after leaf presenting itself to me, just as it was written out by the reality of the flitting hour, and vanishing as fast as written, only because my brain wanted the insight and my hand the cunning to transcribe it."[32] A testament confirmed by one of Straub's favorite poets, Wallace Stevens, in words we encountered in the opening chapter of this book:

> To say more than human things with human voice,
> That cannot be; to say human things with more
> Than human voice, that, also, cannot be...[33]

Indeed, one often gets the sense that Straub is yearning to move past the denotative and connotative functions of language altogether, as the painters Malevich and Robert Rauschenberg abstained from representation altogether and displayed their "White on White" and "White Paintings" canvases in 1918 and 1951, respectively; and as composers Schumann and John Cage stripped away musical sounds from their compositions in the finale to the *Papillons*, Op. 2 and the piano piece, "4 minutes 33 Seconds."[34]

There are moments in *Shadowland* when the meanings of events "would have been impossible to reconstruct into ordinary flawed human speech" (407). Likewise, the horrors witnessed in *A Dark Matter* are ultimately revealed by Lee Harwell to be beyond language, beyond even music. He can only fall back "in dim wonder at its insufficiency," a reality "expanded beyond our capacity for understanding, therefore unbearable ... too utterly unknowable to be contemplated for longer than a nanosecond" (384).

The ink disappears on the page.

Music Sound and Music Silence

Which brings us to music. Inevitably. As noted several times throughout this book, even the most casual reader must be struck by Straub's numerous, even insistent references to music and musicians everywhere in his stories. Although Straub is neither a composer nor performer, he possesses a keen musical ear and a lifelong passion for music in all forms. In the *Doppelgänger* chapter it was demonstrated how he finds in the structure and performance of "program," or "descriptive" music tonal analogues to characters, scene, and situation. Here, however, we consider a far more complicated endeavor, i.e., Straub's attempts to grapple with music *as music*, as an autonomous expression unrelated to anything outside of itself. Lawrence Kramer in his exemplary *Musical Meaning*, considers that music can be investigated beyond contingency, "entirely unaffected by the things with which it mixes, no matter how they may direct or even coerce its expressivity. Subtract them from music, or music from them, and there remains music itself, music on its own, pure music, ineffably present to sense or memory." In other words, concludes Kramer, "music adds something to other things by adding itself, but loses nothing when it takes itself away."[35] But *how* to describe it?

Consider this curious passage near the end of the book at hand, *The Hellfire Club*, when Nora escapes her captor, Dick Dart, and runs across a meadow at night. Suddenly, she hears music—at least a *kind* of music: "On the other side of the meadow, high-pitched voices swooped and skirled, climbing through chromatic intervals, introducing dissonance, ascending into resolution, shattering apart, uniting into harmony again, dividing and joining in an endless song without pauses or repeats" (432). References to unresolved tonalities, pitch intervals, tonal centers, lapses in meter are *musicologically* meaningful, but they tell us nothing about the surrounding scene, situation, and mood—or do they? Are there literal and narrative contingencies, even here?

"In the end, music did explain everything," realizes Tom Pasmore in *Mystery* (32). Well. Wherever we are, there we are. Tom has just "died," i.e., endured a near-death experience. He hears a song—just "some song"—that he doesn't recognize. Tom has been in another place. The music *is* in another place. That's all we know. Or need to know, quoth the Poet. And perhaps that is all Straub knows. In *Under Venus*, composer Elliott Denmark, who is writing a song cycle, *Words for the Wind*, speaks for Straub when he admits his closest feelings are for music. "'I've spent all my life listening to it and trying to understand it, analyzing it, but I could never feel that I owned it or possessed it'" (414). Straub himself admitted as much in some of his jazz criticism:

> Music itself has meaning, even if you don't exactly know what it is. Jazz can evoke a state of being toward which words can only grope. If you're moved by it or thrilled by it, you know it's not just random sounds distributed in a way that sounds pleasant. It's hard to write about music, and jazz is no exception. You can only do it if you know enough technically, but then that wouldn't mean anything to anybody who didn't know what a B-flat note or an augmented triad sounds like. The only way to do it is through metaphor. You have to soft-pedal it and not be too aggressive about it, or the metaphors fall flat.[36]

Significantly, music, no matter how sophisticated, can connect with even the unversed and the unlettered to a degree beyond academic analysis. Bill Sheehan reminds me of those marvelous moments in *Mr. X*, when the four-year old Cobbie Hatch entreats Ned Dunstan into listening to his "favorite music." Cobbie's mother expresses bewilderment at the selections: "'I am baffled,'" she says. "'Cobbie is *fixated* on the last section of *Estampes*, a Debussy piano thing, a Monteverdi madrigal called 'Confitebor tibi' sung by [Emma] Kirkby, and Frank Sinatra doing 'Something's Gotta Give.'" While Ned remarks the "flowing, regular meter" of the Monteverdi, the "high percussive E" that ends the Debussy, and the "rhythm after the instrumental break" of the Sinatra, the boy falls directly into the heart of the music when, displaying perfect pitch, he accurately picks out the notes on a piano. He doesn't know what the notes are called; but he *does* know that E and B are "colored red and blue." Ned muses in wonderment, "I don't know what I felt most like doing, giggling in delight or applauding, but I think I did both" (194, 212).

And in perhaps the most remarkable example of Straub's skirmishes with language and music, the long story "The Ballad of Ballard and Sandrine" presents a race of "We" creatures who "speak in the high-pitched, musical language of birds. They sing their notes "of the utmost liquid purity," Straub writes at the end of the story. "We know what they mean, though they have long since passed through the realm of words and gained again the transparency of music. We love and accept the weight and the weightlessness of music" (92).

Has language failed him? Is language, as Susan Sontag has alleged, "the most impure, the most contaminated, the most exhausted of all the materials out of which art is made?"[37] Other writers have grappled with this dilemma. On more than one occasion Samuel Beckett said that his goal was to put an end to language, to get past language itself. In his *German Letter* (1937), he says: "More and more my own language appears to me like a veil that must be torn apart in order to get at the things behind it…. I cannot imagine a higher goal for a writer today."[38] More than a hundred years earlier, Novalis had already tried to explain what "the things behind it" might be: "The ridiculous and amazing mistake people make is to believe they use words in relation to things. They are unaware of the nature of language—which is to be its own and only concern, making it so fertile and splendid a mystery."[39]

Maybe the movement, or evolution—or devolution—in the arts toward unintelligibility does not negate their power and authority. Perhaps, for example, suggests Sontag, the written word continues, but in a manner which the reader cannot read; the blank, or negative space of a painting incites us to appreciate the positive shapes that have been broken off; and the silence of music, as Cage has noted, provokes us to realize that there is always something that is happening that makes a sound.[40]

Ear Language

When ink runs dry, when it vanishes from the page, what remains is the sheer sensuousness and intoxication of the *sounds* of language—the *sung* and *spoken* word. Straub frequently refers to the "melody of the English language."[41] Call this *ear language*. In one of Straub's brief sketches in *Houses Without Doors*, "The Poetry Reading," a woman listens to an old man reading his lines, but "the next day, she could remember the sound of his voice, but the poems were only a golden blur" (108). In the final confrontation in *The Floating Dragon* the singing of a foolish little song "When the Red, Red Robin," plays a crucial part in the defeat of evil: "The song didn't matter, the song was ridiculous; it was the fact of *singing* that was powerful" (491; italics added). We recall in *A Dark Matter* that the character of Lee Harwell has an epiphany when he hears Nathaniel Hawthorne's words read aloud. It gives him "entry to a lost realm." The historian-musician Charles Rosen has written that

> learning a language, being forced to attach a meaning to a sound, is a burden to the child, who, in reaction, strings together senseless rhyming noises as a form of escape. Even for adults, understanding speech is not devoid of effort, and can be a source of fatigue. With a

silly play on words, there is a split second when a word suspended between to incompatible senses briefly loses all meaning and becomes pure sound, and for a lovely moment we revert to the delighted state of the child freed from the tyranny of language.[42]

And Arthur Machen, a writer we already know who has had a great influence on Straub, writes in *Hill of Dreams*: "Language ... was chiefly important for the beauty of its sounds, by its possession of words resonant, glorious to the ear, by its capacity, when exquisitely arranged, of suggesting wonderful and indefinable impressions, perhaps more ravishing and further removed from the domain of strict thought than the impressions excited by music itself."[43]

Indeed, Straub has an "ear" for the acoustic implications of his prose. One of his characters, Hootie in *A Dark Matter*, is a veritable talking book. It's entirely apt that *Shadowland*, a book about fairy stories, was derived, in part, from the tradition of the spoken word. In *Sides*, Straub explains that after writing much of the book in long-hand, he then dictated the manuscript to a typist: "[She] typed every word I read aloud to her from my journal. Together, we sailed along to the end of the novel. The immense satisfaction of this process can be explained in a phrase— it was exactly like telling a story" (155).

This appreciation came early as Peter and his wife Susan emphasized the value of *reading aloud* stories to their children. The following exchange came during a recent interview with both of them. Susan commented[44]:

Peter Straub and wife Susan, Milwaukee, 1975 (courtesy Fales Archive).

We both read aloud to our two children practically from birth. We found it to be a win-win situation, an amazing experience, how tiny babies, maybe younger than six weeks, do feel safe in hearing their parent's voice. You can read them anything. They hear the rhythm of the sentences. You don't have to read them just baby books—just *read* to them. And there's the turning of the pages, the stopping to ask questions. I think reading aloud is the best way of inculcating literacy culture.[45] Peter was a wonderful storyteller with the kids when they were very young. All of us, after Thanksgiving or Christmas would sit around and wind down and Peter would say inventive stories about living in the forest, the "Eagle Bear" stories, do you remember? They were so much fun—

"Yes, the bedtime stories for Ben," responds Straub. "Emma from her bedroom in the house in Westport could tune in" if the doors were left open:

She would sneak up to the top bunk so she could hear more easily. Starting in London when Ben was two years old, I discovered in myself a capacity for fairy-tale-like stories. I wish I had written them down. Damn it! I was writing *Shadowland* at the time and I put one of them in, about why frogs croak and why they hop. That was a story I told Ben. Eventually, I settled in to a pattern of stories about an old eagle and an old bear who lived in the deepest, darkest forest. It was great fun. I opened the door, turned the key in the lock, and tried not to get in the way!

"Yes," continues Susan, "I remember when my parents used to come live with us for a week at a time … all of us sat transfixed at those stories. Really too bad you didn't write all of them down!"

Benjamin Straub, now 40 years old and working as a film and television producer in Los Angeles, recalls with great affection these early readings: "Reading and being read to as a child was of significant importance in our family because of the *joy* it provided all of us." How fortunate he and his sister, Emma, were to have a father so gifted at storytelling:

My father is a master storyteller, and generously shared his gift with us at bedtime each night. After tucking me and Emma in, he would weave literary tapestries—unwritten and 100% original—that he likened to the improvised jazz solos his heroes were belting out in the records he listened to while working. He told his "The Eagle and Bear Stories." They were our gift for getting through each day. Complete with a beginning, middle and ending, he was tapping into an internal waterfall of creativity. The Eagle and Bear lived in the deepest part of the deepest, darkest forest and looked for each other on adventures and quests. Emma and I were captivated. We LOVED every second of it. We looked forward to bedtime each night for this reason. If he had taken the time to write down "The Eagle and Bear Stories" they would probably rival those written by JR Tolkien in their detail laden inventive beauty.[46]

The practice inspired Susan Straub's "Read to Me" program, which she instituted in 1990[47]: "The non-profit foundation which my mother started," explains Benjamin, "the 'Read To Me' foundation, is as much about infant reading and learning as it is about bonding with your child and the beautiful shared experience that only books can bring. The baby who still cannot understand formal language understands *sounds* and *inflection*, and reacts accordingly. The parent is disseminating information to their beloved baby through sounds, colors found in the books and the loving hold they cradle the infant in while the process is happening."[48]

Susan Straub is the creator and director:

> Because of Peter, I was able to develop a program so I could leave clinical social work and develop a program specifically to create pathways into the pleasurable experience of reading to babies. I started with teenaged parents. It was a project that at first was just me. I made books for my babies, with construction paper and luggage tags and baggies. Cloth books, too; really amazing. I collected wordless picture books. And I had a couple if children's writer friends. And we went to the local public library. Each of these components parts came together. And I got adopted by a non-profit arts organization, called Teachers and Writers Collaborative. Their offices were on Union Square West. They gave me my street cred; otherwise, I was this nice lady in the neighborhood, peddling books. Because I was under their umbrella, I was eligible for grants, donations, and tax deductions. I made two videos because of that connection, and had training programs. I hired staff. I got even written up in Oprah Winfrey's O Magazine, which was the apotheosis of success. We had people nationwide writing me, wanting to expand into their own neighbors.

Libraries, that vanishing breed, are playing their part.

> Libraries are serious cooperative partners. I come in with picture books, some of which I give to families. And there's an amnesty for books that are lost. And they get a library card. The baby can get a library card! Libraries are still one of the finest resources in America for books for young children. As you know, there are these middle-grade books and YA books that are an explosion in the industry. Getting more and more popular. We have a number of very successful YA authors. I remember *Mrs. Piggle-Wiggle's Magic*, one that I remember reading and loved. The *Mary Poppins* books and the *Oz* books, all of them. My dad read me all the Sunday comics.

Peter himself has childhood memories of being read to: "I also remember my parents reading the Sunday comics. "I asked my parents to read comic books to me so often that I memorized them. I began to realize that I was reading after awhile, the sound just happened to appear on the page, somehow!"

Susan Straub maintains that a professionally-trained voice is not necessary to tell children a story. "Not at all. The one thing is, if you're making up a story, you have to remember what you made up. The kids like it the way you did it the first time. You can drive a small child nuts, if you make changes. They really catch you out. I learned such things with my own kids. And now we have a baby boy grandson. And he uses books all day long! They have books everywhere he goes, in the crib, in the family space, the bathroom."

Perhaps not altogether unlike Dick Dart in *The Hellfire Club*, Peter Straub enjoys reading his works to audiences, ever alert to how the sound and rhythms of his speech inflects their meanings. "When I read out loud, I try to let the inner workings of the sentences come through loud and clear. If

A Benevolent American Gothic: Peter and Susan Straub at home in New York City, 2014 (photograph by John C. Tibbetts).

there are a series of tricky spins off the verb into a series of independent clauses, I do my best to read the sentences so everything is all of a piece, so the person listening isn't confused. I want the turns and swerves and straightaways to be *felt*. Over time, I've gotten to be pretty good at that. I read slower now, though some sentences should be read fairly quickly because of some internal necessity."

The Flâneur in the Shadows

Indeed, in the "invisible ink" of Peter Straub are stories that sometimes reside not on the page, not in music, not even in the spoken voice. Like a modern-day *flâneur*, in the tradition of Baudelaire and Poe, Straub finds them on the street, in the faces and actions of passersby.[49] He says, "To me, a *flâneur* is a gentleman who walks around his city, keeping his eyes open, sitting in cafes watching the parade go by while making mental notes. I spend a great deal of time looking at people in a way that I hope they don't notice or think rude, where you're a part of a stream of people going back and forth, throwing off hints about their lives. I helplessly imagine context and plot."[50]

Many of his writer-protagonists describe themselves essentially as observers. Graham Williams in *Floating Dragon* explains that he carries "a little notebook in which I'd scribble my ideas, and I'd take long walks ... and write down the things I thought of" (410). For professor William Standish in "Mrs. God," "Other people's lives were like novels. You saw so little, you had only a small window to peek through and then you had to guess about what your peek had shown you" (44). And Lee Harwell in *A Dark Matter* chooses his "own little angle" on the world: "It's like standing on the sidewalk, looking in through someone's picture window, and trying to make sense of what I see" (250).

Straub sees himself like the fairytale character of Pippin Little in *The Hellfire Club*, who "wandered from character to character, hearing stories." His account of who Pippin meets, what he finds, and what results, nicely describes the special qualities of his own books:

> Some of these characters were human and some were monsters, but they were fine storytellers one and all. Their tales were colorful and involved, full of danger, heroism, and betrayal. Some told the truth and others lied. Some wanted to help Pippin Little, but even they were not always truthful. Some of the others wanted to cut him up into pieces and turn him into tasty meat loaf.... The truth Pippin required as a mosaic to be assembled over time and at great risk [317].

Once ideas suggest themselves, the process is only beginning. "I'll think about books for months before I start to write. Then, when I'm really tired of doing that, and I can no longer postpone writing the first sentence, I start writing."

The Writer's Life

We can imagine him now, husband, father, and novelist, in his new digs in Brooklyn, after a recent move away from Manhattan. His daughter, Emma, is now an established novelist in her own right. His son Ben works as a producer in Hollywood.[51] And he can point with pride to a valuable archive of his personal and private papers that has been established for scholarly research at the Fales Archive at New York University (it is a requisite port of call for every Straubian enthusiast!).[52] And now, back from one of his rambles, Peter bends to his desk. New books are waiting for his pen and his street people. Before him is an advance copy of *Interior Darkness*, just out from Doubleday, a collection of sixteen stories that includes several that have not previously appeared in book form (see the "Magic Taxi" chapter). Reviews in *Publishers Weekly*, *Salon*, and *The Los Angeles Times* (among others) greet it with raptures. Its exploration of grief and loss, enthuses the *Publishers Weekly* critic, "has elevated Straub's fictions above those that place a premium at evoking shrieks of terror, or repulsion. His approach is a powerful counter to the position an editor once shared with him: that horror fiction is only ever about good versus evil."[53]

Typically, Peter Straub will work from mid-morning until a two-hour lunch. Nearing completion is a new novel, contracted from Doubleday, formerly entitled *The Way It Went Down*, now retitled, simply, *Hello, Jack*. Could it be about a modern-day "Jack the Ripper"? In the planning stages is the long-awaited third volume in the so-called *Talisman* series with collaborator Stephen King. Straub pauses, pen suspended over the paper. He confesses he's at an impasse on *Hello, Jack*, that he's "baffled" at the moment; but soon "the whole thing will be not only clear but filled with light."[54] Then, it's back to work until supper hour, around 6:00. In that time he might write five pages, or maybe ten. It all depends, but it's usually somewhere in that range. He reads over the work at night and corrects the "limp metaphors" then inputs all that into the processor, reprints the pages, and continues. "I always write pretty much from the first page to the last," he confides. "Sometimes I go in and take out or fill in, but I'd be sort of lost if I had a whole bunch of parts lying around that I had to glue together somehow." Yet, for his larger canvases, his most complex narratives, like *Mystery* and *Hellfire Club*, "it just seems natural to divide up the plot and tell it in little bits and pieces. I think that's just the way my mind works, because I don't much plan out this aspect of things. It just evolves in the writing.... I know that I have a natural tendency toward complexity, rather than simplicity, and part of what I'm trying to do now is make things a little more simple."[55]

The experience for him—not to mention the reader—is, in his own words, like exploring one of those wonderfully haunted Gothic houses, like Coleman Collin's mansion in *Shadowland*, or Esswood House in "Mrs. God"—the ones "filled with hidden passages and trap doors, also an entire wing sometimes but not always entered by a certain flight of stairs." One moment you may find the stairs to the wing, but another time "you cannot even find the stairs." Or, perhaps, they just lead to a "blank wall." How to negotiate the impasse? "You require another story" and "rearrange your concerns in a different order"; and the results might be "as dubious and unreliable as the others" and will constitute "both a beginning and an ending."[56]

The risk, of course, and the pleasure, is that both writer and reader might get lost in the process. We might lose our bearings in the normative world.

Is it just a trick of the light … or is Straub's figure growing *dim*, then dimmer … almost vanishing altogether?

Are our ears playing tricks on us—or do we hear the faint *blat* of a Magic Taxi outside?

"For a long time," muses Straub, "I have felt that fiction's secret desire is to take over the world, to replace it with itself, though I've never been sure of how this process was to work, exactly." Straub admits this process affects his own life: "Fiction would send its tendrils into more and more of my life, it would consider and consider, and as it considered it would subsume. It seems to me that fiction WANTS to do this, wants to take over."[57]

"A Magellan of the Interior"
An Interview with Straub[1]

The secret that resides in the life and work of the man who has written some of the darkest, most complex, and most disturbing tales of literary horror (he staunchly defends the genre), is that Peter Straub is a kind, generous, and sensitive man, esteemed among his peers and would-be writers alike.

Moreover, he's *funny*. He smiles a lot.[2]

Take that as you please. I think it might be the most authentically enigmatic thing about him.

I've come to interview Peter on a bright sunny day in late May. We are in his five-story townhouse on West 85th street on Manhattan's Upper West Side. We had first met and conversed twenty years ago, just after his first story collection, *Houses Without Doors* (1990), was published. Since then, bridging the gap between the novels *Mystery* (1990) and his latest, *A Dark Matter* (2010), we have gathered at a few horror and fantasy conventions, shared numerous telephone conversations, and shared joint appearances on radio shows.

Peter Straub is a big man, over six feet, sturdily built, with a round face that irrepressibly breaks into quick bursts of laughter. The night before, he had given a public reading of a new story at a Manhattan bookstore, "The Ballad of Ballard and Sandrine" (it appears in issue 56 [2011] of the literary journal, *Conjunctions*).

"It's a very strange piece of work," Straub confides, as we settle ourselves on a couch in the sitting room. We have just taken a brief tour. A lamp is burning. The shutters are drawn ("I never look out the window unless I have to"). Stacks of books and CDs are everywhere. Adorning one wall are two graphics by R.B. Kitaj ("He's a graphic designer and painter, from Cleveland, who went to the Royal Academy of Art at the same time as David Hockney"). A visit to his study upstairs discloses a very crowded desk with a computer; a leather couch; a number of private journals (one of which has a title page

Peter Straub (right) and the author (photograph by James A. Tibbetts).

with a collage of images bearing the inscription, "The Strange Fate of the Mind's Eye"); a copy of John Ashbery's new book, *Flow Chart*; and a manuscript of *The Throat*.

"After my reading," Straub is saying, "I met my great friends, Leo and Diane Dillon." Abruptly, he pauses and leans forward confidentially: "Diane told me about something very strange. She told me that once she saw from her apartment window something that looked like a flying saucer that was moving across the sky. It was disc-shaped and enormous; and bands of light were flashing across its surface. She called Leo over. He saw the same thing."

Straub pauses, gauging my reaction. "Now, this is a woman who is not out of her mind! She's very sensible, totally sane, and has great taste and possesses every decent human quality. Yet … she *saw this thing*? What do we make of that???"

Straub sits back in his chair.

"*The world is unknowable!*" he proclaims, with a satisfied smile.

The Interview

JCT: That reminds me that long ago a lot of us boys spent delicious nights dreaming of flying saucers outside our window. Surely there were monsters hiding under the beds. Were you also like that?

Not like that, exactly. As a boy I wasn't worried about monsters or UFOs so much; but I do remember a big empty meadow beyond my house during the years seven to fourteen; and there was a dark forest 'way at the back of it. At the center of the woods was some sort of mansion made of stone. I had many fantasies about the place and had a lot of fun playing there. I cooked up some pleasurable fears, mainly involved with playing soldiers, or cowboys and Indians, or spies, or Things from Outer Space…. Nowadays you can't be afraid of such things anymore. Take the movie, *District 9* [2009]: The aliens aren't frightening at all, although they're grotesque enough. They're too easily confined, too buried in social commentary. No, there was always a lot going on in my life, and there was always a lot of tension. And the child I was is still fairly present inside me. I have to keep him under control and treat him well while not letting him get the upper hand.

You were writing, already, as a child?

I wrote my first stories while I was in the second and third grades. I always wanted very much to write. I loved the whole idea of the blank page, of pencils, of a desk. Sort of a "sacred space" where you could go and make something up. There were stories about a spy who tried to kill himself by jumping out a window, which was pretty bleak and full of a sense of self-betrayal. Hmm. And my teacher didn't know what to do about *that*. It turned her against me, I'm afraid. That was the only case in my whole grade school life where my teacher didn't like me. And then, my next story was about Judas wandering from place to place and being stoned and driven away. I must admit that looking back it seems odd that a child's imagination would fasten on something like betrayal so early. That is mysterious to me. Anyway, my parents, when they had opportunities, advised me very strongly against making a living as a writer. I thought it was good advice, until the time came when I had to ignore that advice!

This brings up something. Parenting is a real problem in your stories. Children grow up damaged. They suffer trauma. They become violent. You know, I had wonderful parents. I had a wonderful upbringing…. Did I miss out on something?

Oh, you have no idea what you missed out on, John!

I'm actually quite serious. I could not have asked for a better set of parents. Have I suffered a price for that?

It's a blessing! It means you can go through life in a stable fashion. At least you know you were loved, you were supported. You were not undone, you were not orphaned. You didn't suffer physical or mental abuse. Nothing luckier could happen to *anybody*. Also, you were born white and male, which is an immense privilege. That should be questioned, and it is being questioned, but still, in the '50s and '60s there was a whole mess of things you weren't aware of and didn't need to be aware of. Most writers have had sketchy childhoods, in which something went awry, something went amiss, or they became aware of sexual dysfunctions which had to be concealed.

Or retreat to what you call in one of your books "a special place."

Indeed. You're always looking at the world through the eyes of the fictional character you're pretending to be. When I was a kid, I was a fictional character. But the fictional character was *myself*, the self my parents wanted me to be, the self I would have been perhaps had I not been injured and abused as a small boy. I didn't want to be the person who was injured and abused. It didn't fit my *idea* of myself. I always experienced myself as a person of some integrity and wholeness; and also of a certain mental or spiritual force of some kind. I didn't see myself as being victimized. It was a horrible insult; it made me angry and humiliated and ashamed. So I had to pretend it wasn't true. I wasn't in the same ballpark as my friends. We could talk about baseball cards and my new toy gun, but I realized, that's *all* we can do.

In my early teenage years, in a suburb called Brookfield in Milwaukee, I used to walk down the street and ring doorbells of houses where there was a woman alone, and I would introduce myself and hope we could just talk about things. And they would invite me in for a glass of cocoa would just talk. I would listen to them talking about *their* mothers and about their children (they never talked about their husbands!). We'd gab like a couple of old ladies, and then I'd go home. I suppose some of the women thought it was creepy that I could talk eye-to-eye to them, and they didn't want that from a twelve-year-old boy. Others knew it was totally innocent.

This was a different sort of boyhood than you see in, say, Ray Bradbury.[3] I kinda envy that. What I had was *interesting*, at least when my father wasn't blocking the sun. But when I wasn't doing that, things were *boring*. I hated the 'burbs. I wanted to go downtown where there were bigger buildings and people stayed awake at night. As soon as I could, I discovered things that demanded I investigate them on my own—things like jazz and science fiction (which I got into very heavily when I was twelve). I got out of that when I read a novel for adults, Thomas Wolfe's *Of Time and the River* [1935]. One of the great books of wounded boyhood and romantic adolescence. I thought, this book is about *me*…. What could be better when you're fourteen?! And then I never looked at science fiction again. My parents would say, "Put down that book! Don't you want to go outside?!" Soon, there was no use in trying to persuade me to do things I didn't want to do. I was listening to records and going to jazz clubs.

Speaking of books…. Your books are all about books! As an academic myself—curse the word!—I can't help but wince when you come down pretty hard on academia and academics. "Mrs. God" really speaks to those of us who find ourselves buried in libraries and archives in pursuit of God-knows-what arcane subjects and research. Who knew the horrors awaiting us!

Any reader of H. P. Lovecraft will tell you how dangerous that is! "Mrs. God" allowed me a chance to express those glimpses I had had in my youth of the academic life. I had always wanted to do something involving a big English country house. So I made up one of my own, Esswood House, and gave it a huge library modeled after the Adams Library at Kenwood House at the top of Hampstead Heath, which is open to the public, and where we used to go a lot while we lived in England. Professor Standish's pursuit of the hopelessly elusive poet Isobel Standish is really a pursuit into something very dreadful in his recent past.

I didn't want anything in that book to be very clear at all. I wanted there to be the *possibility* of old people being cared for, of big dollhouses down in the basement where tiny, malformed, people lived, of certain mysterious burials out on the lawn. All of that was a product of my having finished four years of really concentrated work on *Koko*. I felt that something marvelous happened to me. My level had gone up. I was working better than before.

Before that, my relationship to my writing had begun awkwardly, and I hadn't written for a year. I couldn't remember how to do a bunch of things. I couldn't remember the things that I couldn't remember how to do. It was like needing to do "finger exercises" on a "keyboard" that had become too limited, you know? Like Beethoven, I needed to find a few extra octaves. Over the three years I spend writing *Koko*, everything came back to me, much more. So one thing that also happened upon finishing *Koko* was a terrible sense of grief. What I then started to do was write a short story which became "Mrs. God," about a man who was driven crazy because he thought his wife was having an affair; and when she became pregnant, he forced her have an abortion because he thought the baby was another man's. But it wasn't another man's. It was *his* baby, and he had had it killed. At the end Standish himself has become a *huge* baby, all covered in grease.

So in all of this, you're saying...?

This is really Peter Straub saying about finishing and leaving behind *Koko*—"*Where's my baby??? I want my baby back!*" I wanted all that to be hidden in "Mrs. God," because it was hidden from Standish himself. Any chance I could get, I put in implications of the *power* of the dead baby, the power of an *angry* baby...

Small wonder, I guess, if some readers and critics don't know what to make of your stories!

Not just critics, but readers out there who send me hostile notes.

In all your work you and your characters attempt to evoke, or describe the indescribable, whether it be the horrific or the transcendent. Shades of H. P. Lovecraft! Lovecraft will expend hundreds of pages in the attempt, but usually lapse at the end into inarticulate words and ellipses on the page. Are you up to something like that in your books?

Maybe you mean *A Dark Matter*. It came out of a tremendous struggle and uncertainty and some pain. For a time I was at "half-candle," and I felt that I was trying to build a house out of just a few planks and windows. That's part of the reason it's a strange book. But I'm very pleased with that book. It's visionary in a way I could not have expected. The central characters have all denied or forgotten something crucial and determining about the event in the Meadow. It boils and smokes inside them. They're imprisoned inside their own repressed worlds. You can only approach truth in *A Dark Matter* in a sidelong way, from many angles. And then near the end, Lee Hayward's wife, who is blind, says, "Shut up! And I'll tell you exactly what happened!" And she does! Sort of. And we do tend to believe her! She's the source of wisdom in the book.

We've been waiting for her!

Yes, she's been lying in wait the whole time, just ticking away. The whole structure of *A Dark Matter* is intended to set up something at the bottom of the book that keeps shifting about and is essentially indeterminate. I didn't exactly intend this. It starts off with a kind of synopsis. In doing that I disobeyed the great rule of writing—don't *tell, describe.* So I give you lots of pages with Lee Hayward *explaining* things, with a few bits of dialogue and movement in the past thrown in. And then he's back to summarizing it all! And you have these images that are very important, like the glass of water shining on the tabletop. It's an image of immense mystery: you can see through it, it's pure and nourishing, it gives life, it's inert, yet somehow magical, laden with inexpressible yearnings and meanings. Anyway, after that, we get a short story written by the guy who described everything the first time around! And that clearly displaces everything. And then you split off into the various characters, all of whom present the same event in their own style. The event itself depends upon things I read in a book by Cornelius Agrippa.

This was a real person?

Yes! Henry Cornelius Agrippa was the *man*. He was a Renaissance magician and had a very turbulent life. He wrote four great books of magic, including *Magical Ceremonies* [1565]. He died too young in a monastery, watched over by a bunch of priests who thought he was a heretic, even satanic character. He's inexplicable. He described spirits conjured up that were beautiful and dangerous. I sucked them into my book. But this also seems dubious— where did Agrippa *get* this stuff? He's describing stuff that would alter our own understanding of the world. Even if we're not sure what that meaning is!

The way you write, the way you tell a story, is very interesting. Sometimes you just stop *the action and will describe whole scenes in great detail.*

I guess if you look at anything long enough, even the most ordinary of surface details, something almost hallucinatory can result.... *Paranormal Activity* [2009] is a recent film that plays with that, don't you think? What I like about that is you have a situation when you're forced to have *patience*, to just *look*. The world is its own meaning. You try to translate the actual world onto your page in the same way that the painter Corot set up his canvas in a field. I'm thinking of a writer like Flaubert—especially in *Madame Bovary*—where the details of observation are chosen so carefully and described so perfectly that the words disappear.... And you find yourself right there on the page with them. Or there's Matisse. In one of his diaries, when he was living on the Mediterranean, he wrote about a mystical sense of *presence* in the physical world, which he wanted to represent in paint. There's a thrill that comes through the words or strokes of paint because of the *seamlessness* of the illusion. It's so good that it isn't an illusion, after all, I think. That's a sacred obligation for any artist. You must *attend* to things, as one is asked to do with those Andy Warhol movies in the '60s. You experience almost a supernatural payoff. Is it a hidden radiance or a hidden nothing? There's no question which side of the duality I have chosen as the truth. That's why I'm fond of the films of Robert Bresson, his pace, the way he speaks without shouting. I just try to write *well*. My notion of what good writing has evolved a great deal over the years. I used to try to write "pretty," and I think you can see some perfect examples of that in my *Ghost Story*. But those kinds of rhetorical moments don't work for me anymore. I'd rather just draw the readers into my stories with their eyes wide open.

Do you see yourself as a modern-day flâneur, like Baudelaire or Poe?[4]

Hmm. To me, a *flâneur* is a gentleman who walks around his city, keeping his eyes open, sitting in cafes watching the parade go by while making mental notes. I spend a great deal of time looking at people in a way that I hope they don't notice or think rude. I'm fascinated by what you can pick up from the way people move and the way they gesture and treat other people, what sort of dramas you can imagine.

In an interview I had once with August Wilson, he said he writes his plays while sitting in coffee shops, just watching, and listening.[5]

Sometimes I've done things like that, but mainly in hotel lobbies, where you're a part of a stream of people going back and forth, throwing off hints about their lives. I helplessly imagine contexts and plot, all of which I'm sure are wildly wrong.

We think the writer's life is a lonely one. But you get out there, don't you, out and about?

Well, it's hard to spend your whole life alone. And that is a demand the job makes on you. But the ultimate reward is that you're not alone at all. You make up this whole world—or you go exploring for it—and it's full of extremely interesting, entertaining folks. Whether you go out or stay in, you listen to them talk and you watch what they do. All the time you're exploring some inner country, like a "Magellan of the Interior," as I say in one of my stories. You get these ideas that are full of excitement because you don't know what they mean yet, or quite know where they're going. But you go along, anyway.

I tell you something, though, my daughter, Emma, is a writer, and she does the same thing.[6] But she's *not* wildly wrong. She's published a collection of short stories called *Other People We Married* (available from a small press). She's got a deal with Riverhead Press and an editor named Megan Lynch for a novel. It'll come out next year. I think it's called *Laura Lamont's Life in Pictures*—a book about a movie star in the golden years of Hollywood. Emma can look at people very often and determine their entire sociology, where they're from, what their parents are like, how well off they are, etc. She's proven this to me many times in airports. I'll see some scruffy dude hanging around the airport ticket counter, and I'll say, "Emma, look at that loser; he's probably getting a ticket to Nowheresville." But she'll say, "Dad, that guy was raised in Cape Cod, is a surfer and has an enormous trust fund and a wealthy mother!" And sure enough, a well-dressed, "waspy" dame will walk over and take him by the arm. I wish I could do that sort of thing as well as she. But as long as I can invent things, I'm okay.

Did you resist Emma becoming a writer the way an actor resists a child becoming an actor?

Almost. But there wasn't much choice with her!

You have said you enjoy doing poetry readings. I guess poetry has always been important to you.

Oh, yes! One of the things that I think is true about poetry is that you can tell, if your ear is good, if a poet is any good or not, even if you don't understand what he is saying. There's something about the way John Ashbery uses language that has *authority*. His work couldn't have had more authority, even though he questioned the very idea of authority itself. I was dazzled, and I remain dazzled.

When you speak your texts out loud, what is happening? Are we hearing them as sounds *as well* as their *sense?*

One wonders! When I read out loud, I try to let the inner workings of the sentences come through loud and clear. If there are a series of tricky spins off the verb into a series of independent clauses, I do my best to read the sentences so everything is all of a piece, so the person listening isn't confused. I want the turns and swerves and straightaways to be *felt*. Over time, I've gotten to be pretty good at that. I read slower now, though some sentences should be read fairly quickly because of some internal necessity.

So this really is a musical experience?

In a way, yeah. I wish it were *more* musical! But we do what we can with what we have. Music itself has meaning, even if you don't exactly know what it is. If you're moved by it or thrilled by it, you know it's not just random sounds distributed in a way that sounds pleasant.

Your love of jazz, in particular, is obvious in stories like "Pork Pie Hat."

Oh yes, "Hat" is based on Lester Young, of course.

And it seems to me there are two people who write so eloquently about jazz—that's you and Charles Beaumont.

Thank you! I included Beaumont's "Black Country" in my double anthology for Library of America of American fantastic tales. It's a knockout story. Just now I watched a documentary film by Jason Brock about Beaumont. I hadn't known that when "Black Country" came out, it flattened everybody. All of that circle of his, Bill Nolan, Harlan Ellison, Ray Bradbury read it, and it knocked them off their chairs. It's hard to write about music, and jazz is no exception. You can only do it if you know enough technically, but then that wouldn't mean anything to anybody who didn't know what a B-flat note or an augmented triad sounds like. The only way to do it is through metaphor. You have to soft-pedal it and not be too aggressive about it, or the metaphors fall flat. At the end of *Mr. X*, I tried my best to describe an alto sax solo by Paul Desmond of "These Foolish Things," and it sounded like I was talking about a landscape painting of mountain ranges. That was the best I could do.

I know you collect jazz recordings. Do you identify with your character of "Little Red" in "Little Red's Tango"? He keeps stacks and stacks of jazz recordings everywhere in his little house—

—I used to keep my jazz records like that, all labeled and catalogued.... Little Red is based on a guy I know, a wonderful character named Jay Andersen who lives on the corner of West 55th and Eighth, in an amazing, warren-like apartment with huge mounds of unnameable stuff all around him. He's such an extraordinary character. Just *staying alive* for this guy is a miracle. He's never been forced out of that apartment, although he has no visible means of support. *That's* a miracle. There's something both alarming and *blessed* about him. I took the best parts of him and used those as the basis for whatever inspiration I had. I gave him the story in manuscript, and he told me he laughed and cried at the same time, which is the best possible response.

Gary K. Wolfe says somewhere there is "a seed of exaltation in extremity" in your work. The experience of torture and sexual abuse is disturbing, but it can come across as somehow wondrous or transformational. You use the words "alarming" and "blessed" interchangeably. I admit that sometimes the extremes of violence and horror in your stories—like Harry Beever's tortures of his little brother in "Blue Rose"—make me uneasy, squeamish.

Sometimes you are asked to go to places that nobody else has ever seen. That's exciting. That's what keeps me coming back to my desk. Yes, of course there are things that I've written that make me feel squeamish. When that happens, I know I'm on to something. "The Juniper Tree" spooked me so much that I didn't even look at it for two years after I wrote it. I didn't even type it up! I revised it very carefully and just put it away and didn't want to look at it. Finally, I took it off the shelf and rewrote it again by hand.

I'm also thinking now of lost boy lost girl. *Despite the violent tortures and brutal deaths that have been revealed, we find in the conclusion that Tim Underhill, his nephew, and Lucy have all received some kind of, well, call it a transfiguration.... At least, I felt something like that, too!*

I'm very glad. At one point I thought I was going to subtitle it "The Uses of Horror." A way of dealing with grief. Certainly I felt as though something good descended upon *me* when I was writing the ending of that, when you finally see the ghosts—or, "remains," as I call them—of Tim's nephew and Lucy Cleveland (Lily Kalender) together at last. I wanted to do a book with more about her. *In the Night Room*, a kind of sequel, if you will, offers a monocular vision of *lost boy lost girl*. The climax has Tim and his own fictional character drive in a car to where the real Lily Kalender is living. It's at the end of a cul-de-sac, backed up against some woods. They see through the window this blonde woman carrying a cup of tea. And you're supposed to think, *"Oh, my God, that's her! There she is! And what a piece of work she is!"*

There's sometimes a touching, even beautiful reality to your ghosts, or whatever they are, isn't there? They're not just the result of some human psychological aberration.

I wrote somewhere ["Hunger, an Introduction"] that although we all have to die sooner or later, we know surprisingly little about ghosts!

No kidding! But in your stories we get glimpses of them out of the corner of our eye.

That's because Tim [Underhill] *wants* to see them, and he knows he wants to see them. One of the great advantages of an imagination is that it can give you possibilities that you know aren't possible, but nonetheless are real because they're in your mind. [Pause] It makes us emotional. And don't forget about my friend, Diane Dillon, who is completely sane, who reported seeing something completely inexplicable. I think the human mechanism, as profound and mysterious as it is, doesn't take in *everything*. There are sounds we cannot hear, colors we cannot see, and that argues for another kind of dimensionality that passes through or in front of us.

Maybe the only way we can cope with the inexplicable is to laugh in its face. We are always surprised by your diabolical sense of humor. The sort of thing you often find in John Collier. We get flashes of that in your stories, especially in "Mr. Clubb and Mr. Cuff." Who knew that torture could be funny?

Thank you! Although I'm not a big fan of John Collier, I do admire some of his short stories and the novel, *His Monkey Wife* [1931]. I began to realize I could be funny in *The Hellfire Club*, when Dick Dart started flapping his tongue. I didn't have much control over that. I just wrote what I heard him say, which was always so surprising, as scabrous and wicked as he was. He could be really funny. Here I was, asking readers, fifty percent of whom were women, to laugh at the utterances of a serial killer who rapes and murders women. That's a tough thing to ask! But I did ask. Now, these days about all we hear about are the tortures of Guantanamo and Abu Ghraib. But there's another side to torture, you know! Think about Clubb and Cuff. They come out of nowhere. They give you what you really want, even though you didn't know what you wanted! It's their business and it's a sick, bloody business. It's an art form for them. They understand themselves to be artists, and who's to say they're not! They certainly get to where they're going, unlike most of us. When they get their hands on you, they're going to get the results they want.

And the narrator ends up suffering the very tortures he's hired them to do to others! Yet, you imply it's a kind of a transforming experience for him! Wow!

That's right. And he would never have gotten there had he not been maimed and broken. You know, John Keats said something in a letter to the effect that in the creation of a soul, things that injure us affect the way our soul is written upon, the way our soul is able to expand. This is a guy speaking on the verge of death. He knew what was in store for him. He could understand what suffering had given him, which was a depth of understanding you don't get unless you are profoundly beaten up by the world. We are *all* maimed.

Care to share any perspectives on your career at this stage in your life?

I don't see any book from now on as my last, but I do know I'm in the late phases of my career. And I think I'm writing really well. But here I am, filled with infirmities, without the stamina I have been used to. My wife says, "Remember, Peter, you're not forty anymore!" [laughs] Okay, I don't write as fast as I used to, and it takes me longer. But right now I'm trying to write a book which I hope I can finish in two years. I'm thinking of calling it *Hello, Jack!*[7] And Stephen King and I want to do another book together. He doesn't shilly-shally around. It's obvious *he* hasn't slowed down. Although I use the good old iMac and even of late have dictated some things, I still sometimes write in long hand. In moments of stress or trouble, I always revert to that.

Chapter Notes

Introduction

1. Peter Straub, "The Juniper Tree," in Straub, *Houses Without Doors* (New York: E.P. Dutton, 1990), 72–90.

2. *Ibid.*, 80.

3. Peter Straub interview with the author, NYC, 2011.

4. Among the most famous of the Grimms' *Tales*, "The Juniper Tree" tells of a woman who abuses her stepson, decapitates him, chops his corpse into pieces, and serves them up to the family in a stew. Later, the victim's stepsister places the bones under the juniper tree. The tree moves and absorbs the bones. A beautiful bird then appears on the topmost branch, soars aloft, drops a millstone onto the head of the stepmother, killing her, and flies away, singing. Philip Pullman attributes the story to the painter, Philipp Otto Runge, although it always appears in the Grimm collections. "For beauty, for horror," writes Pullman, "for perfection of form, this story has no equal." See Philip Pullman, *Fairy Tales from the Brothers Grimm* (New York: Viking, 2012), 198.

5. Peter Straub, *Mr. X* (New York: Random House, 1999), 258.

6. Quoted in Douglas E. Winter, "Peter Straub," in *Faces of Fear* (New York: Berkeley Books, 1985), 232.

7. *Ibid.*, 222.

8. *Ibid.*, 224.

9. Peter Straub, *Shadowland* (New York: Coward, McCann & Geoghegan, 1980), 159.

10. Writing in 1850 in the Preface to *The Scarlet Letter*, Hawthorne described the effect of a "neutral territory" that is "somewhere between the real world and fairy-land, where the Actual and the Imaginary may meet, and each imbue itself with the nature of the other." *The Scarlet Letter*, in Norman Pearson, ed., *The Novels and Selected Tales of Nathaniel Hawthorne* (New York: The Modern Library, 1937), 105.

11. Peter Straub, *In the Night Room* (New York: Random House, 2004), 282.

12. Peter Straub, *Sides*, 165.

13. John Fetzer interview with John Tibbetts, in Tibbetts, *Schumann: A Chorus of Voices* (New York: Amadeus Press, 2010), 35–37.

14. "Affect horror," explains historian and critic John Clute, in *The Darkening Garden* (2006), "may be very profitably applied to non-supernatural texts" and refers to the experience of the visceral affect, "the atrocity of the thing itself." No other genre, he continues, "has been defined in terms of the affect it generates in the reader" (9–10). Historically, the French *grand guignol* dates from roughly the late 19th century to the 1960s. Unlike the Gothic tale, this graphic and gory form of entertainment was based on real-life criminal stories from newspapers and laboratory reports. In his *The Grand Guignol: Theater of Fear and Terror* (New York: Da Capo Press, 1997), Mel Gordon reports: "The shocking stage display was a more truthful unveiling of the savage human soul than anything available elsewhere on stage or in the cinema. Only life matched the horror of the *grand guignol*" (2).

15. Roz Kaveney, "Hiring Jack Ketch," *Times Literary Supplement*, 2 March 2001, 23.

16. See Jack Zipes's *The Irresistible Fairy Tale* (Princeton: Princeton University Press, 2012), 42–44, for a detailed account of the Bluebeard story, "a memetic icon" of the serial killer narrative. See also Harold Schechter's *Savage Pastimes* (New York: St. Martin's Press,

2005), 1–14, for a gruesome catalogue of such archetypcal horrors in the fairy tale tradition and in the literary narratives osf 18th- and 19th- century America.

17. Schama goes on to note, regarding the "Martyrdom": "As St. Lawrence went on cooking, so the legend had it, the smell of scorching human flesh turned, miraculously, into the most intensely sweet fragrance. Brutish nostrils quivered; incredulous pagans were converted; souls were saved." See Simon Schama, *The Power of Art* (New York: HarperCollins, 2006), 78–103.

18. See the discussion of the impact of the 2004 Abu Ghraib atrocities and sexual abuse on film and television in Hilary Naroni, *The Subject of Torture: Psychoanalysis & Biopolitics in Television and Film* (New York: Columbia University Press, 2015). The representations of torture in the Abu Ghraib photographs has brought the reality of torture to the public eye. A striking aspect of them is the obvious enjoyment of the American soldiers in inflicting these abuses. Consequently, the narrative structures of the *Saw* and *Hostel* series "remain steeped in horror genre expectations" but do not push the films "in such a way as to make larger social critiques by upending genre traditions…. They present torture in the way that pornography presents sex" (72–73).

19. Gary K. Wolfe, *Evaporating Genres: Essays on Fantastic Literature* (Middletown, CT: Wesleyan University Press, 2011), 135.

20. Gary K. Wolfe and Amelia Beamer, "Peter Straub and Transcendental Horror."

21. In *The Wound and the Bow* (New York: Oxford University Press, 1970) Edmund Wilson discusses the *Philoctetes* of Sophocles and a more modern version, Andre Gide's *Philocteté*. The hero Philoctetes, who possesses the enchanted bow of Herakles, suffers from an incurable wound from a snake bite. Not until Philocotetes returns to Troy with the bow is he healed and Troy captured. His pain is "a dignity and an interest" for Sophocles. Philoctete's misfortune, writes Wilson, "has enabled him to perfect himself": "I come to know more of the secrets of life than my masters had ever revealed to me" (236).

22. Quoted in Paul Tremblay, "The Whole Ball of Wax in a Nutshell," *Los Angeles Review of Books*, 21 February 2016. See *lareviewofbooks.org/author/peter-straub*.

23. *Ibid.*

24. Peter Straub, *A Special Place* (New York: Pegasus Books, 2010), 94.

25. Peter Straub interview with the author, NYC, 2014.

26. *Ibid.*

27. Peter Straub, "Inside Story," in David Shields and Bradford Morrow, eds., *The Inevitable: Contemporary Writers Confront Death* (New York: W.W. Norton, 2011), 215–216.

28. *Ibid.*, 208–219.

29. For information about Chris Van Allsburg and his books, see my "The Mysteries of Chris Van Allsburg," *The World and I*, Vol. 6, No. 12 (December 1991), 252–261.

30. For a discussion of Emerson's thoughts on the humanism of ecstasy, see Robert D. Richardson, Jr., *Emerson: The Mind on Fire* (Berkeley: University of California Press, 1995). In "The Method of Nature," for example, Emerson writes that ecstatic states are natural, not supernatural, and are experiences open to everyone: "Every man has had one or two moments of extraordinary experience, has met his soul, has thought of something which he never afterward forgot, and which revised all his speech, and moulded all his forms of thought" (353).

31. China Miéville, "M.R. James and the Quantum Vampire," 29 November 2011, *Weird Fiction Review*. See http://weirdfictionreview.com/2011/11/m-r-james-and-the-quantum-vampire-by—china-miéville/. No pagination.

32. China Miéville. "M.R. James and the Quantum Vampire."

33. *"J'ai seul la clef de cette parade sauvage"* is the last line of Rimbaud's prose poem, *Parade*. As translated by John Ashbery, the passage reads: "They act out ballads, tragedies of thieves and demi-gods…. Their eyes flame, the blood sings, the bones swell, tears and trickles of red descend." Quoted in Michael Wood, "We do it all the time," *London Review of Books*, 4 February 2016, 9.

34. Eagleton, "Allergic to Depths," 7. www.ameliabeamer.com/short-fiction-poems-nonfiction/. Reprinted as "Peter Straub and the New Horror," in Wolfe, Gary K., *Evaporating Genres*, 151–163.

35. Quoted in Michael Schumacher, "Ghost Storyteller," *Writer's Digest*, January 1985, 30–34.

36. China Miéville, "M.R. James and the Quantum Vampire."

37. Paul Newman in his *History of Terror* pursues the differences between the terror sublime and the real horror of pain and imminent death: "One is essentially a *recreation*, the other all too real. We are taught to *enjoy* fear, it is important to only *half* believe in it. More than that would make it a threat to sanity" (xi).

38. Douglas E. Winter, ed., *Faces of Fear: Encounters with the Creators of Modern Horror* (New York: Berkley Books, 1985), 232. These categories are taken from John Clute's taxonomy in *The Darkening Garden: A Short Lexicon of Horror.*

39. Quoted in Paul Tremblay, "The Whole Ball of Wax in a Nutshell."

40. Peter Straub, "Something about a Death, Something about a Fire," in Straub, *Houses Without Doors*, 215–219.

41. Peter Straub interview with the author, NYC, 2011.

42. Bill Sheehan, *At the Foot of the Story Tree* (Burton, MI: Subterranean Press, 2000), 29.

43. Peter Straub, *Shadowland*, 200–201. In an interview with the author, Kansas City, 1986, Maurice Sendak talked about the Grimm's ambivalence regarding the readership of their Tales: "The Tales did find a readership among children, that's true. Children have naturally good taste! But when these stories came out, the Brothers were appalled at first at the response by children. They had no idea that children were going to like them and read them so much. The question is, why did they like them so much? Because they had been given a lot of homilies and pap to read previous to that; and suddenly, here were marvelous stories that were linguistically available to them and were simply told. And, too, they were about life and death and murderous impulses and sex and passion and all the things children are interested in but hadn't been allowed access to. So of course they fell in love with the tales! It was a form that everybody loved…. The early Romantics were more insightful than that. They saw in these Tales the natural to-and-fro between the business of being a child and being a grownup. There was naivete, yes, but there were also premonitions of terrors, too. There was nothing eccentric or cute about it. It was just a natural state of things. Now, we have corrupted the folk and fairy tales into what are called 'children's

books.' This was not the Brothers' idea at all. They didn't see them as something specifically for children; they were for *people*. It's hard to put ourselves back into that frame of mind, because we have so corrupted the form into idiocy, which is known as the 'kiddie book.'"

44. Gary K. Wolfe, *Evaporating Genres*, 28.

45. Peter Straub interview with the author, NYC, 2014.

46. *Ibid.*

47. Charles Baudelaire called the flâneur "l'homme des foules" (the man of the crowd), after the short story of that name by Edgar Allan Poe (1840). This figure drifts about the streets, observing without being observed. "To Poe," writes Walter Benjamin, "the flâneur was, above all, someone who does not feel comfortable in his own company. This is why he seeks out the crowd; the reason he hides in it but is probably close at hand." See Walter Benjamin, *The Writer of Modern Life* (Cambridge: Harvard University Press, 2006), 79.

48. The redoubtable—and wholly fictitious—Putney Tyson Ridge has long been acknowledged, asserts Straub, tongue planted firmly in cheek, as "an essential figure in the field of Popular Studies." for a substantial body of Putney's criticism. For example: "*Houses without Doors* comes complete with an insufferably pretentious epigraph and an 'Authors Note' stained with the deepest self-regard…. An undigested mysticism pervades all, many times with hilarious and completely unintentional results." Peter Straub, *Sides* (Baltimore: Cemetery Dance, 2007), 305.

49. Quoted in William Sheehan, *At the Foot of the Story Trees*, 345.

50. Peter Straub interview with the author, NYC, 2011.

Chapter One

1. In the "Note" appended to *Houses Without Doors* (New York: Dutton, 1990), 357–358, Straub generously acknowledges the many sources and circumstances for these stories. Some were inspired by readings of Herman Melville, Gabriel Garcia Márquez, Marguerite Duras, Joseph Brodsky, and Robert Aickman. Others were reactions to screenings of *films noir*. And others were cutting and rewritings of episodes cut from the Vietnam-related novels *Koko* and *The Throat*.

2. Neil Gaiman, cover blurb for *Interior Darkness*.

3. Paul Tremblay, "The Whole Ball of Wax in a Nutshell," *Los Angeles Times*, 21 February 2016. See *lareviewofbooks.org/author/peter-straub*.

4. Peter Straub interview with the author, NYC, 1990. The Márquez short story is "A Very Old Man with Enormous Wings" (*Un senor muy viejo con unas alas enormess*), first published in 1955.

5. Peter Straub interview with the author, NYC, 1990.

6. Quoted in Paul Tremblay, "The Whole Ball of Wax in a Nutshell," *Los Angeles Times*, 21 February 2016. See *lareviewofbooks.org/author/peter-straub*.

7. Peter Straub interview with the author, Providence, RI, 1990.

Chapter Two

1. As I state in my book *The Gothic Imagination* (New York: Palgrave Macmillan, 2011), I apply the term "Gothic" in its most loose-limbed sense, that is, as a mode of speculation that grew out of the 18th century that situates terror instead of love at the heart of the narrative, and which shares critical themes and effects with fairy tales, Romanticism, and science fiction. Standard histories of the literary Gothic include Donna Heiland, *Gothic & Gender* (Maldon, MA: Blackwell, 2004); Jerrold E. Hogle, ed., *The Cambridge Companion to Gothic Fiction* (Cambridge: Cambridge University Press, 2002); Paul Newman, *A History of Terror* (London: Sutton, 2000); David J. Skal, *Screams of Reason: Mad Science and Modern Culture* (New York: W.W. Norton, 1998); Ann Williams, *Art of Darkness: A Poetics of Gothic* (Chicago: University of Chicago Press, 1995); Eino Railo, *The Haunted Castle* (London: Routledge, 1927); Montague Summers, *The Gothic Quest* (London: Fortune Press, 1938); Varma P. Davendra, *The Gothic Flame* (London: Arthur Baker, 1957).

2. Robert K. Martin in *American Gothic* says studies of this kind are indebted to Leslie Fiedler's *Love and Death in the American Novel* (New York: Stein and Day, 1966) and his insistence on the dialogic relation between the American national symbolic and the tendencies of the gothic: "How could one tell where the American dream ended and the Faustian nightmare began?" Here, admits Martin, is a fundamental irony—"an 'essentially gothic' culture produced by a civilization driven 'to be done with ghosts and shadows.'" See Martin and Eric Savoy, eds, *American Gothic: New Interventions in a National Narrative* (Iowa City: University of Iowa Press, 1998), viii. As for Straub's place in America's ongoing interrogation of the Gothic, historian S. T. Joshi raises objections. Although Joshi is enthusiastic about Straub's *Ghost Story*, which forms the core of this chapter, and praises his "literary elegance," he is generally dubious about Straub's avowed allegiance to and possible identification with the Gothic masters: "This kind of self-flattery is regrettably common in Straub's various comments about himself," writes Joshi, "suggesting that he has a pretty high regard for his own talents. Whether that regard is justified is the question." S. T. Joshi, *Unutterable Horrors: A History of Supernatural Fiction*, Vol. 2 (New York: Hippocampus Press, 2014), 657.

3. William Sheehan, *At the Foot of the Story Tree* (Burton, MI: Subterranean Press, 2000), 80.

4. Problems beset both adaptations. *Julia*, which was initially released in 1977 under the title *Full Circle* and later retitled *The Haunting of Julia*, suffers from excessive streamlining of the book's plot. Screenwriter Harry Porter Davenport inexplicably omits the crucial plot point of the connection between the two dead girls, Kate and Olivia (they are half-sisters). Arch villain Magnus's designs on Julia's inheritance is scantily depicted; and his death halfway through the film removes him entirely from the action. There is little sense of Julia's mounting hysteria and, likewise, scant evidence of the house's comparable deterioration. The direction by Richard Loncraine (*Brimstone and Treacle*) lacks the necessary nasty edge; if anything, it is too careful and too respectful of the material. The saccharine music score by Colin Town embalms the action. Worst of all, the book's spectacular scene of Julia's death by a fall from the rooftop after a battle with Olivia's ghost—suicide or murder?—is eliminated.

Perhaps the biggest problem with John Irvin's movie adaptation of *Ghost Story* is the lack of a cloaking atmospheric horror so important to the book's mounting terror. Yes, the village exteriors look great, if too much like a greeting card, but the wintry storm is seldom in evidence, and the apocalyptic horror lurking everywhere scarcely acknowledged. The blizzard here is nothing more than a mild snowfall, a mere bystander to the action. There is only one haunted house, that belonging once to Eva, and there are only two subsidiary villains, Fenny and Greg Bate. The latter two are not supernatural manifestations at all, but just a couple of louts newly escaped from a lunatic asylum. Alma and Eva don't seem to be incarnations of a malevolent demon woman, but merely two women who look alike, one possessed by the other. Alma's accidental demise is clumsily handled in a scene that is dramatically slack (like the impotence of Edward). In short, Straub's rich complex of plot, moods, and characters is redacted to a Hollywood shilling shocker.

Straub himself commented on the *Ghost Story* adaptation in our 1990 interview in Providence, Rhode Island: "I did feel almost personally wounded after I really realized what had happened to my book. I don't want to point any fingers because many, many people went into it with good feelings and with good intentions…. But somebody didn't and the thing didn't work right. So that has made me a little wary about film versions of my books, and I have turned down some projects because of that…. I have no wish to be made ridiculous and I don't need the money."

5. William Sheehan, 92.

6. See the discussion of this transition in Jacques Barzun, *Classic, Romantic, and Modern*, rev. ed. (Chicago: University of Chicago Press, 1961), 1–18. Cultural historian and critic John Clute has an interesting interpretation of the appearance of horror and fantasy at this time: "Horror is born at a point [after 1750] when it has begun to be possible to glimpse the planet itself as a drama: a very dangerous time in the history of the West, because it is at this point that (to put it very crudely) Enlightened Europeans were beginning to know it all, were beginning to think that glimpsing the world was tantamount to owning it. Horror is (in part) a subversive response to the falseness of that Enlightenment ambition to totalize knowledge and the world…" See John Clute, *The Darkening Garden: A Short Lexicon of Horror* (Cauheegan: Payseur & Schmidt, 2006), 87–88.

7. An exhaustive overview of this history can be found in S.T. Joshi, *Unutterable Horror: A History of Supernatural Fiction*, Vol. 1 (Hornsea, UK: PS Publishing, 2012).

8. Alfred Kazin, *An American Procession* (New York: Alfred A. Knopf, 1984), 90.

9. Nathaniel Hawthorne, "Young Goodman Brown," in *The Celestial Railroad and Other Stories* (New York: Signet, 1963), 98.

10. Leslie A. Fiedler, 303–304.

11. Nathaniel Hawthorne, *The Marble Faun*, in Norman Holmes Pearson, ed., *The Complete Novels and Selected Tales of Nathaniel Hawthorne* (New York: The Modern Library, 1937), 681–682.

12. Peter Straub letter to the author, NYC 2011.

13. Nathaniel Hawthorne, "My Kinsman, Major Molyneux," in *The Celestial Railroad and Other Stories*, 46.

14. In *A Dark Matter* Straub "throws" the voice of Hawthorne into several characters. Searching for meanings behind the horrors of the Meadow, Lee Harwell confesses that "Nathaniel Hawthorne turned the key; Hawthorne gave me entry to the lost realm—not the idea of reading him aloud, but that of hearing his words recited: the sound of his writing" (11). And Lee's friend, the strangely withdrawn Hootie Bly (note the allusion to Bly House in *Turn of the Screw*), parrots passages from *The Scarlet Letter* as his only way of communicating with the world: When accosted by a bully, he replies: "'Art thou like the Black Man that haunts the forest round about us?'" And in another quote that references the climax on the scaffold in *The Scarlet Letter* (and at the same time obliquely prefigures the horrific finale of the novel), Hootie declaims: "'In the dark night-time , he calls us to him, and holds thy hand in mine, as when we stood with him on the scaffold yonder!'" (11).

15. "Peter Straub and John Crowley in Conversation," International Conference of the Fantastic in the Arts, 18 March 2005. Moderated by Gary Wolfe. Unpublished transcription. Fales Archive. Series 1, Box 36, Folder 22.

16. Henry James, *The Turn of the Screw*, in Leon Edel, *The Ghostly Tales of Henry James* (New Brunswick: Rutgers University Press, 1948), 550.

17. Jacket copy, *Ghost Story* first edition (New York: Coward, McCann & Geoghegan, 1979).

18. Quoted in Michael Schumacher, "Ghost Storyteller," *Writer's Digest*, January 1985, 32.

19. Peter Straub interview with the author, NYC, 2011.

20. Nathaniel Hawthorne, *The Marble Faun*, in Norman Holmes Pearson, ed., *The Complete Novels and Selected Stories* (New York: The Modern Library, 1937), 590.

21. For example, James expressed a rather different opinion of America, writing in 1888, in a letter to Charles Eliot Norton: "It's a complex fate, being an American, and one of the responsibilities it entails is fighting against a superstitious valuation of Europe" (34). Quoted in Colm Tóibín, "Henry James's New York," *The New York Review of Books*, 9 February 2006, 33–37.

22. Camille Paglia, *Sexual Personae* (New York: Vintage, 1991), 573.

23. Maggie Kilgour, "Dr. Frankenstein Meets Dr. Freud," in Robert K. Martin and Eric Savoy, eds., *American Gothic: New Interventions in a National Narrative* (Iowa City: University of Iowa Press, 1998), 40–41.

24. Debate continues as to whether the idea of an "American" Gothic is an oxymoron. Two recent scholars continue the debate. Michael Cody, for example, asserts categorically that as early as Charles Brockden Brown we find a "Gothic frontier" identified as "distinctly American, and that frontier's wild isolation intensifies … frightening experiences … set in liminal spaces: the frontier between hearth and hinterland, the threshold between psychological coherence and chaos" (98–99). Moreover, in place of Old World institutions, Brown and Hawthorne "substituted republican decorum and Puritanism as sites of Gothic anxiety" (105). On the other hand, Lesley Ginsberg qualifies the dichotomy, reminding us that the colonial America that haunts *The House of the Seven Gables* was a British colony whose inhabitants considered themselves English culturally. English Gothic fiction, moreover, proliferated and was widely consumed in pre-1850 America; and that, for example, Hawthorne's *The Scarlet Letter* and *House of the Seven Gables* present a "New England" that "bears the trace of its double, the England of old" (33). See Michael Cody, "'As Kinsmen, Met a Knight': Charles Brockden Brown and Nathaniel Hawthorne as American Gothic Romancers," *Nathaniel Hawthorne Review*, Vol. 30, No. 2 (Fall 2012), 93–114; and Lesley Ginsberg, "Hawthorne's Transatlantic Gothic House of Fiction: *The House of the Seven Gables*," *Nathaniel Hawthorne Review*, Vol. 30, No. 2 (Fall 2012), 27–46.

25. H. P. Lovecraft, "Supernatural Horror in Literature," in August Derleth and Donald Wandrei, eds., *The Outsider and Others* (Sauk City, WI: Arkham House, 1939), 516.

26. Charles Brockden Brown, "To the Public," in *Edgar Huntly* (New Haven: Yale University Press, 1973), 29.

27. *Ibid.*, 165–166.

28. Harold Schechter letter to the author, 19 January 2011.

29. *Ibid.*

30. For an examination of the bonds between Brown and Hawthorne, see Michael Cody, "'As Kinsmen, Met a Knight," 93–114.

31. H. P. Lovecraft, *Supernatural Horror in Literature*, 531–532.

32. *Ibid.*, 533.

33. Both Poe and Hawthorne are commonly associated with a "New England Renaissance" in early to mid-19th-century America. "For all of Poe's posturing efforts to distance himself from Hawthorne," write Elbert and Marshall, "various critics paired Hawthorne and Poe for much of Gothic literary history." However, contemporary critics asserted that the "heavy-handed" Poe too often veered "into the realm of the improbably and outrageous." Moreover, by contrast to Poe's attempts to make the "weird" seem normal, the more subtle Hawthorne "makes the familiar seem supernatural by making the commonplace seem mysterious" (iii–iv). See Monika M. Elbert and Bridget M. Marshall, "Haunted Hawthorne, Hawthorne's Hauntings," *The Nathaniel Hawthorne Review*, Vol. 30, No. 2 (Fall 2012), iii–xvi. Lovecraft will come to privilege Poe's intense sense of horror over Hawthorne's.

34. *Ibid.*, v–vi.

35. S. T. Joshi, *Unutterable Horrors*, vol. 1, 218.

36. Nathaniel Hawthorne, "Young Goodman Brown," in *The Celestial Railroad and Other Stories*, 95.

37. *Ibid.*, 100.

38. Nathaniel Hawthorne, "The Devil in Manuscript," in Pearson, ed., 1204.

39. Nancy F. Sweet, "'The glory roundabout her': Hawthorne, Feminism, and the 'Serious Business' of the Aged Crone," *The Nathaniel*

Hawthorne Review, Vol. 41, No. 1 (Spring 2015), 47.

40. Nathaniel Hawthorne, "The Devil in Manuscript," in Pearson, ed., 1204–1205.

41. In Elbert and Marshall, ii. This 1871 commentary by Alexander Japp strangely presages our picture of the solitary rambles of H.P Lovecraft's in his native Providence, RI.

42. Brenda Wineapple, *Hawthorne: A Life* (New York: Random House, 2003), 69.

43. Nathaniel Hawthorne, *The Marble Faun*, in Pearson, ed., 645.

44. In 1692 the Massachusetts Bay Colony executed fourteen women, five men, and two dogs for witchcraft. After allegations surfaced of sorcery in January, the first hanging took place in June, the last in September. An estimated 144–185 witches and wizards were named in 25 villages and town. The youngest was five years of age; the oldest, nearly eighty. For a recent overview, see Stacy Schiff, "The Witches of Salem," *The New Yorker*, 7 September 2015, 46–55.

45. While historian S.T. Joshi writes that *House of the Seven Gables* is, in general, "as far from terrifying as it is possible to be," he nonetheless cites Chapter 18 ("Governor Pyncheon") as an exception—as "the true acme of horror in the novel.... I know of nothing like this chapter in the entire range of horror literature, before or since" (Joshi, Vol. 1, 220).

46. Nathaniel Hawthorne, *The House of the Seven Gables,* in Pearson, ed., 258.

47. Nathaniel Hawthorne, in *The House of the Seven Gables*, in Pearson, ed., 247.

48. *Ibid.*, 288.

49. *Ibid.*, 254.

50. *Ibid.*, 258.

51. Horace Walpole, *The Castle of Otranto* (New York: Holt, Rinehart & Winston, 1963), 9–10.

52. Donna Heiland, *Gothic & Gender* (Oxford: Blackwell, 2004), 14.

53. Wanderley's is quoting Hawthorne via the pages of an essay he is reading by Professor R.P. Blackmur (see Blackmur's "Afterword," in *The Celestial Railroad*, 289). The original quotation can be found in the opening page of "The Threefold Destiny," from *Twice-Told Tales*.

54. Gagne, Paul, "An Interview with Peter Straub," in *American Fantasy*, 1 February 1982, 8–26.

55. Quoted in Pearson, ed., xv.

56. Nathaniel Hawthorne, "Wakefield," in *The Celestial Railroad*, 75. Scholar Ellen Weinauer regards "Wakefield" as "a story about the frightful power that matrimony has to make, and unmake, a man" (98). See "Perilous Proximities: The Meanings of Marriage in 'Wakefield,'" *Nathaniel Hawthorne Review*, Vol. 39, No. 1 (Spring 2013), 94–115.

57. Nathaniel Hawthorne, *The Marble Faun*, in Pearson, ed., 696.

58. Nathaniel Hawthorne, *The Scarlet Letter*, in Pearson, ed., 238.

59. Nathaniel Hawthorne, *The Marble Faun*, 840.

60. *Ibid.*, 690–691.

61. *Ibid.*, 663.

62. Nathaniel Hawthorne, "The Minister's Black Veil," in *The Celestial Railroad*, 101–114.

63. Nathaniel Hawthorne, *The Marble Faun*, in Pearson, ed., 856.

64. Quoted in Wineapple, 326–327. Behind many of the secrets in Hawthorne, suggests critic Leslie Fiedler, could be that arch trope of the Gothic, the perversion of love, "the sin of incest, for which [Hawthorne's] mother's family, the Mannings, had once been publicly disgraced" (229). The notoriously private Hawthorne never publicly revealed what could be construed as a family curse, but commentators like Fiedler and, latterly, Philip Young in *Hawthorne's Secret* (1984), allege it surfaces everywhere in his stories. Certainly, incestuous implications—psychological as well as physical—so prevalent in the erotic couplings of Eva Galli in Straub's *Ghost Story*, are everywhere in Hawthorne, from the early "Alice Doane's Appeal" to his last story fragments. Hawthorne's fascination with "forbidden love," in turn, followed in the "deviant" footsteps of the Europeans Horace Walpole (*The Mysterious Mother*), Matthew Lewis (*The Monk*), Lord Byron (*Manfred*), and Percy Shelley (*The Cenci*); and the American Edgar Allan Poe ("The House of Usher," "Beatrice," Ligeia," etc.). See Leslie Fiedler, *Love and Death in the American Novel*; and Philip Young, *Hawthorne's Secret: An Un-Told Tale* (Boston: David R. Godine, 1984).

65. William Sheehan, *At the Foot of the Story Tree*, is careful to remind us that another important literary precedent for Eva Galli is Arthur Machen's classic "The Great God Pan," 90–91. Published in 1894, it remains an important precedent for this type of malevolent,

shape-shifting female. Straub frequently mentions this story as influential on his own work. Known by many names, she is described several times by the men she has corrupted as "at once the most beautiful woman and the most repulsive they had ever set eyes on. She seems to have been a sort of enigma" (82). Of uncertain gender and form, her death is described as a horrifying series of evolutionary regressions, "changing and melting before your eyes from woman to man, from man to beast, and from beast to worse than beast" (115). See "The Great God Pan," in *Tales of Horror and the Supernatural by Arthur Machen* (New York: Alfred A. Knopf, 1948), 61–115.

Remarkably, three other classic Gothic novels featuring these demon women of voracious and malignant sexuality appeared within two years of "The Great God Pan"—Lucy Westernra in Bram Stoker's *Dracula*, The Woman of Songs in Richard Marsh's *The Beetle*, and the priestess Ayesha in H. Rider Haggard's *She*. See the discussion of these three novels in Patricia Murphy, *The New Woman Gothic* (Columbia: University of Missouri Press, 2016), 252–266.

66. The term New Woman was deployed in contradistinction to the so-called Cult of True Womanhood, which was emerging in the first half of the 19th century and which privileged the qualities of piety, purity, submissiveness, and domesticity. Despite—or because of—this ideal status, the True Woman found herself denied Jacksonian society's qualities of education,, success at work, and political participation. By mid-century The New Woman, led by active political and social reformers, were speaking out against domestic confinement and submission to male patriarchy. For a discussion of the New Woman as social activist, see Jill Conway, "Woman Reformers," *The Journal of Social History*, Vol. X, No. 2 (Winter 1971–1972), 169.

67. Camille Paglia, 621–622.

68. Harold Bloom, *The Daemon Knows: Literary Greatness and the American Sublime* (New York: Spiegel and Grau, 1915), 190–191.

69. Camille Paglia, 630–636.

70. Howard Kerr, *Mediums and Spirit-Rappers and Roaring Radicals* (Urbana: University of Illinois Press, 1963), 183. Kerr devotes many pages to Victoria Woodhull's life and her influence on the female trance mediums in Hawthorne, James, Melville, Twain, and Howells.

71. For contexts of this famous quote, see *Truth's Ragged Edge*, by Philip Gura (Farrar, Straus and Giroux, 2013), 126.

72. Nathaniel Hawthorne, *The Blithedale Romance*, in Pearson, ed., 556.

73. Moers defined "female gothic" as one in which "woman is examined with a woman's eye, woman as girl, as sister, as mother, as self" and in which women "give *visual* form to the fear of self." See the discussion in Donna Heiland, 57–58. A recent examination is in Patricia Murphy, *The New Woman Gothic: Reconfigurations of Distress*. See also Sandra M. and Susan Gubar, *The Madwoman in the Attic* (New Haven: Yale University Press, 1979), 17. A sinister, even malignant female agency, like Eva Galli in Straub's *Ghost Story*, had been evident as far back as the Apocrypha, in the monstrous Lilith of Hebrew mythology and in the major women of tragedy, Euripides' Medea and Phaedra, Shakespeare's Lady Macbeth, Racine's Phèdra. "The will-to-power," claims Camille Paglia in *Sexual Personnae*, in her typical hair-raising rhetoric, places the actions of these female demons "under a chthonian cloud." Moreover, they are a conduit of the irrational, opening the genre to intrusions of the barbaric force." In Buddhist culture, for example, the Indian nature-goddess Kali is creator *and* destroyer, "granting boons with one set of arms while cutting throats with the other. She is the lady ringed with skulls." Indeed, from the beginning of time, pursues the irrepressible Paglia, "woman has seemed an uncanny being. Man honored but feared her. She was the black maw that had spat him forth and would devour him anew.... [Her] body is a labyrinth in which man is lost.... Men, bonding together, invented culture as a defense against female nature. Think of Coleridge's terribly deformed Geraldine in 'Christabel' ('A sight to dream of, not to tell') and Keats's poems of sexual danger, from *Endymion* through 'Lamia' to 'La Belle Dame Sans Merci.' In the latter, she is Keats's 'woman without mercy,' a Circean sexual predator, 'full beautiful,' a 'faery's child,' but with 'wild' eyes.' Poor, gentle Keats, in love with Fanny Brawne, but who can still write to his friend Bailey, 'When I am among Women, I have evil thoughts, malice spleen—I cannot speak or be silent—I am full of Suspicions and there listen to nothing—I am in a hurry to be gone.'" Quoted in Paglia, 7–9, 384.

74. Nancy Sweet, 45.

75. Nathaniel Hawthorne, *The Scarlet Letter*, in Pearson, ed., 249.

76. Brenda Wineapple, 175.

77. Nathaniel Hawthorne, *The Blithedale Romance,* in Pearson, ed., 510.

78. Alfred Habegger, *Gender, Fantasy, and Realism in American Literature* (New York: Columbia University Press, 1982), 340.

79. Peter Buitenhuis, *The Grasping Imagination: The American Writings of Henry James* (Toronto: University of Toronto Press, 1973), 144.

80. *Ibid.*, 149.

81. Alfred Habegger, *Gender*, 255.

82. Alfred Habegger, *The Father: Henry James, Sr.* (New York: Farrar, Straus and Giroux, 1994), 231–233.

83. Gerald E. Myers, *William James: His Life and Thought* (New Haven: Yale University Press, 1986), 15–23.

84. Quoted in Sarah B. Daugherty, *The Literary Criticism of Henry James* (Athens: Ohio University Press, 1982), 98.

85. Howard Kerr, *Mediums and Spirit-Rappers and Roaring Radicals*, 209.

86. Deborah Blum, *Ghost Hunters,* 228.

87. Quoted in Deborah Blum, *Ghost Hunters: William James and the Search for Scientific Proof of Life after Death* (New York: Penguin, 2006), 313.

88. Lyndall Gordon, *A Private Life of Henry James* (London: Chatto and Windus, 1998), 337.

89. Henry James, "De Grey," in Leon Edel, ed., *The Ghostly Tales of Henry James* (New Brunswick: Rutgers University Press, 1948), 65.

90. Leon Edel, in *The Ghostly Tales of Henry James*, 429.

91. Henry James, *The Turn of the Screw*, in Leon Edel, ed., 472.

92. Henry James, "Sir Edmund Orme," in Leon Edel, ed., 158.

93. S. T. Joshi, *Unutterable Horrors*, vol. 1, 296. However, Joshi applauds *The Turn of the Screw* as "the ultimate refinement of the Christmas ghost story" (296) and comes down squarely in favor of the "reality" of the apparitions haunting Bly House.

94. Quoted in Leon Edel, *The Ghostly Tales of Henry James*, xxv.

95. Nathaniel Hawthorne, *The Blithedale Romance*, in Pearson, ed., 502.

96. China Miéville, "M.R. James and the Quantum Vampire," http://weirdfictionreview. com/2011; and interview with Joan Gordon, http://www.depauw.edu/sfs/interviews/ miievilleinterview.htm.

97. R. P. Blackmur, R.P., "Afterward," in *The Celestial Railroad and Other Stories*, 50.

98. Leon Edel, *Ghostly Tales*, xxix.

99. Henry James, Preface to Vol. 17 of the 1909 New York Edition (London: Macmillan, 1909), xvi.

100. R.P. Blackmur, Afterword, in *The Celestial Railroad and Other Stories*, 48–49.

101. See my "Men, Women, and Ghosts: The Supernatural Fiction of Edith Wharton," *Helicon Nine: The Journal of Women's Arts and Letters*, No. 9 (Winter l983), 44–53.

102. A particularly Jamesian example of this is Edith Wharton's short story "Miss Mary Pask." A painter while on tour in Brittany decides to visit the spinster sister of a friend. It is a stormy night before he finally reaches her house—only to find it dark. Then he suddenly remembers: Miss Pask had died some time ago and for some reason he had forgotten all about it. But then, much to his horror, the door opens and there is Miss Pask, looking ghastly and wraith-like in the candlelight. The apparition invites him in. She talks to him of gaining "such a sense of freedom" from her death. And the man has to agree that Miss Pask seems "so much more real to me than ever the living one had been." Miss Pask talks of her loneliness and beseeches the man not to leave her. The man, bent upon quitting the place, is surprised to hear her entreaty: "Oh, stay with me, stay with me … just tonight…. It's so sweet and quiet here…. No one need know … no one will ever come and trouble us." Aghast, he retreats out the door, leaving behind him a pitiful whimper from Miss Pask. He shudders to think that the unuttered loneliness of a lifetime was now welling up in her ghost, express¬ing "at last what the living woman had always had to keep dumb and hidden." But this terror is as nothing to what the man later feels, when he learns that Miss Pask had not really died, but was living quietly in her little house by the sea. For the man, as well as for us, the fact that Miss Pask had had to *pretend* to be a ghost to express her innermost desires is an irony that is almost unbearable. Even in this little story that seemed at first to be a charming trifle in

Wharton's ghostly oeuvre, there is a terrible social insight that is devastating. See *The Ghost Stories of Edith Wharton* (New York: Charles Scribner's Sons, 1976).

103. Henry James, "The Jolly Corner," in Leon Edel, ed., *The Ghostly Tales*, 742.

104. *Ibid.*, 755–757.

105. Scholar Eric Savoy's "The Queer Subject of 'The Jolly Corner,'" advances a rather different interpretation of Brydon's new awareness, i.e., of his *renewed awareness*: Brydon has returned to America as a self-knowing gay man whose identity is now contested by his "differently closeted" double. In effect, Brydon's heterosexuality is "reclaimed" in the arms of Alice Staverton (3). See Eric Savoy, "The Queer Subject of 'The Jolly Corner,'" *Henry James Review*, Vol. 20, No. 1 (Winter 1999), 1–21.

106. Harold Bloom, *The Daemon Knows*, 19. Edmund Burke first formulated the "terror sublime" in his *Philosophical Inquiry into the Origin of Our Ideas of the Sublime and Beautiful* in 1757. Imaginative transport is not desirable, it is a mental and physical *necessity*. The sublime is an apprehension of danger in nature or art without the immediate risk of destruction: "When danger or pain press too nearly, they are incapable of giving any delight, and are simply terrible; but at certain distances, and with certain modifications, they may be, and they are, delightful." See Hogle, 14–15, 28.

107. Keith Neilsen, in his essay on the novel, rhetorically asks why the child-creature, knowing full well the danger it faces from Wanderley, didn't try to escape him. "In the end," Neilsen writes, "inhuman, almost invincible, evil makes itself vulnerable" through its own arrogance. From which there is no final escape, for, in the end, Eva is merely a pathetic insect crushed beneath the knife. See Nielsen, "Ghost Story," in Frank N. Magill, ed., *Survey of Modern Fantasy Literature*, Vol. Two (Englewood Cliff, NJ: Salem Press, 1983), 607–611.

108. R.P. Blackmur, "Afterword," in *The Celestian Railroad and Other Stories*, 292.

Chapter Three

1. Peter Straub, *Sides* (Baltimore: Cemetery Dance, 2007), 152. The eminent fairy-tale historian Jack Zipes describes the origins and evolution of what we loosely call "fairy tales," a term first coined in 1697: "The fairy tale was first a simple, imaginative oral tale containing magical and miraculous elements and was related to the belief systems, values, rites, and experiences of pagan peoples." It underwent numerous transformations before "the innovation of print led to the production of fixed texts and conventions of telling and reading. But even then, the fairy tale refused to be dominated by print and continued to be altered and diffused around the world by word of mouth up to the present." See Zipes, *The Irresistible Fairy Tale* (Princeton: Princeton University Press, 2012), 21.

2. Philip Pullman, *Fairy Tales from the Brothers Grimm* (New York: Viking, 2012), xvii–xix.

3. William Sheehan, *At the Foot of the Story Tree* (Burton, MI: Subterranean Press, 2000), 101.

4. For details of the Schumann cycle, see Eric Sams, *The Songs of Robert Schumann* (London: Faber and Faber, 1993), 197–217.

5. In a 1988 interview with the author, Maurice Sendak talked about the Grimm's ambivalence regarding the readership of their Tales: "The Tales did find a readership among children, that's true. Children have naturally good taste! But when these stories came out, the Brothers were appalled at first at the response by children. They had no idea that children were going to like them and read them so much. The question is, why did they like them so much? Because they had been given a lot of homilies and pap to read previous to that; and suddenly, here were marvelous stories that were linguistically available to them and were simply told. And, too, they were about life and death and murderous impulses and sex and passion and all the things children are interested in but hadn't been allowed access to. So of course they fell in love with the tales! It was a form that everybody loved.... The early Romantics were more insightful than that. They saw in these Tales the natural to-and-fro between the business of being a child and being a grownup. There was naivete, yes, but there were also premonitions of terrors, too. There was nothing eccentric or cute about it. It was just a natural state of things. Now, we have corrupted the folk and fairy tales into what are called 'children's books.' This was not the Brothers' idea at all. They didn't see them as something specifically for children; they were for *people*."

6. Nathaniel Hawthorne, *The Marble Faun*, in Norman Pearson, ed., *The Complete Novels and Selected Tales of Nathaniel Hawthorne* (New York: The Modern Library, 1937), Chapter XLIX (845–851).

7. See Bruno Bettelheim, *The Uses of Enchantment* (New York: Vintage, 1977), 8.

8. Richard Dadd painted *The Fairy Feller's Master Stroke* and other bizarre "fairy" paintings, notably *Contradiction: Oberon and Titania*, in the years 1854–1864 in Bethlem Royal Hospital for the Insane, where he had been committed after murdering his father. For this and many more images of Dadd and his contemporaries, see Jeremy Mass, *Victorian Fairy Painting* (London: Merrell Holberton, 1998).

9. Critic and historian Bill Sheehan notes that John Fowles's *The Magus* has had a decided influence on Straub's *Shadowland*. See *At the Foot of the Story Tree* (Burton, MI: Subterranean Press, 2000), 103–105.

10. The cultural historian, Vladimir Propp, notes that one of the essential aspects of the "wonder tale" is the "initiation of a young man or woman that takes the form of a quest.... [He or she] lacks something, must abandon or is banished from home, receives help in the form of advice or magical objects ... is tested, and either happily survives or dies" (quoted in Zipes, 66–67).

11. Peter Straub, *Sides*, 151–152.

12. Quoted in Francesca Wade, "Pigs for Life," *Times Literary Supplement*, 13 March 2015, 3–5.

13. Maria Tatar, *The Hard Facts of the Grimm's Fairy Tales* (Princeton: Princeton University Press, 1987), 25.

14. Quoted in Cristina Bacchilega, *Postmodern Fairy Tales: Gender and Narrative Strategies* (Philadelphia: University of Pennsylvania Press, 1987), 25.

15. *Ibid.*, 4.

16. In this spirit Straub has written a baffling tale in tribute to Aickman, "Robert Aickman's Air Rifle."

17. Peter Straub, *Sides*, 152.

18. Nathaniel Hawthorne, *The Marble Faun*, in Pearson, ed., 642.

19. Peter Straub, *Sides*, 149.

20. *Ibid.*, 149.

21. Schiffman claims that in the fourth chapter of *The Marble Faun* Hawthorne "likened his own method of storytelling to

E.T.A. Hoffmann's and Tieck's" (42). Moreover, "comparing Novalis's and Hawthorne's works reveals several inverted and other parallels," particularly in comparing Novalis's *Heinrich von Ofterdingen* and Hawthorne's "Rappaccini's Daughter" (46). See Robyn Schiffman, "Novalis and Hawthorne: A New Look at Hawthorne's German Influences," *Nathaniel Hawthorne Review*, Vol. 38, No. 1 (Spring 2012), 41–55.

22. Gordon Birrell, "Introduction," to Frank G. Ryder and Robert M. Browning, eds., *German Literary Fairy Tales* (New York: Continuum, 1983), xv. This is an invaluable collection of English translations of *Kunstmärchen* by Goethe, E.T.A. Hoffmann, Novalis, Clemens Brentano, Franz Kafka, and others. Fairy tale historian Jack Zipes, deploys the term "literary fairy tale" in more general terms for any story that displays "a symbiotic relationship of oral and literary and currents." "[They] emanated from the oral traditions through the mediation of mauscripts and print, and continue to be created today in various mediated forms around the world." See Jack Zipes, 2–3.

23. William J. Lillyman, *Reality's Dark Dream: The Narrative Fiction of Ludwig Tieck* (New York: Walter de Gruyter, 1979), 78.

24. E.T.A. Hoffman, "The Golden Pot," in Leonard J. Kent and Elizabeth C. Knight, eds., *Selected Writings of E. T. A. Hoffmann*, Volume One (Chicago University Press, 1969), 20.

25. Novalis, *Heinrich von Ofterdingen*, trans. Palmer Hilty (New York: Frederick Ungar, 1982), 156.

26. Chesterton, G.K., "The Ethics of Fairyland," *The Speaker*, 12 October 1901; reprinted in A.L. Maycock, ed., *The Man Who was Orthodox* (London: Dennis Dobson, 1963), 174–176.

27. Novalis, *Heinrich von Ofterdingen*, 77. For a detailed examination of Novalis's extraordinarily complex narrative, see Eric A. Blackall, *The Novels of the German Romantics* (Ithaca: Cornell University Press, 1983), 107–130.

28. *Ibid.*, 106.

29. William Sheehan, *At the Foot of the Story Tree*, 103.

30. Peter Straub, *Sides*, 148.

31. Giordano Bruno was a 16th-century Dominican monk much given to the Epicurean philosophy, whose subversive teachings held that the world has no limits in either space or

time, that the grandest things are made of the smallest, that atoms, the building blocks of al that exists, link the one and the infinite. "We have the knowledge," he wrote, "not to search for divinity removed from us if we have it near; it is within us more than we ourselves are." Quoted in Roger Greenblatt, *The Swerve* (New York: W.W. Norton, 2011), 237.

32. "Peter Straub and John Crowley in Conversation," International Conference of the Fantastic in the Arts, 18 March 2005. Moderated by Gary Wolfe. Unpublished. Fales Archive. Series 1, Box 36, Folder 22.

33. A noted historian of the early Church, Elaine Pagels, has produced a cogent introduction to the subject of Gnosticism, a belief system declared heretical by the orthodox church by the start of the second century after Christ. When the Gnostic writings were unearthed in 1945 near Nag Hammadi in Upper Egypt, including the Gospel of Thomas, they revealed a counter-Christianity which disputed common Christian beliefs, such as the virgin birth and the bodiy resurrection of Jesus as "naïve misunderstandings." Instead of coming to save us from sin," writes Pagel, "he comes as a guide who opens access to spiritual understanding. But when the disciple attains enlightenment, Jesus no longer serves as his spiritual master: ;the two have become equal—even identical. Pagel speculates, "Does not such teaching—the identity of the divine and human, the concern with illusion and enlightenment, the founder who is presented not as Lord, but as spiritual guide—sound more Eastern than Western?" Elaine Pagels, *The Gnostic Gospels* (New York: Vintage, 1989), xx–xxi.

34. "Straub and Crowley in Conversation."
35. Bettelheim, 179.
36. *Ibid.*, 282.
37. The Pied Piper legend, dating from an alleged true incident in 1284, and documented and adapted by the Brothers Grimm as "The Children of Hameln" (No. 245) in 1812, the poet Robert Browning as "The Pied Piper of Hamelin" in 1842, animator Walt Disney in "The Pied Piper" in 1933, and filmmaker Atom Egoyan in *The Sweet Hereafter* in 1997, told the story of a mysterious piper clad in motley who enticed 130 children out of the city of Hamelin to an undisclosed fate. Magician, artist, pedophile? Robert Browning's description is sardonically mysterious:

His queer long coat from heel to head.
Was half of yellow and half of red.
And he himself was tall and thin.
With sharp blue eyes, each like a pin.
And light loose hair, yet swarthy skin.
No tuft on cheek nor beard on chin.
But lips where smile went out and in;
There was no guessing his kith and kin [58–64].

Of the adaptations cited above, leave it to Walt Disney in his 1933 cartoon "The Pied Piper" to have the Piper lead the children away from their uncaring parents into the "joyland" of a magic mountain, where they live happily ever after.

38. Geoffrey Chaucer, *The Canterbury Tales* (New York: The Heritage Press, 1946), 256–268.
39. Harold Frederic, *The Damnation of Theron Ware* (Chicago: Stone & Kimball, 1896), 330.
40. William Dean Howells, *The Leatherwood God* (New York: Harper and Brothers, 1916), 232.
41. Susan Kuhlmann, *Knave, Fool, and Genius* (Chapel Hill: University of North Carolina Press, 1973), 90.
42. Peter Straub interview with the author, NYC, 2011.
43. Philip Pullman says that the blinding of the stepsisters was not included in the 1812 version, but added in the 1819 version. See Pullman's version, *Fairy Tales from the Brothers Grimm* (New York: Viking, 2012), 116–127.
44. See "Pierre Menard," by Jorge Borges, in Hurley, Andrew, trans., *Jorge Luis Borges: Collected Fictions* (New York: Viking, 1998), 95.
45. G.K. Chesterton, "The Ethics of Elfland," 96–97.
46. Peter Straub, "Fearful Places," *Locus*, July 2006, 7, 78–79.

Chapter Four

1. James Hogg, *The Private Memoirs and Confessions of a Justified Sinner* (Koln: Koenemann, 1999), 218.
2. Significantly, both the King and Oates novels concern writers confronted with their own Doubles. Most of Straub's characters are also writers involved in similar situations.

3. Gary K. Wolfe, *Evaporating Genres* (Middletown, CT: Wesleyan University Press, 2011), 28.

4. Quoted in William Sheehan, *At the Foot of the Story Tree* (Burton, MI: Subterranean Press, 2000), 303.

5. *Ibid.*, 311.

6. August Strindberg, "Author's Note," from *A Dream Play*. In *Six Plays of Strindberg*, trans Elizabeth Sprigge (New York: Doubleday, 1955), 193.

7. Gary K. Wolfe, *Evaporating Genres*, 315.

8. To be more precise, the German term, *Entwicklungsroman*, applies. While *Bildungsroman* refers to the development of the mind and the personality, *Entwicklungsroman* considers the development of the whole person, how one develops through experiences in the mind and in reality and sensuality. In such novels, the protagonist travels and encounters experiences of the senses, the mind, of spirituality. He changes into a more complete human being." See the discussion by Professor Wolfgang Nehring, of UCLA, in John C. Tibbetts, *Schumann: A Chorus of Voices* (New York: Amadeus Press, 2010), 40–41.

9. See Ronald R. Thomas, "The Strange Voices in the Strange Case: *Dr. Jekylll, Mr. Hyde*, and the Voices of Modern Fiction," in William Veeder and Gordon Hirsch, *Dr. Jekyll and Mr. Hyde after One Hundred Years* (Chicago: University of Chicago Press, 1988), 74.

10. H. P. Lovecraft, "The Haunter of the Dark," in August Derleth and Donald Wandrei, eds, *The Outsider and Others* (Sauk City, WI: Arkham House, 1939), 193.

11. Michel Foucault, "What Is an Author?" trans. Donald R. Bouchard and Sherry Simon, eds, in *Language, Counter-Memory, Practice* (Ithaca: Cornell University Press, 1977), 117.

12. In his celebrated essay "The Death of the Author," Roland Barthes declares that "writing is the destruction of every voice, of every point of origin. Writing is that neutral, composite, oblique space where our subject slips away, where all identity is lost, starting with the very identity of the body writing.... The voice loses its origin, the author enters into his own death, writing begins" (142). See Barthes, *Image Music Text*, trans. Stephen Heath (New York: Hill and Wang, 1977), 142.

Many of Beckett's characters, like those of Straub, seem uncertain about their own reality,

wondering aloud if they really exist. Beckett's *Molloy* is a novel with two narrators, Molloy and Moran, who may be the same person or they may be unwitting "collaborators" on a text that is itself a doubling of two different versions of the same events. It that wise, its formal structure and characters recall Hogg's *Private Memoirs*. All three novels in the trilogy have monologists who, like the shifting personae that is Straub's "Mr. X," are revealed to be aliases, each story the alibi of its successor. Ultimately, only a disembodied voice is left: "I am neither, I needn't say.... I can't even bring myself to name them, nor any of the others whose very names I forget, who told me I was they, who I must have tried to be." Quoted in Benjamin Kunkel, "Sam I Am," *The New Yorker*, 7 & 14 August 2006, 88.

13. *Ibid.*, 83.

14. Ramsay Campbell's first published book was, he confesses, "a direct imitation of Lovecraft, *The Inhabitant of the Lake*, in 1964 when he was just eighteen years old. It was a series of stories written wholly in the style of Lovecraft, using his ideas and his alien being.... I set it in a mythical location in the Severn Valley. That was my version of Lovecraft's Arkham." Later years and novels like *Obsession* (1985) released him from Lovecraft's influence: "I decided that maybe some of the ideas I was working with didn't really need the Lovecraft crutch, so I didn't need to put the names that Lovecraft had invented, and the stories could do without them. I hadn't been happy with that." See my interview with him in *The Gothic Imagination* (New York: Palgrave Macmillan, 211), 36–38.

15. An indefatigable correspondent, Lovecraft drew around him a circle of young, aspiring writers with whom he corresponded voluminously and to whom he extended valuable advice, criticism, and encouragement. They included August Derleth, Frank Belknap Long, Clark Ashton Smith, Donald Wandrei, R.H. Barlow, and Robert Bloch, to name just a few. They not only carried on the Lovecraft tradition but went on to distinguished careers of their own. Indeed, long after his death, writers like Ramsey Campbell, Basil Copper, and Brian Lumley have continued and developed the Lovecraftian style and subject matter.

Due to the untiring efforts of the aforementioned friend and former protégé, August Derleth, Lovecraft's stories were rescued from obscurity in several volumes from Arkham House publishers (named after the mythical town in which Lovecraft set many of his tales), beginning in 1939 with *The Outsider and Others*. Five other volumes from Arkham House of Lovecraft's *Selected Letters* have documented the amazing number, extent and variety of his correspondence with the above-named writers. However, it should be noted that Derleth's longstanding preoccupation with his mentor has produced some curious—even controversial—results. What he termed the "Cthulhu Mythos" of Lovecraft has produced many stories written either in collaboration with Lovecraft or suggested by notes and sketches Lovecraft left behind. Biographer Joshi, for example, calls Derleth's Mythos "a perverted understanding" of Lovecraft's work, which has resulted in "a whole series of truly dreadful pastiches that unwittingly parodied the author he claimed to be honoring." Specifically, he attacks Derleth's claim that Lovecraft's "gods" can be divided into forces of "good" (the Elder Gods) and evil (the Old Ones, i.e., Cthulhu, Yog-Sothoth, Azathoth, Nyarlathotep, Shub-Niggurath, etc.). "Derleth, a Catholic, could not endure Lovecraft's bleakly atheistic cosmic vision, so he deliberately perverted his pseudo-mythology to make it more amendable to a religious worldview" (Tibbetts, 16).

Nonetheless, as John D. Haefele has noted in his extensive volume on the subject, *A Look Behind the Derleth Mythos*, "that a Cthulhu Mythos *industry* exists today is undeniable," writes John D. Haefele. "Derleth did not invent the Mythos all by himself, but is responsible for what now flies under its various banners, not only for having provided the framework that made it easily adaptable to all sorts of media, but for preserving and promoting the very concept for over forty years" (442–443). See John D. Haefele, *A Look Behind the Derleth Mythos* (Odense: Cimmerian Press, 2014).

16. Letter from Lovecraft to Clark Ashton Smith, October 3, 1933. In August Derleth and Jim Turner, eds., *H.P. Lovecraft: Selected Letters, 1932–1934* (Sauk City, WI: Arkham House), 27.

17. Quoted in the Preface by August Derleth and Donald Wandrei to *The Outsider and Others* (Sauk City, WI: Arkham House, 1939), xiii. Does the unpronounceable name "Cthulhu" owe its derivation to the word "chthonian"? Camille Paglia writes: "What the west represses in its view of nature is the chthonian, which means 'of the earth'—but earth's bowels, not its surface.... I adopt it as a substitute for Dionysian.... It is the chthonian realities which Apollo evades, the bind grinding of the subterranean force, the long slow suck, the murk and ooze. It is the dehumanizing brutality of biology and geology, the Darwinian waste and bloodshed, the squalor and rot we must block from consciousness to retain our Apollonian integrity as persons." See Camille Paglia, *Sexual Personae* (New York: Vintage, 1991), 5–6.

18. Wilson quoted in Michael Saler, "Strange tales of alien incursions," *Times Literary Supplement*, 4 March 2005, 19.

19. Joyce Carol Oates, "The King of Weird," *The New York Review,* 31 October 1996, 46–53.

20. Stephen King, *Danse Macabre* (New York: Everest, 1981), 72.

21. S. T. Joshi Interview with John C. Tibbetts, 26–27 September 2010, in Tibbetts, *The Gothic Imagination*, 12. Joshi knows more about H.P. Lovecraft than anyone on the planet—and perhaps in The Great Beyond, as well. Winner of numerous awards, including the Bram Stoker Award for his *H.P. Lovecraft: A Life* (1996), the Distinguished Critic Award from the International Association for the Fantastic in the Arts in 2003, and the World Fantasy Award for Professional scholarship from the Science Fiction and Fantasy Writers of America, Joshi has edited five volumes of Lovecraft's *Collected Essays* (2004–2007), several Lovecraftian journals, and many volumes of Lovecraft's *Letters*. His massive, two-volume biography of Lovecraft, *I Am Providence* (New York: Hippocampus Press, 2010). A prolific scholar, he has also researched and published on writers as various as John Dickson Carr, Ambrose Bierce, and H.L. Mencken. See also *Lovecraft: A Life*, 1996; Frank Belknap Long's *Lovecraft: Dreamer on the Night Side*, 1995; and L. Sprague de Camp's *Lovecraft: A Biography*, 1995.

22. Joshi in Tibbetts (13). This shadow on Lovecraft's name is threatening to remove his likeness from the bust that designates the annual World Fantasy Awards. The controversy is reviewed by Monica S. Kuehler in "Retiring Lovecraft," *Rue Morgue*, No. 163 (Jan.-Feb. 2016), 51: "Changing [the award's likeness]

doesn't diminish what winning the what the award meant, that's ridiculous—it's about the message the WFAs want to send to current and future nominees.... Surely in 2016 there are better and more inclusive ways to celebrate excellence in writing," 51.

23. Peter Straub papers, Fales Collection, Series 1, Box 36, Folder 22, New York University. No pagination.

24. In a letter dated 14 June 2003 to Robert Kelly, Straub cites Derleth's influence: "On rereading Lovecraft for the first time in about thirty years, I have discovered that he is much, much better than I remembered him.... Derleth must have done a great deal of damage to Lovecraft's reputation. I've been struck over and over by how good the man's writing really was." Peter Straub papers, Fales Collecction, Series III, Box 42, Folder 77, New York University. No pagination.

25. In the Author's Note appended to *Mr. X*, Straub acknowledges he has taken liberties with the publication history of Lovecraft's story "The Shunned House" (483). The story's first appearance in hard covers was in the Derleth-edited anthology from Arkham House, *The Outsider and Others* in 1939. It appeared later in another collection entitled *The Dunwich Horror and Others*, also from Arkham House in 1963.

26. Lovecraft seems to have employed the place name of "Arkham" for the first time in 1920 in the story, "The Picture in the House." The narrator says, "I had been travelling for some time amongst the people of the Miskatonic Valley ... [and] now I found myself upon an apparently abandoned road which I had chosen as the shortest cut to Arkham." See H. P. Lovecraft, "The Picture in the House," in August Derleth and Donald Wandrei, eds., *The Outsider and Others*, 127. Lovecraft once declared that the name was a fictional analogue of Salem, Massachusetts, but some scholars, according to Lovecraft's biographer, S. T. Joshi, "conjecture that the name Arkham was founded on the central Massachusetts town of Oakham"; while others claim "the source was an archaic Rhode Island town of Arkwright" (374). Joshi concludes, "Until further evidence emerges, we shall have to remain in the dark as to the precise origin of the name Arkham" (374). See Joshi, *I Am Providence: The Life and Times of H.P. Lovecraft*. Vol. One, 374.

27. Kingsley Amis, *New Maps of Hell* (New York: Arno Press, 1974), 43.

28. H.P. Lovecraft, *The Dunwich Horror and Others*, ed., S.T. Joshi (Sauk City, WI: Arkham House, 1982).

29. "The Jolly Corner" was James's last published work of short fiction and the last story he set in his native New York. The city had haunted James for many years, just as it haunted Spencer Brydon in the story. "There was something unresolved and haunting in James's dislike of New York and his fear of it," writes Colm Tóibín. "In 'The Jolly Corner,' written after his American sojourn of 1905, James found a new doubled self to dramatize, the man who had left New York and lived in England, and his double, still haunting him, who had never left, who still wandered in those same rooms" (36). Colm Tóibín, "Henry James's New York," *The New York Review*, 9 February 2006, 33–37.

30. Henry James, "The Jolly Corner," In *Leon Edel, ed., The Ghostly Tales of Henry James* (New Brunswick: Rutgers University Press, 1948), 755.

31. Langan, John, "Interview: Peter Straub," *Nightmare Magazine*, October 2012, No. 1. http://www.nightmare-magazine.com/non fiction/interview-peter-straub-part-1.

32. William Sheehan, *At the Foot of the Story Tree*, 317.

33. Peter Straub, *Sides* (Baltimore: Cemetery Dance, 2007), 148.

34. Quoted in Bill Sheehan's letter to the author, 3 February 2016. See Fernando Pessoa, trans. Richard Zenith, *The Book of Disquiet* (New York: Penguin, 2002). See also the discussion of Pessoa in Tim Parks, "Italy's Seriously Playful Genius," *The New York Review of Books*, 4 June 2015, 63–65.

35. Robert Kramer, *Musical Meaning: Toward a Critical History*. Berkeley and: University of California Press, 2002), 202.

36. Peter Straub interview with the author, NYC, 2014.

37. "The Walk to the Paradise Garden" is a musical interlude during Frederick Delius' 1907 opera, *A Village Romeo and Juliet*. Two young lovers, Sali and Vreli, are thwarted in their union. As they walk to the Paradise Garden—not a garden, but a village inn—they determine on a pact to die together. The music reflects the lovers' quandary: it falters and

soars, alternating between languor and ecstatic release. See Gloria Jahoda, *The Road to Samarkand: Frederick Delius and His Music* (New York: Charles Scribner's Sons, 1969), 136–137.

38. The deployment of Doubles in the novels of Jean Paul Richter (1763–1825) finds its direct correlative in Schumann's music and critical writings. Schumann's biographer, John Daverio, points out that Jean Paul first coined the word *"Doppelgänger"* in the novel, *Siebenkäs* (1796–1797). The notion, Daverio says, "is an unsettling one, yet it was precisely to the disturbing qualities in the writer's works that Schumann was particularly drawn" (38). The most obvious connection between Jean Paul and Schumann is the novel that linked them both, Jean Paul's *Flegeljahre* (1804–1805), which is also the source for Schumann's piano cycle, *Papillons*, Op. 2 (1830–31). In the book, the Harnisch twins Walt (the the aggressive, "masculine" personality) and Vult (the dreamy, "feminine" personality) contend for the hand of the fair Wina, the daughter of a Polish general. They are musically realized in Schumann's twin personae of, respectively, Florestan and Eusebius, who likewise grew out of a very troubling period in Schumann's life as he was deeply conflicted in matters of career between literature and music and from his frustrated love for Clara Wieck. Thus, Florestan and Eusebius are writers and musicians. Their contrasts in mood and gesture not only inform the abrupt shifts in musical tempo and tonality, but inscribe their signatures onto the music criticism Schumann wrote for his journal, *Neue Zeitschrift für Musik*. These two personalities appear elsewhere in many works, particularly the piano cycles, *Papillons*, Op. 2, and *Carnaval*, Op. 9, wherein they are joined by many more musical personalities, derived from both real and imaginary sources. Schumann even expressed a third "voice," that of "Master Raro," the balance, or arbiter, or *containment* of the conflicting Florestan and Eusebius. That balancing was to disappear as Schumann lapsed into psychotic episodes in which his personality further fragmented and eventually was obliterated altogether.

Moreover, Jean Paul provides Schumann with many structural models that relate literature and music—and which we see in the narratives of Peter Straub. As historian John Dav-

erio explains, Jean Paul's work was laden with baffling metaphors and digressions and narrative embeddings—or even embeddings within embeddings: "Decipherment is a necessary condition for even a basic comprehension of the Jean-Paulian text.... He stubbornly refused to adhere to the accepted principles of unity of plot, if only because he passionately believed that life itself was a motley, variegated affair." Through it all, moreover, he juxtaposes prosaic and poetic styles, pigtails and moonlight" with the "uncanny ability to give a humorous twist to the most solemn subjects" (37). In her book on the relationships between Schumann and Jean Paul, Erika Reiman demonstrates how Schumann aligns the structure and aesthetic of Jean Paul with his experiments with fragmentary musical forms. "The sleight-of-mind required to traverse the dense, digressive prose of Jean Paul may find useful application to the fragmentary, enigmatic, harmonically, and rhythmically surprising tendencies in Schumann's piano cycles" (Reiman, 3). She outlines the following devices of literary and musical doubling: (1) *Focalization*. To tell a narrative not just from a particular point of view but frequently from multiple points of view. Exterior and interior viewpoints may shift unexpectedly. The author of the story may himself be a character *in* the story, or intruding to comment *on* the story. Similarly, Straub habitually employs multiple narrative voices. (2) *Intertextuality*. This refers to the practice of breaking down the boundaries of separate works, rendering them porous, so that characters and situations reappear are doubled in a variety of contexts. Schumann will do the same with melodies, which cross boundaries and appear and reappear in numerous works. Similarly, Straub's Tim Underhill and other characters migrate from story to story, novel to novel. (3) *"Witz"* and *"Zweite Welt."* The first connotes the collision of opposites, finding commonalities between two seemingly opposite things. This is a kind of "Defamiliarization." It captures familiar things from unusual perspectives. This corresponds to the Gothic "uncanny." The second presents alternate worlds, parallel realities. Schumann likewise keeps two or more melodies in a kind of suspension, shifting back and forth among them. Straub frequently deploys parallel realities, particularly in the

Stephen King collaborations. (4) *Disappearance*. Jean Paul's characters may literally vanish and fade from view. Schumann's music sometimes fails to find a tonal resolution, as when a piece may end on an unresolved chord, as in "Child Falling Asleep"; or when the music literally lapses into a few scattered notes, then into silence altogether, as in the conclusion to *Papillons*. There are even moments, as in the *Humoreske*, when the music is *inaudible*, i.e., inscribed on the page but, in directions to the performer, *not to be heard*. Many of Straub's characters exist in various states of substance and visibility. They may be characters in a meta-text who appear and reappear, depending upon the status of the author; or as they shift in and out of an expanded state of consciousness. And language frequently lapses into a kind of gibberish or fails to connote meanings at all. See John Daverio, *Robert Schumann: Herald of a "New Poetic Age"* (New York: Oxford University Press, 1997); Erika Reiman, *Schumann's Piano Cycles and the Novels of Jean Paul* (Rochester: University of Rochester Press, 2004); and John C. Tibbetts, *Schumann: A Chorus of Voices* (New York: Amadeus Press, 2010).

39. See the topic, known generally as "The Schumann Problem," debated by a group of psychologists, biographers, and physicians in my *Schumann: A Chorus of Voices*, 369–391.

40. Peter Straub interview with the author, NYC, 2015.

41. Peter Straub interview with the author, NYC, 2011.

42. Peter Straub, "Inside Story," in David Shields and Bradford Morrow, eds., *The Inevitable: Contemporary Writers Confront Death* (New York: W.W. Norton, 2011), 208–219.

43. William Sheehan, *At the Foot of the Story Tree*, 334.

Chapter Five

1. Max Frisch, *Don Juan and the Love of Geometry*, in *Three Plays*, trans. James L. Rosenberg (New York: Hill & Wang, 1967), 37–39.

2. Dickens, Charles, *The Mystery of Edwin Drood* (New York: Heritage Press, 1941), 14.

3. Chesterton presided over a meeting of the Dickens Fellowship on 7 January 1914, in which a mock trial found John Jasper guilty of the murder of Edwin Drood. The identity of Datchery was also examined, and Helena Landless and a clerk named Bazzard were both interrogated. The foreman of the "jury" was George Bernard Shaw! The "proceedings" of the event were recorded and published in 1914. For a reprint, see *Trial of John Jasper, Lay Precentor of Cloisterham Cathedral in the County of Kent, for the Murder of Edwin Drood, Engineer*, printed on demand by the Leopold Classics Library.

4. Vincent Starrett declares that Datchery "is indeed one of the most fascinating figures of the narrative. It is possible that with Datchery correctly identified the mystery of Drood's fate would be somewhat less of a mystery and perhaps no mystery at all." See Starrett's Introduction to the Heritage Press's 1941 edition of *The Mystery of Edwin Drood*, xxi. Meanwhile, a valuable overview of numerous attempts to "solve" the Drood Case are documented in Philip Collins, *Dickens and Crime* (London: Macmillan, 1962).

5. G.K. Chesterton, *Appreciations and Criticism of the Works of Charles Dickens* (London: J. M. Dent & Sons, 1911), 218–219. Even if Dickens is chary to identify Dick Datchery as an actual detective, he did provide one bona-fide example in the person of Inspector Bucket in *Bleak House* (1853), the first detective to appear in an English novel. Placed in charge of the murder investigation of the lawyer, Mr. Tulkinghorn, Bucket is also instrumental in settling the great case of Jarndyce and Jarndyce.

6. Gary K. Wolfe, *Evaporating Genres* (Middletown, CT: Wesleyan University Press, 2011), 154.

7. William Sheehan, *At the Foot of the Story Tree* (Burton, MI: Subterranean Press, 2000), 12.

8. The term "blue rose" holds a biographical and thematic importance for Straub. It recurs frequently in many different contexts throughout s life and work. It clearly holds much significance to him. Although we know it primarily as a short-hand designation for the serial killings in *Mystery*, *Koko*, and *The Throat*, it also appears earlier as the title for his first published novella in 1985 (San Francisco: Underwood-Miller), in which young Harry Beavers, son of "Maryrose" Beavers uses the term as a post-hypnotic suggestion he had found in a book about hypnotism: "*Blue Rose*—Harry did not know why, but he liked

the sound of that" (21). Young Harry's discovery of the term, which incites his future career as a serial killer, likely matches the same time and date that Straub himself discovered it in a book. Straub explains in a letter to the author, 22 January 2016, that "blue rose" is a post-hypnotic suggestion in a book on hypnosis he had read as a boy of thirteen in 1956. Moreover, the story is dedicated to Rosemary Clooney, who recorded a Duke Ellington number called "Blue Rose" in 1956.

Meanwhile, references to "blue rose" recur frequently in his stories in both literary, painterly, and musical contexts: In *The Throat*, a secondary character, a painter, draws blue roses into his canvases. Also in *Mystery* and *The Throat* there are references to an incidental character, a saxophonist named Glenroy Breakstone, who has recorded a jazz album under the name "Blue Rose." "Bunny Is Good Bread" serial killer Bob Bandalier tells his son, Fee, about a concentration camp guard he met who cultivates a peculiar genus of *blue roses*. Bandalier then bestows the words upon his son, a serial-killer-in-training: "You know what you are? You're a little blue rose, that's what you are" (129). Regarding the latter, Straub relates that a builder of his acquaintance once told him about meeting a prison guard in Dachau who grew blue roses (letter to the author, 28 June 2015).

9. William Sheehan, *At the Foot of the Story Tree*, 191.

10. *Ibid.*, 184.

11. Samuel Beckett frequently employs this metaphor of invisibility to convey liminal identity: "There is something essentially missing at [the characters'] center; and, as we will see what is missing is precisely that, a center." They exist "just at the threshold of the recognizable, at the limit of what we expect to be the human … always on the verge of fading out of existence." Quoted in Jonathan Boulter. *Beckett: A Guide for the Perplexed* (New York: Continuum, 2008), 83.

12. Peter Straub interview with the author, NYC, 2015.

13. William Sheehan, 207.

14. Peter Straub interview with the author, NYC, 2015.

15. John Langan, "Interview: Peter Straub," in *Nightmare Magazine*, www.nightmare-maga zine.com/nonfiction/interview-peter-straub.

16. Babar the Elephant is a fictional character who first appeared in 1931 in the children's book, *Histoire de Babar*, by Jean de Brunhoff. French composer Francis Poulenc wrote a setting for voice and piano in 1940.

17. David Mathew, "Dancing Architecture: An Interview with Peter Straub," *Infinity Plus*, www.infinitypus.co.uk/nonfiction/intstraub. hem. n.p.

18. Peter Straub, "The Path of Extremity, *Locus*, January 1994, 65.

19. Ross Macdonald, "The Writer As Detective Hero," in Francis M. Nevins, Jr., *The Mystery Writer's Art* (Bowling Green, OH: Bowling Green State University Popular Press, 1970), 297.

20. Jacques Barzun, "Introduction," in Barzun, ed., *The Delights of Detection* (New York: Criterion Books, 1961), 10–14.

21. This was the mandate enforced by The Detection Club in London, founded by Anthony Berkeley in 1928, and including as its exclusive membership Dorothy Sayers, E.C. Bentley, and G. K. Chesterton. It celebrated the "fair-play" of their stories with an oath including the admonition, "*Do you solemnly swear never to conceal a vital clue from the reader?*" The introduction of the supernatural in a detective story was regarded as a cheat. No matter how bizarre the scene of the crime, how elaborate the array of clues, how numerous the incidental characters and subplots, how securely the murder chamber was locked and bolted *from the inside*, everything must point through sheer logic and ingenuity of deduction to one—and only one—rational solution. Carr applauded these writers and their detectives as "the aristocrats of the game, the old serpents, the gambit-devisers and trap-baiters whose strokes of ingenuity make the game worth playing." For a complete text of the Detection Club Oath, see Howard Haycraft, ed., *The Art of the Mystery Story* (New York: Simon & Schuster, 1946), 197–198.

22. Carr's biographer, Douglas Greene, declares *The Burning Court* is among Carr's finest works, surpassing even *The Three Coffins* and *The Crooked Hinge* in its cumulative power. Its distinction resides in what Greene says is its "startling combination of fair-play puzzling making and witchery." It's suggestion of a supernatural conclusion was far more overt than such suggestions in his other books. "Rather

than shut the supernatural horrors back in their box," the novel's epilogue reveals that the murderer is actually a witch. "Only in *The Burning Court* did [Carr] indicate that fundamentally there is no material order in creation…. Carr never wrote another novel with a supernatural ending." See Greene, *John Dickson Carr: The Man Who Explained Miracles* (New York: Otto Penzler Books, 1995), 170–172. Critic S.T. Joshi gives the novel high marks and points out that "*all* aspects of the case cannot be explained except by recourse to the supernatural" and that the "novel expands the realm of logic to include the supernatural…. Whatever our final conclusions are about this enigmatic and disturbing novel, we can scarcely deny it a very high—perhaps the highest—place in Carr's *oeuvre*." See Joshi, *John Dickson Carr: A Critical Study* (Bowling Green, OH: Bowling Green State University Popular Press, 1990), 123–124. See also John Dickson Carr, "The Grandest Game in the World," in Michael Nevins, ed., *The Mystery Writer's Art* (Bowling Green, OH: Bowling Green State University Popular Press, 1970), 229.

It is worth noting that Carr's "master of miracles," Dr. Gideon Fell, was modeled after the paradoxical manner and enormous girth of Carr's idol, G.K. Chesterton. "Chesterton knew that he was the original of Carr's detective," writes Carr's biographer, Douglas Greene, "but he did not mind, perhaps because Carr resolves never to allow Fell to do or say anything which might have embarrassed Chesterton or his acquaintances" (311). See Douglas G. Greene, "A Mastery of Miracles: G.K. Chesterton and John Dickson Carr," *The Chesterton Review*, Vol. X, No. 3 (August 1984), 307–315.

23. G.K. Chesterton, *The Man Who Was Thursday* (New York: Dodd, Mead, 1917), 140. It is tempting to test Straub's works against Chesterton's detective stories, especially what is, I believe, the greatest detective story ever written, *The Man Who Was Thursday* (1908). Although Straub says he has not read Chesterton, suffice to say that everywhere in Straub we find a mysterious complicity with Chesterton. Do they share a commonality in The Realm? Is there, for example, a better description of Straub's work anywhere than in Chesterton's evocation of Shakespeare's *A Mid-*

summer Night's Dream: "Here is the pursuit of the man we cannot catch, the flight from the man we cannot see; here is the perpetual returning to the same place, here is the crazy alteration in the very objects of our desire, the substitution of one face for another face, the putting of the wrong souls in the wrong bodies, the fantastic disloyalties of the night." See G.K. Chesterton, "A Midsummer Night's Dream," in *The Common Man* (New York: Sheed and Ward, 1950), 61.

24. In his "Imp of the Perverse," Poe suggested that perversity and criminal behavior are inextricably linked to the "faculties and impulses" of the human soul. Everyone has within him the "overwhelming tendency to do wrong for the wrong's sake" he wrote. "I am not more certain that I breathe, than that the assurance of the wrong or error of any action is often the one unconquerable *force* which impels us, and alone impels us to its prosecution," even to the point of self-annihilation." *Tales of Edgar Allan Poe* (New York: Random House, 1944), 437–444.

25. Historian Frank D. McSherry, Jr., describes the "Janus Resolution as "deliberately leaving the question open." The writer "may skillfully and cleverly plot his story in such a way that a natural explanation and a supernatural one account equally well for all the facts. Making the weight of the evidence on one side as equal as possible to that on the other, and deliberately failing to state which explanation he considers or intends to be correct, the author leaves the reader to decide for himself." See McSherry, "The Janus Resolution," in Francis Nevins, Jr., ed., *The Mystery Writer's Art*, 263–271.

26. E.T.A. Hoffmann, *Kater Murr*, in Leonard J. Kent, Leonard J. and Elizabeth C. Knight, eds., *Selected Writings of E. T. A. Hoffmann*, Volume Two (Chicago University Press, 1969, 141.

27. Charles Brockden Brown, *Wieland* (Philadelphia: David McKay, 1889), 199–204.

28. G.K. Chesterton, "How to Write a Detective Story," *G.K.'s Weekly*, 17 October 1925; reprinted in *The Chesterton Review*, Vol. IX, No. 2 (May 1984), 111–118, 113. Chesterton's play, *Magic*, affirms the point. Originally produced at Gertrude Kingston's Little Theatre in London in December 1913, the play features a parlor magician who confounds a skeptic cler-

gyman and an atheist when he changes the color of a red lamp to blue, then back again to red. He confesses it was done by magic, that he had discovered that devils and evil spirits actually exist and serve him when bidden. At the same time, to keep his atheist auditor from going mad, he reluctantly decides he will concoct a "natural explanation." "'You cannot think how that trick could be done naturally,'" he explains. "'I alone found out how it could be done—*after* I had done it by magic!'" In a splendid irony, just as he had refused to explain the magic, now he conceals his *natural* explanation. See Chesterton, *Magic: A Fantastic Comedy in a Prelude and Three Acts* (London: Martin Secker, 1913).

29. G. K. Chesterton, "The Tremendous Adventures of Major Brown," in Chesterton, *The Club of Queer Trades* (New York: Harper Brothers, 1905), 28.

30. Jorge Borges, "On Chesterton," in *Other Inquisitions, 1937–1952* (New York: Washington Square Press, 1966), 86–88.

31. G. K. Chesterton, "The White Pillars Murder," in *Thirteen Detectives* (New York: Dodd, Mead, 1987), 27.

32. G. K. Chesterton, "The Blue Cross," in *The Innocence of Father Brown* (New York: The Macaulay Company, 1911), 31.

33. G.K. Chesterton, "The Secret of Father Brown," in *The Secret of Father Brown* (New York and London: Harper & Brothers, 1927), 11.

34. G.K. Chesterton, "The Chief Mourner of Marne," in *The Secret of Father Brown* (New York: Harper & Brothers, 1927), 266.

35. William J. Scheick, "The Twilight Harlequinade of Chesterton's Father Brown Stories," *The Chesterton Review*, Vol. IV, No. 1 (Fall-Winter 1977–78), 109. See G. K. Chesterton's "The Vanishing of Vaudrey," in *The Secret of Father Brown*.

36. *Ibid.*, 112.

37. Gary Wills, *Chesterton* (New York: Doubleday, 1975), 275.

38. Raymond Chandler, "The Simple Art of Murder," in Howard Haycraft, ed, *The Art of the Mystery Story* (New York: Random House, 1946), 222–244.

39. Frank MacShane, ed. *Selected Letters of Raymond Chandler* (New York: Columbia University Press, 1981), 135.

40. Critic Michael Dirda observes that Hammett's Sam Spade "remains essentially a

cipher.... We see Spade, and hear him talk, but we never know what he's actually thinking or feeling. The wholly external third-person approach allows him to keep the reader constantly intrigued about the meaning of Spade's actions and utterly in the dark about how things will finally play out." See Dirda, "Dashiell Hammett," in Dirda, *Classics for Pleasure* (New York: Harcourt, 2007), 290–293.

41. See Frank MacShane, ed., *Selected Letters of Raymond Chandler*, 99.

42. Gary K. Wolfe., "Afterword: Fractal Evil," in Peter Straub, *A Special Place* (New York: Pegasus Books, 2010), 130.

43. Historian Ron Goulart reports that by the mid–1930s 200 separate pulp magazines flooded the newsstands. *Black Mask* was number one, helmed by Joseph T. Shaw, who first published Hammett and Chandler. See Goulart, *The Hardboiled Dicks* (Los Angeles: Sherbourne Press, 1965).

44. Quoted in Tom Nolan, *Ross Macdonald: A Biography* (New York: Scribner, 1999), 139.

45. 'Crime novelist Jim Thompson granted us this memorable insight from the viewpoint of a serial killer: "Plenty of pretty smart psychiatrists have been fooled by guys like me, and you can't really fault 'em for it. There's just not much they can put their hands on, know what I mean? We might have the disease, the condition; or we might just be cold-blooded and smart as hell; or we might be innocent of what we're supposed to have done. We might be any of those three things, because the symptoms we show would fit any one of the three." See Thompson, *The Killer Inside Me* (London: Orion, 1952), 201.

46. Peter Straub, "The Path of Extremity," 65.

47. The recent notoriety of the television series, *Making a Murderer*, plays up this general perception. See Lorrie Moore, "TV: The Shame of Wisconsin," *The New York Review of Books*, 25 February 2016, 10, 12. Straub's near contemporary, the regional writer August Derleth, also utilized Wisconsin for many of his novels and stories—many of them of a Gothic nature—in his "Sac Prairie Saga," the fictive place name for his native Sauk City, which is located just a hundred miles north and west of Milwaukee.

48. John Langan, "Interview: Peter Straub," in *Nightmare Magazine*, www.nightmare-

magazine.com/nonfiction/interview-peter-straub.

49. Dashiell Hammett, *The Maltese Falcon* (New York: Alfred A. Knopf, 1957), 54.

50. Straub uses this memorable phrase frequently in his writings. For example, in his account of his debilitating accident and its protracted aftermath, he writes, "One of the first questions that I asked my mother afterward in the hospital, was if I could have the clothing I wore that day. I wanted to wear my own blood.... I wanted to walk around in the costume of my worst, most decisive, most mysterious and appalling moment.... I wanted to plug myself back into the fearful story to recover what had been lost. The wish to dress myself in that ruined clothing, it strikes me now, represented a childish, cartoonlike attempt at self-analysis." (215–216). See Straub, "Inside Story," in David Shields and Bradford Morrow, eds., *The Inevitable: Contemporary Writers Confront Death* (New York: W.W. Norton, 2011), 215–216.

51. Peter Wolfe, *Something More than Night: The Case of Raymond Chandler* (Bowling Green, OH: Bowling Green State University Popular Press, 1985), 2.

52. Ross Macdonald, "Foreword," to *Archer at Large* (New York: Knopf, 1970), viii–ix.

53. See Robert I. Edenbaum, "The Poetics of the Private Eye: The Novels of Dashiell Hammett," in Mike Nevins, ed., *The Mystery Writers Art* (Bowling Green, OH: Bowling Green State University Popular Press, 1970), 98–121. Certain aspects of the hard-boiled formula were immediately embraced and/ or criticized on both sides of the Atlantic by such literary luminaries as Albert Camus, Jacques Barzun, and Samuel Beckett. Critic Jonathan Boulter reports that Beckett's novel *Malloy* novel is both a parody and critique of the epistemological assumptions of the classically formal detective novel, with its specified time and place, integrated characters, a plot with actions and consequences, and solutions to a mystery. "The primary assumption is that the there is order in the universe, that the world is knowable, is open to the power of the detective's observation and reason. [The detective] makes sense of what appears at first glance to not make sense. The crime is committed in the past, and it is solved in the present. The detective/narrator is reliable. There is a clear onto-

logical and moral distinction between pursuer and pursued." However, from the outset, Beckett questions and sometimes overturns these assumptions. The reader is confronted with unknowable characters who recount unstable and uncanny narratives. The detective is one "Moran," who is searching for "Molloy," a search that ends in a violent encounter in the woods with a man who may or may not be Molloy. Here, the detective never really finds his object. He undergoes a dismantling of his authority. "Not only is the narrative as a whole an unstable structure, but individual sentences threaten to undermine themselves." See Jonathan Boulter, *Beckett: A Guide for the Perplexed* (New York: Continuum, 2008), 112.

Albert Camus rejects outright this form of detective story. In *The Rebel*, he wrote that the hard-boiled's rejection of sentiment, particularly in Hammett, is to reject psychology and everything that comprises the inner life. In words echoing Chesterton's Basil Grant, Camus charges that the analysis of character and behavior is rejected in favor of observations of exterior appearances, factual data, and "daily automatisms": "On this mechanical level men, in fact, seem exactly alike, which explains this peculiar universe in which all the characters appear interchangeable, even down to their physical uliarities.... The unity thus obtained is a degraded unity, a leveling off of human beings and of the world. It would seem that for these writers it is the inner life that deprives human actions of unity and that tears people away from one another." He is, moreover, "the symbol of the despairing world in which wretched automatons live in a machine-ridden universe, which American novelists have presented as a heart-rending but sterile protest." See Camus, *The Rebel* (New York: Vintage, 1984), 265–266.

Jacques Barzun, while admitting his admiration for the hard-boiled school, goes on to say, "The detective tale is not the place to make us appreciate the moral burdens of the times by presenting a detective who... gives glimpses of man's callous indifference to man." See Barzun, 19.

54. Peter Straub, "Mr. Clubb and Mr. Cuff," in *Magic Terror* (New York: Random House 2000), 321–323.

55. Both men held the prestige of academia and the popularity of the mainstream in a love-

hate relationship. A writer of mysteries, Chandler feared, "could never rival serious mainstream novelists; by working in a suspect, if not despised subgenre, the mystery writer either confirms his own triteness or goes slumming artistically." See Peter Wolfe, 2. As for Macdonald, he admits, "When I took up the hardboiled novel, beginning in 1946 with *Blue City*, I was writing in reaction against a number of things, among them my strict academic background." See Macdonald, Foreword, x.

56. In *The Long Goodbye* rich playboy Terry Lennox is suspected of the murder of his wife. He asks Marlowe to drive him to Tijuana. Marlowe does, and is later questioned by the cops and jailed as an accessory. Released after Lennox's apparent suicide in Mexico, Marlowe continues to investigate his supposed death. He is visited by mobsters who think he has the money Lennox was carrying. Meanwhile, in a related case, Marlowe is hired by Eileen Wade to track down her missing husband a successful writer. He also is found dead, an apparent suicide. Eileen is implicated in his death. Lennox, who has undergone many identity changes and aliases, finally reappears at the end, very much alive, his identity altered by facial surgery.

In *The Galton Case* Archer is hired to track down Anthony Galton, the long-lost son and heir of a dying woman. He finds a Canadian actor named John Brown, who is posing as Galton—but who also goes under the name Theo Fredericks. The novel's climax is the revelation that Brown/Fredericks was in fact impersonating himself. In a switcheroo of Chestertonian paradox, he actually *is* who he has impersonated!

57. Peter Straub, "The Fantasy of Everyday Life," in *Sides* (Baltimore: Cemetery Dance, 2007), 167–168.

58. Peter Straub interview with the author, NYC, 2015.

59. Peter Straub, "The Fantasy of Everyday Life," in *Sides,* 167–168.

60. Peter Straub interview with the author, NYC, 2015.

61. Raymond Chandler, *The Long Goodbye* (New York: Vintage, 1992), 273.

62. Peter Wolfe, *Something More Than Night: The Case of Raymond Chandler* (Bowling Green, OH: Bowling Green State University Popular Press, 1985), 216.

63. Quoted in Ross Macdonald, "The Writer as Detective Hero," in Francis M. Nevins, Jr., ed., *The Mystery Writer's Art* (Bowling Green, OH: Bowling Green State University Popular Press, 1970), 301.

64. Quoted in Tom Nolan, *Ross Macdonald,* 183.

65. Peter Straub interview with the author, NYC, 2015.

66. For a particularly fine overview of the American *film noir,* see Terry Curtis Fox, "City Knights," *Film Comment,* October 1984, 30–39. And for an overview of Chandler's years in Hollywood, see Paul Jensen, "Raymond Chandler: The World You Live in," *Film Comment,* November-December 1974, 18–26.

67. Altman was on record as having not read the book all the way through. Yet, according to biographer Patrick McGilligan, "One feels from Altman an identification with Marlowe [Elliott Gould], a misfit in Hollywood, an underachiever, a loner betrayed by his friend. The theme of treachery aroused this director... " See Patrick McGilligan, *Robert Altman: Jumping off the Cliff* (New York: St. Martin' Press, 1989), 365.

68. Quoted in Al Clark, *Raymond Chandler in Hollywood* (London: Proteus, 1982), 103.

69. Peter Straub, "A Special Place," 2 0–21.

70. Peter Straub, "Author's Note" in Straub, *5 Stories* (Baltimore: Borderlands Press, 2008), 124.

71. *Ibid.,* 124.

72. Peter Straub interview with the author, NYC, 2015.

73. Fielding Bandolier makes an appearance in a graphic novel, *The Green Woman* (Vertigo Comics, 2010), co-written by Peter Straub and Michael Easton and graphically designed by John Bolton. Haunted by the female victims of his past and memories of his war crimes in Vietnam, Fee is pursued by a tough, jaded cop named Bob Steele.

74. Gary K. Wolfe, *Evaporating Genres,* 155.

75. Even earlier examples of an occult investigation include Miles Coverdale's exposure of the fraudulent psychic practices of the spiritualist Westervelt in Nathaniel Hawthorne's *The Blithedale Romance* (1852); Mr. Latimer's disclosure of a murder plot against him in George Eliot's *The Lifted Veil* (1859); and Basil Ransome's rescue of the medium, Verena Tarrant, from the clutches of her father in Henry

James's *The Bostonians* (1886). One of the first haunted-house investigations—the prototype of Shirley Jackson's *The Haunting of Hill House* (1959)—transpired in Edward Bulwer-Lytton's *The Haunted and the Haunters* (1859).

76. At the same time, other researchers, amateur and professional, exposed and discredited the spiritualists. In 1858 poet Robert Browning accused the medium D.D. Home of fraud in sittings involving his wife, Elizabeth Barrett. The newly formed British and American Societies for Psychical Research, established, respectively, in 1882 and 1884, documented numerous instances of hoax and fraud. Magician J.N. Maskelyn, and later Harry Houdini, revealed to a shocked public that the machinery of stage illusion included ventriloquism, the use of accomplices, hidden phonographic devices, rigged "spirit cabinets," hypnosis, and the nauseating practice of trance mediums who secretly regurgitated materials in order to produce seance materializations. Worst of all, just forty years after her involvement with the Hydesville Rappings, Margaret Fox confessed to her own fraudulent practices. Yet the public remained loyal to the spiritualists' claims. Evolutionary theory had recently delivered a severe blow to fundamental religious doctrines, and spiritualism seemed to come to the rescue, offering a timely and badly needed reaffirmation of life after death. As Henry Sidgwick, one of the founders of the British SRO explained: "The dilemma is clear and certain to me. Either one must believe in ghosts, modern miracles, etc., or there can be no ground for giving credence to the Gospel story." Moreover, thinkers like William James realized that what had begun—and been exposed—as a public craze was nonetheless producing an impressive mass of data—evidence of clairvoyance, psychometry, mesmeric trance, paranormal activity, even reincarnation—for further research. What might have seemed "magic" to a past generation was now the foundation of a new "science" to the present one. See John C. Tibbetts, "Phantom Fighters: 150 Years of Occult Detection," *The Armchair Detective*, Vol. 29, No. 3 (Summer 1996), 340–345.

77. *Ibid.*, 340–345.

78. The most interesting psychic sleuth, in my opinion, is John Carnacki. William Hope Hodgson's stories about "Carnacki the Ghost-

Finder" appeared in 1913. While Carnacki didn't possess any special psychic gifts, he was the "Craig Kennedy" of the occultists, utilizing ingenious scientific apparatus to battle the uncanny. Indeed, some of the eight stories read like early forms of science fiction. Despite occasional allusions to occult spells and an arcane volume of lore called the "Sigsand Manuscript," Carnacki generally prefers modern technology in his battles against the Dark. In his first case, "The Thing Invisible," he exposes a fraudulent haunting of a chapel by means of a camera. In "The House Among the Laurels" and "The Haunted 'Jarvee,'" he constructs wireless transmitters to beam "vibrations" into the ether to "insulate" and protect the targets of psychic attack. In his greatest case, "The Hog," he invents an early kind of television device by which he can "hear" and "see" his client's nightmares. He also devises what he calls a "Spectrum Defense," which consists of seven concentric circles of vacuum-tubing, each circle a different hue of the color spectrum. The "cool" colors like blue and indigo repulse invasive entities, while the "warm" colors like orange and red attract them. In this way Carnacki is able to entrap and destroy hostile forces. "It's a kind of colour organ upon which I seem to play a tune of colour combinations that can be either safe or infernal in its effects," he explains. "You know, I have a keyboard with a separate switch to each of the colour circles." Occasionally in the stories Carnacki even quotes his own academic treatises, a la Holmes, like the "Lecture on Astarral Vibrations Compared with Matter-Involuted Vibrations Below the Six-Billion Limit"! See Tibbetts, "Phantom Fighters," 340–345. Obscure references to other Carnacki cases have been expanded into a new series of Carnacki stories in A.F. Kidd and Rick Kennett, *No 472 Cheyne Walk* (Ashcroft, British Columbia: Ashtree Press, 2002).

79. William Sheehan, *At the Foot of the Story Tree*, 232.

80. Zack Handlen, "Peter Straub," in *The A.V. Club*, www.avclub.com/article/peter—straub-38322.

81. Peter Straub interview with the author, NYC, 2011.

82. Allbert Camus is referring to Franz Kafka's views on multiple viewpoints in narration, "in forcing the reader to *reread.*" See Camus, *The Myth of Sisyphus*, 92.

83. Eric Larson's nonfiction book, *The Devil in the White City* (2003), revived interest in Holmes and his "Murder Castle." It juxtaposed an account of the planning and staging of the Chicago's Columbian Exposition with Holmes's story.

84. Gary K. Wolfe, *Evaporating Genres*, 153.

85. Straub is probably inserting a sly reference to Margaret Millar's classic novel of psychological suspense, *Beast in View* (1955).

86. Gary K. Wolfe, *Evaporating Genres*, 160.

87. Rene Magritte,"Not to Be Reproduced," 1937.

88. Peter Straub interview with the author, NYC, 2015.

89. Nathaniel Hawthorne, "Introduction" to *The Scarlet Letter*, in Norman Holmes Pearson, ed., *The Complete Novels and Selected Tales of Nathaniel Hawthorne* (New York: The Modern Library, 1937), 106.

90. Peter Straub interview with the author, NYC, 2011.

91. Gary K. Wolfe, "Fractal Evil," in Peter Straub, *A Special Place* (New York: Pegasus Books, 2010), 127–128.

92. David Mathew, "Dancing Architecture."

93. Charles Baudelaire, "Crowds," in *Paris Spleen*, trans. Louie Varese (New York: New Directions, 1970), 20.

Chapter Six

1. "Quoted in Michael Schumacher, "Ghost Storyteller," *Writer's Digest*, January 1985, 34.

2. Peter Straub, "Meeting Stevie," in Tim Underwood and Chuck Miller, eds,. *Fear Itself: The Horror Fiction of Stephen King* (San Francisco: Underwood-Miller, 1982), 12. Straub's comparison of himself and King with Chandler and Hammett is very much to the point. As writers all too often consigned to the marginalized "Horror" markets, they have occasionally chafed over the years at the lack of critical recognition. Hammett and Chandler, likewise, had labored in the back alleys and "mean streets" of the detective story. In his study of Raymond Chandler, Peter Wolfe noted the writer's insecurity about his position as an artist: "Being a mystery writer probably brought him as much embarrassment and hence anger as it did satisfaction. His letters bristle with self-conscious references to literary detection. A writer of mysteries, he feared, could never rival serious mainstream novelists." See Wolfe, *Something More than Night: The Case of Raymond Chandler* (Bowling Green, OH: Bowling Green State University Popular Press, 1985), 2. Chandler himself defended the "literary" potentials of his craft in his classic essay "The Simple Art of Murder" (1944). Because the detective story "is difficult to write well," that "good specimens of the art are much rarer than good serious novels" (223). Chandler went on to assess the work of Dashiell Hammett. "He wrote at first (and almost to the end) for people with a sharp aggressive attitude to life. They were not afraid of the seamy side of things; they lived there. Violence did not dismay them; it was right down their street" (234). See the complete essay in Haycraft, Howard, *The Art of the Mystery Story* (New York: Simon & Schuster, 1946), 222–237.

3. Critic Matthew Bevis notes that this quality of the ambiguous nature of good deeds and mystery is essential to this poem and to Elizabeth Bishop's poetry in general. See Bevis, "the lighthouse stares back," *London Review of Books*, 7 January 2016, 9–10.

4. Gary K., Wolfe, "The Talisman" and "Black House," in *Bearings: Reviews, 1997–2001* (Essex: Beccon Publications, 2010), 393.

5. William Sheehan, *At the Foot of the Story Tree* (Burton, MI: Subterranean Press, 200), 159–160.

6. See Sheehan for an examination of the two books' connections with Twain's *Tom Sawyer* and *Huckleberry Finn*.

7. In an interview with Douglas E. Winter, Straub acknowledge the "Dickensian" model for his books. See "Peter Straub," in Winter, ed., *Faces of Fear* (New York: Berkley Books, 1985), 231.

8. G. K. Chesterton, "Bleak House," in Chesterton, *Appreciations and Criticisms of the Works of Charles Dickens* (London: J.M. Dent & Sons, 1911), 151.

9. Albert Fish was one of America's most notorious serial killers. He was a child rapist and cannibal who was executed in the electric chair in 1936.

10. Conceived as early as 1970, Stephen King's Dark Tower is an Aleph, a point in time, space, and reality where all dimensions meet—the spindle of creation" (22). The first installment in 1970 was *The Gunslinger*, which takes

place in Mid-World, which might be the future of a world much like ours or a separate reality entirely. Like a medieval kingdom it is separated into baronies, some ruled by honorable men called Gunslingers. At the center of all things is the Dark Tower, the spindle on which reality turns, has been somehow tainted and corrupted, and as the knight and adventurer named Roland views the devastation around him, Roland decides that he must devote his life to saving the Tower (23). For a useful overview of the Dark Tower stories, see Stanley Wiater, Christopher Golden and Hank Wagner, eds., *The Stephen King Universe* (Los Angeles: Renaissance Books, 2001), 21–30. (Note: King purportedly bases his stories on a high school reading of Robert Browning's "Childe Roland to the Dark Tower Came" [1855], itself inspired by the legends surrounding the death of the real-life Count Roland, nephew of the Emperor Charlemagne. See the overview in Wiati, 21–31.) His associates are called "ka-tet," fellow gunslingers, gathered from various worlds connected to his own by "thin" barriers. His ultimate enemy is the Crimson King. The "beams" of power emanate from the Tower and hold time, space, and all realities together are being corrupted. As a result, the barriers among the various realities begin breaking down.

11. William Sheehan letter to the author, 26 August 2015.

12. In "The Aleph," Borges describes this "mirror" as revealing "all the places of the world, seen from every angle…. What my eyes saw was *simultaneous*…. In this glass the entire universe was reflected." Andrew Hurley, trans., *Jorge Luis Borges: Collected Fictions* (New York: Viking, 1998), 285.

13. E.T.A. Hoffmann, "The Golden Pot," in Leonard J. Kent and Elizabeth C. Knight, eds., *Selected Writings of E. T. A. Hoffmann,* Volume One (Chicago: Chicago University Press, 1969), 20.

14. Peter Straub," "Meeting Stevie," 13.

15. Stephen King, *Danse Macabre* (New York: Everest House, 1981), 242–252.

16. Quoted in Douglas E. Winter, *The Art of Darkness* (New York: New American Library, 1984), 139.

17. Peter Straub, "Meeting Stevie," 7–10. Just two years later Straub amplified these early impressions. King's work ethic inspired him "simply to work harder." Even though at the time

he recognized that next to King he was the "Number Two Man" in the public perception of top horror writers, he accepted the position with good humor. "I have always thought that Steve deserved every success he has had. He is incredibly gifted. Back when nobody ever heard of him, I used to go around telling people, 'You really ought to read this guy, because he's great.' So I do sometimes feel as though ironic revenge has been visited upon me. But I don't think I envy Steve his success, because first, I think he more than deserves it, and second, the 'phenomenon' took over and it eventually began to have as much to do with celebrity as with books. I am just as happy that, when I walk down the street, people don't rush up to me for autographs. I don't think Steve likes that" (Winter 229).

18. William Sheehan, 146.

19. Michael Schumacher, "Ghost Storyteller," *Writer's Digest*, January 1985), 34.

20. *Ibid.*, 30–34.

21. Peter Straub interview at the World Fantasy Convention, Ottawa, Canada, 1984; quoted in Tim Underwood and Chuck Miller, eds., *Bare Bones: Conversations on Terror with Stephen King* (New York: McGraw-Hill, 1988), 172.

22. Michael Smith, "Peter Straub and Stephen King Team Up for Fear," *Hellfire Newsletter*, 21 September 2001. n. p. Fales Collection, New York University.

23. Gary K. Wolfe, "'Talisman'" and 'Black House,'" 392–393.

24. Quoted in Underwood and Miller, *Bare Bones,* 91.

25. *Ibid.*, 173–175.

26. Peter Straub interview with the author, NYC, 2015.

27. *Ibid.*

28. In Samuel Beckett's *Molloy* there is a moment when a character describes at length the mysterious buzzing dance of bees, controlled by "determinants of which I had not the slightest idea." In his essay, "Sam I Am," Benjamin Kunkel declares it may be the happiest, most fruitful moment in Beckett: "'And I said, with rapture, here is something I can study all my life, and never understand.'" See Kunkel, "Sam I Am," *The New Yorker*, 7 & 14 August 2006, 89.

29. Gary K. Wolfe, "'The Talisman'" and "'The Black House,'" 395.

30. The atrocities were committed by soldiers from Company C of the 1st Battalion, 20th Infantry Regiment, 11th Brigade, 23rd Infantry Division. The victims included men, women, children, and infants. Twenty-six soldiers were charged but only Lt. William Calley was convicted. His life sentence was reduced to only three and a half years under house arrest.

31. Stephen King, "Low Men in Yellow Coats," in King, *Hearts in Atlantis* (New York: Scribner, 1999), 426- 498.

32. *The Throat*, whose characters and incidents relate it to *Koko*, is rich with accounts of Tim Underhill's experiences in Vietnam. His platoon includes soldiers we met in *Koko, Michael Poole, Tina Pumo*, and M.O. Dengler. One episode involves the discovery of a "ghost village" of Bong To, a site reeking of cannibalism and evidence of the torture of children.

33. William Sheehan, *At the Foot of the Story Tree*, 168.

34. Peter Straub interview with the author, NYC, 2015.

Chapter Seven

1. Straub quotes Thomas Nashe's "In Time of Pestilence" (1593) at length in *The Floating Dragon*. Dick Dart's "adaptation" of it in *Hellfire* is singularly apt, considering the horrors lurking in the past at Shorelands. These lines apply:

All things to end are made;
The plague full swift goes by;
I am sick, I must die—
Lord, have mercy on us!

2. Peter Straub interview with the author, NYC, 2011. It is my opinion that Dart's manglings of poetry bears at least a passing resemblance to the movement known as the "Language Poets," which emerged in the late 1960s and early 1970s in the work of Charles Bernstein, Leslie Scalapino, Stephen Rodefer, Ron Silliman, etc. The movement emphasizes the role of the *reader* in interpreting the *construction* of a poem, rather than its purported *expression*—just as the *montage* movement in the Soviet Cinema of Sergei Eisenstein in the 1920s relied on the viewer to construct meanings from the stream of shots in a sequence. See Charles Bernstein, ed., *The Politics of Poetic Form: Poetry and Public Policy* (New Yorki: Roof, 1990).

3. *Desert Music and Other Poems*, by William Carlos Williams, was published in 1954.

4. Peter Straub, "Toward a New Edition of William Carlos Williams's *The Desert Music*," Straub's Masters Thesis for Columbia University. The Fales Collection, New York University, Series V, Box 52, Folder 1.

5. These brief quotes are from an insightful discussion of Williams's work in William M. Ober, M.D., "William Carlos Williams, M.D.: Physician as Poet," in Ober, *Boswell's Clap & Other Essays of Literary Men's Afflictions* (New York: Harper and Row, 1988), 206–232.

6. Peter Straub letter to the author, 5 May 2015.

7. William Sheehan, *At the Foot of the Story Tree* (Burton, MI: Subterranean Press, 2000), 14.

8. Peter Straub interview with the author, NYC, 2011.

9. From Thom Tessier's Afterword to the 1995 Gauntlet Publications deluxe limited hardcover edition of *Shadowland*.

10. Unpublished note by Peter Straub, "The Good Karl," 29 December 1996. Straub Archive, Fales Collection, New York University, Series 1, Box 35, Folder 34.

11. "Tracking," *Open Air* (Shannon: Irish University Press, 1972), 16.

12. Peter Straub interview with Stanley Wiater, in *Hauntings: The Official Peter Straub Bibliography* (Woodstock, GA: Overlook Connection Press, 1999), 21–23.

13. Quoted in William Sheehan, *At the Foot of the Story Tree,* 339.

14. Quoted in Walter Benjamin, *The Writer of Modern Life* (Cambridge: The Belknap Press of Harvard University Press, 2006), 98.

15. "The Writer's Credo," from "The Juniper Tree," 84.

16. *Fence* is a print and online journal of experimental and avant-garde material. Conceived by Rebecca Wolff in 1997, it is currently affiliated with the New York State Writers Institute.

17. Laura Sims has published three volumes of poetry for Fence Books: *Stranger* (2009), *Restraint* (2005), and *my god is this a man* (2014). She teaches literature and creative writing at NYU.

18. "In writing this book," Sims says in her "Author's Note" to *my god is this a man*, "I read

the confessions, interviews, letters and journal entries of, with, and by convicted (or suspected) murderers."

19. Peter Straub letter to the author, 9 March 2011.

20. Laura Sims letter to the author, 19 March 2015.

21. Peter Straub interview with the author, NYC, 1990.

22. Quoted in Douglas E. Winter, *Stephen King: The Art of Darknesss* (New York: New American Library, 1984), 139.

23. Peter Straub interview with the author, NYC, 1990.

24. Quoted in William Sheehan, *At the Foot of the Story Tree*, 345.

25. "[The novel] was a conscious attempt to get back to the landscape I knew as a child. It was a wonderful experience to conjure all of that up in my head, to wander those little streets and look at the woods and the streams and the farmhouses in my mind, and then to try to work out their emotional nuances on paper." Straub interview in Douglas E. Winter, in *Faces of Fear* (New York: Berkley Books, 1985), 225.

26. The great British art critic John Ruskin celebrated what he termed "the desire of my eyes": "The greatest thing a human soul ever does in this world is to *see* something, and tell what it *saw* in a plain way. Hundreds of people can talk for one who can think, but thousands can think for one who can see. To see clearly is poetry, prophecy, and religion—all in one." Quoted in Wolfgang Kemp, *The Desire of My Eyes: The Life and Work of John Ruskin* (New York: Farrar, Straus and Giroux, 1990), 258. One also thinks of Virginia Woolf's story, "The Mark on the Wall," and its "worshipping solidity, worshipping reality, worshipping the personal world which is a proof of some existence other than ours." It was published by the Hogarth Press in 1917.

27. I am indebted to Bill Sheehan for pointing this out. Letter to the author, 3 February 2016.

28. Quoted in Paul Tremblay, "The Whole Ball of Wax in a Nutshell," *Los Angeles Review of Books*, 21 February 2016. See *lareviewofbooks.org/author/peter-straub*.

29. Peter Straub, "The Fantasy of Everyday Life," in Straub, *Sides* (Baltimore: Cemetery Dance, 2007), 165.

30. Quoted in Paul Tremblay.

31. Quoted in William Sheehan, *At the Foot of the Story Tree*, 345.

32. Nathaniel Hawthorne, Preface to *The Scarlet Letter*, in Norman Holmes Pearson, ed., *The Complete Novels and Selected Tales of Nathaniel Hawthorne* (New York: The Modern Library, 1937), 106.

33. Wallace Stevens, "Chocorua to Its Neighbor."

34. The concept behind Rauschenberg's "White Paintings" has been compared in an essay by Nick Richardson to Cage's "4–33": "Cage recognized that the 'emptiness' of Rauschenberg's painting was no such thing, writing later that he saw them as 'airports for the lights, shadows and particles'" that "turned visual minutiae that would usually go unnoticed into objects of aesthetic appreciation." In the same essay, Richardson also describes the first "performance" of John Cage's "4'33," 19 August 1952: "Four minutes and 33 seconds without a note played and Cage had stamped himself on music history with the most radical contribution of his generation" (18). See Nick Richardson, "Rain, Blow, Rustle," *London Review of Books*, 19 August 2010, 18.

35. Lawrence Kramer, *Musical Meaning: Toward a Critical History* (Berkeley: University of California Press, 2002), 2–5.

36. Peter Straub, "The Modern Jazz Quartet," 10 May 1987 (no attribution). Fales Papers, New York University, Series 1, Box 40, Folder 19.

37. Susan Sontag, "The Aesthetics of Silence," in Sontag, *Styles of Radical Will* (New York: Farar, Straus, and Giroux, 1969), 7.

38. Jonathan Boulter, *Beckett: A Guide for the Perplexed*. New York: Continuum, 2008, 59. Beckett's early novel, *Watt* (1941), is more or less a traditional narrative about a person who descends into madness, and whose language disintegrates as he speaks backward, reverses the order of words, reversing the order of letters in words, then the order of words and letters (Jonathan Boulter, *Beckett: A Guide for the Perplexed* [New York: Continuum, 2008]).

39. Novalis quoted in Jeremy Adler, "News of the Golden Age," *Times Literary Supplement*, 15 June 2012, 3–5.

40. In an interview with this writer, 15 April 1988, John Cage described the experience: "I think more and more people are hearing the

environmental sounds and enjoying them. You know, one of the first ones to make publicly clear that that was a pleasure was Henry David Thoreau. And I just received in the mail a post-card from [Richard Castellanos], who'd come across a remark of Glenn Gould to the effect that listening to the sounds, such as the sounds that are coming in the window now, is in fact a musical pleasure. It's been that way for me all along. People ask me what music I prefer, and I tell them, no music at all. Just what happens to be audible wherever I am."

41. Peter Straub, *Mystery*, 56.

42. Charles Rosen, "Freedom and Art," *The New York Review of Books*, 109 Ma 2012, 18.

43. Quoted in Vincent Starrett, *Buried Caesars* (Chicago: Covici-McGee, 1923), 16–17.

44. Peter and Susan Straub interview with the author, NYC, 2014.

45. Storyteller/artist Chris Van Allsburg (*The Polar Express* and *Jumanji*) expressed to me his thoughts on the process of reading aloud: "At first, I was in favor of the audio cassette, because the book descriptions of lots of sounds, and I thought it could be successful, artistically. But then, having agreed to do it, I had hoped it wouldn't displace the family reading. I disliked the thought of a family gathering around the hearth and then booting up the compact disc instead of opening up the book and reading it aloud. It's not as bad as a video cassette of a Yule log in a fireplace, but it gave me some of those concerns. Now, my concern is that when the film version comes out on DVD, which it will, that some people will decide to view the DVD on Christmas Eve instead of reading the book. And I don't think I want that to happen. I have kids. The stimulation that comes out of a television set is pretty irresistible. You have to make an effort to expose your children to the values and satisfactions of hearing words in a quiet bedroom and seeing how that special stimulation works instead." See John C. Tibbetts, "The Mysteries of Chris Van Allsburg," *The World and I*, Vol. 6, No. 12 (December 1991), 252–261.

46. Benjamin Straub letter to the author, 17 January 2016.

47. In a recent statement, Susan Straub has announced that Read to Me has been retired: "We would like to thank you all for the 25 years of shared reading with babies. We are retiring, but will continue to promote reading with ba-bies everywhere we can. The store is closed too. We have sold our last Reading With Babies and the RTM Video DVDs. Although the visual guidance given to us by those babies and toddlers is timeless, the little ones on the actual video are now teenagers. The ones with whom we are still in touch are avid readers and doing brilliantly well in school! If you need DVDs and Guide Books please contact our excellent colleague Isabel Baker:

President.

The Book Vine for Children.

3980 W. Albany St., Suite 7.

McHenry, IL 60050.

Tel: 800 772–4220.

Fax: 815 363–8883.

www.bookvine.com

info@bookvine.com

48. Benjamin Straub letter to the author, 17 January 2016.

49. Edgar Allan Poe wrote of this kind of detached observer/storyteller in "The Man in the Crowd." And Baudelaire in his sketch "Crowds" described himself as "one of those wandering souls who goes looking for a body" and who "enters as he likes into each man's personality." See Charles Baudelaire, "Crowds," in *Paris Spleen*, trans. Louise Varese (New York: New Directions, 1970), 20.

50. Peter Straub interview with the author, NYC, 2015.

51. In 2013, Peter and Benjamin Straub formed Seafront Productions, LLC, and are in the process of translating his novels and short stories into feature films and tv series. "We had the good fortune of working with Hollywood companies, large and small," says Benjamin, "from NBC/Universal to independent Film and Production companies. Hollywood, if nothing else, is an exercise in patience. In the 8 projects that we have running concurrently, I have no doubt that at some point in the near future, we will once again get the trilling opportunity to see that which was born in the mind of Peter Straub on the big screen and TV." Benjamin Straub letter to the author, 17 January 2017.

"My children are doing well," Straub adds. "Emma as a flourishing young novelist and Ben as a sort of human-dynamo film agent. I am immensely proud of both of them, and grateful that I can be. My marriage is a lovely, solid relationship without which my life would be both impoverished and imperiled. One lives through so much, and after a while things sort of settle down, and most of what one wishes for is a long calm continuance, with work and love, friendship and art, clear-headedness, laughter, and an unbroken awareness of how fragile and threatened any such blessedness must be. As dear Ben Sidran says, Everything is broken, and nothing is gonna be all right. Cue the drummer." Peter Straub letter to the author, 2015.

52. In an interview on 13 November 2014, with this writer, Straub talked about the Archive: "Mike Kelly was the person responsible for the acquisition of my papers at the Fales. The book dealer who represented my papers went to Mike and some other private and university libraries, around 2007. He got a very interested customer in Mike, who connected me with Marvin Taylor, who then acquired my papers…. I am glad the papers are there. They cover many years of my writing life. I'm glad that I saved all my drafts, many of them in my handwriting, which is awful! I hope that any academic or independent scholar interested in my work would communicate with Fales and ask to be allowed to come and look it all over. They previously were deeply private, but they are now there and available." The Fales Library is located at 70 Washington Square South, NYC 1002. Fales.library@nyu.edu.

53. Lenny Picker, "Things That Go Bump into the Night," *Publishers Weekly*, 8 February 2016.

54. Peter Straub letter to the author, 12 February 2016.

55. Michael Schumacher, "Ghost Storyteller," *Writer's Digest*, January 1985, 32–33.

56. Peter Straub, "Preface to *Shadowland*," *Sides*, 153.

57. Letter to the author, 15 December 2015.

Appendix

1. This interview contains excerpts from a longer conversation with Peter Straub at his home on 22 May 2011 in New York City. Update as of 2016: He has since relocated to Brooklyn.

2. Straub's colleagues and friends—they seem to be synonymous—all attest to this. Jack Ketchum, for example, recalls amusing times together on the road and over drinks: "We laugh a lot. Peter's laughter, which ranges all the way from booming baritone to an alarming counter-tenor, is pretty much a constant. And having heard that laugh along the many miles of highway or back home in my neighborhood bar—hearing it distinctly now as I write this—I'm not exactly sure how the hell I ever got along without it." See "A Short Peter Straub Companion," in Ketchum, *What They Wrote* (Crossroads Press, 2013), 82–84.

3. Bradbury's *Dandelion Wine* (1957) is a semi-autobiographical account of a twelve-year-old's coming of age in the fictitious Green Town, Illinois (modeled after Waukegan). By contrast to Straub's boyhood, its homespun memoir is infused with a nostalgic and affectionate tone.

4. In his essay, "Crowds," Baudelaire described the *flâneur*: "The solitary and thoughtful stroller finds a singular intoxication in this universal communion. The man who loves to lose himself in a crowd enjoys feverish delights that the egoist locked up in himself as in a box … will be eternally deprived of. He adopts as his own all the occupations, all the joys and all the sorrows that chance offers." See Charles Baudelaire, trans. Louis Varese, *Paris Spleen* (New York: New Directions Books, 1970), 20.

5. John C. Tibbetts, "August Wilson Interview," *Literature/Film Quarterly*, Vol. 30, No. 4 (2002), 238–242.

6. Update as of 2016: Emma Straub is the author of the novels *The Vacationers* and *Laura Lamont's Life in Pictures*, and the short story collection *Other People We Married*. Her fiction and nonfiction have been published in *Vogue*, *New York Magazine*, *Tin House*, *The New York Times*, *Good Housekeeping*, and *The Paris Review Daily*. She lives with her husband and son in Brooklyn.

7. Update as of 2016: *Hello, Jack* is still unfinished and unpublished.

Bibliography

Works by Peter Straub

For the ease and convenience of the reader (and not to clutter up this book with more chapter notes than is absolutely necessary), this book includes page numbers in parentheses from the following editions of Peter Straub's novels and stories:

POETRY

Open Air. Shannon: Irish University Press, 1972.

NOVELS

Black House (with Stephen King). New York: Pocket Books, 2001.

A Dark Matter. New York: Doubleday, 2010

Floating Dragon. New York: G.P. Putnam's Sons, 1983.

Ghost Story. New York: Coward, McCann & Geoghegan, 1979.

The Hellfire Club. New York: Random House, 1996.

In the Night Room. New York: Random House, 2004.

Koko. New York: E.P. Dutton, 1988.

lost boy lost girl. New York: Random House, 2003.

Mr. X. New York: Random House, 1999.

Mystery. New York: E.P. Dutton, 1990.

Shadowland. New York: Coward, McCann & Geoghegan, 1980.

The Talisman (with Stephen King). New York: Pocket Books, 1984.

The Throat. New York. E.P. Dutton, 1993.

Wild Animals. New York: G. P. Putnam's Sons, 1984. Includes the novels *Under Venus*, *Julia*, and *If You Could See Me Now*.

STORIES

"The Ballad of Ballard and Sandrine." Burton: MI: Subterranean Press, 2011.

Five Stories. Baltimore: Borderlands Press, 2008. Note: Quoted in this volume are the following stories: "Little Red's Tango." "Lapland, or Film Noir." "Mr. Aickman's Air Rifle."

"The General's Wife." West Kingston, RI. Donald M. Grant, 1982.

Houses Without Doors. New York: E.P. Dutton, 1990. Note: Quoted in this volume are the following stories: "Blue Rose." "In the Realm of Dreams." "The Juniper Tree." "A Short Guide to the City." "The Poetry Reading." "The Buffalo Hunter." "Something about a Death, Something about a Fire." "The Veteran." "Mrs. God."

Interior Darkness. New York: Doubleday, 2016. Note: Quoted in this volume are the following stories: "Mallon the Guru." "The Collected Stories of Freddy Prothero."

Magic Terror. New York: Random House, 2000. Note: Quoted in this volume are the following stories: "Ashputtle." "Isn't It Romantic?." "The Ghost Village." "Bunny Is Good Bread." "Porkpie Hat." "Hunger, an Introduction." "Mr. Clubb and Mr. Cuff."

"A Special Place." New York: Pegasus Books, 2010. One story unattached to this is "Mr. Electricman Lives in New York." It is appended to the volume of essays *Sides* (Forest Hill, MD: Cemetery Dance, 2007).

PETER STRAUB INTERVIEWS WITH THE AUTHOR

Providence, Rhode Island, 1990.
New York City, 2011.
New York City, 2014.
New York City, 2015.

Other Sources

Adey, Robert C.S. *The Locked Room Murders*. Minneapolis: Crossover Press, 1991.

Adler, Jeremy. "News of the Golden Age." *Times Literary Supplement*, 15 June 2012, 3–5.

Aickman, Robert. *The Wine-Dark Sea*. Introd. Peter Straub. New York: William Morrow, 1988.

Ashbery, John. *Selected Poems*. New York: Viking Penguin, 1985.

Bacchilega, Cristina. *Postmodern Fairy Tales: Gender and Narrative Stragegies*. Philadelphia: University of Pennsylvania Press, 1997.

Barthes, Roland. *Image Music Text*. Trans. Stephen Heath. New York: Hill and Wang, 1977. 142–148.

Barzun, Jacques, ed. *The Delights of Detection*. New York: Criterion Books, 1961.

Baudelaire, Charles. "Crowds." *Paris Spleen*. Trans. Louise Varese. New York: New Directions, 1970.

Benjamin, Walter. *The Writer of Modern Life*. Cambridge: Harvard University Press, 2006.

Bettelheim, Bruno. *The Uses of Enchantment*. New York: Vintage, 1976.

Bevis, Matthew. "The Lighthouse Stares Back." *London Review of Books*, 7 January 2016, 9–20.

Blackmur, R.P. "Afterward." *The Celestial Railroad and Other Stories*. New York: Signet Classics, 1963.

Blackmur, R.P. *Studies in Henry James*. New York: New Directions, 1983.

Blum, Deborah. *Ghost Hunters: William James and the Search for Scientific Proof of Life after Death*. New York: Penguin, 2006

Borges, Jorge. "On Chesterton." *Other Inquisitions, 1937–1952*. New York: Washington Square Press, 1966.

Bosky, Bernadette. "Peter Straub: From Academe to Shadowland." Schweitzer, Darrell, ed., *Discovering Modern Horror Fiction II*. Berkeley Heights, NJ: 1999. 3–17.

Boudreau, Kristin. "*Is* the World Then So Narrow? Feminist Cinematic Adaptations of Hawthorne and James." *Henry James Review*, Vol. 21, No. 1 (Winter 2000), 43–53.

Boulter, Jonathan. *Beckett: A Guide for the Perplexed*. New York: Continuum, 2008.

Buitenhuis, Peter. *The Grasping Imagination: The American Writings of Henry James*. Toronto: University of Toronto Press, 1973.

Camus, Albert. *The Rebel*. New York: Vintage, 1984.

Carr, John Dickson. "The Grandest Game in the World." Nevins, Francis, ed., *The Mystery Writers Art*. Bowling Green, OH: Bowling Green State University Popular Press, 1970. 227–247.

Chandler, Raymond. "The Simple Art of Murder." Haycraft, Howard, ed., *The Art of the Mystery Story*. New York: Simon & Schuster, 1946.

Chandler, Raymond. *The Long Goodbye*. New York: Vintage Books, 1992.

Chesterton, G.K. "The Ethics of Elfland." *Orthodoxy*. New York: Dodd, Mead, 1943. 96–97.

Chesterton, G.K. "The Ethics of Fairyland." *The Speaker*, October 12, 1901; reprinted in Mayock, A.L., ed., *The Man Who Was Orthodox*. London: Dennis Dobson, 1963. 174–176.

Chesterton, G.K. "The Honour of Israel Gow." *The Innocence of Father Brown*. New York: The Macaulay Company, 1911.

Chesterton, G.K. "How to Write a Detective Story." *G.K.'s Weekly*, 17 October 1925; reprinted in *The Chesterton Review*, Vol. IX, No. 2 (May 1984), 111–118.

Chesterton, G.K. *Magic: A Fantastic Comedy in a Prelude and Three Acts*. London: Martin Secker, 1913.

Chesterton, G. K. "A Midsummer Night's Dream." *The Common Man*. New York: Sheed and Ward, 1950.10–21.

Chesterton, G.K. "The Mystery of Edwin Drood." *Appreciations and Criticism of the Works of Charles Dickens*. London: J.M. Dent & Sons, 1911. 218–228

Chesterton, G.K. "The Tremendous Adventures of Major Brown." *The Club of Queer Trades*. London and New York: Harper, 1905.

Clark, Al. *Raymond Chandler in Hollywood*. London: Proteus, 1982.

Clute, John. "Beyond the Pale." *Conjunctions* No. 39 (2002), 420–433.

Clute, John. *The Darkening Garden: A Short Lexicon of Horror*. Cauheegan: Payseur & Schmidt, 2006.

Cody, Michael. "'As Kinsmen, Met a Night': Charles Brockden Brown and Nathaniel Hawthorne as American Gothic Romancer." *Nathaniel Hawthorne Review*, Vol. 30, No. 2 (Fall 2012), 93–114.

Collings, Michael R. *Hauntings: The Official Peter Straub Bibliography*. Woodstock, GA: Overlook Connection Press, 1999.

Corrigan, Maureen. "A Dark Matter." *The Washington Post*, 8 February 2010. n.d. Straub Papers, NYU.

Daugherty, Sarah B. *The Literary Criticism of Henry James*. Athens: Ohio University Press, 1982.

Daverio, John. *Robert Schumann: Herald of a "New Poetic Age."* New York: Oxford University Press, 1997.

Derleth, August, and Donald Wandrei. *The Outsider and Others.* Sauk City, WI: Arkham House, 1939.

Dickens, Charles. *The Mystery of Edwin Drood.* New York: Heritage Press, 1941.

Eagleton, Terry. "Allergic to Depths." *London Review of Books*, 18 March 1999, 7–8.

Edel, Leon, ed. *The Ghostly Tales of Henry James.* New Brunswick: Rutgers University Press, 1948.

Edenbaum, Robert I. "The Poetics of the Private Eye: The Novels of Dashiell Hammett." Nevins, Mike, ed., *The Mystery Writers Art.* Bowling Green, OH: Bowling Green State University Popular Press, 1970. 98–121.

Elbert, Monika M., and Bridget M. Marshall. "Introduction: Haunted Hawthorne, Hawthorne's Hauntings." *Nathaniel Hawthorne Review*, Vol. 30, No. 2 (Fall 2012), ii–xvi.

Fiedler, Leslie A. *Love and Death in the American Novel.* New York: Stein & Day, 1966.

Fiedler, Leslie A. *What Was Literature?* New York: Simon & Schuster, 1982.

Gagne, Paul. "An Interview with Peter Straub." *American Fantasy*, February 1982, 8–26.

Gilbert, Sandra M., and Susan Gubar. *The Madwoman in the Attic.* New Haven: Yale University Press, 1979.

Ginsberg, Lesley. "Hawthorne's Transatlantic Gothic House of Fiction *The House of the Seven Gables.*" *Nathaniel Hawthorne Review*, Vol. 30, No. 2 (Fall 2012), 27–46.

Gordon, Lyndall. *A Private Life of Henry James.* London: Chatto and Windus, 1998.

Gordon, Mel. *The Grand Guignol: Theater of Far and Terror.* New York: Da Capo Press, 1997.

Green, Graham. *The Lost Childhood.* New York: Viking, 1962.

Greene, Douglas G. "A Mastery of Miracles: G.K. Chesterton and John Dickson Carr." *The Chesterton Review*, Vol. X, No. 3 (August 1984), 307–315.

Greenblatt, Stephen. *The Swerve: How the World Became Modern.* New York: W.W. Norton, 2011.

Gregory, Jay. "TZ Interview: Peter Straub." *Twilight Zone Magazine*, May 1981, 13–16.

Gura, Philip. *Truth's Ragged Edge.* Farrar, Straus and Giroux, 2013.

Habegger, Alfred. *The Father: Henry James, Sr.* New York: Farrar, Straus and Giroux, 1994.

Habegger, Alfred. *Gender, Fantasy, and Realism in American Literature.* New York: Columbia University Press, 1982.

Haefele, John D. *A Look Behind the Derleth Mythos.* Cimmerian Press, 2014.

Handlen, Zack. "Peter Straub." *The A.V. Club*, www.avclub.com/article/peter—straub-38322.

Heiland, Donna. *Gothic & Gender.* Oxford: Blackwell, 2004.

Hogle, Jerrold E., ed. *The Cambridge Companion to Gothic Fiction.* Cambridge: Cambridge University Press, 2002.

Jahoda, Gloria. *The Road to Samarkand: Frederick Delius and His Music.* New York: Charles Scribner's Sons, 1969.

Joshi, S.T. *Unutterable Horror: A History of Supernatural Fiction*, Vol. 1. Hornsea, UK: PS Publishing, 2012.

Joshi, S.T. *Unutterable Horror: A History of Supernatural Fiction*, Vol. 2. New York: Hippocampus Press, 2014.

Kent, Leonard J., and Elizabeth C. Knight, eds. *Selected Writings of E. T. A. Hoffmann*, volume one. Chicago: Chicago University Press, 1969.

Kerr, Howard. *Mediums and Spirit-Rappers and Roaring Radicals: Spiritualism in American Literature, 1850–1900.* Urbana: University of Illinois Press, 1973.

King, Stephen. *Danse Macabre.* New York: Everest House, 1981.

King, Stephen. *Hearts in Atlantis.* New York: Scribner, 1999.

Kirk, Russell. "The Moral Conservatism of Hawthorne." *The Contemporary Review*, Vol. 182 (December 1952), 361–366.

Kramer, Robert. *Musical Meaning: Toward a Critical History.* Berkeley: University of California Press, 2002.

Kuhlmann, Susan. *Knave, Fool, and Genius.* Chapel Hill: University of North Carolina Press, 1973.

Kunkel, Benjamin. "Sam I Am." *The New Yorker*, 7 & 14 August 2006, 84–88.

Langan, John. "Interview: Peter Straub." *Nightmare Magazine*, October 2012, No. 1. http://www.nightmare-magazine.com/nonfiction/interview-peter-straub-part-1.

Lillyman, Wiliam J. *Reality's Dark Dream: The Narrative Fiction of Ludwig Tieck.* New York: Walter de Gruyter, 1979.

Lovecraft, H.P. "Supernatural Horror in Literature." Derleth, August, and Donald Wandrei, eds., *The Outsider and Others.* Sauk City, WI: Arkham House, 1939, 509–553.

Macdonald, Ross. "The Writer as Detective Hero." in Nevins, Francis M, Jr., ed., *The Mystery Writers's Art*. Bowling Green, OH: Bowling Green State University Popular Press, 1970. 295–305.

Macdonald, Ross. "Foreword." to *Archer at Large* (New York: Knopf, 1970).

Machen, Arthur. "The Great God Pan." *Tales of Horror and the Supernatural by Arthur Machen*. New York: Knopf, 1948, 61–115.

MacShane, Frank, ed. *Selected Letters of Raymond Chandler*. New York: Columbia University Press, 1981.

Martin, Robert K. "Ages of Innocence: Edith Wharton, Henry James, Nathaniel Hawthorne." *Henry James Review*, Vol. 21, No. 1 (Winter 2000), 56–62.

Martin, Robert K., and Eric Savoy, eds. *American Gothic: New Interventions in a National Narrative*. Iowa City: University of Iowa Press, 1998.

Mathew, David. "Dancing Architecture: An Interview with Peter Straub." *Infinity Plus*, http://www.infinityplus.co.uk/nonfiction/intstraub.htm.

Matthiessen, F.O. *American Renaissance*. New York: Oxford University Press, 1941.

McGilligan, Patrick. *Robert Altman: Jumping off the Cliff*. New York: St. Martin's Press, 1989.

Miéville, China. "M.R. James and the Quantum Vampire." http://weirdfictionreview.com/2011; and interview with Joan Gordon, http://www.depauw.edu/sfs/interviews/miievilleinterview.htm.

Murphy, Michael, ed. *Starrett vs. Machen*. St. Louis: Autolycus Press, 1977.

Mussell, Kay. *Women's Gothic and Romantic Fiction*. Westport, CT: Greenwood Press, 1981.

Myers, Gerald E., *William James: His Life and Thought*. New Haven: Yale University Press, 1986.

Neroni, Hilary. *The Subject of Torture: Psychoanalysis & Biopolitics in Television and Film*. New York: Columbia University Press, 2015.

Nevins, Francis M., Jr., ed. *The Mystery Writer's Art*. Bowling Green, OH: Bowling Green State University Popular Press, 1970.

Newman, Paul. *A History of Terror*. London: Sutton, 2000.

Novalis. *Heinrich von Ofterdingen*. Trans. Palmer Hilty. New York: Frederick Ungar, 1982.

Pagels, Elaine. *The Gostic Gospels*. New York: Vintage, 1989.

Paglia, Camille. *Sexual Personae*. New York: Vintage, 1991.

Parks, Tim. "Italy's Seriously Playful Genius." *The New York Review of Books*, 4 June 2015, 63–65.

Pearson, Norman Holmes, ed. *The Complete Novels and Selected Tales of Nathaniel Hawthorne*. New York: The Modern Library, 1937.

"Peter Straub and John Crowley in Conversation." International Conference of the Fantastic in the Arts." 18 March 2005. Moderated by Gary Wolfe. Unpublished. Fales Archive. Series 1, Box 36, Folder 22.

Picker, Lenny. "Things That Go Bump in the Night." *Publishers Weekly*, 8 February 2016.

Pullman, Philip. *Fairy Tales from the Brothers Grimm*. New York: Viking, 2012.

Quinn, Joseph. "The Club of Queer Trades." *The Chesterton Review*, Vol. V, No. 1 (Fall-Winter 1 978–79), 79–86.

Rainey, Stephen Mark. "Are the Old Monsters Dead?" *Horror Magazine*, No. 9 (1997), 38–39, 43.

Reiman, Erika. *Schumann's Piano Cycles and the Novels of Jean Paul*. Rochester: University of Rochester Press, 2004.

Richardson, Nick. "Rain, Blow, Rustle." *London Review of Books*, 19 August 2010, 18–20.

Richardson, Robert D. *Emerson: A Mind on Fire*. Berkeley: University of California Press.

Robinson, Bruce. *They All Love Jack*. New York: HarperCollins, 2015.

Rosen, Charles. "Freedom and Art." *The New York Review of Books*, 10 May 2012, 28, 39.

Ryder, Frank G., and Robert M. Browning, eds. *German Literary Fairy Tales*. New York: Continuum, 1983.

Saler, Michael. "Strange Tales of Alien Incursions." *Times Literary Supplement*, 4 March 2005, 19.

Saler, Michael. "Then It's Weird Again." *Times Literary Supplement*, 9 January 2015, 17–18.

Savoy, Eric. "The Queer Subject of 'The Jolly Corner." *Henry James Review*, Vol. 20, No. 1 (Winter 1999), 1–21.

Schechter, Harold. *Savage Pastimes*. New York: St. Martin's Press, 2005.

Scheick, William J. "The Twilight Harlequinade of Chesterton's Father Brown Stories." *The Chesterton Review*, Vol. IV, No. 1 (Fall-Winter 1977–78), 104–114.

Schiff, Stacy. "The Witches of Salem." *The New Yorker*, 7 September 2015, 46–55.

Schiffman, Robyn. "Novalis and Hawthorne: A New Look at Hawthorne's German Influences." *Nathaniel Hawthorne Review*, Vol. 38, No. 1 (Spring 2012), 41–55.

Schumacher, Michael. "Ghost Storyteller." *Writer's Digest*, January 1985, 30–34.

Schama, Simon. *The Power of Art*. New York: HarperCollins, 2006.

Sheehan, William. *At the Foot of the Story Tree*. Burton, MI: Subterranean Press, 2000.

Sheick, William J. "The Twilight Harlequinade of Chesterto's Father Brown Stories." *The Chesterton Review*, Vol. IV, No. 1 (Fall-Winter 1977–78), 104–114.

Skal, David J. *Screams of Reason: Mad Science and Modern Culture*. New York: W.W. Norton, 1998.

Sontag, Susan. "The Aesthetics of Silence." *Styles of Radical Will*. New York: Farrar, Straus and Giroux, 1969, 3–34.

Starrett, Vincent. *Buried Caesars*. Chicago: Covici-McGee Co., 1923.

Stillinger, Jack. *Romantic Complexity*. Urbana: University of Illinois Press, 2009.

Stone, Donald David. *Novelists in a Changing World*. Cambridge: Harvard University Press, 1972.

Straub, Peter. "Fearful Places." *Locus*, July 2006, 7, 78–79.

Straub, Peter. "Inside Story." Shields, David, and Bradford Morrow, eds. *The Inevitable: Contemporary Writers Confront Death*. New York: W.W. Norton, 2011 208–219.

Straub, Peter. "Introduction." *Poe's Children*. New York: Anchor Books, 2008.

Straub, Peter. "Meeting Stevie." Underwood, Tim, and Chuck Miller, eds., *Fear Itself: The Horror Fiction of Stephen King*. San Francisco: Underwood-Miller, 1982.

Straub, Peter. "The New Wave Fabulists." *Conjunctions* No. 39 (2002), 6–7.

Straub, Peter. "The Path of Extremity." in *Locus*, January 1994, 4, 65.

Straub, Peter. Papers. Fales Archives, New York University.

Straub, Peter. "Seeing Double." *Locus*, December 1998, 4–5.

Straub, Peter. *Sides*. Baltimore: Cemetery Dance, 2007.

Straub, Peter, ed. *H.P. Lovecraft: Tales*. New York: Library of America, 2005.

Sweet, Nancy F. "'The glory roundabout her': Hawthorne, Feminism, and the 'Serious Business' of the Aged Crone." *The Nathaniel Hawthorne Review*, Vol. 41, No. 1 (Spring 2015), 33–56.

Tatar, Maria. *The Hard Facts of the Grimms' Fairy Tales*. Princeton: Princeton University Press, 1987.

Thomas, Ronald R. "The Strange Voices in the Strange Case: Dr. Jekyll, Mr. Hyde, and the Voices of Modern Fiction." Veeder, William, and Gordon Hirsch, eds., *Dr. Jekyll and Mr. Hyde after One Hundred Years*. Chicago: University of Chicago Press, 1988, 73–93.

Tibbetts, John C. "G.K. Chesterton (1874–1936)." Winks, Robin, ed., *Mystery and Suspense Writers* New York: Scribner's, 1998. 181–194.

Tibbetts, John C. *The Gothic Imagination*. New York: Palgrave Macmillan, 2011.

Tibbetts, John C. "Locked Rooms and Mean Streets." *The World and I*, Vol. 7, No. 5 (May 1992), 313–325.

Tibbetts, John C. "Men, Women, and Ghosts: The Supernatural Fiction of Edith Wharton." *Helicon Nine: The Journal of Women's Arts and Letters*, No. 9 (Winter l983), 44–53.

Tibbetts, John C. "Miracles of Rare Device: Chesterton's Miracle Crimes." Ahlquist, Dale, ed., *The Gift of Wonder: The Many Sides of G.K. Chesterton*. Minneapolis: American Chesterton Society, 2001. 101–109.

Tibbetts, John C. "Phantom Fighters: 150 Years of Occult Detection." *The Armchair Detective*, Vol. 29, No. 3 (Summer 1996), 340–345.

Tibbetts, John C. "Psychic Sleuths." Herbert, Roseman, ed., *The Oxford Companion to Crime and Mystery Writing*. New York: Oxford University Press, 1999. 358–359.

Tibbetts, John C. *Schumann: A Chorus of Voices*. New York: Amadeus Press, 2010.

Tóibín, Colm. "Henry James's New York." *The New York Review*, 9 February 2006, 33–37.

Tremblay, Paul. "The Whole Ball of Wax in a Nutshell." *Los Angeles Review of Books*, 21 February 2016. See lareviewofbooks.org/author/peter-straub.

Underwood, Tim, and Chuck Miller. *Fear Itself: The Horror Fiction of Stephen King*. San Francisco: Underwood-Miller, 1982.

Underwood, Tim, and Chuck Miller, eds. *Bare Bones: Conversations on Terror with Stephen King*. New York: McGraw-Hill, 1988.

Wade, Francesca. "Pigs for Life." *Times Literary Supplement*, 13 March 2015, 3–5.

Wiater, Stanley, Christopher Golden and Hank Wagner, eds. *The Stephen King Universe*. Los Angeles: Renaissance Books, 2001.

Williams, Anne. *The Art of Darkness: A Poetics of Gothic*. Chicago: University of Chicago Press, 1995.

Wills, Garry. *Chesterton*. New York: Doubleday, 1975.

Wineapple, Brenda. *Hawthorne: A Life*. New York: Random House, 2003.

Winter, Douglas E. *Faces of Fear: Encounters with the Creators of Modern Horror*. New York: Berkley Books, 1985.

Wolfe, Gary K., and Amelia Beamer. "Peter Straub and Transcendental Horror." www.ameliabeamer.com/short-fiction-poems-nonfiction/, Reprinted as "Peter Straub and the New Horror" Wolfe, Gary K., *Evaporating Genres*, 151–163.

Wolfe, Gary K. *Evaporating Genres: Essays on Fantastic Literature*. Middletown, CT: Wesleyan University Press, 2011.

Wolfe, Gary K. "The Talisman" and "Black House." in *Bearings: Reviews, 1997–2001*. Essex: U.K.: Beccon Publications, 2010, 392–395.

Wolfe, Gary K. "Mr. X." in *Bearings: Reviews, 1997–2001*. Essex: U.K.: Beccon Publications, 2010, 226–228.

Wolfe, Gary K. "Malebolge, or the Ordnance of Genre." *Conjunctions* No. 39 (2002), 405–419.

Wolfe, Gary K. "Afterword: Fractal Evil." Peter Straub, *A Special Place*. New York: Pegasus Books, 2010, 123–136.

Wolfe, Peter. *Something More Than Night: The Case of Raymond Chandler*. Bowling Green, OH: Bowling Green State University Popular Press, 1985.

Young, Philip. *Hawthorne's Secrets: An Un-Told Tale*. Boston: David R. Godine, 1984.

Zipes, Jack. *The Irresistible Fairy Tale: The Cultural and Social History of a Genre*. Princeton: Princeton University Press, 2012.

Index

Numbers in **bold italics** refer to pages with illustrations.

Starrett, Vincent 223*n*4
Stevens, Wallace 17, 120–121
Stevenson, Robert Louis 72; *Dr. Jekyll and Mr. Hyde* (novel) 72
Stoker, Bram 29
Straub, Benjamin Bitker (son) *147*, 188–192, 234*n*51; on bedtime reading 189
Straub, Emma (daughter) 202–203, 235*n*6; on her father's writing processes 189; *Laura Lamont's Life in Pictures* (novel) 202
Straub, Peter *6*, *69*, *79*, *97*, *147*, *179*, *188*, *191*, *196* and "affect" horror 9; and ambiguity 9, 22, 38, 60, 140, 199, 200–201; and American Gothic 14, 26, 29, 32–33, 35, 49; "Ashputtle" 22, 40, 67; "The Ballad of Ballard and Sandrine" 11. 23–24, 186, 195; *Black House* 13, 16, 146, 150–153, 182; and "Blue Rose" 11, 16, 21, 22, 97–98, 107–109, 130, 113*n*8, 223–224*n*8; and boyhood 197–199; "The Buffalo Hunter" 10, 20, 88, 117; "Bunny Is Good Bread" 11, 23, 27, 65, 88, 109, 123, 180; "Collected Stories of Freddy Prothero" 23–24, 183; *A Dark Matter* 16, 24, 66, 118, 126–129, 173, 182, 185, 187, 192, 195; and "Dark Tower" cycle 154–156; *Desert Music* 174, 232*n*3, 232*n*4; and *Doppelgängers* 72, 85; and "ear language" 187–192; and fairy tales 51–52, 58–59, 64; and Fales Archive 235*n*52; and family life 188–194, 195–206; "Fearful Places" 70; and Fernando Pessoa 17, 86; and film noir 121–123, 125; and the *flâneur* 192, 202; *Floating Dragon* 13, 49, 65, 88, 126, 127–128, 157, 187, 188, 192, 200; "The General's Wife" 23–24, 87–88; and *Ghost Story* (film) 27, 210*n*4; 211*n*4; *Ghost Story* (novel) 14, 26–29, 48–49, 127, 162, 180, 202; "The Ghost Village" 20; and G.K. Chesterton *see* Chesterton, G.K.; and Gnosticism 63–64; and H.P. Lovecraft *see* Lovecraft, H.P.; *Hellfire Club* 15, 67, 88, 124, 168–173, 177, 185, 192, 206; *Hello Jack* 11, 193, 206; and Henry James *see* James, Henry; and home life 188–192, 234*n*57; and humor 13, 17, 93, 119, 166–167, 195, 205–206, 209*n*48; "Hunger, an Introduction" 22, 128, 181, 205; *If You Could See Me Now* 26, 40, 87, 126, 181, 184; *In the Night Room* 16, 66, 110, 114, 121, 125, 134–145, 173, 182, 183, 205; and influences of Hawthorne and James 29–49; "Inside Story" 91–92, 227*n*50; and jazz 6, 17, 23, 57, 88, 107, 176, 183, 186, 189, 199, 204; and jazz criticism 186; and John Ashbery *see* Ashbery, John; *Julia* (*Haunting of Julia* film) 210*n*4; *Julia* (novel) 26, 40, 87, 126, 180; "Juniper Tree" 5–17, 21, 22, 66, 109, 123, 180, 204, 207; *Koko* 16, 89, 97, 104–106, 117, 133, 163–165, 181–182; and language 17, 25, 136, 171–172, 180–185, 201; "Lapland, or Film Noir" 23. 24. 122, 194; and Laura Sims 177–179 and *My God Is This a Man* 178–179; *Leeson Park and Belsize Square* 176; "Little Red's Tango"

23, 204; *lost boy lost girl* 16, 110, 114, 121, 125, 130–135; and the "Magic Taxi" 25, 193–194; "Mallon the Guru" 23; *Marriages* 7; as "Merry Prankster" of language, 24; and metafiction 27, 70, 137–138, 141–145, 173, 223*n*38; and Milwaukee 7, 21, 36, 116–117, 118, 123, 176, 198, 226; "Mr. Aickman's Air Rifle" 23–24; "Mr. Clubb and Mr. Cuff" 23, 119, 205; *Mr. X* 72–94, 126, 128, 204; "Mrs. God" 21, 88, 92, 128, 177, 179, 182, 192, 199–200; and music 185–187, 203; *Mystery* 16, 92, 97, 98–104, 109, 186, 195; and Nathaniel Hawthorne *see* Hawthorne, Nathaniel; *The Night Journey* (novel) 67, 124, 170, 172–173, 184; *Open Air* 176; and poetry 17, 86, 168–170, 174–177, 203; "The Poetry Reading" 187; "Porkpie Hat" 23; and prose style 8, 12, 17, 22, 46, 60, 123, 133, 146, 160–161, 167, 174–179, 180, 181, 182, 188, 183; and Putney Tyson Ridge as alter-ego 17, 92, 93–94, 209*n*4; and Raymond Chandler *see* Chandler, Raymond; and Robert Aickman *see* Aickman, Robert; and Robert Schumann *see* Schumann, Robert; and Ross Macdonald *see* Macdonald, Ross; and serial killers 11, 69, 91, 116, 118–119, 133, 151, 165, 177, 226*n*45; *Shadowland* 15, 50–70, 86, 87, 173, 179, 185, 188; "Short Guide to the City" 21, 22, 116, 117, 161, 183; *Sides* 24, 86; "Something About a Death, Something About a Fire" 14, 20; "A Special Place" 11, 66, 118; and Stephen King *see* King, Stephen; *The Talisman* 16, 146–153; on Thomas Tessier *see* Tessier, Thomas; *The Throat* 16, 27, 65, 88, 92, 96, 97, 106–109, 116, 122, 123; and Tim Underhill as alter-ego 104–109, 118, 124, 130–134, 134–145, 205; and torture and transcendence ("the uses of horror") 9, 10, 23, 28, 36, 89, 98, 119, 125, 130, 132, 139, 153, 208*n*21, 204–205, 208*n*30; *Under Venus* 186; and Vietnam 89, 104–106, 163, 166; and Wallace Stevens *see* Stevens, Wallace; and William Carlos Williams *see* Williams, William Carlos; and the *Wound and the Bow* (book) 208*n*21; and writers' colonies 170–171
Straub, Susan (wife) *188*, *191*; on the Read to Me program 189–190, 134*n*47; on reading aloud 188–192
Sublime *see* Burke, Edmund
Strindberg, August 74
Swedenborg, Emanuel *see* James, Henry

The Tennis Court Oath (poems) *see* Ashbery, John
Tessier, Thomas 175, 176
Thompson, Jim: *The Killer Inside Me* 226*n*45
Tibbetts, James A. 196
Tibbetts, John C. *196*; *The Gothic Imagination* (book) 210*n*1, 219*n*14, 220*n*21
Tieck, Ludwig 29